American Portraits

Biographies in United States History

VOLUME II
Third Edition

Stephen G. Weisner
Springfield Technical Community College

William F. Hartford
Independent Scholar

Mc
Graw
Hill

Boston Burr Ridge, IL Dubuque, IA Madison, WI New York
San Francisco St. Louis Bangkok Bogotá Caracas Kuala Lumpur
Lisbon London Madrid Mexico City Milan Montreal New Delhi
Santiago Seoul Singapore Sydney Taipei Toronto

Higher Education

AMERICAN PORTRAITS: BIOGRAPHIES IN UNITED STATES HISTORY, VOLUME II
Published by McGraw-Hill, a business unit of The McGraw-Hill Companies, Inc., 1221 Avenue
of the Americas, New York, NY, 10020. Copyright © 2008, 2002, 1998 by The McGraw-Hill
Companies, Inc. All rights reserved. No part of this publication may be reproduced or
distributed in any form or by any means, or stored in a database or retrieval system, without
the prior written consent of The McGraw-Hill Companies, Inc., including, but not limited to, in
any network or other electronic storage or transmission, or broadcast for distance learning.
Some ancillaries, including electronic and print components, may not be available to customers
outside the United States.

This book is printed on acid-free paper.

1 2 3 4 5 6 7 8 9 0 FGR/FGR 0 9 8 7 6

ISBN: 978-0-07-321027-8
MHID: 0-07-321027-7

Vice President and Editor-in-Chief: *Emily Barrosse*
Publisher: *Lisa Moore*
Senior Sponsoring Editor: *Jon-David Hague*
Developmental Editor: *Larry Goldberg*
Editorial Assistant: *Sora Kim*
Executive Marketing Manager: *Sharon Loeb*
Managing Editor: *Jean Dal Porto*
Senior Project Manager: *Becky Komro*
Art Director: *Jeanne Schreiber*
Lead Designer: *Gino Cieslik*

Photo Research Coordinator: *Sonia Brown*
Cover Photos (clockwise from top left):
   AP/Wide World Photos; Reuters/Corbis;
   Stock Montage, Inc.; AP/Wide World Photos;
   © *Bettmann/Corbis; Courtesy of the Archives*
   and Special Collections on Women in
   Medicine, MCP, Hahnemann University
Senior Production Supervisor: *Janean A. Utley*
Composition: *10/12 Palatino by Techbooks*
Printing: *45# New Era Matte, Quebecor World*

Credits: The credits section for this book begins on page 324 and is considered an extension of
the copyright page.

Library of Congress Cataloging-in-Publication Data
American portraits: biographies in United States history / [edited by] Stephen G. Weisner,
William F. Hartford.—3rd ed.
        p. cm.
     Includes bibliographical references.
     ISBN-13: 978-0-07-353455-8 (softcover : v. 1 : alk. paper)
     ISBN-10: 0-07-353455-2 (softcover : v. 1 : alk. paper)
     ISBN-13: 978-0-07-321027-8 (softcover : v. 2 : alk. paper)
     ISBN-10: 0-07-321027-7 (softcover : v. 2 : alk. paper)
     1. United States—Biography.   2. United States—History.   I. Weisner, Stephen G., 1949–
     II. Hartford, William F., 1949–
CT214.A47 2008
973'.099—dc22   2006025152

The Internet addresses listed in the text were accurate at the time of publication. The inclusion of
a Web site does not indicate an endorsement by the authors or McGraw-Hill, and McGraw-Hill
does not guarantee the accuracy of the information presented at these sites.

www.mhhe.com

For my mother,
Anne Weisner, 1921–1993,
Harry Weisner, 1915–1984,
and my sister,
Linda Levine

About the Authors

STEPHEN WEISNER received his BA from Richmond College of the City University of New York and his PhD from the University of Massachusetts at Amherst. He is currently Professor of History and the Honors Programs at Springfield Technical Community College. He is the author of *Embattled Editor: The Life of Samuel Bowles* (1986), *Samuel Bowles and the Springfield Republican in Springfield, 1636–1986* (1987), "Biographical Portraits of Samuel Bowles I and II" in *American National Biography* (1999), "Governor Rueben Fenton" in *The Encyclopedia of the American Civil War* (2000). Dr. Weisner is currently working on a manuscript entitled *Go West Young Man: A Life of Horace Greeley* for young adults. He was the recipient of a Distinguished Service Award at STCC. in 1982, the Outstanding Faculty Member of the Year Award in 1988, and a National Excellence in Teaching Award in 1989.

WILLIAM HARTFORD received his BA and his PhD from the University of Massachusetts at Amherst. Currently, he is a Project Editor at National Evaluations Systems in Hadley, Massachusetts as well as a professional writer. He is the author of the article "Unions, Labor Markets, and Deindustrialization: The Holyoke Textile Industry" in *Labor in Massachusetts: Selected Essays* (1990) and the books *Working People of Holyoke: Class and Ethnicity in a Massachusetts Mill Town, 1850–1960* (1990), *Where Is Our Responsibility? Unions and Economic Change in the New England Textile Industry, 1870–1960* (1996), and *Money, Morals, and Politics: Massachusetts in the Age of the Boston Associates* (2001) and coauthor of *Commonwealth of Toil: Chapters in the History of Massachusetts Workers and Their Unions* (1996).

Contents

PRIMARY PERSPECTIVES   *viii*

PREFACE   *ix*

Part One
INTRODUCTION

1 Philip H. Sheridan by *Paul Andrew Hutton*   3

2 Susan LaFlesche Picotte by *Valerie Sherer Mathes*   23

3 Mary Lease by *Rebecca Edwards*   38

4 Henry McNeal Turner by *John Dittmer*   55

5 John D. Rockefeller by *Robert L. Heilbroner*   75

Part Two
INTRODUCTION

6 Theodore Roosevelt by *Edmund Morris*   95

7 Eugene V. Debs by *Francis Russell*   111

8 W. E. B. Du Bois by *Elliott Rudwick*   129

9 Margaret Sanger by *Margaret Forster*   148

10 Eleanor Roosevelt by *William H. Chafe*   170

11 Huey Long by *Glen Jeansonne*   190

12 George Patton by *Stephen E. Ambrose and Judith D. Ambrose*   200

Part Three
INTRODUCTION

13 Joseph R. McCarthy by *Fred Cook*   215

14 Martin Luther King, Jr., by *Stephen B. Oates*   233

15 Betty Friedan by *David Halberstam*   249

16 Cesar Chavez by *Cletus E. Daniel*   263

17 Ronald Reagan by *James T. Patterson*   285

18 Bill Gates by *H. W. Brands*   305

PHOTO CREDITS   324

Primary Perspectives

The Plains Indians and the Passing of the Buffalo   20

"Americanizing" Native Americans   35

The Omaha Platform   51

Ida B. Wells and the Anti-Lynching Movement   71

Affidavit of George O. Baslington   90

Corporate Regulation   108

Child Labor   126

Booker T. Washington   144

Letters to Margaret Sanger   167

African Americans and the New Deal   187

Address by Father Charles E. Coughlin, 1936   196

D-Day   210

U.S. Cold War Policy   230

Jo Ann Robinson and the Women's Political Council of Montgomery   246

The Feminine Mystique   260

Dolores Huerta   282

The Reagan Revolution   301

Microsoft at the Creation of the IBM PC   320

Preface

American Portraits is a two-volume collection of biographical profiles designed to supplement the textbooks used in college-level survey courses. We adopted this format for several reasons. One is a belief that biography provides a particularly valuable tool for introducing students to the excitement and wonder of history. Life-writing forcefully reminds us that, beneath the abstractions, history is about the aspirations and struggles of flesh-and-blood human beings; it further enables us to identify with these individuals as they seek to give meaning to their lives. In so doing, biography restores a sense of immediacy to the study of the past that is often lost in textbook generalizations. Accordingly, the articles in this anthology have been selected not only for their readability—though that was certainly a consideration—but also for the interest they are likely to generate. It is our hope that, in reading these essays, students will learn more about themselves as well as the people whose lives are profiled.

We also believe that biography provides an especially effective means of exploring the social and cultural diversity that has figured so prominently in the American experience. In the not-too-distant past, U.S. history was largely the study of middle-aged white males who had attained positions of political, military, or social distinction and whose forebears hailed from the British Isles. This is no longer the case, and textbooks today devote increasing attention to both women and men from a variety of cultural groups and social classes.

Biography cannot expand the breadth of this coverage. It can, however, deepen our understanding of these people. To cite but two examples from this anthology, Alvin M. Josephy's examination of the obstacles Tecumseh encountered in his efforts to achieve Indian unity sheds light on the diversity of Native American life; and Cletus Daniel's portrait of Cesar Chavez shows how factors such as religion and ethnicity shaped the development of this leader's unique brand of trade unionism.

On a related matter, biography adds depth to our understanding of major historical themes. Most of the essays selected for this anthology thus have a dual purpose: to profile the life of a given individual and to explore how that person influenced and was influenced by broader historical forces. For example, Patricia Horner's article on Mary Richardson Walker describes the trials and tribulations of a female pioneer in the Oregon Country; however, it also raises important questions about the ways in which environment and culture limited women's self-activity in frontier areas.

New to This Edition

In this revised third edition we have made changes—in large measure based upon suggestions from our reviewers—that strengthen the reader.

In Volume I we have replaced the existing Benjamin Franklin and Phillis Wheatley articles with more current pieces. In the new Franklin essay, Walter Isaacson explores the relevance of Franklinian virtues for contemporary Americans; in the Wheatley essay, Henry Louis Gates not only provides a stimulating look at the poet's life, but also examines changing perceptions of her work. We have also added a new essay on the Lowell mill worker and labor activist Sarah Bagley that broadens the reader's thematic scope through an examination of industrialization in antebellum New England.

In Volume II we have replaced the existing Huey Long article with a more recent portrait that presents a more comprehensive view of his life. In addition, two entirely new essays have been added to take account of important late 20th-century political and economic developments. One is on Ronald Reagan, whose 1980 election to the presidency was the first major triumph of a resurgent conservatism in U.S. political life; the other is on Bill Gates, the software entrepreneur who best personifies the communications revolution of the period.

We have also clarified some questions in retained articles. Updated bibliographies include works through the year 2005, as well as relevant video recommendations. As we continue to look for additional ways to improve the reader, instructors and students are encouraged to offer comments and suggestions. These can be sent to: Professor Stephen Weisner, Department of History, Springfield Technical Community College, Springfield, Massachusetts, 01102-9000.

Structure and Pedagogy

We have divided the essays in each volume into three or four parts. Each part begins with an introductory essay that is designed to help put the portraits into topical and chronological perspective. To provide additional context for the lives profiled in the anthology, we have prepared headnotes for every article. Within each article, definitions are provided for any obscure terms and phrases and high-level vocabulary with which students might not be familiar. We also have selected a document to accompany each chapter and thus broaden the scope of coverage. This feature is called "A Primary Perspective." Discussion questions follow, to help focus attention on the main issues raised in each chapter's portrait. Finally, each chapter concludes with a list of additional resources that includes book and film and video recommendations.

Acknowledgments

We are grateful to reviewers for the third edition, who offered many helpful suggestions for revision: S. Carol Berg, College of St. Benedict; Robert L. Bridwell, Del Mar College; Barbara Dunsheath, East Los Angeles College; Hal Friedman, Henry Ford Community College; Timothy P. Mattimoe, Beaufort County Community College; David R. McMahon, Kirkwood Community College; Jaakko Puisto, California State University, Stanislaus; Glen Vaughn-Roberson, University of Oklahoma; and Matthew Young, Marietta College.

At Springfield Technical Community College, thanks go to President Ira Rubenzahl, Dean Stephen Keller, Vice President Richard Parkin, and the wonderful staff at the STCC library. Thanks also go to Arlene Rodríguez, Dean of Arts, Sciences, and Humanities. Thanks are also in order for Dr. Hugo Cuadra, Dr. David Pierangelo, and Dr. Michael Perlman, MDs not PhDs! Finally, I am grateful for the support of my wife Jane and daughters Sarah and Hannah.

Stephen G. Weisner

William F. Hartford

Introduction

*T*he late 19th century was a period of expansion and growth in most parts of the nation. With the construction of a transcontinental railroad network, enterprise flourished on the agricultural, ranching, and mining frontiers of the West. In the East, cities grew at an astounding rate as new immigrants poured into the country from Eastern and Southern Europe. The pace of industrialization also quickened, propelled by the formation of massive new corporate entities that substantially increased output in numerous industries. By century's end, no informed observer doubted that the United States would soon displace Great Britain as the world's leading economic power.

Not everybody benefited from these advances. Among the casualties, no one suffered more than the Native Americans who stood in the way of westward expansion. Although most tribes agreed to relocate on reservations, they often found that government promises of decent living conditions were a cruel hoax. When some tribes subsequently rebelled, federal forces intervened, ruthlessly suppressing all expressions of dissent. In his essay on Philip Sheridan, the general most responsible for implementing Indian policy in the postbellum West, Paul Andrew Hutton sheds light on the darker side of regional development.

As federal officials gradually recognized that the reservation policy was not working well, they sought to replace it with an assimilation program designed to strip Native Americans of the "barbaric" traditions of their cultural past. The new approach targeted Indian youths, many of whom were placed in off-reservation boarding schools, where they were expected to internalize the values of white society. Despite the patronizing assumptions that informed the program, some students profited from the experience. One of them was Susan LaFlesche Picotte, the daughter of an Omaha chief, who went on to become the nation's first Native American female doctor. Her education and subsequent work on behalf of her people are the subject of an essay by Valerie Sherer Mathes.

Although agricultural output boomed during the Gilded Age, increased production did not necessarily mean greater returns for all American farmers.

In the Plains states, declining crop prices and high interest rates left many farmers with a bulging packet of unpaid loans. Casting aside their reputed conservatism, they turned to politics, forming a radical political movement that sought to redress a wide range of grievances. One of the more colorful and outspoken Populist orators was a Kansas housewife named Mary Elizabeth Lease. In her essay on Lease, Rebecca Edwards provides a lively profile of a forceful woman who devoted her ample energies to a succession of reform causes.

Native Americans were not the only group for whom Gilded Age developments brought more sorrow than fulfillment. This was also a dismal time for African Americans, particularly those ex-slaves who remained in their southern homeland. With the restoration of traditional white rule during the 1870s, the hopes raised by emancipation began to fade amid mounting racial oppression. As they did, southern blacks became increasingly reliant on their own independent institutions. Of these, none had a greater influence on African-American life than the church, whose ministers often provided leadership on political and social as well as spiritual matters. In his essay on African Methodist Episcopal bishop Henry McNeal Turner, John Dittmer examines how one black churchman responded to the deteriorating position of regional African Americans.

In most areas outside the South, where economic development lagged throughout the period, the release of entrepreneurial energies made the Gilded Age an era of extraordinary material growth. Leading the way were huge, multidivisional enterprises that used the latest technology to take advantage of economies of scale. In so doing, some of the new corporations not only crushed smaller competitors but established effective monopolies in given industries. Few Gilded Age firms proved more adept at this often brutal game than John D. Rockefeller's Standard Oil Company, which by century's end refined more than 80 percent of the oil produced in the United States. In his essay on the oil tycoon, Robert Heilbroner attempts to move beyond the robber baron stereotype and furnish a rounded portrait of Rockefeller by exploring his private life and philanthropic activities as well as his business career.

Chapter 1

Philip H. Sheridan

*A*t the start of the Civil War, Native Americans still controlled much of the trans-Mississippi West. But this soon changed, as western Indians found themselves caught between two great population movements. On one hand, miners from the Pacific Coast poured east into the Rocky Mountains. At the same time, a seemingly endless stream of eastern settlers pressed westward onto the Great Plains. Meanwhile, the completion of a transcontinental railroad in 1869 gave added impetus to both migrations. This was only the beginning. As additional railroad lines crisscrossed the region in subsequent years, the buffalo gradually disappeared, thus depriving the Plains Indians of their primary source of food, clothing, and shelter.

Their entire way of life threatened, Native Americans did not passively accept these developments. During the Civil War years, the Plains Indians of Minnesota and the Dakotas killed nearly 1,000 pioneers in attacks on frontier settlements. Afterward, tribes further west sought to protect their hunting grounds by disrupting the road-building activities of the U.S. government. To end the bloodshed, federal authorities initially negotiated treaties that promised to provide Native Americans of the region some measure of security by establishing protected reservation areas. But not all tribes

accepted the policy, and in 1871 Congress arbitrarily declared that the U.S. government had the authority to confine all Plains Indians to reservations, regardless of their wishes.

Even had all western Indians agreed to relocate on reservations, the program probably would not have worked. Because of the mismanagement and corruption that all too often characterized the federal administration of reservation areas, many Native Americans soon found that such life offered a bleak future at best. Not surprisingly, several tribes chose to fight rather than submit. Thus began a new round of Indian wars that continued throughout the 1870s and beyond.

A major figure in those conflicts was an army general named Philip H. Sheridan. One of the great heroes of the Civil War, Sheridan began his military career on the Plains; afterward he returned to the region with fixed ideas about how to deal with his Native American adversaries. In the essay that follows, Paul Andrew Hutton provides an insightful portrait of this sometimes ruthless military commander, whose commitment to order often overrode any ethical considerations that might obstruct the accomplishment of his aims. In so doing, Hutton tells us much about the costs of progress in the postbellum West.

Philip H. Sheridan

Paul Andrew Hutton

They buried Philip Henry Sheridan, commanding general of the United States Army, on August 11, 1888, in Arlington Cemetery. His grave, on a high, green knoll near the Custis-Lee Mansion, faces eastward toward the city of Washington. Lavish eulogies poured forth from that city, where Congress had tardily voted him a fourth star only weeks before his death, and from throughout the nation. They rang with the familiar names of battle sites—Stones River, Missionary Ridge, Winchester, Cedar Creek, Five Forks, Appomattox—that had established Sheridan as the youngest member of the Union's trinity of great captains. But strangely absent from this outpouring of mournful praise was any mention of the task that had dominated the first 7 and last 20 years of the general's career—the conquest of the American frontier.

Phil Sheridan had been, in fact, the republic's preeminent frontier soldier. He had commanded a larger frontier region—the vast Division of the Missouri—for a longer period of time than any other military officer in the

Source: Paul Andrew Hutton, "Phil Sheridan's Frontier," *Montana: The Magazine of Western History* 38 (Winter 1988), pp. 16–31. Reprinted by permission.

nation's history. He had given overall direction to the final, and greatest, Indian campaigns waged on this continent. Between 1867 and 1884, his troops fought 619 engagements with the western Indian tribes, completing the sub-jugation of America's native peoples and the conquest of their lands, which had been set underway almost 400 years before. At the same time he actively promoted the movement of hunters, stockmen, miners, farmers, and rail-roaders into these newly appropriated regions, using his military power and political influence to bring some order to this rapid, oftentimes chaotic, expan-sion westward. The American West during the 1870s and 1880s was in a real sense Phil Sheridan's frontier.

Sheridan's origins gave little hint of the vital role he was to play in his adopted nation's future. The exact place and date of his birth is unknown. He confused the issue himself, claiming both Albany, New York, and Somerset, Ohio, on various official documents, before finally deciding that Albany on March 6, 1831, sounded best. It seems almost certain that he was born either in County Cavan, Ireland, where his parents were tenant farmers, or on the boat en route from Liverpool. He was an infant when his parents, John and Mary Sheridan, settled in the hamlet of Somerset, Ohio.

Sheridan's later life was greatly influenced by the education he received in Somerset's one-room schoolhouse. He particularly admired an itinerant educator named Patrick McNaly, a drunken brute who believed that educa-tion could be beaten into students. Sheridan recalled with admiration that the Irishman consistently punished every "guilty mischief-maker" by whipping the whole class when unable to identify the actual culprit. This effective tac-tic made a deep impression on young Phil, as did the overall power of edu-cation. "The little white schoolhouse of the North made us superior to the South," he later remarked. "Education is invincible."

At 14, his schooling over, Sheridan secured a position as clerk in a local general store at $2 a month. He rose quickly to become bookkeeper in Som-erset's largest dry-goods shop, a mighty responsibility for one so young, for almost all business was transacted on credit. Although dedicated to his book-keeping chores, the lad was often lost in daydreams of martial glory, espe-cially after the outbreak of the Mexican War. His greatest hero as a youth had been Somerset's Revolutionary War veteran who was trotted out every Fourth of July to be admired by the citizenry. "I never saw Phil's brown eyes open so wide or gaze with such interest," noted his boyhood chum Henry Greiner, "as they did on this old Revolutionary relic." On another occasion Greiner and Sheridan interrupted their play to gawk admiringly at a tall, carrot-topped West Point cadet who was courting one of the young ladies at Somerset's St. Mary's Female Academy. The lady, Ellen Ewing, would eventually marry that fledgling soldier from nearby Lancaster, and her beau, lanky William Tecumseh Sherman, made a deep impression on young Phil Sheridan.

Learning that the 1848 appointee from his district to West Point had failed the entrance examinations, Sheridan hurriedly appealed to Congressman Thomas Ritchie offering to fill the vacancy. The congressman, who knew Sheridan's father well, promptly returned a warrant for the class of 1848, which elated Sheridan but horrified his family. Not only was West Point generally viewed by westerners as a bastion of aristocracy, special privilege, and militarism, all out of keeping with the ideals of the republic, but it was also firmly Episcopalian. John Sheridan took Phil in hand to the Church of St. Joseph where Dominican Father Joshua Young advised: "Rather than send him to West Point take him out into the backyard, behind the chicken coop, and cut his throat."

John Sheridan brooded over this sound if drastic advice for some time, but finally relented and allowed the boy to go. Phil traveled to the military academy with future general David S. Stanley. Stanley remembered Sheridan as "small and red faced, [with] long black wavy hair, bright eyes, very animated and neatly dressed in a brown broadcloth suit." At the academy, the long locks were soon shorn and the simple suit replaced by the "plebe skin," or brown linen jacket, of a freshman cadet. Poor Sheridan, Stanley noted, was "the most insignificant looking little fellow I ever saw."

West Point was an unhappy place for Sheridan. Gray buildings melded into a rocky landscape under foreboding wintry skies, reinforcing the discipline and monotonous regimen of cadet life. The traditional hazing frayed his volatile temper, and his grades suffered. The refined mannerisms and aristocratic temperament of the southern clique that dominated academy social life irritated him. While he found solace in the company of three other Ohio cadets—George Crook, John Nugen, and Joshua Sill—his rural, Irish-Catholic, Whig roots left him constantly insecure and ill at ease.

His frustrations broke forth late one afternoon on the drill field in September 1851. Virginian William R. Terrill ordered Sheridan to align himself properly in the ranks. Instead of obeying the order Sheridan lunged at Terrill with his bayonet. When Terrill reported the incident to his superiors, Sheridan sought him out and attacked him, but this time with his fists. An officer intervened and saved the wiry, five-foot-five Sheridan from a thrashing by the much larger Virginian. Saved from expulsion by a previously unblemished record, Sheridan received only a year's suspension. Unrepentant, he harbored deep resentment at all those involved in the incident. He brooded for 9 humiliating months back at his Somerset bookkeeping job before returning to West Point in August 1852, where he compounded his poor grades with a bitter attitude that left him only 11 demerits away from expulsion when he graduated 34th in a class of 52 in July 1853.

Brevet Second Lieutenant Sheridan was assigned to the First Infantry and ordered to Fort Duncan, Texas, perhaps the most desolate and primitive post on the frontier. Nevertheless, he found the fort an improvement over West Point and busied himself with amateur ornithology and hunting expeditions. He was soon transferred to his friend George Crook's regiment, the Fourth Infantry, and sent to Fort Reading, California, at the northern tip of the Sacramento Valley. The region was overrun by the dregs of humanity in search of a quick fortune in the goldfields. The miners and squatters terribly abused the local Indians, while their political representatives—most notably ambitious young Isaac Stevens, governor of Washington Territory—pushed through specious treaties to force the tribes off their coveted lands.

Crook, who had been in the Pacific Northwest since 1853, characterized the situation as "the fable of the wolf and the lamb." It was not infrequent, Crook noted, "for an Indian to be shot down in cold blood, or a squaw to be raped by some brute," and the white criminals to escape unpunished. Then, when the Indians were pushed beyond endurance and struck back, the soldiers "had to fight when our sympathies were with the Indians." Sheridan's sympathies, however, were not with the "miserable wretches" native to the region, for he felt their "naked, hungry and cadaverous" condition to be the natural result of the overthrow of savagery by civilization.

A gold discovery and influx of miners at Colville, Washington Territory, finally drove the Yakima and Rogue River Indians to war. Sheridan marched north in October 1855 with a detachment of 350 regular troops and a regiment of Oregon mounted volunteers under the command of Major Gabriel Rains. Sheridan's introduction to Indian fighting was a dismal affair, with the Yakimas easily avoiding the pursuing troops. On one occasion Sheridan, in command of the advance column, pursued a party of fleeing Indians for two miles before discovering them to be a company of Oregon volunteers. Winter snows mercifully ended the campaign, and Sheridan spent the next few months at Fort Vancouver.

While the reorganized troops were busy preparing for a spring invasion of the Walla Walla Valley, the Yakimas struck the first blow on March 26, 1856, attacking white settlements at the Cascades, a vital portage on the Columbia River. With 40 dragoons and a small cannon, Sheridan rushed upriver to the rescue aboard a little steamboat. Although they outnumbered the soldiers, the Indians only skirmished before withdrawing when more troops arrived on March 28. Slightly wounded by a Yakima bullet that grazed his nose before killing a soldier standing beside him, Sheridan had his first victory over the Indians and his first military honor when General Winfield Scott commended him in general orders.

After his victory at the Cascades, Lieutenant Sheridan and his troops occupied the nearby village of the Cascade tribe, easily rounding up the demoralized Indians. The Cascade men protested their innocence, but Sheridan found freshly burned powder in several of their old muskets. He hauled 13 of the men before Colonel George Wright, and a drumhead court-martial immediately sentenced 9 of them to death. The soldiers fastened a rope to a nearby cottonwood tree, stacked two barrels underneath, and unceremoniously hanged the Indians. Among those executed was Tumult, a Cascade Indian who had warned several settlers of the impending attack and had guided an elderly white man to safety. Sheridan noted with satisfaction that this "summary punishment inflicted on the nine Indians, in their trial and execution, had a most salutary effect on the confederation, and was the entering wedge of disintegration." Somerset schoolmaster McNaly's legacy was ever the directing influence in Phil Sheridan's use of force to effect the will of his government.

Sheridan's remaining years in the Pacific Northwest were spent quietly at the Grande Ronde Indian Reservation, guarding the several tribes who lived there. He learned the Chinook language while there, aided no doubt by Frances, a Rogue River Indian girl who lived with him on the reservation.

This liaison, however, seemed to have no moderating influence on his prejudice toward the natives. He was proud of the harsh tactics he employed on
the reservation to suppress traditional customs. "We made," he later noted,

> a great stride toward the civilization of these crude and superstitious people,
> for they now began to recognize the power of the Government . . . I found
> abundant confirmation of my early opinion that the most effectual measures
> for lifting them from a state of barbarism would be a practical supervision at
> the outset, coupled with a firm control and mild discipline.

It was difficult to concentrate on the duties at hand, for the news from the
East was increasingly worrisome. Pony Express riders carried the sober details
of Fort Sumter westward across the plains to western posts. Sheridan fretted
that the war would end before he could return east. He was delighted to
depart Portland in September 1861 as a newly minted captain in the Thir-
teenth Infantry and was anxious to see action, confiding to a friend that if the
war lasted long enough he might "have a chance to earn a major's commission." The small-framed, 30-year-old frontier captain was a latecomer to the
war. Ulysses S. Grant had already won fame as the victor at Fort Henry and
Fort Donelson, William T. Sherman was now in command of a division, and
George Crook's political connections had secured him the colonelcy of an
Ohio volunteer regiment by the time Sheridan took command of a desk at
General Henry W. Halleck's Missouri headquarters. His bookkeeping skills
paid rich dividends as the young staff officer quickly straightened out the con-
fused accounts of Halleck's predecessor, General John C. Frémont.

Sheridan's impressive staff service brought him to General Sherman's
attention. He recommended Sheridan be given command of one of the Ohio
volunteer regiments, but the governor declined to make the appointment.
Russell Alger, the future secretary of war, then a captain in the Second Michigan
Cavalry, succeeded where Sherman had failed, using his considerable political
influence back home to have Sheridan appointed colonel of his regiment. On
May 27, 1862, Sheridan jumped from regular army captain to volunteer army
colonel, beginning one of the most meteoric rises in American military history.

The new colonel fought a masterful battle at Boonville, Missouri, against
a force over four times the size of his own, prompting General William Rose-
crans and four of his brigadiers to telegraph Halleck that Sheridan deserved
a promotion and was "worth his weight in gold." Promoted to brigadier general of volunteers in September 1862, Sheridan quickly won a high reputation
in army circles for his bulldog tenacity and reckless courage. His fierce counterattack at Stones River turned seeming defeat into an important but grisly
Union victory and won him a second star in the volunteer army. It remained
for his bold charge up Missionary Ridge, however, to secure him General
Grant's esteem and guarantee his future. The press would dub Sheridan's
assault on the seemingly impregnable Confederate positions on the crest of
Missionary Ridge in November 1863 as the miracle at Missionary Ridge.

General Grant, who had watched the assault in amazement, was delighted.
"Sheridan showed his genius in that battle," Grant later declared,

and to him I owe the capture of most of the prisoners that were taken. Although commanding a division only, he saw in the crisis of that engagement that it was necessary to advance beyond the point indicated by his orders. He saw what I could not know, on account of my ignorance of the ground, and with the instinct of military genius pushed ahead.

When Grant went east in March 1864 as commander of all Union forces, he took Sheridan with him to command the Army of the Potomac's cavalry. Sheridan quickly defeated Confederate cavalry commander J. E. B. Stuart at Yellow Tavern and earned an independent command in the Shenandoah Valley. With orders to block the advance of General Jubal Early's Confederates up the valley and seal off the rebel breadbasket once and for all, Sheridan won battles at Winchester and Fisher's Hill and secured a brigadier's star in the regular army as a reward.

His greatest triumph, however, came at Cedar Creek. Sheridan was 14 miles to the north, at Winchester, when his army was taken by surprise on October 19, 1864. Galloping to the sound of the guns, he rallied his routed forces to crush Early's Confederates. "Sheridan's Ride," as it was called, became one of the most memorable episodes of the Civil War, soon celebrated in poem, story, and painting.

With the rebel army destroyed, Sheridan and his "robbers," as his army was thereafter known, ravaged the Shenandoah Valley so that it would never again support an invading army from the south. A crow, Sheridan boasted, would have to carry his own rations when crossing Virginia's most bountiful valley. "I do not hold war to mean simply that lines of men shall engage each other in battle," Sheridan declared, in defining the strategy he would apply both in the Shenandoah and later on the frontier. "This is but a duel, in which one combatant seeks the other's life; war means much more, and is far worse than this." The key to strategic success in war lay in ravaging the enemy's homeland, depriving him of the resources to make war, and destroying the will of the people to resist, "for the loss of property weighs heavy with the most of mankind; heavier often, than the sacrifices made on the field of battle." As he later advised Prussian Count Otto von Bismarck in 1870:

> The proper strategy consists in the first place in inflicting as telling blows as possible upon the enemy's army, and then causing the inhabitants so much suffering that they must long for peace, and force their government to demand it. The people must be left nothing but their eyes to weep with over the war.

President Abraham Lincoln had hesitated to agree to Sheridan's Shenandoah command, believing the general too young and inexperienced. The president had once described Sheridan as "a brown, chunky little chap, with a long body, short legs, not enough neck to hang him, and such long arms that if his ankles itch he can scratch them without stooping." Lincoln now confessed that he had always thought a cavalryman should be "six feet tall, but five feet four seems about right," he declared, subtracting an inch from Sheridan's already diminutive size. His reelection hopes given a timely boost by the victory at Cedar Creek, the president promoted Sheridan to major general in the regular army.

Realizing that the war would soon be over, Sheridan hurried south to rejoin Grant. At Five Forks his troops destroyed the right flank of Lee's army, and at Appomattox he blocked the Army of Northern Virginia's line of retreat. On Sunday, April 9, 1865, 34-year-old Phil Sheridan, the Union's finest combat commander, walked with General Grant into the McLean house at Appomattox to accept the surrender of Lee's army.

The war over, Grant immediately sent Sheridan to the Texas border with orders to provide material and moral support to the forces of Benito Juárez in their struggle with Maximilian, the puppet of the French emperor, Louis Napoleon. Sheridan relished the opportunity to confront French troops in battle, but the Department of State restrained him. Sheridan still aided Juárez by declaring huge quantities of arms and ammunition as surplus or condemning and depositing them on the Rio Grande for Juárez's troops. The French soon abandoned Maximilian, and the imperialist adventure swiftly moved to its melancholy finale.

Although preoccupied with border affairs, Sheridan kept a wary eye on civil matters in Texas and Louisiana. He distributed troops at critical points to suppress night-riding white terrorists and assist civilian authorities in enforcing the law. Before the war, Sheridan's mind, as he put it, had never "been disturbed by any discussion of the questions out of which the war grew" and he had been animated at the outbreak of the rebellion only to preserve the Union. The war had radicalized him, so that by the time of Appomattox he was one of the most stridently Republican and bitterly anti-Southern generals in the army. Enraged by the various vagrancy and apprentice laws—**black codes**—enacted in Texas, Sheridan angrily declared that they resulted in "a policy of gross injustice toward the colored people on the part of the courts, and a reign of lawlessness and disorder ensued." Although hardly enlightened in his racial views, Sheridan determined that he would protect the blacks. Now that they had been given their freedom, "it was the plain duty of those in authority to make it secure" and "see that they had a fair chance in the battle of life."

Sheridan further angered unreconstructed Texans. When asked by a reporter at Brownsville, Texas, what he thought of the Lone Star state, Sheridan acidly replied: "If I owned hell and Texas, I would rent Texas out and live in hell!" Sheridan also argued with Texas Governor James Throckmorton over troop assignments. The governor wanted troops transferred from the interior of the state to protect frontier settlers from raiding Comanches. Sheridan refused to move any men, noting that "if a white man is killed by the Indians on an extensive Indian frontier, the greatest excitement will take place, but over the killing of many freedmen in the settlements, nothing is done."

Sheridan's determined defense of blacks in Texas and Louisiana, his bitter disputes with local politicians, his forceful suppression of white terrorism, and his enthusiastic application of the Reconstruction policies of the congressional Radical Republicans, led President Andrew Johnson to dismiss him from his command on July 31, 1867.

> **black codes** Laws passed in Southern states in 1865–1866 that restricted the rights of newly freed slaves.

Reassigned to command the Department of the Missouri, which included present-day Kansas, Oklahoma (Indian Territory), New Mexico, and Colorado, the embittered Sheridan would find the task of frontier defense equally difficult work, but far more congenial to his temperament.

Peace on the frontier was tenuous at best. Although the 1867 Treaty of Medicine Lodge had established reservations for the Cheyennes, Arapahos, Kiowas, Comanches, and Kiowa-Comanches in the Indian Territory, the Indians had in general failed to settle on the reservations. Congress had been preoccupied with the impeachment of President Johnson and had failed to appropriate the necessary funds to meet the government's treaty obligations. It hardly surprised Sheridan when a Cheyenne war party raided white settlements along the Saline and Solomon rivers in Kansas in August 1868. Sheridan thought that the only way to ensure a lasting peace was to see the Cheyennes "soundly whipped, and the ringleaders in the present trouble hung, their ponies killed, and such destruction of their property as will make them very poor."

Sheridan determined on a winter campaign to crush the Indians. Although campaigning against Indians during winter was hardly a novel idea, Sheridan's campaign was universally greeted as a bold, innovative plan. He was convinced that his well-fed and well-clothed troopers could challenge the severe climate long enough to strike a decisive blow. Winter limited the Indians' mobility, their greatest advantage over the soldiers. With their ponies weakened by scarce fodder they would seek the comfort of their traditional winter camps and be lulled into a false sense of security. Distance and climate had always protected them, but the westward advance of the railroads had ended that advantage, allowing supplies to be shipped rapidly to distant depots and stockpiled for prolonged campaigns.

Sheridan was well aware of the vital role to be played by the railroads in bringing order and peace to the frontier, and he was determined to remove the Indian barrier that impeded the rapid advance of the lines. Thus, he concentrated his forces against the Cheyennes, Arapahos, and Sioux who ranged near the Kansas Pacific and Union Pacific lines and paid only passing attention to the Kiowas and Comanches, who traditionally raided south into Texas and New Mexico. Self-interest and past fellowship tied the soldiers and railroaders together, for most of the railroad construction bosses, surveyors, and engineers were former soldiers with close ties to the military establishment. Grenville M. Dodge, chief engineer of the Union Pacific, had commanded an army corps during General Sherman's Atlanta campaign. William J. Palmer, president of the Kansas Pacific, and W. W. Wright, superintendent of the same line, were both former Union army generals. These personal relationships naturally resulted in close cooperation between the soldiers and the railroadmen. Military escorts for surveying parties and construction crews were readily provided, and Sheridan often made large troop transfers to oblige the needs of the railroads.

This alliance was only natural considering the heavy federal investment in the railroads. It was in the best interests of the government, the military, the capitalists, and the people to have the roads completed as rapidly as possible. For the military, the lines promised rapid and inexpensive transport of troops and supplies and consolidation of numerous scattered posts. More importantly, the transcontinental lines would split the northern Indian tribes from the southern ones, spell doom for the great buffalo herds, and bring in more settlers. In 1867, General Sherman correctly foresaw that the completion of the transcontinental railroad was "the solution of the Indian question."

Throughout late 1868 and early 1869 Sheridan directed a masterful winter campaign against the Cheyennes and allied tribes. In sharp encounters at the Washita in November 1868, at Soldier Springs the following month, and at Summit Springs in July 1869, Sheridan's troopers broke the power of the Cheyennes and compelled them to settle on a reservation in Indian Territory. The campaign won Sheridan an enviable reputation as an Indian fighter.

After Grant took office as president in March 1869, he appointed Sheridan lieutenant general and gave him command of the Division of the Missouri. This vast command extended from Sheridan's Chicago headquarters on the east to the western borders of Montana, Wyoming, Utah, and New Mexico on the west and from the Canadian line on the north to the Rio Grande on the south. Most of the Indian population of the United States lived within the boundaries of Sheridan's division: Sioux, Northern Cheyennes, Southern Cheyennes, Kiowas, Comanches, Arapahos, Utes, Kickapoos, and Apaches all battled Sheridan's troopers. Before he left his frontier post to become commanding general of the army in 1883, Sheridan planned and directed the greatest Indian campaigns of the century.

Sheridan's pragmatism and elastic ethics made him the perfect frontier soldier for an expansionist republic. He ruthlessly carried out the dictates of his government, never faltering in his conviction that what he did was right. He viewed all Indians as members of an inferior race embracing a primitive culture. He felt them to be inordinately barbarous in war, which he attributed to a natural, ingrained savageness of the race. They formed, in Sheridan's mind, a stone-age barrier to the inevitable advance of white, Christian civilization. Sheridan not only favored this advance, but he also proudly saw himself as its instrument.

Although he denied uttering it, the infamous quote that "the only good Indian is a dead Indian" became synonymous with Sheridan and his Indian policy. Although the sentiment certainly did not originate with the general, it nevertheless has the ring of typical Sheridan rhetoric. Exactly as he had done in the Shenandoah Valley in 1864, Sheridan proposed to undermine the Indians' economy and impoverish them, as well as kill warriors in battle. Sheridan believed that the essential first step in his total war against the Indians was the destruction of the great buffalo herds. Not only did buffalo provide a rich commissary for the plains tribes, but the herds also gave the Indians reason to continue their traditional seasonal movements, which led them off their reservations and into collision with whites. Several treaties, such as the 1868 Fort Laramie Treaty with the Sioux, gave the Indians the legal right to hunt in certain areas off the reservation so long as the buffalo ranged in sufficient numbers to justify the chase. Sheridan hoped to quickly reduce the buffalo population and thus terminate this hunting right.

The general applauded the activities of the white hunters who began slaughtering the buffalo in the early 1870s for their hides. In 1875, when the Texas state legislature was considering a bill to protect buffalo in Texas, Sheridan protested. Instead of outlawing the slaughter, Sheridan declared, the legislature should strike a bronze medal with a dead buffalo on one side and a discouraged Indian on the other and bestow it on the hunters. "These men have done in the last two years, and will do more in the next years, to settle the vexed Indian question, than the entire regular army has done in the last 30 years," the general declared.

> They are destroying the Indians' commissary; and it is a well-known fact that an army losing its base of supplies is placed at a great disadvantage. Send them powder and lead, if you will; but for the sake of a lasting peace, let them kill, skin, and sell until the buffaloes are exterminated. Then your prairies can be covered with speckled cattle, and the festive cowboy, who follows the hunter as a second forerunner of civilization.

After the destruction of the southern herd during the early 1870s, Sheridan worked to ensure the same fate for the northern herd. In 1881, when the government considered protecting what was left of the herds, Sheridan vigorously opposed such action. "If I could learn that every buffalo in the northern herd were killed I would be glad," the general wrote the War Department. "The destruction of this herd would do more to keep Indians quiet than anything else that could happen. Since the destruction of the southern herd, which formerly roamed from Texas to the Platte, the Indians in that section have given us no trouble."

Sheridan's sponsorship of several civilian hunting parties onto the plains—such as the millionaire's hunt of 1871 and the Grand Duke Alexis hunt in 1872—furthered his policy of exterminating the buffalo while at the same time he curried the favor of powerful, influential citizens. An avid sportsman, Sheridan liked to combine business with pleasure on these western jaunts. Nevertheless, they were a calculated part of his overall strategy to defeat the defiant western tribes.

With their economic base destroyed, western Indian tribes would have no choice but to retire to the reservations allotted to them by the government. Sheridan believed the concentration of the tribes and their segregation from the whites to be essential to the establishment of order on the frontier. He thus agreed with the reservation policy and supported President Grant's so-called Peace Policy out of loyalty to his old commander, but he vehemently disagreed with what he viewed as the overly mild treatment of the Indians on the reservation. "An attempt has been made to control the Indians, a wild and savage people, by moral suasion," Sheridan noted in 1874, "while we all know that the most stringent laws have to be enacted for the government of civilized white people."

The Civil War had taught Sheridan how easily the social order could be disrupted, and he had come to believe that the application of force was essential to guarantee stability. "I have the interest of the Indian at heart as much as anyone, and sympathize with his fading out race," Sheridan wrote, "but many years of experiences have taught me that to civilize and christianize [sic] the wild Indian it is not only necessary to put him on Reservations but it is also necessary to exercise some strong authority over him." Sheridan believed that only the army could exercise this control, and he repeatedly but futilely recommended that supervision of Indian affairs be transferred from the Department of the Interior back to the War Department where it had been until 1849.

The Indian Bureau's protection of Indians that Sheridan believed were guilty of depredations frustrated him, while the lack of a firm national consensus on the righteousness of his Indian campaigns deeply troubled him. During the Civil War, a grateful nation applauded his every action, but now he drew bitter criticism for pursuing similar tactics against the western Indians. The public condemnation of his direction of **Custer's 1868 Washita fight** and **Baker's 1870 Piegan massacre** on the Marias deeply wounded Sheridan.

Sheridan could never fathom why so many opposed his methods. His experience in previous Indian campaigns where conventional military methods had been employed and failed had convinced him by the early 1870s that the army could not "successfully fight Indians on the principle of high-toned warfare; that is where the mistake has been." "In taking the offensive," he once explained to Sherman in defense of his methods,

> I have to select that season when I can catch the fiends; and if a village is attacked and women and children killed, the responsibility is not with the soldiers but with the people whose crimes necessitated the attack. During the war did any one hesitate to attack a village or town occupied by the enemy because women and children were within its limits? Did we cease to throw shells into Vicksburg or Atlanta because women and children were there?

Sheridan could not cope rationally with eastern criticism, repeatedly relying on a string of Indian atrocity tales to discredit those who opposed his tactics. He pointed to "good and pious ecclesiastics" as the agents of frontier disorder, castigating them as the aiders and abettors of savages who murdered, without mercy, men, women, and children; in all cases ravishing the women sometimes as often as 40 and 50 times in succession, and while insensible from brutality and exhaustion forced sticks up their persons, and, in one instance, the 40th or 50th savage drew his saber and used it on the person of the woman in the same manner.

Custer's 1868 Washita fight A military engagement that pushed the Cheyenne and Arapaho toward final capitulation and removal to a reservation.

Baker's 1870 Piegan massacre Colonel E. M. Baker's attack on Chief Red Horse's camp that killed nearly 200 Indians, including Red Horse and many children, with the loss of only 1 soldier.

He viewed his soldiers as defenders of female virtue—the heart of civilization—who sacrificed everything to destroy "murderers and rapers of helpless women." Sheridan repeatedly trotted out these atrocities—committed by Cheyennes during the 1868–1869 war—in his debates with the eastern humanitarians. "I do not know exactly how far these humanitarians should be excused on account of their ignorance," he wrote, in 1869, "but surely it is the only excuse that gives a shadow of justification for aiding and abetting such horrid crimes."

This use of such graphic diatribes gives some insight into Sheridan's background, his unconventional nature, and his quick reliance on any tactic to discredit his enemies. No story was more traditional in American history or more effective in rallying support to the western army than the plight of captive frontier women. Unmarried until age 44 and then taking a wife young enough to be his daughter, Sheridan fully subscribed to Victorian notions of man as woman's protector. He was mortified when unable to save the captive Clara Blinn and her child, whom the Arapahos murdered at the Battle of the Washita in 1868; and he was elated at Custer's 1869 rescue of two women held by the Cheyennes during the same campaign. Nonetheless, he saw these women as forever tainted by their captivity. In 1872, Sheridan refused to authorize the payment of five ponies to ransom Mary Jordan from the Cheyennes. "I cannot give my approval to any reward for the delivery of this white woman," Sheridan declared. "After having her husband and friends murdered, and her own person subjected to the fearful bestiality of perhaps the whole tribe, it is mock humanity to secure what is left of her for the consideration of five ponies." Mrs. Jordan's captors murdered her.

Sheridan's bizarrely convoluted logic dictated that the Indians be destroyed *before* such outrages could occur, *before* the social fabric could come undone, *before* the race could be polluted. It was a no-win situation for Sheridan. "We cannot avoid being abused by one side or the other," he mused in 1870. "If we allow the defenseless people on the frontier to be scalped and ravished, we are burnt in effigy and execrated as soulless monsters, insensible to the suffering of humanity. If the Indian is punished to give security to these people, we are the same soulless monsters from the other side." Sheridan consciously, even combatively, made his decision to support the settlers who resided on the extended frontier line encompassed by his military division:

> My duties are to protect these people. I have nothing to do with Indians but in this connection. There is scarcely a day in which I do not receive the most heart rendering [*sic*] appeals to save settlers . . . and I am forced to the alternative of choosing whether I shall regard their appeals or allow them to be butchered in order to save myself from the hue and cry of the people who know not the Indians and whose families have not the fear, morning, noon, and night, of being ravished and scalped by them. The wife of the man at the center of wealth and civilization and refinement is not more dear to him than is the wife of the pioneer of the frontier. I have no hesitation in making my choice. I am going to stand by the people over whom I am placed and give them what protection I can.

Such sentiments endeared Sheridan to the westerners, who soon came to regard him as their special advocate. They saw the question clearly. "Shall we Williampennize or Sheridanize the Indians?" asked the Columbus, Nebraska, *Platte Journal* in 1870. An angry Texan's letter in 1870 to the *Chicago Tribune* clearly expressed the position of many westerners: "Give us Phil Sheridan and Send Philanthropy to the devil!" But Indiana Congressman Daniel Voorhees spoke for many in the East when he rose in the House to denounce the "curious spectacle" of President Grant "upon the one hand welcoming his Indian agents in their peaceful garments and broadbrims coming to tell him what they have done as missionaries of a gospel of peace and of a beneficent Government, and upon the other hand welcoming this man, General Sheridan, stained with the blood of innocent women and children!" Wendell Phillips, the famed Boston reformer, could not have agreed more, declaring at an 1870 Reform League meeting: "I only know the names of three savages upon the Plains—Colonel Baker, General Custer, and at the head of all, General Sheridan."

Undeterred, Sheridan planned and directed a series of harsh campaigns during the 1870s that broke the back of Indian resistance and opened the frontier to rapid white occupation. In the largest of these campaigns, the **Red River War** of 1874–1875 on the southern plains and the **Great Sioux War** of 1876–1877 on the northern plains, he employed the same overall strategy that had succeeded in his 1868–1869 winter campaign. In each case he attempted to employ winter as an ally—although both campaigns saw summer fighting—and to have converging columns trap the Indians. Recognizing the difficulties of distance and terrain, he never expected these columns to meet or work in concert. Rather, they would keep the Indians insecure, off-balance, and constantly moving. In neither of these campaigns did the Indians suffer much loss of life in battle, but rather were defeated by starvation, exposure, stock and property losses, and constant insecurity. These campaigns reaffirmed the effectiveness of Sheridan's philosophy of total war, for it was concern over the suffering of their families that brought the warriors in to the reservations to surrender. If Indian women and children had been allowed to find sanctuary on the reservations—which they were not—or if the soldiers had been prohibited from attacking the Indian villages, then Sheridan's strategy could not have been successful. Only by making war on the entire tribe—men, women, and children—could Sheridan hope for quick results. Although brutal, this strategy was eminently successful.

So wedded to his converging-columns, winter-campaign strategy, Sheridan often refused to consider alternatives. Sheridan's conservatism, combined with his underestimation

---

Red River War The war that brought an end to effective Indian resistance on the southern Plains.

Great Sioux War The war in which U.S. troops defeated Sitting Bull and Crazy Horse, but not before Custer and his contingent were annihilated at the Battle of the Little Big Horn.

of the tenacity, courage, and ability of his Indian foes, could lead to disaster, as it did at both the **Rosebud** and Little Big Horn in 1876. In these most conventional of battles, where large numbers of troops and Indians maneuvered for control of open battlefields, the Indians simply outgeneraled Crook and Custer. Only after Sheridan turned to occupying the Sioux hunting grounds, to constant harassing tactics, and to military control over the agencies did the Indians suffer defeat as a result of starvation and exhaustion.

Sheridan, who during the Civil War had proven to be quite original in his approach to military problems, failed for the most part to provide innovative or imaginative leadership for the frontier army. The long shadow cast by the Civil War was part of the problem. Instead of looking to the future, Sheridan and many other army officers were far more captivated by the glorious past. The conflict on the western frontier was simply not a "real" war to the men who had won their stars in the great struggle of 1861–1865. Traditionalism set the tone of Sheridan's little frontier army.

After the Great Sioux War the nature of Indian campaigning changed. Sheridan's soldiers no longer marched into strange country against a foe of unknown numbers. Instead, his troopers ringed the Indian reservations with their forts, guarding against outbreaks. Clearly on the defensive, the Indians never could muster much strength. "Indian troubles that will hereafter occur will be those which arise upon the different Indian reservations," Sheridan declared in 1879, "or from attempts made to reduce the number and size of these reservations, by the concentration of the Indian tribes." The characteristic type of campaign after 1877 was the pursuit of Indian fugitives over a large expanse of territory. Such was the case with Chief Joseph's Nez Perce band in 1877 and with the Northern Cheyennes of Dull Knife and Little Wolf in 1878.

To guard against these outbreaks Sheridan could muster few troops. In the Departments of the Missouri, the Platte, and Dakota, he had but one man for every 75 square miles of territory, while in the Department of Texas he had but one for every 120 square miles of territory. His infantry companies averaged 40 men, while the cavalry and artillery did only slightly better with 60 and 50 men, respectively. Sheridan complained that three or four of his companies were "expected to hold and guard, against one of the most acute and wary foes in the world, a space of country that in any other land would be held by a brigade."

Keeping the peace on the Indian frontier remained Sheridan's primary duty throughout his years as commander of the Division of the Missouri, but even when there was Indian unrest his troops were quickly pulled from the frontier to meet various threats to national order. Sheridan and his troopers were called to duty, for example, during 1875 when he was placed in charge of Louisiana, during the tense

> **Rosebud** A battle against General George Crook's northbound column during the 1876 Sioux campaign that bolstered the Indians' confidence.

election crisis of 1876, and during the railroad labor strife of 1877. Indian wars were already anachronistic to Gilded Age Americans, and the requirements of frontier expansion were usually subordinated to more pressing political or economic needs in the East.

Sheridan spent much of his time with the establishment, construction, maintenance, and abandonment of forts within the Division of the Missouri. A parsimonious Congress never appropriated enough funds to build vital new posts or to keep established forts in even a modest state of repair. Western communities competed for forts, depots, or headquarters offices, and some frontier community boosters even fabricated Indian scares to bring in troops, with a resulting gain to the local economy from construction and supply contracts. Sheridan often confronted irate citizens, congressmen, and even his own officers over troop transfers or the location, construction, and budget of forts and depots. Sheridan guarded his meager resources, spending funds only on those projects that he considered in "the public interest." He resented accusations that his actions retarded development in the western territories, for just the opposite was true. When Montana's territorial delegate chided Sheridan over his refusal to construct new posts, the general angrily reminded him that "nearly everything done for the opening of a way to Montana for the last two years has been ordered by me, or on my recommendation."

Sheridan was one of the West's greatest boosters, actively promoting western lands and constantly encouraging settlement. Despite his warm approval of the activities of western capitalists, he never sold his favor to any business interest and his name was never tainted with scandal. He was quick to point out to frontier promoters that "if the wishes of the settlers on the frontier were to be gratified, we would have a military post in every county, and the Army two or three hundred thousand strong." He had enormous power over the frontier economy, and when he could justifiably do so he worked to assist struggling western communities. One of his proudest accomplishments was to "have been connected with the great development of the country west of the Mississippi River by protecting every interest so far as in my power, and in a fair and honorable way, without acquiring a single personal interest to mar or blur myself or my profession."

Along with his promotion of western growth, Sheridan also developed a deep interest in the cause of conservation during his final years as commander of the Division of the Missouri. He had long had a special interest in the Yellowstone National Park region and had sponsored several exploring expeditions into the area. During an 1882 trip to Yellowstone National Park, Sheridan was enraged to learn of the slaughter of the park's wildlife by hide hunters. He was further disturbed to learn that the Department of the Interior had granted monopoly rights to develop the park to a company affiliated with the Northern Pacific Railroad. In contradiction to his earlier encouragement of the slaughter of the buffalo and his long support of the Northern Pacific, Sheridan now vigorously raised his voice in opposition. "The improvements in the park should be national," he declared in 1882, and if the Department of the Interior could not operate and protect the park, he would. "I will engage to keep out skin hunters and all other hunters," he told the administration, "by use of troops from Fort Washakie on the south, Custer on the east, and Ellis on the north, and, if necessary, I can keep sufficient troops in the park to accomplish this object, and give a place of refuge and safety for our noble game." . . .

As part of his crusade to protect Yellowstone National Park, Sheridan organized a presidential excursion to the park during the summer of 1883. President Chester Arthur's trip, which was guided by Sheridan and accompanied by Secretary of War Robert Lincoln, Senator Vest, Governor Crosby, and other dignitaries, attracted wide publicity. It resulted in blocking efforts by the railroad to run a spur line into the park, reducing the company's leases in the park from 4,400 acres to only 10 acres, and defeating an attempt to return the park to the public domain. Sheridan failed to expand the park, but in August 1886 he had the satisfaction of ordering a company of the First Cavalry to take charge of the park, inaugurating 32 years of able military administration. When Sheridan rode to Yellowstone's rescue he achieved the finest moment of his last years and secured a national treasure for posterity.

On November 1, 1883, General W. T. Sherman retired from the army and Phil Sheridan moved to Washington to assume the position of commanding general. By law, however, Sherman's four stars retired with him, leaving Sheridan with the rank of lieutenant general. Sheridan found his new position frustrating, for the office was devoid of any real authority. The commanding general had no vital responsibilities in time of peace, because various bureau chiefs actually administered the army and reported directly to the secretary of war. Despite his relative youth, Sheridan's health had been slipping for years and he now withdrew more and more from the public limelight to spend time with his wife, Irene Rucker Sheridan (they were married in 1875), and their four young children. He spent much of this time working on his memoirs, which he completed in March 1888. . . .

On May 22, 1888, just after his return from Chicago to inspect the site for Fort Sheridan, the 57-year-old general collapsed from a severe heart attack. A string of heart attacks of increasing seriousness followed. This news prompted Congress to revive the grade of general of the army, and President Grover Cleveland promptly signed the commission so that Sheridan joined Washington, Grant, and Sherman in holding the four-star rank. His spirits buoyed by the promotion, even though his body was now frail and emaciated, he requested that he be taken to his seaside cottage at Nonquitt, Massachusetts. Throughout July he calmly waited, looking out over the lovely summer sea of Buzzard's Bay, as his condition worsened. He faced the end without fear or despair, for Sheridan knew neither. He had dealt in death all of his adult life—he was too familiar with it to fear it when it came for him on the Sabbath evening of August 5, 1888.

His legacy, as with all of humankind, is a mixed one. Hardly cerebral, he nevertheless possessed a truly continental vision for the republic. He was determined to open up the West and unite it with the rest of the nation. He could be cruel and vindictive in this enterprise, and this found expression in his frontier military policies. Knowing nothing but a soldier's life, Sheridan tended to view every situation in light of how military power could establish order. Deeply affected by the chaos of Civil War, he was quick to apply force against all those who opposed his government's wishes—be they unreconstructed rebels in the South, striking laborers in the East, or Indians in the West.

Despite his racism, brutality, and conservatism he was in many ways the perfect soldier for his times. He ruthlessly carried out the dictates of his government, confident that his harsh tactics brought on a quicker peace and thus an end to warfare for all. He conquered and subjugated the Indians, opening their rich lands to a wildly expansive and exploitative generation. He then sought, in his simple, blunt way, to impose order on that mad push westward and was at times somewhat successful.

By the time Phil Sheridan passed from the scene his frontier was gone as well. That final, rapid push westward—in all its brutality and all its glory—remains his great legacy. "He was," as the Bard said, "a man, take him for all in all, I shall not look upon his like again."

A Primary Perspective

THE PLAINS INDIANS AND THE PASSING OF THE BUFFALO

Most of the Plains Indians' economic and cultural activities revolved around the buffalo. In addition to being their main source of food, clothing, and shelter, the buffalo also played a central part in their ceremonial practices. When Philip Sheridan decided to target the great herds for extermination, he could not have done more to disrupt the traditional way of life of his Native American foes. In the selection below, taken from an Indian folktale related to anthropologist Alice Marriott, a Kiowa woman named Old Lady Horse tells us what the loss of the buffalo meant to her people.

The End of the World: The Buffalo Go

Everything the Kiowas had came from the buffalo. Their tipis were made of buffalo hides, so were their clothes and moccasins. They ate buffalo meat. Their containers were made of hide, or of bladders or stomachs. The buffalo were the life of the Kiowas.

Most of all, the buffalo was part of the Kiowa religion. A white buffalo calf must be sacrificed in the Sun Dance. The priests used parts of the buffalo to make their prayers when they healed people or when they sang to the powers above.

So, when the white men wanted to build railroads, or when they wanted to farm or raise cattle, the buffalo still protected the Kiowas. They tore up the railroad tracks and the gardens. They chased the cattle off the ranges. The buffalo loved their people as much as the Kiowas loved them.

There was war between the buffalo and the white men. The white men built forts in the Kiowa country, and the woolly-headed buffalo soldiers [the Tenth Cavalry, made up of Negro troops] shot the buffalo as fast as they could, but the buffalo kept coming on, coming on, even into the post cemetery at Fort Sill. Soldiers were not enough to hold them back.

Then the white men hired hunters to do nothing but kill the buffalo. Up and down the plains those men ranged, shooting sometimes as many as a hundred buffalo a day. Behind them came the skinners with their wagons. They piled the hides and bones into the wagons until they were full, and then took their loads to the new railroad stations that were being built, to be shipped east to the market. Sometimes there would be a pile of bones as high as a man, stretching a mile along the railroad track.

The buffalo saw that their day was over. They could protect their people no longer. Sadly, the last remnant of the great herd gathered in council, and decided what they would do.

The Kiowas were camped on the north side of Mount Scott, those of them who were still free to camp. One young woman got up very early in the morning. The dawn mist was still rising from Medicine Creek, and as she looked across the water, peering through the haze, she saw the last buffalo herd appear like a spirit dream.

Straight to Mount Scott the leader of the herd walked. Behind him came the cows and their calves, and the few young males who had survived. As the woman watched, the face of the mountain opened.

Inside Mount Scott the world was green and fresh, as it had been when she was a small girl. The rivers ran clear, not red. The wild plums were in blossom, chasing the red buds up the inside slopes. Into this world of beauty the buffalo walked, never to be seen again.

QUESTIONS

1. Why did Sheridan have such a negative opinion of the Plains Indians? In what ways did his views of African Americans differ from his views of Native Americans? In what ways were they similar?

2. To what extent did Sheridan's Civil War experience influence his conduct of the Indian wars? How would you describe his philosophy of war?

3. What role did railroads play in Sheridan's military strategy against the Plains Indians? What prompted such an ardent proponent of progress to become a conservationist?

4. What were Sheridan's views of women? In what ways did these views shape Sheridan's conception both of himself and of his mission on the post–Civil War frontier?

5. What influence did Sheridan have on the times in which he lived? What challenges does a biographer who has chosen to write about Sheridan confront? Would your portrayal of the famous general be positive or negative?

ADDITIONAL RESOURCES

The most recent biography of Sheridan is Roy J. Morris, Jr., *Sheridan: The Life and Wars of General Phil Sheridan* (1992). Studies that focus on Sheridan's post–Civil War career on the Plains include Paul Andrew Hutton, *Phil Sheridan and His Army* (1985); Randolph Keim, *Sheridan's Troopers on the Borders: A Winter Campaign on the Plains* (1985); and Stan Hoig, *The Battle of the Washita: The Sheridan–Custer Indian Campaign of 1867–1869* (1976). For more general treatments of the late nineteenth-century Indian wars, see Robert M. Utley, *Frontier Regulars: The United States Army and the Indian, 1866–1891* (1973); William H. Leckie, *The Military Conquest of the Southern Plains* (1963); and Dee Brown, *Bury My Heart at Wounded Knee: An Indian History of the West* (1970), which examines the conflicts from a Native American perspective.

For Philip Sheridan, the landmark documentary *The Civil War* by filmmaker Ken Burns supplies the best coverage of that conflict. Released in 1990, the series comes in nine parts. Another Ken Burns documentary, the multi-episode *The West*, puts Sheridan's post–Civil War activities in a larger historical context. For a dramatic representation of the Army–Native American encounter, the 1990 film *Dances With Wolves*, starring actor Kevin Costner, furnishes a modern interpretation.

Chapter 2

Susan LaFlesche Picotte

*T*he Indian wars had ramifications that extended well beyond the Plains region. They were also felt in Washington. During the early 1880s, government officials gradually recognized that federal inability to protect Indian lands from the incursions of white settlers had made a mockery of the reservation policy. In its place, Washington moved toward an assimilation program designed to "civilize" Native Americans: by dissolving their tribal organizations and by integrating them into the broader society. The legislative centerpiece of this new approach was the Dawes Severalty Act of 1887, which broke up communally controlled tribal lands and provided 160-acre allotments to individual families. To ensure that Native Americans remained on these plots and did not sell them to speculators, the government retained title to the allotments for 25 years.

Although many federal officials doubtless believed assimilation would improve the lives of Native Americans, no one bothered to consult them about the change of policy. And the assumptions underlying the new program represented the worst forms of cultural chauvinism. Having to maintain their own property, it was believed, would both force Native Americans to discard the "barbaric" habits of their tribal past and promote acquisition of those moral-pecuniary values—temperance, thrift, industry, and the like—that white society so highly prized.

In implementing the new policy, Indian Bureau officials took a number of steps to speed the pace of assimilation. One was the suppression of traditional tribal rituals such as the Sun Dance. Another focused on Native American youths, many of whom were dispatched to off-reservation boarding schools, where they received instruction designed to separate them from their cultural past. For many students the experience left much to be desired. All too often they found themselves in a miserable situation for which they were totally unprepared: Those who resisted the school routine had a terrible time; yet those who adapted were frequently considered outsiders when they returned home.

There were, however, some exceptions. One was Susan LaFlesche Picotte. The daughter of an Omaha chief who believed Native Americans had no alternative but to accept assimilation, she made the most of her years at Virginia's Hampton Institute, later becoming the nation's first Indian woman doctor. Despite her accomplishments, Picotte did not forget where she came from, and her subsequent career demonstrated that assimilation did not require an abandonment of one's past. In the essay that follows, Valerie Sherer Mathes describes the obstacles Picotte had to surmount in order to become a physician, while providing an in-depth examination of this remarkable woman's selfless work among her people.

Susan LaFlesche Picotte

Valerie Sherer Mathes

"Plenty of air and sunshine—that is Nature's medicine, but I have hard work to make my people understand," Susan LaFlesche, the first Indian woman physician, once remarked. Susan's people, the Siouan-speaking Omaha, had their origins in the Ohio and Wabash River area but had subsequently migrated westward to eastern Nebraska. Following the passage of the Indian Removal Act in 1830, they began ceding their claims to eastern lands. By 1854 they gave up their rights to hunting grounds west of the Missouri River and retained only a small tract bordering the river. In return for ceded lands, they received annuities, a grist mill, a blacksmith shop, and protection from hostile tribes. The treaty also gave the Board of Foreign Missions of the Presbyterian Church four quarter sections of land to continue missionary work among the tribe.

Source: *Nebraska History*, Winter 1982, pp. 502–25. Reprinted by permission of Nebraska State Historical Society.

The Presbyterians had established their first permanent mission at Bellevue, Nebraska, in 1845, but when the Omaha cession required the Indians to move to their new reservation, the missionaries followed. In 1858 they built a new mission house as well as a boarding and day school where Omaha children, including those of Joseph LaFlesche, were educated.

The son of a French fur trader and his Indian wife, Joseph in 1853 was the last recognized chief of the tribe. Aware that the Indians would eventually have to learn the ways of the whites, in the 1850s he hired white carpenters to construct a two-story frame house near the site of the new mission. By abandoning the Omaha traditional earthen lodge, Joseph became an example for his people to follow. He laid out a town site, fenced 100 acres, and divided the land into smaller fields in order that each man in his village could farm.

Joseph took another step in adopting white ways when he refused to have his daughters tattooed and his son's ears pierced. He explained, "I was always sure that my sons and daughters would live to see the time when they would have to mingle with the white people, and I determined that they should not have any mark upon them that might be detrimental in their future surrounding."

Joseph was remarkably astute, for several of his seven children not only mingled with whites but played important roles in bridging the gap between the two cultures. One son, Francis, became a well-known ethnologist with the Bureau of American Ethnology; Susette, the eldest daughter, became a prominent Indian-rights leader; and Susan, the youngest daughter, became the first Indian woman to graduate from a medical college and practice modern medicine. . . .

Susan's education began at the Omaha Agency and the Presbyterian Mission School. In September 1879 she and her sister Marguerite entered the Elizabeth Institute for Young Ladies in Elizabeth, New Jersey. In 1882, after three years in New Jersey, the sisters returned to the reservation. Susan spent the next two years working at the mission school and for a six-month period taught a class of small children. In 1884 Marguerite and Susan entered Hampton Normal and Agricultural Institute in Hampton, Virginia.

The education of Indians at Hampton began in 1879 when Richard Henry Pratt, a young Army officer, arrived with 22 Indian students from Fort Marion, Florida. Well known for its education of Negro freedmen, Hampton had been established by General Samuel Armstrong in 1868. Armstrong welcomed the Indian students warmly, thus beginning a long and successful experiment in Indian education at Hampton.

For the next two years Susan and Marguerite, dressed in uniforms, drilled on the parade ground and were imbued with the educational philosophy of Armstrong. He believed that labor was "a spiritual force, that physical work not only increased wage-earning capacity, but promoted fidelity, accuracy, honesty, persistence and intelligence." . . .

Graduating from Hampton on May 20, 1886, as salutatorian, Susan's address was entitled "My Childhood and Womanhood." General Byron M. Cutcheon,

Civil War medal of honor winner, also presented her with the Demorest prize, a gold medal awarded by the faculty to the graduating senior who had achieved the highest examination score in the junior year. Dressed simply but neatly, "Susan looked well, spoke clearly and everyone was delighted with her," wrote Alice Cunningham Fletcher, an ethnologist who had journeyed from Washington, D.C., to join the more than 1,000 people in the audience.

Susan's education to this point was little out of the ordinary, but her decision to attend medical college was unique. The fact that she eventually became a medical practitioner was not unusual, for in some western tribes there were medicine women and female shamans. All native medical practitioners gained their skills through visions and trances brought on by fasting as well as by special training. While Indians could acquire healing skills at any point in their lives, women could not engage in healing until after menopause. What set Susan apart was her desire to graduate from a medical college, an accomplishment few women could hope to achieve, especially Indian women. Later, too, she would practice medicine many years before the onset of menopause on the Omaha reservation.

At Hampton, Susan had been encouraged to concentrate on academic subjects rather than vocational skills. Both General Armstrong and Dr. Martha M. Waldron, the school physician, believed Susan capable of attending medical college. But first it was necessary to raise funds for tuition and expenses. Alice Cunningham Fletcher and Sara Thomson Kinney, wife of the editor of the *Hartford* (Connecticut) *Courant,* would solve that problem.

Alice Fletcher was familiar with the LaFlesche family, having worked closely with Francis as her major informant on Omaha culture, and having been tended by young Susan during an attack of inflammatory rheumatism in 1883. While serving as missionary, teacher, and government official for the tribe, Miss Fletcher had also been a frequent visitor to reform gatherings at Lake Mohonk, New York. There she met Sara Kinney who, after some persuasion, agreed to approach the commissioner of Indian Affairs about the possibility of Susan's continued education.

The Woman's Medical College of Pennsylvania, located in Philadelphia, ultimately admitted Susan as a "beneficiary student." Established initially as the Female College of Pennsylvania "to instruct respectable and intelligent *females* in the various branches of medical science," it opened its doors on October 12, 1850. By the time of Susan's attendance, it was known as the Woman's Medical College of Pennsylvania. . . .

On learning of her good fortune, young Susan wrote to Mrs. Kinney from Hampton in June that it made her happy to have so many mothers caring for her. "It has always been a desire of mine to study medicine ever since I was a small girl," she wrote, "for even then I saw the needs of my people for a good physician." She intended to teach the women of her tribe a few practical points about cleanliness, cooking, nursing, and housekeeping. In closing Susan noted that she and Marguerite hoped to spend most of the summer working among the sick at the church.

Suffering from motion sickness, a weary Susan alighted from the train in Philadelphia in early October. She was met by Mrs. Seth Talcott, chairman of the business committee of the association and Dr. Elizabeth Bundy, an instructor of anatomy at the college. Susan was placed in suitable housing at the YWCA, with which she was extremely pleased, and was provided with necessary supplies and clothing. For the next three years she sent home lively and interesting letters to her sister Rosalie about the people she met, her courses, and the sights she saw. . . .

In her first year Susan attended lectures in chemistry, anatomy, physiology, histology, materia medica, general therapeutics, and obstetrics. Students were expected to take notes. Apparently Susan had difficulty with chemistry, for she borrowed a chemistry notebook almost every morning after lecture from a second-year student, Sarah Lockery. Although attendance was not mandatory, Susan and the others rarely missed classes, especially on examination day, for they had to pass 90 percent of their tests.

In addition to attending lectures, the students went to a weekly clinic at the Woman's Hospital. Susan humorously described an incident in which female students had been joined by male students of the Jefferson Medical College. Just as the surgeon prepared to operate, a young man fainted and had to be removed from the room. "I wasn't even thinking of fainting," wrote Susan, nor for that matter were any "of the girls." Susan and her fellow students must have truly enjoyed that day, for they had often been teased about being faint hearted. Apparently Susan never minded dissecting cadavers and jokingly informed Rosalie she was "going to wield the knife tonight—not the scalping knife though." . . .

Unlike most Indian women of the 19th century, Susan was afforded the opportunity to learn about mainstream cultural activities. She frequented the Philadelphia Academy of Art, commented on the paintings of Benjamin West, became fond of musical performances, and attended literary and theatrical events, including "The Mikado" and a performance of Lily Langtry in "Wife's Peril." Accompanied by her brother Francis, she witnessed the Philadelphia Mummer's Parade, commenting that the masqueraders dressed as Indians looked "pretty well for Indians."

She especially enjoyed getting out of the city and walking through Fairmount Park collecting pine cones, but she did not ignore her Indian friends and visited Marguerite at Hampton at every opportunity. She also visited the Indian boys at the Educational Home in West Philadelphia as well as the Indian children at Philadelphia's Lincoln Institute. She attended missionary meetings, went to church, and joined her friends in various social activities. Well respected by her fellow students, Susan was chosen corresponding secretary of the Young Women's Christian Association. Out of a feeling of indebtedness for their support, she spoke before several branches of the Connecticut Indian Association. In October 1887 she visited the Hartford group, meeting for the first time many of the women whom she lovingly called her "mothers." . . .

Susan graduated on March 14, 1889, at the head of a class of 36 young women. In his commencement address Dr. James B. Walker praised Susan highly:

> Thoughtful of a service to her people, child though she was, she permits not the magnitude of her task to stay the inspiration, but bravely, thoughtfully, diligently pursues the course, and to-day receives her fitting reward. All this without a precedent. She will stand among her people as the first woman physician. Surely we may record with joy such courage, constancy, and ability.

Following a competitive exam, Susan was elected one of six women to intern at the Woman's Hospital for four months beginning in May. She took a brief vacation before her internship. Spending several days with her Connecticut "mothers," she was kept busy speaking before branches in Farmington, Guilford, New Britain, Norwich, Waterbury, and Winsted before she made a quick trip home.

Susan returned to the reservation permanently in late 1889. She accepted an appointment as physician at the government boarding school on August 5, but in December Omaha Agent Robert Ashley requested that she be allowed to treat the adults of the tribe as well. Commissioner Thomas Morgan complied with his request. Although there was already another physician at the reservation, within three months of her coming, Susan cared for most of his Indian patients because she spoke their language. When the other doctor left, she was in charge of the health care of all the 1,244 tribal members.

The government built an office for her at the school. A spacious building, it contained a drug counter, cabinets full of games and scrapbooks and picture books as well as magazines. Some branches of the Women's National Indian Association donated books and other reading matter to her library. Before long her office was full not only of school children but of adults, who came to ask her advice on business matters, personal affairs, and questions of law. Especially on cold rainy days, the older Omaha could be found spending a pleasant hour either visiting with Susan or looking through the magazines.

Susan's living quarters were provided at the government school, where Marguerite was the principal teacher. Although most of their work was centered at the school, Susan and Marguerite also carried on their father's work, directing the tribe along the path to assimilation. They advised the tribe, encouraging couples to marry by license and with the sanction of the church. Christian services were soon being held over the dead. Thus Susan was serving not only as physician but also as nurse, teacher, social worker, general adviser, and interpreter for church services.

Religion had always been an important part of Susan's life, and partly for that reason the Women's National Indian Association appointed her medical missionary to her tribe. She attended church services on Sunday mornings, where she and Marguerite often assisted by singing and interpreting. Sometimes they spoke before church groups on various topics. Christian Endeavor meetings were held for the young people on Sunday evenings, prayer meetings were held on Wednesdays, and Sunday school was held for the children in the schoolhouse before church.

But it is the medical record of this young Omaha woman that is legendary. Her patients, scattered over the 30x45-mile reservation, were reached by a network of poor, dirt roads. During her first year she was unable to make as many house calls as she wished because she did not have a team. If a patient was only a mile or so away, she walked. If the distance was greater, she hired a team, but patients often came to her. She finally purchased a team and buggy. In a talk at Hampton in 1892, Susan told her audience that the roads were so bad that a single horse could not pull a wagon. "After trying for some time to go about on horseback," she said, "I broke so many bottles and thermometers that I had to give that up."

During the first winter there were two epidemics of influenza. Although there were no fatalities among the adults, two babies died. With the arrival of summer, her patient load lessened. During July 1891, she saw only 37 patients; in August the number rose to 111; and by September it soared to 130. She started out every morning before eight o'clock, drove six miles in one direction, returned to the office by noon and then set out again on more rounds, returning sometimes as late as 10 P.M. with an exhausted team. Although she never spoke of her own weariness, her reports began to reflect more and more days taken off because of illness. She treated both acute and chronic cases ranging from influenza, dysentery, and cholera, to an epidemic of conjunctivitis, an eye ailment spread because of unsanitary conditions. After she had instructed her patients to use separate towels and basins, the epidemic subsided. At the end of her second year, she summed up her experiences by saying, "I am enjoying my work exceedingly, and feel more interest in, and more attached to my people than ever before. I have not a single thing to complain of, for . . . my life here is a very happy one."

December 1891 brought an especially bad epidemic of influenza, *la grippe* as she called it. Susan saw a total of 114 patients that month during the epidemic. She wrote that the disease

> raged with more violence than during the two preceding years. . . . Some families were rendered helpless by it, sometimes all the family but one or two being down with it. Almost every day during the month I was out making visits. Several days the thermometer was 15 to 20 degrees below zero, and I had to drive myself.

. . . January 1892 brought no relief as Susan cared for 120 cases in three weeks. The last week of the month she took off to care for members of her immediate family. When ladies from the Morristown, New Jersey, auxiliary of the Women's National Indian Association sent Susan money for the sick, she added it to funds of her own to buy food for her patients. From October 1891 to the spring of 1892, Susan saw more than 600 patients. The hard rides were becoming increasingly exhausting, but she never refused to make a call unless she was bedridden herself.

With the arrival of summer 1892, Susan took a well-deserved month of rest and attended Hampton's 24th anniversary. She gave the commencement address, entitled "My Work as Physician Among My People." While in the East, she had an opportunity to meet more members of the Women's National Indian Association. As their medical missionary, she now had to make annual reports. In May she spoke before the Washington, D.C., auxiliary on the spread of intemperance among her people. One of her earlier reports had stressed the drinking problem, noting that the Omaha could obtain whisky almost as easily as water. Laws were needed to prevent crimes attributed to alcoholism, she believed: "If a drunken Indian smashes a buggy and assaults a woman and child by beating them and nothing is done, what can prevent him from doing it again." The temperance movement was beginning to occupy much of her thought.

During the fall of 1892, Susan continued her arduous round of house calls, attending to children and numerous walk-in patients, but her own health began to suffer. She had complained of numbness and breathing difficulties in college but thought it was psychological. Possibly it was an early indication of the disease that would later take her life. By the first of January 1893, she was bedridden. "Susie has been sick for several weeks, her ears have been troubling her very much, she says she has pain in her head and the back of her neck constantly," wrote Rosalie to Francis. On October 20, 1893, she resigned as government physician because of her health and that of her mother, who had recently become critically ill.

In the summer of 1894, Susan surprised her family by announcing her forthcoming marriage to Henry Picotte, a Sioux Indian from the Yankton Agency and brother of Marguerite's late husband, Charles. Charles had died in 1892, and probably sometime shortly thereafter Thomas Ikinicapi, Susan's first love, died of tuberculosis. Only Marguerite and Rosalie knew of "TI," as Susan called him, for she had placed her education and career before marriage. After she graduated and began to practice, she met Henry, "a handsome man with polite, ingratiating manners, and a happy sense of humor." Susan fell in love with him. When she expressed her desire to marry, her friends and the Heritages [close family friends] were upset. Learning of the intended betrothal on June 30, Mrs. Heritage wrote expressing regret, for she did not think it wise owing to Susan's poor health. Marian also wrote Rosalie of her concern over the matter. "It is because I wish for Susie only the best things in this world with the least suffering and trouble that I wish she had decided not to take this step," she wrote.

Personal letters written by Susan about her romance with Henry have not survived, but there are numerous letters in which she revealed her feelings for TI. They had met at Hampton, and although he was deeply interested in Susan, she had decided that her career must come first. She visited Hampton several times while a student at the Woman's Medical College and spent as much time as possible with TI. She was afraid that he might return to Hampton already married but wrote Rosalie that [this] would not break her heart, for she was not "made that way." She added, however, "He was *without exception* the handsomest Indian I ever saw."

Her 1886 Christmas visit to Hampton found TI constantly by her side, as handsome as ever. They attended a band concert, and brought in the New Year together. At one point during her visit, TI was so overcome with emotion on seeing her that "he had his handkerchief up to his face and his eyes were shining—I felt so sorry for him—I felt like crying," she wrote. When her carriage departed Hampton, he stood with a handkerchief over his eyes again. He looked so forlorn that Marguerite broke down and another friend wrote that he "acted as if he had lost his right hand."

In his letters TI told Susan he thought of her constantly. Her good friend, Hampton teacher Cora M. Folsom, was convinced that there was no one good enough for Susan, and encouraged her to have only a "platonic friendship" with TI, for she feared he was getting into "deep waters" over her. "He is so respectful to me & I like him for that & for his faithfulness," wrote Susan in reply.

In January 1887, Susan and a friend had gone to the Educational Home in West Philadelphia to visit the Indian boys. While there a young Dakota Sioux had paid a great deal of attention to her, but Susan wrote she did not "care to go with any one and . . . remembered someone at Hampton and wondered what he would think to see so much attention lavished upon [her]." When she attended morning service and Sunday school in the afternoon, the young Sioux sat next to her holding out his hymnal. She remarked to Rosalie, "That is the end of it I hope. I haven't any time or patience for such things nowadays. Doctors don't have much time, you know, and he will have to keep his place."

Several days later she wrote, "I shall be the dear little old maid you know and come and see you . . . and doctor and dose you all." In the very next sentence, nevertheless, she spoke of TI: "Sometimes it seems to me I can see *him* looking at me with such a look—sometimes a smile on his face as he says, 'Come on Susie.'" But afraid her older sister might become concerned, Susan assured her that TI had helped her, had been a good influence, and that she only hoped her influence over him would be half as good. "I want to be his *friend*," she wrote, "and help him—I am a better girl for having gone with him." She ended by assuring Rosalie that "nothing will come of it dear, so be easy and at rest." One wonders if her life would have been the same had TI lived and had they married, but that was not to be.

Susan, when almost 30, apparently decided she was tired of being an old maid. Following her marriage to Henry, she began to participate more directly in Indian life. She and Marguerite, who had remarried, drew even closer, both having their first babies within a few months of each other. Within a year Susan was seriously ill again. "Susie had been very sick; I had given up all hopes of her when she commenced to improve," wrote Rosalie to Francis. . . .

Despite her poor health she became an active temperance speaker in place of her father. In 1856 Joseph LaFlesche had organized a police force of Omaha Indians who administered corporal punishment to any member of the tribe found drunk. Until his death in 1888, there was very little liquor on the reservation, but since that time liquor flowed freely, church attendance suffered, and farm work was often neglected.

As a young student at the medical college, Susan had attended lectures by noted temperance leaders including Frances O. Willard. She was, therefore, exposed to the temperance movement and the effects of alcoholism early in her medical career. Later as a physician she saw the effects of alcohol from both medical and personal angles. Tragically, her husband had begun to drink excessively, and consequently she became even more active in the movement. During the four years she had tended the ill of the Omaha tribe, Susan always felt perfectly safe in making her appointments, but the increased use of alcohol had begun to change the situation. "Men and women died from alcoholism, and little children were seen reeling on the streets of the town," she wrote. "Drunken brawls in which men were killed occurred and no person's life was considered safe." Women pawned their clothing, and men spent rent money on liquor instead of provisions and machinery. Congress passed a law that improved the situation and a commissioner or deputy was assigned to enforce it, but his removal encouraged bootleggers to return. A death caused by alcoholism on January 26, 1900, prompted Susan to write to William A. Jones, commissioner of Indian Affairs, asking what advantage any money saved from the removal of the deputy would be if her "people . . . [were] to be demoralized mentally, morally, and physically. . . ."

Domestic brawls were common, and Indian lands were sold for money to purchase liquor. One Indian, she explained, sold his land in 1904 for $6,000, and in one year spent the money, treating his friends to liquor, giving them money, and buying himself three buggies. She enumerated the deaths attributed to liquor from 1894 to 1914, beginning with an individual who fell from a buggy and was not missed by his drunken companions until the next morning, when his frozen body was discovered. The government's efforts to keep liquor off the reservation had failed miserably. Susan urged that the detectives appointed to patrol the reservation not be local men, and above all, should be moral, impartial, and above receiving bribes.

Whatever small victories she achieved elsewhere were not equalled at home, and in 1905, owing to complications from drinking, Susan's husband died. She was left as the sole support of an invalid mother and two small boys. For the remainder of her life, she continued her struggle against alcohol. Following her husband's death, the Presbyterian Board of Home Missions appointed her missionary to her tribe, the first Indian to hold such a position. She was furnished housing along with a small stipend.

The degenerative ear disease from which she had suffered for years made her increasingly deaf; and the pain now extended down into her back. She continued, nevertheless, serving as teacher, preacher, field worker, and physician at the agency's Blackbird Hills Presbyterian Church. She held church services, read the Bible in her native tongue, interpreted hymns, and held simple Christian services for those who died.

In November 1906, Susan and Marguerite's husband, Walter Diddock, purchased house lots in the newly established town of Walthill, carved out of Indian land by the railroad. Largely through Susan's work, the Secretary of the Interior Department ruled that no liquor could be sold in towns once a part of the Omaha Reservation, another small victory in her long struggle over alcohol. On her town lot Susan had a modern home built, complete with fireplace, furnace, windows for light and fresh air, and an indoor bathroom. Upon its completion, Susan, her sons Pierre and Caryl, and her mother moved in. Once settled, Susan and Marguerite entered the social structure of the town, becoming charter members of the new chapter of Eastern Star. Susan, a major organizer of the new Presbyterian Church, also taught in its Sunday school. Her home was on occasion filled with family and friends, for she enjoyed entertaining.

The two sisters supported community projects, lectures, concerts, and special events at the county fair. At the latter Susan was in charge one year of the Indian department. She continued to be active as president of the church missionary society, urging townspeople and businessmen of Walthill to become sufficiently interested in projects to give freely of their money and time. Soon many people began attending the monthly church meetings of the study circle, which held talks on topics ranging from Mexicans to Negro freedmen. Concerts were held to raise money for missionary work.

Susan also became politically involved when the government arbitrarily decided to extend the trust period for the Omaha an additional 10 years because it considered Indians in general uneducated and backward. This was, however, not true of the Omaha, who had a higher literacy rate than most tribes. "They are independent and self reliant . . . [and] as competent as the same number of white people," noted Susan. Their last allotment papers had been delivered in 1885, and the 25-year trust period, during which time they could not alienate their land, should have ended in 1910. The decision to extend the trust term caused numerous hardships for the Omaha. In addition, a new system of supervised farming was instituted. The Winnebago and Omaha Agencies were consolidated, thus requiring longer travel distance for tribal members to transact agency business. A. G. Pollock, well-respected Omaha superintendent, was removed. Protests arose from both whites and Indians over the additional supervision. "Every business action of the individual is supervised and hedged about with red tape and paternal restrictions," wrote the editor of the *Walthill Times.* All the Omaha wanted was to lease their lands and draw upon their monies themselves. But, as Susan had predicted, the entire tribe rebelled, depending upon her to free them of these new regulations. . . .

In February she was the unanimous choice of the Omaha men and women as one of the delegates to argue their case before the Secretary of the Interior Department and the attorney general of the United States. When she originally declined to do so because of poor health, tribesmen threatened to place her bodily on the train. "The Omahas depend on me so, and I just have to take care of myself till this fight is over," she wrote to her friend Miss Folsom. Despite a severe case of neurasthenia (nervous frustration), which prevented her from digesting food, Susan protested the red tape which made it difficult for the Indians to get their own money and the problems imposed in travel to the new combined agency. Her efforts and those of the rest of the delegation were successful, and most of the Omaha were deemed competent to rent or lease their lands and to receive monies.

Susan occasionally wrote articles which contained light humor. Invited by the Burt County Farmer's Institute to speak on "Primitive Farming among the Omaha Indians," she put the history of tribal farming on paper. "There was no need for suffragettes in those days," she wrote, "for the produce of these gardens always belonged to the woman." Her final draft was read by Marguerite on February 13, 1912, in Decatur, Nebraska, during one of the most successful meetings the association had ever held. Susan continued recording the traditions of her people by writing an article on the origin of corn for the local newspaper.

Susan always returned, nevertheless, to her first love, medicine. She was one of the organizers of the Thurston County Medical Association, served several terms on the health board for the town of Walthill, and was a member of the State Medical Society. For three years she served as chairman of the state health committee of the Nebraska Federation of Women's Clubs, working to get health-related bills through the state legislature. She began to study tuberculosis more intensively, giving lectures on the subject at the Indian church as well as to local townspeople. . . .

Another one of Susan's important successes was the campaign to eradicate the "troublesome household pest," the fly. Describing it as the filthiest of all vermin, Susan designed an attractive anti–house fly poster encouraging people not to allow flies in their houses or near food. By sprinkling lime or kerosene where flies might collect, she pointed out, their breeding places could be eliminated; she also encouraged the use of screens for doors and windows. Fly traps were soon available at local hardware stores.

Susan had always dreamed of a hospital where she could care for her patients and avoid the long trips to hospitals in Omaha or Sioux City. After several efforts to interest local philanthropic organizations in building a hospital, she approached the Home Mission Board of the Presbyterian Church. It granted $8,000. The Society of Friends (Quakers), through the Presbyterian Church, gave an additional $500. Marguerite and her husband donated an acre of land, and equipment and furnishings came from other individuals and organizations. A benefit concert was held to raise additional funds, and the hospital opened in January 1913. It contained two general wards with a capacity of 12 beds, five private wards, maternity ward, operating room, two bathrooms, kitchen, and reception room. Both Indians and whites were admitted, and in 1915 a total of 448 patients were cared for, 126 of them Indians. The presence of the hospital made it possible for Susan to reduce her patient load and avoid long drives in inclement weather.

Death took Susan LaFlesche on September 18, 1915. The infection in her ears had worsened steadily, and by 1914 was diagnosed as "decay of the bone," probably cancer. Susan underwent two operations, the first in February 1915 and the second the following March. By June her brother had been informed by the surgeon that she had only a month or so to live. Her sons, Caryl and Pierre, were home from school that summer and they and Marguerite's eldest daughter helped care for her. Caryl was the only one Susan would trust to give her hypodermic injections and medicines.

Her value to the community had been so profound that the *Walthill Times* of September 24 added an extra page to carry special eulogies of Susan. Funeral services were held on Sunday morning, September 19, in her home, where friends and relatives surrounded her casket. The simple service was performed by three Presbyterian clergymen, the Reverend C. H. Mitchelmore, pastor of the Walthill Presbyterian Church, which Susan had helped to organize; the Reverend George A. Beith, pastor of the Blackbird Hills Mission, where she had spent years of hard work; and Dr. D. E. Jenkins, a member of the Presbyterian Board of Home Missions, which she had served for many years. The closing prayer was given in the Omaha language by one of the older members of the tribe. Interment took place at the Bancroft Cemetery, where she was laid to rest beside her husband. The Amethyst Chapter of the Eastern Star conducted a moving graveside service.

> Hardly an Omaha Indian is living who has not been treated and helped by her, and hundreds of white people and Indians owe their lives to her treatment, care and nursing . . . We are confronted here with a character rising to greatness, and to great deeds out of conditions which seldom produce more than mediocre men and women, achieving great and beneficial ends over obstacles almost insurmountable.

After her death the Walthill Hospital was in tribute renamed the Dr. Susan Picotte Memorial Hospital by the Home Mission Board.

A Primary Perspective

"AMERICANIZING" NATIVE AMERICANS

Though often well meaning, the people in charge of late 19th-century Indian policy viewed Native American culture through an ethnocentric prism that distorted all their plans. This was especially so with regard to educational matters, as can be seen in the excerpt below from the 1880 report of the Board of Indian Commissioners. Given the assumptions behind such programs, it was little wonder that so many Native American youths resisted the assimilationist teachings encountered in government schools.

Report of the Board of Indian Commissioners (1880)

The most reliable statistics prove conclusively that the Indian population taken as a whole, instead of dying out under the light and contact of civilization, as has been generally supposed, is steadily increasing. The Indian is

Source: Twelfth Annual Report of the Board of Indian Commissioners (1880), pp. 7–9, in Francis Paul Prucha, ed., *Americanizing the American Indians: Writings by the "Friends of the Indian," 1880–1900* (Cambridge: Harvard University Press, 1973), pp. 193–96.

evidently destined to live as long as the white race, or until he becomes absorbed and assimilated with his pale brethren.

We hear no longer advocated among really civilized men the theory of extermination, a theory that would disgrace the wildest savage.

As we must have him among us, self-interest, humanity, and Christianity require that we should accept the situation, and go resolutely at work to make him a safe and useful factor in our body politic.

As a savage we cannot tolerate him any more than as a half-civilized parasite, wanderer, or vagabond. The only alternative left is to fit him by education for civilized life. The Indian, though a simple child of nature with mental faculties dwarfed and shriveled, while groping his way for generations in the darkness of barbarism, already sees the importance of education; bewildered by the glare of a civilization above and beyond his comprehension, he is nevertheless seeking to adjust himself to the new conditions by which he is encompassed. He sees that the knowledge possessed by the white man is necessary for self-preservation. He needs it to save him from the rapacity and greed of men with whom he is forced to come in contact; he needs it just as much to save him from himself.

It is this, supplemented and reinforced by a pure morality and the higher principles of Christianity, that is to enable him to resist the old currents of habit, which, like a mighty river, would otherwise sweep him to certain destruction. . . .

If suitable boarding and industrial schools could be established and properly managed, a compulsory attendance of the youth enforced, as is practiced by some of the governments of Europe, the next generation of Indians would unquestionably be found far in advance of what may be expected from many years of schooling under the present, imperfect, and unsatisfactory methods.

To expect them to attain civilization without these advantages is to look for impossibilities; to deny them these opportunities is to perpetuate their present helpless semibarbarous condition.

The influence of the education of the child is most beneficial to the parents. Gradually they come to perceive the immense advantages of education over ignorance, and they are eager to encourage their children to secure a boon which will eventually enable them to compete successfully with the more favored white man.

The Indian has demonstrated his record for courage, endurance, and loyalty, elements of true manhood, and with proper facilities will show himself equally capable of a true civilization.

Industrial schools once established, the methods suggested by experience as the wisest and most successful should be adopted for bringing them to the highest possible state of efficiency; these are the dictates of economy as well as justice and humanity.

If the common school is the glory and boast of our American civilization, why not extend its blessings to the 50,000 benighted children of the red men of our country, that they too may share its benefits and speedily emerge from the ignorance of centuries?

QUESTIONS

1. What influence did her years at Hampton Institute have on Picotte's life? Why did her white sponsors show such great interest in Picotte? Why do you think Picotte was able to overcome the internal conflicts that troubled so many Native American youths who attended off-reservation boarding schools?
2. Why did Picotte want to become a physician? Why did other Omahas consult Picotte on business and legal matters as well as medical problems?
3. What were the greatest problems that Picotte encountered as a practicing physician? Why did she become an ardent temperance advocate? What steps did Picotte take to reduce alcohol consumption among the Omahas?
4. In what ways did Picotte's medical practice most likely differ from that of white physicians of the period? What were her most important achievements as a doctor?
5. How do you think Picotte would have responded to the sentiments expressed in the 1880 report of the Board of Indian Commissioners? What would the commissioners have thought of Picotte?
6. Which aspects of Picotte's life did you find most interesting? If you were asked to write a biographical profile about Picotte, in what ways would your portrait differ from the one presented in this chapter?

 # ADDITIONAL RESOURCES

The best study of Picotte's life is Benson Tong's recent work, *Susan LaFlesche Picotte, M.D.: Omaha Indian Leader and Reformer* (1999). There are no other full-length biographies of Picotte, but her family is the subject of Norma Kidd Green's *Iron Eye's Family: The Children of Joseph LaFlesche* (1969). Also see Dorothy Clarke Wilson's fictionalized biography of her sister, *Bright Eyes: The Story of Susette LaFlesche, an Omaha Indian* (1974). Studies of late nineteenth-century Indian policy and the operation of the assimilation program include Francis Paul Prucha, *American Indian Policy in Crisis: Christian Reformers and the Indian, 1865–1900* (1976), and Robert Winston Mardock, *The Reformers and the American Indian* (1971). For more on female physicians during the period, see Mary Walsh, *"Doctors Wanted: No Women Need Apply": Sexual Barriers in the Medical Profession, 1835–1975* (1977), and Regina Markell Morantz-Sanchez, *Sympathy & Science: Women Physicians in American Medicine* (1985).

The eight-part series from PBS *The West*, by Ken Burns, provides one of the most comprehensive treatments available on the settlement of the American West and the resulting impact on the original inhabitants of that area. Episodes 6, "Fight No More Forever," and 8, "One Sky Above Us," especially deal with the white–Native American contest for the West.

Chapter 3

Mary Elizabeth Lease

*I*n the late 19th century, more than 40 million people lived and worked in America's agricultural regions. Despite dramatic increases in urban population, the United States remained a nation of farmers. If statistics on farm productivity meant anything, it should have been a prosperous time for most of them. Between 1860 and 1890, improvements in agricultural machinery and the adoption of scientific farming methods enabled land cultivators to grow ever larger crops. In the Midwest and Plains states during this 30-year period, wheat production increased nearly threefold, while corn harvests rose from 800 million to 1.6 billion bushels. In the South, cotton output more than doubled to 8.6 million bales. Meanwhile, expansion of the railroad network linked the most distant farm areas to burgeoning urban markets.

Unfortunately, prices did not keep pace with productivity, and the period witnessed a steady decline in farm returns. The same bushel of wheat that brought $1.96 in 1865 sold for 90 cents a quarter-century later; other crops did no better. As prices plummeted and debt increased amid mounting mortgage foreclosures, farmers turned to a growing literature on agricultural economics in an effort to find out what had gone wrong. One focus of their attention was the money supply. Increasing the amount of money in circulation, they believed, would not only raise price levels but reduce interest rates in farm areas. Hard times also prompted them to take a close look at railroad operations. Here they found that shipping rates in the West and South were considerably higher than those charged in eastern areas, where railroad companies faced stiffer competition for freight.

Discussion of these and related problems soon led to organization. When various economic self-help projects failed to produce desired changes, farmers looked increasingly to government; and when the two major parties largely ignored their grievances, they began to field candidates of their own. These political initiatives culminated in the formation of the People's or Populist Party. Founded in 1892, it adopted a broad platform that called for legislation on land, money, markets, taxes, and railroads. Believing that the political process itself needed reforming, the Populists also sought a secret ballot and direct election of senators; and in an effort to forge ties with urban working people, they supported labor demands for shorter hours and higher wages.

Although men took the political lead in farm country, women shared the economic burdens of rural life. Apart from their vital role in child care and household maintenance, many farm families depended on the cash income derived from the butter, eggs, cloth, and other goods that they produced and sold. As rural discontent spread, many women added their voices to the growing clamor for reform. One of these women was a Kansas housewife named Mary Elizabeth Lease, who in 1892 alone made as many as 160 appearances before Populist gatherings. Her activities are the subject of the essay that follows. In it, Rebecca Edwards furnishes an inspiring account of an energetic woman whose contributions to the Populist movement occupied only a small part of a lifetime dedicated to making this a more just and humane world.

Mary Lease and the Sources of Populist Protest

Rebecca Edwards

In the 1890s Mary Lease was one of the most famous women in the United States, so well known that newspapers called her simply "Mrs. Lease of Kansas." The decade of her fame coincided with a deep economic depression,

Source: "Mary Lease and the Sources of Populist Protest" by Rebecca Edwards from Ballard G. Campbell, ed., *The Human Tradition in the Gilded Age and Progressive Era* © 2000.

mass unemployment, and hundreds of strikes. By 1900, Americans were uneasily conscious of growing divisions between rich and poor. Lease won her fame by speaking to these issues with anger, humor, and eloquence. As a leader of the Populist Party, she helped shape a movement of farmers, workers, and reformers that challenged the political and economic status quo. Today, Lease is largely forgotten, receiving only an occasional mention as the woman who urged American farmers to "raise less corn and more hell."

Historians have written a great deal about the Populists' ideas and identities. For the most part they have described populism as a movement of native-born, Protestant, Anglo-American farmers whose cause failed because of the fraud and intimidation practiced by southern Democrats and because the new party never won a following in the Midwest and Northeast. Yet although the Populist party disappeared in a few years, it left an important legacy. Much of its program won passage in the Progressive Era and New Deal, having been taken up by other reformers. Before Mary Lease died in 1933, she witnessed federal regulation of banks and railroads, government aid to farmers, direct election of U.S. senators, and a national progressive income tax, all of which the Populists had proposed.

The Populists, then, have not been forgotten, but Mary Lease has, perhaps because she remains an ambiguous figure. Her life contradicts much of what we think we know about populism. Born in Pennsylvania less than a year after her parents arrived from Ireland, Lease was heir to her father's legacy of agricultural poverty. A Catholic by birth and education, she had become an **agnostic** by 1900, contradicting historians' picture of populism as an evangelical Protestant crusade. Only briefly a farmer's wife, Lease gained an eclectic political education from the Woman's Christian Temperance Union, the women's suffrage movement, labor unions, and the Irish nationalist cause. A champion of "equal rights for all, special privileges for none," she nonetheless made anti-Semitic remarks and endorsed U.S. colonization of Latin America. When, in Lease's opinion, the Populists caved in to the Democratic party, she turned against them. She then divorced her husband, moved to New York City, and worked as a journalist, lawyer, and advocate of birth control.

Perhaps Lease was an oddity, a woman whose background and beliefs lay outside the mainstream of her movement. If so, she was a very influential oddity. Her claim that she single-handedly brought the Kansas Populists to power was only a slight exaggeration. She sat in Populist inner councils, played a pivotal role in two national conventions, and conducted speaking tours across the nation from Georgia to Minnesota and Montana to New York. Her life tells us a great deal about the political and economic reshaping of the United States between the Civil War and the New Deal. It also tells us a great deal about how these changes affected women and how women themselves became agents of change. Lease was that much-feared figure, an angry woman. She helped build up populism, and then in bitter disillusionment she helped destroy it, exiling herself from history's ranks of Populist heroes. She remains, today, a

> **agnostic** One who is uncertain whether God exists.

complicated figure: courageous, ambitious, immensely talented, alternately petty and visionary, a woman of small prejudices and great dreams.

Mary Lease, born Mary Clyens, experienced poverty and loss from her earliest childhood. Her parents came to the United States in 1849 from County Monaghan, Ireland, during the devastating potato famine that reduced Ireland's population by 2.5 million through emigration, starvation, and disease. Mary's two older sisters and one of her older brothers died in the famine, probably from cholera. Her father joined other tenant farmers in protesting British policies in Ireland; his absentee landlord finally got rid of this "objectionable" tenant by paying the family's passage to America. Mary was born a year after the Clyens' arrival in northwestern Pennsylvania. Her parents had barely scraped together enough money to buy a farm when her father and brother enlisted in the Civil War. Both died—her father of scurvy and dysentery in a Confederate prison camp—and Mary's mother was forced to sell the land. Only through the help of family friends did Mary receive an education at St. Elizabeth's Academy in nearby Allegany, New York.

Twenty-year-old Mary Clyens, like many Americans of the postwar period, decided that a better future lay in the West. She had been an excellent student, and in 1871 the nuns at St. Elizabeth's arranged a teaching post for her at Osage Mission in eastern Kansas. Saying good-bye to her younger brother and sister and her widowed mother, Mary boarded the train and apparently never looked back. After three years teaching in Kansas, where the ratio of men to women was high, Mary fulfilled the contemporary prophecy that an unmarried woman, once west of the Mississippi, would soon write home as a bride. Surrounded by her new friends in Osage Mission, she married Charles Lease in January 1873.

Charles owned a successful drugstore, sat on the board of a local bank, and a year after the wedding became the mayor of Osage Mission. The Leases had many friends, and Mary seemed destined for respectable small-town prosperity until, in May 1874, her fortunes came crashing down with those of her new husband. In the wake of a severe financial panic, Charles Lease lost his store under circumstances that left him not only bankrupt but under a cloud of suspicion. When the scandal broke, Mary was four months pregnant with their first child. Embarrassed both financially and socially, the couple moved to Denison, Texas, where Charles found work as a pharmacy clerk. They stayed nine years.

For Mary, the poverty of these years was a sad repetition of her mother's troubles. She probably knew little of her husband's business affairs when they first married, but his financial ruin and the subsequent disgrace and social ostracism must have made a deep impression on her. She later asserted that the key source of women's oppression was economic dependence on their husbands—a conviction surely born of personal experience. Other shocks were in store. Less than a year after moving to Denison, she received news of her mother's death in Pennsylvania. After the birth of Charles, her first child, she became pregnant five more times and watched two of her children die in infancy—an event not uncommon at the time. On her husband's meager salary,

Mary struggled to raise the surviving children, Charles, Louisa, Grace, and Ben. Like her own mother she valued education, and she took in other families' laundry in order to pay for her children's school clothes and books. Publicly, at least, she never expressed bitterness or anger toward her husband for the crisis into which they had plunged, but the couple grew increasingly distant.

By 1884 the Leases had saved enough money to move back to Kansas and pursue Charles's old dream of farming in the dry lands west of Wichita. During the post–Civil War years, frontier "boosters" offered glowing descriptions of the future prosperity of farms on the Great Plains. Fresh from Union victory, the nation abounded in optimistic editors, politicians, businesspeople, and railroad managers, the latter of whom needed to sell lands granted to them by Congress to finance a flurry of railroad construction in the largely unsettled West. Even scientists joined in, arguing that settlement would create more and more rainfall because the crops and trees planted by pioneers would attract atmospheric moisture. This prediction was not true, of course, but "rain follows the plow" became a Plains axiom. A settlers' guide commissioned by the Missouri Pacific Railroad, and published in the year Mary Lease first arrived in Osage Mission, made extravagant claims about Kansas's climate and the certainty of its economic growth. "Every year there has been a noted increase in the fall of rain," the guide reported, "unquestionably brought about by the cultivation of the soil, and planting of forest trees and orchards."

The Leases, along with thousands of other settlers, were shocked by the actual conditions in western Kansas. Staking a claim in Kingman County, Charles and Mary took the government up on its offer, under the Homestead Act of 1862, to provide 160 free acres to anyone who lived on the land for three consecutive years. Because the policy encouraged settlement on lands of marginal quality, free land was not necessarily the road to prosperity. Like many others, the Leases found that rain did not follow the plow. A 160-acre farm could provide a good living in Pennsylvania, but it was not large enough to sustain a family on the Plains, especially during periods of drought. The Leases soon resettled in Wichita, little better off financially than at the start of their marriage. Charles found a job as a pharmacy clerk, and Mary continued to take in laundry.

Driven by her hardships, Mary began as early as 1880 to seek a public role in movements for political and economic change. While still in Texas she joined a local chapter of the Woman's Christian Temperance Union (WCTU), the most successful women's organization of the 1870s and 1880s. Though prohibition of liquor may today seem a **quixotic** or narrow-minded goal, the WCTU construed it broadly. Refusing to trivialize the costs of alcoholism, WCTU leaders argued that thousands of women and children suffered neglect and abuse at the hands of drinking husbands and fathers. For Mary Lease, as for many women, temperance was a way to begin speaking tentatively about women's rights. The WCTU also addressed economic injustice. By the 1890s the WCTU's charismatic national president, Frances Willard of

---

quixotic Foolishly idealistic or impractical.

Illinois, described herself as a Christian Socialist and cited poverty as the chief cause of alcoholism. Mary Lease's ideas developed along the same lines.

Lease became immersed in a host of reform organizations after moving to Wichita. First, she organized a women's study club, whose members sought to cultivate their intellectual talents. In 1886 she cofounded the Wichita Equal Suffrage Association (WESA), which asserted women's right to vote. Suffrage was a radical demand, and WESA was subject to immediate ridicule in the columns of Wichita newspapers, all of whose editors were men. When these men poked fun at the "pants-wearing" women who wanted to vote, Lease riposted with witty poems and letters. She learned, however, that suffrage was an uphill battle and its supporters had to bear public insults, including claims that they were aggressive, "unwomanly," and bad mothers to boot.

By the late 1880s, Lease's interests expanded in other directions. She re-claimed her Irish-American identity, which she seems to have downplayed or even hidden during her early quest for respectability. Wichita had a large working-class Irish community, many of whom had arrived to work in rail-road construction. Invited to address Irish social and political clubs, Lease began to give stirring speeches advocating the end of British colonial rule in Ireland as well as fair treatment for Irish tenant farmers. Around the same time, not coincidentally, she joined a local assembly of the largest and most inclu-sive labor union in the United States, the Knights of Labor. In 1886 the Knights organized a massive strike against the Southwestern Railway System, operated by wealthy New York financier Jay Gould. At many points along Gould's rail-roads, including Wichita, local members of the Knights of Labor blocked trains and disabled engines. Though the governor of Kansas called in the National Guard to put down the strike, Lease had witnessed a vivid episode of collec-tive protest against low wages, layoffs, and dangerous working conditions.

Three years later, well practiced in stump speaking and organizing, Lease also joined the Wichita branch of the Farmers' Alliance and Industrial Union, or "the Alliance," as it was widely known. At the time, the Alliance was sweeping across the South and the Great Plains in response to the problems of drought, low crop prices, and heavy farm debts. The Alliance sought allies among union members, including the Knights of Labor. These two groups saw themselves as sharing the same enemies, especially railroad owners such as Jay Gould, whom angry farmers accused of monopolizing key routes and overcharging farmers for the transport of crops to market. (Gould's Missouri Pacific, among others, had promised Kansans "rain would follow the plow.")

More broadly, Knights and Alliance members shared a common set of beliefs that historians have called "producerism." In the decades after the Civil War, railroads and large industrial corporations gained unprecedented power; farm-ers and laborers increasingly found their fate in the hands of faraway managers and shareholders. Influential thinkers such as Henry George, author of *Progress and Poverty*, identified the income from land rentals, bonds, and other invest-ments as the cause of growing disparities between rich and poor. Lenders were growing rich on high interest rates, such thinkers argued, while borrowers were falling into hopeless debt. Thus, economic reformers began to draw a sharp distinction between bankers and bondholders on the one hand (viewed as parasites who lived on the labor of others) and farmers and the working class on the other. Both the Knights and the Alliance, along with organizations of international scope such as the Irish National League, spoke for the interests of "producers": men and women who did hard, physical work.

Lease's activities on behalf of temperance, women's suffrage, Irish nationalism, and farmers' and workers' rights thus were not as scattered as they might seem. The immigrant men and women who cheered Lease's speeches on behalf of Irish freedom were, in many cases, the same people she met in Knights of Labor meetings. They saw a connection between their parents' poverty in the Old World and labor exploitation in America. Many, like Lease, came from families experienced in protest, and they had emigrated from parts of Ireland where Ribbonmen and other secret societies organized to defend tenants' rights. In these movements, Irishwomen had long played an important role, so it was natural for Irish-American women to play prominent roles in both the Knights and Irish nationalist organizations.

In the meantime, many temperance leaders such as Frances Willard emphasized poverty and unemployment as causes of alcohol abuse, and the Knights and Farmers' Alliance promoted temperance among their members. Furthermore, male leaders of the Knights and the Alliance gave lectures, as Lease had done, to encourage women to join the movement. The strongest justification for women's entry into such public activities was the view, widespread at the time, that women were morally purer than men. Both the WCTU and many suffragists emphasized women's special role as mothers and wives, seeking to extend "housekeeping" and maternal love into the public sphere. Lease found this rhetoric to be powerful and applicable to the problems of poor laboring women and farm families. "After all our years of toil and privation, dangers and hardships upon the Western frontier," she told one WCTU audience, "monopoly is taking our homes from us by an infamous system of mortgage foreclosure. . . . Do you wonder the women are joining the Alliance? I wonder if there is a woman in all this broad land who can afford to stay out."

Both the Knights and Farmers' Alliance were divided on the question of women's suffrage; conversely, not all WCTU members agreed on the importance of poverty and unemployment as causes of intemperance. In Wichita, however, Mary Lease found sympathetic allies on all sides, and many of her fellow organizers agreed on the need for a grand, unified movement that would work for economic and social reform. By the late 1880s, many activists were furiously debating whether a political party was the best vehicle for collective action. The WCTU had already helped to build up the Prohibitionist party, and its leaders were seeking alliances with other reform-minded groups. In 1888, at a Knights convention in Kansas City, Mary Lease argued vigorously that the union should make partisan endorsements and even run its own candidates. In the fall elections, like-minded Knights ran a fledgling campaign as the Kansas Union Labor party, on whose behalf Lease gave her first partisan speeches. By 1890 the Kansas Farmers' Alliance was also frustrated by the failure of its cooperative stores and other self-help measures, and its members declared their readiness for electoral politics. Thus Kansas populism was born, and Mary Lease with her multiple affiliations and her experience as a speaker and organizer found herself on center stage.

From the start, Populists sought to remedy America's problems through electoral means, challenging Republicans and Democrats with a new program of government activism. Opposing Republicans' constriction of the money supply (a policy beneficial to lenders), Populists called for currency expansion to stimulate credit and ease the burdens of borrowers. They also demanded government regulation—if not outright ownership—of the railroads and telegraphs, which made up the nation's basic infrastructure. At the local level, Populist editors and orators suggested a host of other measures to rescue farmers and industrial laborers from poverty and foreclosure. Like any movement embracing hundreds of thousands of people, populism contained tensions and contradictions; yet all Populists agreed that the "money power" (meaning Wall Street financiers and the politicians whose influence they bought) threatened the interests of hardworking Americans.

Populists' first testing ground was the Kansas election of 1890, a campaign in which Lease played a key role. Incensed at Republican senator John J. Ingalls—who ridiculed the Populists and told women their proper place was at home, not in politics—Lease went on the stump, giving an estimated 160 speeches in three months. Like her fellow Populists, Lease saw the new party as a movement not of farmers only but of all the producing classes. She excoriated bankers, corporate managers, and those who lived on income from their investments. In broader terms she spoke out against government and corporate policies that were rapidly making the rich richer while the poor stayed poor. "I hold to the theory," she said, "that if one man has not enough to eat three times a day and another man has $25 million, that last man has something that belongs to the first."

Lease quickly emerged as one of her party's most effective orators. She had a low, powerful voice—described by listeners as resonant, masculine, or even hypnotic—along with a keen memory for statistics, a sense of humor, and the ability to think on her feet. In an era when political speeches were mass entertainment, she excelled at holding audiences' attention, often for two hours or more. "One of the best addresses, if not the best and most eloquent address I ever heard from a woman," a Nevada newspaperman wrote in his diary after hearing her speak. "Splendid style, voice and elocution." "She is the greatest natural orator of the female sex (or of either sex) that has appeared on earth," wrote another admirer. Lease laced her speeches with quotations from Shakespeare and the Bible, and she learned to handle hecklers with scathing sarcasm or disarming wit.

Hailing "Our Queen Mary," the upstart Kansas Populists won five of the state's seven congressional districts and a majority of seats in the legislature. Because state legislatures elected U.S. senators until the Seventeenth Amendment, ratified in 1913, the new legislature promptly unseated John Ingalls and chose William Peffer as the nation's first Populist senator. It was a stunning victory. The events of 1890 in Kansas brought national fame to the new party and to Lease, and they persuaded Alliance members and Knights in other parts of the country that electoral politics was worth a try.

Thus, there was hardly time to celebrate the Kansas victory as organizers hastened to build the movement nationwide. A proven orator, Lease spent little time in Kansas over the next two years. Leaving her four teenage children in Wichita with their father, she represented the party all over the nation. In February 1892, her speech in St. Louis provoked wild enthusiasm from a gathering of thousands. The following June, as the lone woman in the Kansas delegation, Lease participated in the Omaha convention that established a national People's party. She helped craft parts of the platform in committee, and she gave the seconding speech for James B. Weaver, the party's presidential nominee. In the famous Omaha Platform, the new party presented a bold program for reform. "The conditions which surround us best justify our cooperation," argued the platform's preamble.

> The fruits of the toil of millions are boldly stolen to build up colossal fortunes for a few, unprecedented in the history of mankind; and the possessors of these, in turn, despise the republic and endanger liberty. . . . We believe that the powers of government—in other words, of the people—should be expanded . . . as rapidly and as far as the good sense of an intelligent people and the teachings of experience shall justify, to the end that oppression, injustice, and poverty shall eventually cease in the land.

The 1892 campaign was, in retrospect, the height of populism and of Mary Lease's fame. By this time a member of the party's top inner circle, she accompanied Weaver and his wife on grueling campaign tours around the country. In August they spoke to huge audiences in the West with Lease making as many as eight speeches in a day. "A mortgaged home, an empty stomach and a ragged back know no party," she told a San Francisco audience, urging it to make the "nonpartisan" choice and vote for populism. "We will live to write the epitaphs of the old parties: 'Died of general debility, old age and chronic falsehoods.'"

Populists' greatest difficulty lay, however, in capturing support beyond the West. This they failed to do. Though a Populist coalition emerged in Chicago, most urban workers in the Midwest and Northeast did not respond to appeals from a movement depicted as a "farmers'" revolt." Eastern newspapers alternately ridiculed the party and warned that its leaders were anarchists and Communists. Both Republicans and Democrats, wherever they were entrenched at the state and local levels, commanded vastly greater funds and patronage than did the upstart party and were not averse to using it. Lease herself apparently received offers of bribes to work for the Republicans. Many Northeasterners apparently stayed loyal to the Grand Old Party (GOP) for other reasons: Republicans still took credit for preserving the Union in the Civil War, and they argued that their protective tariff policies sheltered workers in the textile and other industries from low-wage competitors overseas.

The South was the site of populism's most tragic failures. Before 1892, thousands of southern farmers had built a strong Farmers' Alliance ranging from North Carolina to Texas, including a segregated but active Colored Farmers'

Alliance. Yet this activism never translated into Populist strength. Black South-erners' voting rights were increasingly restricted through poll taxes and disfran-chisement laws, and white farmers were reluctant to abandon the Democrats, who pronounced themselves the champions of (white) "home rule" for the South and of resistance to federal intrusion. Those Southerners who became Populists often did so at great risk. Weaver and Lease vividly experienced southern Democrats' fear and hatred when they arrived in Georgia in Septem-ber 1892. In Macon, only a few miles from the place where Lease's father had died in a Confederate prison camp, she and Weaver were hooted down and pelted with rotten vegetables and eggs. At Albany, the speakers and their entourage hid in their hotel, unsure for hours whether the angry crowd outside intended to lynch them. Within a week Weaver and Lease had canceled the rest of their southern tour. In November, Democrats retained control of almost every southern state—by persuading Populist voters where they could and, where necessary, by using overt violence and fraud.

Weaver's defeat—though he won more than a million votes—was only the beginning of Mary Lease's troubles. Though Kansas Populists won many offices in 1892, including the governorship, they did so through ticket-splitting (or "fusion") arrangements with Democrats. To Lease, who spent less and less of her time in Kansas, such an alliance was a betrayal of populism. Democrats were the men she had encountered in Georgia, many of whom were former Confederates, and in her view they were responsible for killing her father.

Furthermore, Democrats in Kansas and elsewhere were staunch oppo-nents of women's suffrage and prohibition, and Populists had to give up these goals in order to appease their new friends. For some Populists this apparent compromise was not a problem, since they had never supported such mea-sures in the first place. But many others, Lease included, wanted the party to articulate a much broader vision. Outside the former Confederacy, in almost every state where they had held a convention in the early 1890s, Populists had adopted women's suffrage planks. Some had also made favorable mention of prohibition. Yet at the 1892 National Populist Convention these planks had been dropped, largely in deference to the party's more conservative southern wing. Lease observed the same Populist-Democratic fusion in her home state of Kansas: the men in power dismissed women's suffrage and prohibition as side issues at best or even as extremist, illegitimate demands. Small wonder that some Kansas Populists began bitterly denouncing the fusionists, claim-ing they were no longer Populists at all. Those who favored fusion responded, with some justification, that unless the new party allied itself with Democrats, it could not win; with fusion, it had elected a Populist governor.

For Lease, the biggest affront was the division of appointments after the 1892 state campaign. She let it be known that she was interested in Kansas's second U.S. Senate seat, which the new legislature would fill. Lease's candi-dacy created a nationwide sensation: in only two states (Wyoming and Col-orado) were women allowed to vote for national offices, and the idea of a woman senator was entirely new. To many progressive-minded onlookers, this issue was a test of the party's true colors. Women's suffrage leader Susan B.

Anthony offered a public endorsement. James Weaver and other Populists also wrote letters of support, stating that the Constitution clearly allowed women to serve in Congress. But Kansas's new governor and legislators had no desire to appoint either a woman or a "mid-roader," a Populist who avoided fusion with either the Democrats or the Republicans. Their victory had been at best a shaky one, and they calculated that Lease's strongest supporters among the citizenry of Kansas were Alliance women, who had no future votes with which to retaliate if they were displeased. Lease was shunted aside and offered a lesser appointment as state superintendent of charities. No American woman had ever held such a prominent office, and the new governor, Lorenzo Lewelling, no doubt thought he was making a suitable offer. Lease, who rightly considered herself one of her party's most valuable assets, took a different view.

She nonetheless accepted the post Lewelling offered and for a year oversaw the state's asylums for orphans, the mentally retarded, and elderly veterans. With little experience in such work, Lease attended national conferences and listened to the advice of experts, but at the same time she continued to jockey for power within the Kansas party. When Lewelling tried to appoint two Democrats to the Board of Charities as part of the new fusion agreement, Lease protested vigorously and even criticized the governor in her interviews with reporters. Populists who supported Lewelling began to criticize her for disloyalty; many mid-roaders hailed her as a hero. Facing division within Populist ranks, Lewelling dismissed Lease from her post in December 1893. Lease fought an expensive legal battle for reinstatement, but she lost.

By 1895, Lease was also worn down by opponents' attacks. As a woman who spoke for new, radical ideas, she was an outsider to the world of politics, and from the first she received treatment as such. Republican and Democratic editors and politicians branded her as ugly, loud, aggressive, and "unwomanly"—terms of abuse that activist women of all political persuasions have faced. After Kansas's 1892 inauguration ceremony, *Harper's Weekly* ignored Lease's speech for the occasion, reporting instead that she was too flat-chested to wear a ballgown. Some opposition newspapers hinted that Lease "prostituted" her talents; one snidely remarked that her voice was the only thing marketable about her. As Kansas Populists split between fusionists and mid-roaders, some Populists joined in such attacks. Lease claimed in 1894 that Governor Lewelling, when Lease had begun to expose corruption in his administration, had threatened to buy evidence purporting to prove that she and James Weaver had slept together during their 1892 campaign tour. As a poor woman, Lease was particularly vulnerable to such charges, in part because her use of words such as "hell" (even though she was quoting from the Bible) shocked many a respectable citizen.

Angry and isolated, Lease found herself cut off from many former allies as the Populist party fell apart. She first tried to reestablish her influence by publishing a book, *The Problem of Civilization Solved*, which appeared in 1895. It was a rambling work that foreshadowed the logic of the most extreme imperialists in the next decade. Lease argued that European-American farmers needed new land and resources in order to prosper; their future lay in Central and South America, and "enterprising white men from the North" should "colonize the valley of the Amazon and the tropical plateaux." How they would acquire this land remained unclear; Lease repeatedly denounced war and helped found the National Peace Society. In contrast, she praised the U.S. Army for its wars against the Sioux and Cheyenne on the northern plains, and she later gave her wholehearted endorsement to imperialism. With her muddled thinking and overt racial condescension, Lease was lucky that her book was largely ignored.

In 1896, she recommitted herself to stump-speaking tours in one of the most important presidential elections in U.S. history. Democrats nominated William Jennings Bryan for president on a platform that borrowed a few planks from the Populists, most notably in advocating currency expansion. Despite strenuous objections from Lease and others, the Populist national convention seconded Bryan's nomination, adopting a fusion strategy again. Lease spent most of the autumn in New York and Minnesota, speaking for Bryan but noting in an occasional aside that Bryan's platform offered only the barest of reform measures. By the time the Republican candidate, William McKinley, won the White House in November, Lease was declaring herself a Socialist. She was one of the first prominent Populists to do so, and many other Populists (including Eugene Debs, later a famous Socialist candidate for the U.S. presidency) soon followed her lead.

In the wake of McKinley's election the Populist party fragmented and fell into decline. Bitter about the effects of fusion, Lease probably also agreed with former Colorado governor Davis Waite, another Populist who had exhausted himself for the cause. "I have done traveling 1000 miles to make a single speech," Waite wrote Ignatius Donnelly in 1896, "or attempting to fill spasmodic appointments with spasmodic speeches. I want some organization, to make a regular daily series of appointments, provide halls & pay actual living & travel expenses from day to day." The Populist leadership, presiding over a shrinking party, could not offer even these shreds of support.

At the age of forty-eight, so financially desperate that on one occasion her luggage was repossessed, Lease decided to leave Kansas and start a new life. She secured an amicable divorce from Charles and moved with her children to New York City. Having studied law and passed the bar in Wichita during the 1880s, she established a part-time legal practice in New York's Lower East Side, largely serving the immigrant poor. She also taught evening classes on history and literature for the New York Board of Education, and she lectured occasionally on literary, economic, and political topics. In the 1910s she joined a group of reformers working for women's reproductive rights—no doubt recollecting her harsh experiences as a frontier wife and mother. At the end of her life, looking back Lease considered her efforts on behalf of the National Birth Control League, headquartered in New York, among her most important works of public service.

After 1900, Lease never quite found another political home. As early as 1896 she had identified herself as a Socialist, and she became a friend of American

Socialist party leader Eugene Debs, for whose ideas and candidacies she spoke on many occasions. At the same time, Lease was painfully aware of the difficult position of third parties, which had meager campaign funds and no patronage posts to distribute and whose enemies increasingly sought to exclude them from the ballot altogether. Lease retained a fierce hatred of Democrats, based on her father's death and her own touring experiences in Georgia, and she remained hopeful that Republicans would take up new reforms. She admired Theodore Roosevelt, and when he made his Progressive party presidential bid in 1912, she made a series of speeches on his behalf. In a typical move, she afterward sued the campaign for not paying her as much as they had promised—reminding male party leaders, as always, that they could not take her services for granted.

In 1905, Lease suffered another personal tragedy when her beloved oldest son, Charles, died suddenly of appendicitis. In her last years, however, she found the financial security she had sought for so long and proudly watched her three surviving children graduate from college, fulfilling the dream of her own mother, Mary Clyens, that her American grandchildren be well educated. Louisa, Grace, and Ben settled comfortably in Brooklyn. Ben, ironically, became a stockbroker; Louisa married a writer; and Grace followed her mother into politics, becoming a district organizer for the Republicans. In 1932 Mary Lease purchased a farm in Sullivan County, New York, along the Delaware River, where she spent the final year of her life.

Before she died, Lease witnessed the implementation of many policies she had espoused even though Progressive Era economic reforms fell far short of what Populists had dreamed of, leaving the "money power" more entrenched than reformers had hoped. Lease lived to see national women's suffrage, and she watched a one-time Populist ally, Rebecca Felton, become the first woman to sit in the U.S. Senate, albeit if only briefly to serve out her deceased husband's term.

Lease died in 1933 at the age of eighty-three. William Allen White, an old foe who had grown more sympathetic to some of Lease's views, wrote upon her death that "as a voice calling the people to action she has never had a superior in Kansas politics. . . . She was an honest, competent woman who felt deeply and wielded great power unselfishly." Lease did, indeed, seek public solutions to private problems, impoverishing herself in the 1890s by working for measures that would aid millions of Americans rather than only herself. In her long life she experienced many reversals of fortune. Poverty and the deaths of three children were griefs she shared with millions of women; other sufferings—including the countless attacks on her as a public speaker, in which she heard herself called everything from a harlot to a harpy—she shared with only a few. Her restless search for reform continued despite it all.

In her private life, Lease continually reinvented herself. She remained open to new ideas and willing to start again from scratch in the face of bankruptcy, a failed marriage, public scorn, and the loss of those close to her, from the death of her father when she was thirteen to that of her oldest son when she was fifty-five. In her public life she displayed the same willingness to start

over when the causes she worked for crumbled to dust and had to be resur-
rected or reshaped under new names. "Keep your eye fixed upon the mark,"
she once remarked, "and don't flinch when you pull the trigger." Not all her
views were admirable, but they were bold and often ahead of her time, and
throughout her career she kept a sustained focus on inequities of class and
gender. Her eloquence moved tens of thousands of listeners to share—whether
for a few moments, a few years, or a lifetime—a vision of a future America
in which citizens would demand that their government guarantee equality to
women and justice to the poor.

A Primary Perspective

THE OMAHA PLATFORM

Though primarily a farmer's movement, Populism sought to address the concerns
of "the plain people." No party statement makes this clearer than the Omaha Plat-
form of 1892, which is the best-known expression of Populist philosophy and aims.
The document's preamble, from which the excerpt below is taken, was written by
Ignatius Donnelly, a former Radical Republican who was then a leading figure in
Minnesota Populism.

The Omaha Platform

Assembled upon the 116th anniversary of the Declaration of Independence,
the People's Party of America, in their first national convention, invoking
upon their action the blessing of Almighty God, puts forth, in the name and
on behalf of the people of this country, the following preamble and declaration of principles:—

   The conditions which surround us best justify our cooperation: we meet
in the midst of a nation brought to the verge of moral, political, and material
ruin. Corruption dominates the ballot-box, the legislatures, the Congress, and
touches even the ermine of the bench. The people are demoralized; most of
the States have been compelled to isolate the voters at the polling-places to
prevent universal intimidation or bribery. The newspapers are largely subsi-
dized or muzzled; public opinion silenced; business prostrated; our homes
covered with mortgages; labor impoverished; and the land concentrating in
the hands of the capitalists. The urban workmen are denied the right of organization for self-protection; imported pauperized labor beats down their wages;

Source: Reprinted from *National Economist* (Washington, D.C.), July 9, 1892, and in all of the leading Populist newspapers in the weeks following the convention. The *People's Party Paper* (Atlanta)
often ran the entire document as late as 1893 and 1894.

a hireling standing army, unrecognized by our laws, is established to shoot them down, and they are rapidly degenerating into European conditions. The fruits of the toil of millions are boldly stolen to build up colossal fortunes for a few, unprecedented in the history of mankind; and the possessors of these, in turn, despise the republic and endanger liberty. From the same prolific womb of governmental injustice we breed the two great classes—tramps and millionaires. . . .

We have witnessed for more than a quarter of a century the struggles of the two great political parties for power and plunder, while grievous wrongs have been inflicted upon the suffering people. We charge that the controlling influences dominating both these parties have permitted the existing dreadful conditions to develop without serious effort to prevent or restrain them. Neither do they now promise us any substantial reform. They have agreed together to ignore in the coming campaign every issue but one. They propose to drown the outcries of a plundered people with the uproar of a sham battle over the tariff, so that capitalists, corporations, national banks, rings, trusts, watered stock, the demonetization of silver, and the oppressions of the usurers may all be lost sight of. They propose to sacrifice our homes, lives and children on the altar of mammon; to destroy the multitude in order to secure corruption funds from the millionaires.

Assembled on the anniversary of the birthday of the nation, and filled with the spirit of the grand general and chieftain who established our independence, we seek to restore the government of the Republic to the hands of "the plain people," with whose class it originated. We assert our purposes to be identical with the purposes of the National Constitution, "to form a more perfect union and establish justice, insure domestic tranquillity, provide for the common defence, promote the general welfare, and secure the blessings of liberty for ourselves and our posterity." We declare that this republic can only endure as a free government while built upon the love of the whole people for each other and for the nation; that it cannot be pinned together by bayonets; that the civil war is over, and that every passion and resentment which grew out of it must die with it; and that we must be in fact, as we are in name, one united brotherhood of freemen.

Our country finds itself confronted by conditions for which there is no precedent in the history of the world; our annual agricultural productions amount to billions of dollars in value, which must, within a few weeks or months, be exchanged for billions of dollars of commodities consumed in their production; the existing currency supply is wholly inadequate to make this exchange; the results are falling prices, the formation of combines and rings, the impoverishment of the producing class. We pledge ourselves, if given power, we will labor to correct these evils by wise and reasonable legislation, in accordance with the terms of our platform. We believe that the powers of government—in other words, of the people—should be expanded (as in the case of the postal service) as rapidly and as far as the good sense of an intelligent people and the teachings of experience shall justify, to the end that oppression, injustice, and poverty shall eventually cease in the land.

While our sympathies as a party of reform are naturally upon the side of every proposition which will tend to make men intelligent, virtuous, and temperate, we nevertheless regard these questions—important as they are—as secondary to the great issues now pressing for solution, and upon which not only our individual prosperity but the very existence of free institutions depends; and we ask all men to first help us to determine whether we are to have a republic to administer before we differ as to the conditions upon which it is to be administered; believing that the forces of reform this day organized will never cease to move forward until every wrong is remedied, and equal rights and equal privileges securely established for all the men and women of this country.

QUESTIONS

1. In what ways did Lease's experience as a housewife shape the development of her feminism? What prompted her to take an increasingly expansive view of women's rights?
2. What effect did Lease's Irish-American identity have on her emerging radicalism? Of the various reform causes that she supported, what common threads tied them together?
3. What were Lease's greatest strengths as a reformer? What obstacles did she face as a reformer and political activist?
4. In what ways did Populist leaders seek to forge bonds with the labor movement? What issues and concerns provided a basis for an alliance between the two groups? Were any Populist demands at odds with the interests of urban working people?
5. What did the Populists hope to achieve by turning to politics? Why did Populism fail as a national movement?
6. Why did Lease find the alliance between Kansas Populists and Democrats so troubling? How did proponents of fusion justify the alliance? Do you think fusion was a good idea?
7. A comparison of Lease's life with that of Susan LaFlesche Picotte raises interesting questions about gender in late nineteenth-century America. Which of the two women posed a greater challenge to the society in which she lived?

ADDITIONAL RESOURCES

The author of this essay, Rebecca Edwards, is currently at work on a book-length portrait of Lease. When completed, it should be the standard biography for some time to come. In the meantime, there is a rich and growing literature that readers seeking additional information on women's activities during her lifetime can consult. Two fine accounts of their experiences in the postbellum West are Julie Roy Jeffrey, *Frontier Women: The Trans-Mississippi West, 1840–1880* (1979), and Joanna Stratton, *Pioneer Mothers: Voices from the*

Kansas Frontier (1981), which contains generous excerpts from a rare collection of autobiographical writings. For more on women's involvement in the temperance crusade, see Ruth Bordin, *Women and Temperance: The Quest for Power and Liberty* (1981), and Barbara Leslie Epstein, *The Politics of Domesticity: Women, Evangelism, and Temperance in Nineteenth-Century America* (1981); women's contributions to the socialist movement are examined in Mari Jo Buhle, *Women and Socialism, 1870–1920* (1981). In their studies, Peter H. Argersinger, *Populism and Politics: William Alfred Peffer and the People's Party* (1974), Scott G. McNall, *The Road to Rebellion: Class Formation and Kansas Populism, 1865–1900* (1988), and Jeffrey Ostler, *Prairie Populism: The Fate of Agrarian Radicalism in Kansas, Nebraska, and Iowa, 1880–1892* (1993), look at various features of Kansas Populism, while Robert C. McMath, Jr., provides an excellent survey of the broader movement in *American Populism: A Social History* (1993).

Although *The Wizard of Oz* (1939) might at first appear to be an unusual recommendation, the film, based on Frank L. Baum's book *The Wonderful Wizard of Oz* is an allegory of the silver movement that inflamed the prairies in the late 19th century. When seen as an allegory, and after Dorothy's ruby slippers in the film are replaced with the original silver, the connection to Populism becomes more apparent. The yellow brick road represents the gold standard, the Wicked Witch of the East represents the Eastern money power, while the Scarecrow represents the farmer, the Tin Woodman is the industrial worker, and the Cowardly Lion is William Jennings Bryan. Perhaps most appropriately, the story is set in Kansas, where Lease gained her political reputation.

Chapter 4

Henry McNeal Turner

ollowing the end of Reconstruction in 1877, the position of African Americans in southern society steadily deteriorated. To be sure, major changes did not occur overnight. The region's white-dominated governments were initially restrained by fears of northern reaction and uncertainty as to what system of race relations they wished to institute in place of slavery. But such questions were soon resolved. During the 1880s, the new system began taking shape, as state after state enacted a wide range of Jim Crow laws that required physical separation of the races at public facilities. Nor was this all. Beginning in Mississippi in 1890, southern state governments also moved to deprive African Americans of their voting rights through a combination of devices such as poll taxes, white primaries, and racially biased literacy tests.

Socially isolated and forced to rely on their own resources, southern blacks turned increasingly to what would become the most important institution in postbellum African-American society: the church. With emancipation, the secret churches of slavery came out of hiding and experienced tremendous growth. As they did so, black churches not only met the spiritual needs of their parishioners but took on a broad range of secular functions: promoting economic cooperation and development; providing food and shelter to the poverty-stricken; educating people of all ages; and serving as a general haven in a hostile white world.

Churches further served as an important training ground for the development of a leadership class. Not allowed to participate in the broader society, ambitious African Americans sought advancement by channeling their energies into racially based institutions. The ministry thus became a primary avenue for social mobility, and ministers were highly respected and powerful members of their communities, whose influence extended to secular as well as religious matters. That black clergymen later played a dominant role in the modern civil rights movement was hardly surprising.

One of the most prominent—and the most controversial—black churchmen of the late nineteenth century was an African Methodist Episcopal bishop named Henry McNeal Turner. After service as a Civil War army chaplain, Turner settled in Georgia, where he struggled to give the promise of emancipation real meaning. He soon found, however, that all too little had changed. And as discrimination and oppression obliterated earlier hopes, he became a leading proponent of African emigration ventures that would enable southern blacks to flee "this bloody, lynching nation." In the essay that follows, John Dittmer traces the evolution of Turner's thought, showing how it was informed by a theological interpretation of history that merged religious themes and secular concerns in a coherent whole.

Henry McNeal Turner

John Dittmer

Outside of the African Methodist Episcopal **(AME) church,** where he is venerated as one of the pillars of that denomination, Henry McNeal Turner is best known today (when he is known) as a combative black nationalist who promoted ill-fated schemes to send black Americans "back to Africa." He was the "forerunner of **Marcus Garvey.**" But important as that was, Turner's significance as a black leader rests upon much more than his impassioned advocacy of African emigration. More than any other public figure of his day, he encouraged identification with the

> **AME church** A black church founded by Richard Allen in 1816 following a confrontation over segregated seating in a Philadelphia white Methodist church.
> **Marcus Garvey** A black nationalist leader who emphasized black pride and achievements and founded a "back to Africa" movement in the early 1920s.

African homeland, instilling confidence and pride among Afro-Americans "inferiorated" by centuries of slavery. Yet Turner also committed himself to the ongoing black struggle for freedom and dignity inside white America. His public life encompassed one of the most turbulent periods in Afro-American history, from the latter days of slavery to the nadir of black life at the outbreak of World War I.

Viewed in terms of individual achievement, Turner's career was a nineteenth-century American success story. Rising from humble origins, he gained national recognition as an important Reconstruction politician and, after the failure of that democratic experiment, quickly moved up through the ranks of the AME church hierarchy. Later, as senior bishop, he became one of the most influential and outspoken black churchmen. Turner believed that in the post-war South religious leaders must become involved in the secular life of the community, and thus he saw his mission as both spiritual and political. In the 1880s Turner emerged as a leader of the African emigration movement, and his unrelenting support of that cause gained him a wide audience and a major voice in the debate over the Afro-American's future. He was the preeminent black nationalist of the period, and his appeals to race consciousness and pride, coupled with his blistering attacks on white society, won him the respect of thousands of American blacks.

At the same time Turner was one of the most paradoxical public figures of his era. The champion of the inarticulate black masses, he did not effectively represent their interests during the early period of his political ascendancy after the Civil War. The same man who pleaded for black unity was unwilling to compromise with other leaders and was himself a divisive force in the black community. His criticism of white America, as it developed over the years, was more biting and incisive than that of his contemporaries, yet Turner openly consorted with racist politicians, not all of whom supported his emigrationist platform. It is difficult, even today, to reconcile many of these apparent con-tradictions. Turner kept his own counsel and did not leave behind memoirs or correspondence that might shed light on the complexity of his thought.

The contradictions in Turner's public life were reflected in his personality. A large, powerful man, crude and awkward of manner, Turner evoked the image of the two-fisted frontiersman. He was a spellbinding orator whose cruel irony and penetrating sarcasm withered his ideological enemies. Yet this rough facade masked a sensitive, deeply religious man whose spiritual mission was to alleviate the suffering of his people. This messianic vision at first manifested itself in the optimistic belief that white political leaders would live up to the promises made in the immediate postwar period. The collapse of Reconstruc-tion and the subsequent failure of the federal government to safeguard black Americans' constitutional rights dashed Turner's hopes, left him profoundly cynical about the motivations of all white people, and reinforced his convic-tion that blacks could achieve their just destiny only by returning to the African homeland. The contrast between his youthful optimism and later bitter disil-lusionment tells us as much about America in the half century after Appo-mattox as it does about the intellectual odyssey of Henry McNeal Turner.

On Emancipation Day in 1866 a large audience of freed slaves turned out in Augusta to hear a young preacher named Henry Turner deliver the commemorative address. At 32 already one of the major figures in black Georgia, Turner had worked his way up from the cotton fields to a position of state leadership in the AME church. He was clearly a man to be reckoned with, and his presence in Augusta was proof of how far blacks might carry their aspirations. Emancipation itself had created an atmosphere of excitement and anticipation, and the citizens attending this meeting were expecting an oration equal to the joyous occasion. Their speaker did not disappoint them.

In his address Turner rehearsed the history of racial injustice in America, but his tone was upbeat, focusing on the contributions of Africans and Afro-Americans to the advancement of civilization. He urged his listeners to take pride in achievements won in the face of adversity. The young minister saw the Civil War as a turning point and, along with many other black activists, looked to the future with optimism. Using the American flag as his symbol, Turner observed that while in the past "every star was against us; every stripe against us," now "we can claim the protection of the stars and stripes. The glories of this faded **escutcheon** will ever bid us go free." He concluded with the advice that, so far as southern whites are concerned, blacks should "let by-gones be by-gones. . . . Let us show them we can be a people, respectable, virtuous, honest, and industrious, and soon their prejudice will melt away, and with God for our Father we will all be brothers."

That Turner would face the dawn of Reconstruction with such misguided optimism was due in part to his own successful rise from obscurity. Although he was born free in South Carolina in 1834, family necessity dictated that Henry be sent to work alongside slaves in the cotton fields, so he too felt the overseer's lash. Determined to escape the plantation environment, Turner saw education as a way out. With the help of several friendly whites, he learned to read and write, and while still in his teens he caught the attention of officials of the white Methodist Episcopal Church-South, who enlisted him as an itinerant minister. Turner traveled freely throughout the Deep South in the mid-1850s, preaching to slaves and free blacks, and his powerful sermons attracted whites to his meetings as well. Then in 1858 he learned of the AME church, and the idea of an all-black denomination exerted strong appeal. Assigned to the AME mission in Baltimore, Turner began a rigorous program of educational training, studying Latin, Greek, Hebrew, and theology with several professors at Trinity College. Appointed deacon in 1860 and elder two years later, the young minister moved to Washington, where he pastored Union Bethel Church, the largest black congregation in the city.

In Washington, Turner developed friendships with leading antislavery congressmen such as Benjamin Wade, Thaddeus Stevens, and Charles Sumner, contacts he would cultivate during his years as an active politician. He gained national attention when Abraham Lincoln appointed him the first black army chaplain. Turner served with distinction, accompanying troops into

---

escutcheon   A coat of arms, made to resemble a shield.

battle while ministering to their spiritual needs. After the war he moved to Georgia to work with the Freedmen's Bureau, but racial discrimination soon led to his resignation. He then accepted Bishop Daniel A. Payne's offer to become presiding elder and superintendent of the AME missions in Georgia.

Banned from the South for over 30 years, the AME wasted no time in dispatching over 70 missionary-organizers into the states of the Old Confederacy in a massive effort to win over the former slaves who had been members of white-run denominations. Returning to Georgia in 1865, Turner found many freedpeople still prisoners of old slave habits. They exhibited little racial pride and were fearful of antagonizing their former masters. From the outset Turner realized that by necessity his mission would be political as well as religious. A largely self-educated intellectual, he retained the common touch and sought by courageous example to raise the consciousness of free blacks. Throughout his life he would speak to the condition of impoverished blacks, and they would remain his natural constituency and major base of support.

Turner threw himself into his organizational work with unsurpassed energy and enthusiasm. Of his efforts in the field one black Georgian wrote: "I never saw a man travel so much, preach and speak so much and then be up so late of nights . . . drilling his official men. Surely if he continues this way, and lives the year out . . . he has nine lives." There was some question as to whether Turner would "live the year out," for many southern whites did not take kindly to this invasion of black organizers. Tempers flared on both sides. In Macon, after white Methodists won a court victory giving them control of church property, they awoke to find the church burned to the ground. Turner received a number of death threats and welcomed protection from armed supporters as he traveled throughout the rural South. (What was at stake here was more than church property or the souls of freedpeople. For whites, the sight of black men and women organizing to take charge of their destiny did not bode well for the future of white supremacy.)

Turner saw the necessity of striking fast, while the South was off-balance, and he licensed preachers "by the cargo," declaring that "my hastily made preachers have been among the most useful." The efforts of the AME missionaries met with instant and spectacular success, as they recruited thousands of converts. Early in 1866 Turner claimed that Georgia had been secured for the AME church, stating, "I have visited every place it was safe to go, and sent preachers where it was thought I had better not venture."

A man of Turner's talents quite naturally became involved in secular matters, including the burning question of civil and political rights. When asked by the Republican Executive Committee to organize black voters in Georgia, he retraced his steps across the state, writing campaign broadsides, organizing **Union leagues,** and speaking at freedpeople's conventions. His message was always the same: "We want power, it can only

> **Union leagues** Organizations originating in the North during the Civil War that insisted upon equality before the law and full participation by blacks in the political and economic life of the South.

come through organization, and organization comes through unity." Crucial to his success in mobilizing the black vote were the AME churches he had founded the previous year. In these often isolated communities the minister, in addition to preaching the gospel, educated and politicized parishioners. The church was the only institution capable of providing secular leadership, and it quickly became the focal point of black political life as well.

Describing himself as "a minister of the gospel and a kind of politician—both," Turner could look back with satisfaction on the two years since the war's end. He had established the AME church in Georgia on a solid footing and laid the groundwork for his future leadership of that denomination. While his claim that he "organized the Republican party in this state" was somewhat exaggerated, his grass-roots organizing campaign was unprecedented; indeed Georgia would not again see anything like it until the civil rights movement a century later. At 33 Turner was the most influential black religious and political leader in Georgia, the state with the largest black population. As an elected member of the state constitutional convention in late 1867, he looked forward to working with white men of good will to shape a new government responsive to the needs of all its citizens.

Like many grass-roots organizers who would follow him, Turner proved more effective in the field than in the legislative halls. Throughout the long deliberations leading to Georgia's Reconstruction constitution, his stance was both conservative and accommodationist. Consistently supporting planter interests, he introduced a resolution to prevent the sale of property of those owners unable to pay their taxes, and he supported a petition to Congress to grant $30 million for planter relief. He also introduced a resolution providing financial assistance for banks, supported poll tax and education requirements for suffrage, and even attempted to persuade the convention to take up a petition for the pardon of Jefferson Davis. Perhaps Turner summed up his convention performance best when he later ruefully observed that "no man in Georgia has been more conservative than I. 'Anything to please the white folks' has been my motto. . . ."

Aside from his key convention role in establishing a public school system, Turner did not address the concerns of his black constituents. He avoided the issue of land reform, despite widespread interest among freedpeople for "40 acres and a mule." Indeed, by protecting planter property he helped reduce the amount of land for purchase at reasonable prices. His stand for suffrage restrictions would have drastically reduced the potential black electorate, and his failure to push for a constitutional amendment making absolutely clear the right of blacks to hold public office contributed to the expulsion of all black members of the state legislature.

The accommodationist position taken by Turner and the other black delegates rested in part on political expediency. Over three-fourths of the nearly 170 convention delegates were conservative white southerners. Blacks, who made up no more than 20 percent of the total, felt the need to compromise to maintain any political influence. But such assumptions also stemmed from the rather naive faith of Turner and most other blacks at the convention that white

Georgians would agree to meaningful black participation in government. As members of the educated black elite they assumed to know what was best for the illiterate black masses, and they were confident of their ability to deal with seasoned and powerful white politicians. They were wrong on both counts.

After satisfying the requirements of the Congressional Reconstruction Acts of 1867, Georgia was readmitted to the Union and in April 1868 held elections for governor and state legislators. Conservative white Democrats and Republicans dominated the new General Assembly, but 32 blacks did win election, including Henry Turner. During his brief tenure in the legislature, Turner served with greater distinction than he had at the constitutional convention. Now openly suspicious of the agenda of white lawmakers, he increasingly saw his role as that of defender of the rights of freedpeople. Along with other black legislators he introduced bills to provide state subsidies for black higher education, to charter black cooperative stock companies, and to create a black militia to offer some protection against Klan violence. Aware of the nature of economic exploitation against blacks, Turner was among the first to make effective use of the term "peonage" to describe the widespread practice by which many landlords held on to unwilling tenants. He offered legislation to protect sharecroppers, to enact an eight-hour work day, and to abolish the convict lease system.

As he moved away from his accommodationist stance, Turner's relationship with white politicians became confrontational. The state's most articulate black leader, he was singled out for abuse. Angered by slanderous attacks on his character, and upset by the failure of white Republicans to support problack legislation, Turner lashed back at his critics. His speech during the debate that led to expulsion of all black legislators, the most powerful of his career, was a manifesto for human rights: "I am here to demand my rights and to hurl thunderbolts at the man who would dare to cross the threshold of my manhood. . . . Never, in the history of the world has a man been arraigned before a body clothed with legislative, judicial, or executive functions, charged with the offense of being of a darker hue than his fellowmen. . . . The great question, sir, is this: Am I a man?" Turner went on to defend the Negro against charges of inferiority ("I hold that we are a very great people") and to voice contempt for the "treachery" of the white race. At the close of his address he led the black delegation out of the chamber, turned to face his colleagues one last time, and contemptuously scraped the mud off his shoes.

This would not be Turner's legislative swan song. Under protection of federal bayonet the black representatives would gain readmission, and Turner would serve during the 1870 General Assembly session. But by the time he returned, Radical Reconstruction in Georgia had been so effectively undermined that there was little chance for the black delegation to have any impact. The Democrats quickly consolidated their power. After lobbying unsuccessfully for further federal intervention, Turner called upon his old friends in Congress to secure him appointive office. These efforts to obtain federal patronage met such intense white resistance—as when President Grant appointed him postmaster of Macon—that Turner retired from active political life in the early 1870s. Deprived of his political power base, disillusioned by federal indifference to white violence and voter fraud, Turner returned full-time to his religious duties.

Except for church historians, scholars have given Turner's religious career and beliefs short shrift. For over a half century the church was the central concern in his life, providing him with his livelihood and a strong base of operations in the black community. Moreover, his theological interpretation of history laid the foundation for his early political optimism, his evolving black nationalism, and his ultimate obsession with African emigration.

Bishop Turner's theology was grounded in the Bible, particularly in the teachings of the Hebrew prophets and in the gospel of Jesus. A firm believer in the omnipotence and sovereignty of God, Turner said: "There is a God that runs this universe: and a nation and people are no exception." Given this fundamentalist view of the relationship between God and humanity, Turner had to come to terms with the tragic history of the African peoples since the **diaspora.** In so doing he developed a messianic vision which had as its keystone the concept of God's Providential design for people of African descent. Throughout his ministerial career Turner insisted that slavery was a "Providential institution." God was "not asleep or oblivious to passing events" but knew that the slave regime "was the most rapid transit from barbarism to Christian civilization for the Negro." Thus God permitted the enslavement of Africans and placed them under the trusteeship of white Americans. It was whites' brutal treatment of slaves that subverted divine will and purpose and was "an insult to God." It would take the Civil War to "satisfy the divine justice and make slavery despicable in the eyes of a country which loved it so dearly and nurtured it so long." This logic led Turner at first to see Reconstruction as a conversion experience for whites in which they would undergo a change of heart. Convinced that "all great convulsive courses have been succeeded with liberative consequences," he held out the olive branch to southern whites, hopeful that together they would build the new Jerusalem.

The bitter experience of Reconstruction soured Turner on elective politics but did not shake his faith in God's Providential design. The bishop simply adapted the model to fit new circumstances. His experience with the evils of slavery, the racism of northern troops, and the perfidy of both South and North after the war convinced Turner that God's plan for the Negro did not include a positive role for whites. From the outset of his ministry he had believed the church must develop racial pride and consciousness among millions of blacks beaten down by centuries of oppression. Now, beginning in the late 1880s, Turner viewed this mission with a great sense of urgency and began to develop a black theology of liberation grounded in the basic tenets of Christianity.

To achieve this end, Turner realized, blacks must reject all teachings of the white church that confirmed

diaspora The dispersal of a people from their native homeland.

their inferior status. He was particularly sensitive to the symbolic significance of "whiteness" in Christian teachings and discouraged singing of such verses as, "Now wash me and I shall be whiter than snow," explaining that the purpose of washing was to make one clean, not white. More dramatic was his assertion, often repeated, that "God is a Negro." When this statement drew criticism from whites—and from a few blacks—Turner patiently pointed out that historically every race of people had portrayed God in its own image; but he also lashed out at those whites and "all of the fool Negroes" who "believe that God is a white-skinned, blue-eyed, projecting-nosed, compressed-lipped and finely-robed *white* gentleman, sitting upon a throne somewhere in the heavens." Turner was deeply disturbed by the negative influence of white Christianity upon the black psyche: He knew that "Christianity" reflected the values of the greater society, and he despaired of any significant improvement in the self-image of Afro-Americans so long as they were subjected to daily indoctrination by the dominant culture. "As long as we remain among the whites," he wrote in 1898, "the Negro will believe that the devil is black . . . and that he [the Negro] was the devil . . . and the effect of such sentiment is contemptuous and degrading." This is one of the reasons, Turner concluded, "why we favor African emigration."

The black exodus was both the culmination and cornerstone of Turner's theology. It linked his messianic vision of the AME Christian mission and his African dream of a strong and proud black nation, free from the corrupting influence of white society. He had always believed that God's providential plan was to Christianize Africa. As early as 1866 the young minister expressed interest in emigration, and after Reconstruction it became his consuming passion. Contrary to critics' charges, Turner never contended that all Afro-Americans would choose to return to the land of their ancestors. But "millions of the Negro race" would emigrate, bringing with them the message of Christ crucified and (paradoxically) the benefits of Western civilization. To comprehend Turner's black nationalism and the depth of his dedication to Africa, then, one must examine both within the context of his strong religious beliefs.

Turner's election to the bishopric in 1880 culminated 22 years of active service for the AME church in a variety of positions. After five years of religious and political organizing in Georgia, he resigned as elder to become pastor of a large Savannah congregation. In 1876 the Methodist hierarchy called him to Philadelphia to become business manager of the nearly bankrupt AME Book Concern. Turner impressed his superiors with his administrative skills and made good use of the opportunity to write for publications, edit the *Christian Recorder,* revise the church hymnal, and compile the *Catechism of the AME Church.* He also used his position to political advantage, traveling from conference to conference to meet influential black Methodists.

Turner became bishop over the objections of his former patron, Bishop Daniel A. Payne, and other northern-based church leaders. The pious and idealistic Payne was uncomfortable with this crude, awkward preacher-politician from the South. Turner's support came from the southern rank-and-file AME members and their pastors, many of whom he himself recruited into the ministry. In charge of the Georgia Conference, the denomination's largest, Turner and his followers became a powerful voice for the AME church's southern majority.

Church leadership gave Turner a forum denied him in the 1870s. He enjoyed the rough-and-tumble ecclesiastical politics. One of his contemporaries remembers him as "always looking for a fight." Another recalled that he "was no kid glove leader, and no hat box bishop. There was nothing of the smell of the parlor and drawing room about him." Turner saw himself as the leader of the masses but not one of them. He wielded power autocratically, eschewing familiarity. One minister who addressed Turner as "brother" at a convention got a sharp reprimand, as Turner stopped the proceedings with an explosive, "I want you to understand, I am the BISHOP."

Turner's private life centered around his spacious home at 30 Younge Street in Atlanta. Even here the outside world intruded, for amid a mountain of books, journals, and manuscripts, a clerical staff was on hand to do the bishop's bidding. Married four times, Turner survived three wives and all but two of his children. He did not normally refer to his personal tragedies, but in 1893 he did inform newspaper readers that in the 10-year period just ended he had lost his mother, his eldest daughter, his first wife, his youngest daughter, and his second wife. His final marriage at age 73 to his private secretary, Laura Pearl Lemon, a divorcee, evoked a storm of criticism in the AME bishopric, but Turner survived the attempts to remove him from office. A firm believer in the institution of marriage, he once wrote to his son John that "bachelors are a public nuisance."

Although his attitude toward husband–wife relations appears to have reflected the mores of the Victorian age, Turner was ahead of his time in advocating an expanded public role for women. While serving in the Georgia legislature he introduced a bill giving women the vote, and in 1888 he ordained a woman as deacon in the AME church. (The Council of Bishops immediately rescinded the appointment, claiming that the Scriptures did not authorize such action and grumbling that it was an act "without a precedent in any other body of Christians in the known world.") Turner persisted in involving women in the activities of the church, founding the Women's Home and Foreign Mission Society, praising black women because they "intend to make a fight for their rights," and opening the columns of his newspapers to women writers. Turner received strong support and little criticism from women in the AME church; he in turn was proud to recognize their contribution and worth.

As senior bishop for 20 of his 35 years in the episcopacy, Turner put his stamp on the church in numerous ways. An iconoclast at the head of a vast bureaucracy, he scorned regulations that did not serve his purposes. Thus, when faced with the need for strong local leadership in the new AME mission in South Africa, he created the post of vicar-bishop—an office unknown to Methodism. Turner's pragmatism continually caused conflict with his fellow bishops. He also ruffled feathers on the congregational level with attacks on emotionalism in the pulpit and insistence on rituals and [the] use of clerical vestments to promote formality and dignity in worship services.

But his major contributions to the church lay in the fields of education and foreign missions.

Like most black leaders, Turner saw education as the key to progress, and from the beginning of his ministry he stressed the need for well-trained ministers and teachers. Moreover, since he believed that education could be either a means of social control or a potent weapon for liberation, he insisted that schools be organized and run only by blacks, without interference from white teachers or trustees. Under Turner's leadership the AME transferred most of its educational activities to the South, establishing a dozen schools and colleges during the last two decades of the nineteenth century. The centerpiece of the system was Morris Brown College in Atlanta. Turner took special interest in this institution, serving for a time as its chancellor, overseeing its expansion, and at one point mortgaging his personal property to keep the college afloat. In 1900 the college's board of trustees established Turner Theological Seminary in honor of the contributions of the senior bishop.

While not nearly so well publicized as his promotion of African emigration, Turner's missionary work on the continent produced tangible results for the AME church and facilitated the rise of black consciousness in South Africa. The conviction that the AME church had an obligation to Christianize Africa was not original with Turner, but early efforts to do so had failed because of the church's meager economic resources and the more immediate task of evangelizing the freedpeople in the South. The crusade to convert Africans began in earnest in the late 1880s, when Bishop Turner became president of the AME Missionary Department and expanded its jurisdiction to include Africa. Late in 1891 he made his first trip to Africa, drawing upon his considerable organizational skills to establish annual conferences in Sierra Leone and Liberia. Then, and in two subsequent visits in 1893 and 1895, Turner ordained preachers, elders, and deacons, established schools and churches, and won over hundreds of converts to African Methodism. Welcomed by large crowds wherever he went, Turner responded enthusiastically and in a series of widely read letters promoted both African missions and emigration.

The AME church's major gains came in South Africa, where Turner became involved in the racial politics of that strife-torn region on the eve of the **Boer War.** AME church interest stemmed directly from establishment of the South African Ethiopian church in 1892 by African religious leaders upset by the color bar in white churches and stirred by nationalistic feelings of "Africa for Africans." The two religious bodies had so much in common that in 1896 the Ethiopian church sent a delegation to Atlanta to arrange a merger. Turner appointed Reverend James W. Dwane, leader of the Ethiopian group, as superintendent of the newly created AME church in South Africa and authorized his return to Africa to work on the transition of the clergy and members of the Ethiopian mission into the AME denomination.

Two years later Turner made a five-week triumphal tour through

> **Boer War** A war between the British and Dutch for control of South Africa at the turn of the twentieth century.

South Africa, traveling over a thousand miles from Cape Town to Pretoria, meeting with Paul Kruger, the president of the **Orange Free State,** and organizing the Transvaal and Cape Colony conferences. Although he received a polite reception from government officials, they became suspicious that he and American AME missionaries were pursuing goals more political than religious. The "race solidarity" and "race regeneration" messages brought by these missionaries alarmed colonial administrators, who began placing restrictions on the ministers. Turner was specifically accused of arousing nationalist passions among the Zulus, and after the Zulu revolt failed in 1906, AME missionaries were barred from most of Natal and Transvaal.

Turner's South African campaign also got him into trouble with his fellow bishops back home. The controversy erupted with the appointment of Dwane as vicar-bishop. Turner argued that the position was not inconsistent with Methodist tradition, but the AME episcopacy repudiated his action. The Dwane affair was but one of a series of issues that had been dividing Turner and the more traditional bishops (the majority of them did not share his enthusiasm for African emigration), and in the 1890s his power in the church began to decline. But by then Turner had once again reimmersed himself in the secular world, promoting and organizing black migration to Africa, renewing his interest in state and national politics, and making his bid to fill the leadership void left by Frederick Douglass.

For Afro-Americans the decade of the 1890s was the low point of their post–Civil War experience. Acts of racial violence had reached a new high, the courts were continuing their retreat from the constitutional guarantees afforded American citizens, and the depression of 1893 further tightened the chains of crop lien and peonage. Traditional black leaders appeared unable to come to terms with these catastrophic developments. Douglass was now an old man (he would die in 1895), and his assimilationist ideology, based on black political empowerment, had failed to anticipate the depth and virulence of white racist sentiment. The time was ripe for new leadership, and Henry McNeal Turner was ready to make his move.

Save for Douglass, Turner was as well known and as well respected as any black leader. His appeals to black pride and his famous denunciation of the U.S. Supreme Court for its decision in the 1883 civil rights cases had won him a large audience. Turner understood better than most the implications of that ruling, which declared unconstitutional the Civil Rights Act of 1875. That "barbarous" decision should be "branded, battle-axed, sawed, cut and carved with the most bitter epithets and blistering denunciations that words can express. . . . It absolves the allegiance of the Negro to the United States." His position as senior bishop provided a strong power base in the black community, and his organizing skills and oratorical prowess would serve him well in a bid for national leadership. Turner also had a program, one based on the realities of the past three decades of American history: The Afro-American dream of assimilation had failed; it was time for blacks to found their own nation in Africa.

Orange Free State A province in east central South Africa.

Although he continued to demand equal rights for blacks in America, African emigration was the heart and soul of Bishop Turner's program. His first trip to Africa in 1891 was an emotional and exhilarating experience, one that confirmed his feelings about Africa as the homeland. Upon his return he persuaded the AME church to establish a monthly newspaper, the *Voice of Missions*, which quickly became the personal voice of Henry Turner. Under his editorship the *Voice* achieved a wide circulation. The monthly devoted its columns to attacks on racial discrimination, essays on black history and achievement, and, above all, articles promoting African colonization. Turner soon began receiving hundreds of letters from poor southern blacks, eagerly requesting information on passage to Africa. Convinced by this outpouring of interest that his idea was one whose time had come, he pushed forward with plans to settle colonies in Liberia, where the black government would welcome Afro-Americans. Middle-class blacks here remained either lukewarm or hostile to emigration, with their spokespeople usually unequivocal in their opposition.

To rally middle-class support for his crusade, Turner sent out a call for a national convention of Afro-Americans, to meet in Cincinnati in November 1893. With the Democrats back in the White House, the decline of Douglass, and the failure of organizations such as the Afro-American League to unify and galvanize black leadership, a political vacuum now existed that Turner purported to fill. Though the call specifically stated that the convention would "have no application to party politics," he made it clear that "the Negro cannot remain here in his present condition and be a man . . . for at the present rate his extermination is only a question of time."

The response to the convention call was gratifying. Turner's emphasis on the need to rally against racial injustice struck a common chord, and many prominent blacks responded. When the bishop rose to make the keynote address, nearly 800 delegates and a large group of local blacks were in the audience. The occasion afforded Turner a unique opportunity, yet he opened the meeting with a curious speech. He began by reiterating his concept of slavery as a providential institution and then went on to observe that during the Civil War the "Negro was as loyal to the Confederate flag as he was to the federal." Turner devoted much of his talk to the increase in lynching and, more specifically, the question of rape as its primary cause. Though he attacked the "rape defense," Turner did argue that blacks must assume responsibility for dealing with rapists in their midst. Only at the end of his speech did he address the issue of emigration, coupling it with an eloquent plea for the development of a "consciousness that I am somebody, that I am a man . . . that I have rights . . . that I am entitled to respect, that every avenue to distinction is mine."

The audience received Turner's speech warmly, but his somewhat muted emigrationist appeal failed to sway convention delegates, who rejected a committee report recommending that black Americans "turn their attention to the civilization of Africa as the only hope of the Negro race." To avoid a showdown vote he would have lost, Turner sent the report back to committee for revision. Bishop Turner's efforts to unify the delegates around a nationalist and emigrationist program had failed. While he adamantly denied having called the convention to promote his program, the black press was correct in labeling the outcome as a personal defeat for the bishop. Turner was never comfortable in the role of conciliator, and his rebuff by representatives of the black elite in Cincinnati affected him in much the same way as his earlier humiliation at the hands of white Georgia Reconstructionists. Never at home in bourgeois society, Turner reverted after Cincinnati to his familiar polemical style to answer his black critics. . . .

What angered Turner most about the attacks of black opponents was their exaggeration and distortion of his position on emigration and Africa. As early as 1883 he lamented, "Every solitary writer who has been trying to excoriate me for my African sentiments has done so under the hidden idea, 'He wants us all to go to Africa.'" Simply stated, Turner's goal was that a significant minority (his numbers varied) of blacks should "found and establish a country or a government somewhere upon the continent of Africa." Beyond that Turner was vague in his statements concerning the form of government and the nature of the economic system in his proposed African state. There was more truth to the charges that the bishop exaggerated the appeal of Africa to attract emigrants ("And gold dust can be switched up by women and children in marvelous quantities along the shores of rivers and creeks after heavy rains . . . "); yet he did make a point of telling prospective settlers of the difficulties they would initially face and insisted that blacks should not emigrate without sufficient funds to maintain themselves until they found employment.

In the end the most persuasive arguments against African colonization came from the emigrants themselves. In the mid-1890s two boatloads of colonists left the United States for Liberia amid much fanfare and press coverage. Months later reports of disease, malnutrition, and death started filtering back. As the first colonists returned to America with horror stories of life in Liberia, the newspapers reported every tragic detail. Black opponents of emigration seized upon these reports to discredit both the movement and its chief promoter, Bishop Turner. Not all colonists had bad experiences in Africa, however; a few stayed and prospered. But returnees reinforced stereotypes of the "dark continent," and Turner could not dispel that image. His assertions that those who came back had selfish motives, exaggerating their plight to justify their defection and win sympathy back home, were undermined when he labeled them as "shiftless no-account Negroes . . . accustomed to being fed and driven around by white men. . . ." It appeared that Turner, to repair the damage of unfavorable publicity, had resorted to blaming the victim. Although he continued to press for African emigration, the failures of the early expeditions, along with the solid opposition of most black leaders, prevented the bishop from rekindling the spirit of the early 1890s, when thousands of poor southern black sharecroppers shared his African dream of a homeland free from the tyranny of white supremacist rule.

In addition to his work with African missions and for colonization, Turner found time to become active once again in state and national politics. His retirement from active political life in the 1870s had not been total: Occasional comments on national affairs and his widely read denunciation of the U.S. Supreme Court in 1883 had won him a large audience. While he never regained his early zeal for party politics (almost all of his later political pronouncements included the disclaimer that the Afro-American's stay in this country was "a temporary one"), in the 1890s he began to speak out more frequently on issues facing black Georgians. As the decade ended he was vehemently denouncing the new United States imperialism in Cuba and in the Philippines.

For the last quarter century of his life Henry McNeal Turner was a political maverick. The most important black member of the small Prohibition party, he agreed to be a delegate to the party's 1888 national convention. In Georgia, Turner was not alone among black leaders in supporting Democrat William J. Northen for governor in 1892, for Northen was a southern moderate who promised increased funds for black schools and a state antilynching law. The bishop joined most black spokespeople in resisting the appeals of Tom Watson's Populists. More comfortable with powerful Democrats than white insurgents, Turner also questioned the Populist commitment to interracial politics. Ideologically, the Populists had little to offer him, for the bishop never concerned himself much with economic alternatives to corporate capitalism.

Turner received much notoriety—and a degree of political influence—for his support of Democratic candidates running for national office. The bishop was almost alone among blacks in his support of Grover Cleveland's 1892 bid for the presidency. Turner wrote to Cleveland endorsing Georgia editor Hoke Smith for secretary of the interior and was rewarded by having three of his relatives appointed to jobs in the interior secretary's office. (This information surfaced in the 1906 Georgia gubernatorial campaign, embarrassing candidate Smith, by this time one of the state's champion race-baiters.) When Turner actively supported Democrat William Jennings Bryan in his unsuccessful presidential campaigns, the bishop drew fire from black Georgia's political establishment. Republican to the core, leaders such as William A. Pledger, editor of the *Atlanta Age* and the first black Republican state chairman in Georgia, and attorney Judson Lyons, who, as register of the United States Treasury, was the nation's highest black appointee, viewed Turner's actions as heresy, and the black press excoriated him for his crimes.

The bishop's alliance with stand-pat conservative Democrats in Georgia and in Washington does not lend itself to easy explanation, for unlike Senators Morgan and Butler, the Northens and Smiths did not support Turner's plans for African emigration. They were, at best, racial paternalists and had no program for addressing the range of problems facing black Americans. Turner never attempted to reconcile his vehement attacks on American "democracy" with his support of politicians who embraced the status quo in race relations. His endorsement of Democratic candidates enabled him to settle some scores with white and black political foes, provided him with a forum for his emigrationist views in the white press, and gained him some access to important politicians. But in the long run Bishop Turner did not look upon his political activity as preparing the way for meaningful and lasting black participation in the American system. Events at the turn of the century only strengthened his conviction that white America was on a collision course with people of color, both at home and abroad.

Although well into his 60s and in failing health, Turner seemed to grow angrier and more militant with age. Enraged by escalating white violence against defenseless blacks, the bishop responded with a *Voice of Missions* editorial titled, "Negro, Get Guns": "Let every Negro in this country, who has a spark of manhood in him supply his house with one, two, or three guns . . . and when your domicile is invaded by the bloody lynchers or any mob . . . turn loose your missiles of death and blow the fiendish wretches into a thousand giblets. . . ." This was too much for the white press, which accused him of fomenting race war. Although he backed off some here, Turner's nationalistic message remained clear and strong. He carried his analysis a step further when the United States, acting upon its imperialistic impulses, declared war on Spain in 1898.

Turner had opposed American intervention in Cuba, but when the McKinley administration moved to crush the Aguinaldo independence movement in the Philippines, the bishop's rage knew no bounds. Labeling the war there the "crime of the century," Turner castigated blacks who volunteered to help put down the insurrection: "I boil over with disgust when I remember that colored men from this country . . . are there fighting to subjugate a people of their own color. . . . I can scarcely keep from saying that I hope the Filipinos will wipe such soldiers from the face of the earth. . . . to go down there and shoot innocent men and take the country away from them, is too much for me to think about, and I will write no more, for I cannot stand it."

His increasingly outspoken behavior further eroded Turner's support in the church hierarchy, and while he successfully resisted efforts to "encourage" his retirement as senior bishop, he did lose control of the *Voice of Missions* in 1901. Unabashed, he founded his own personal journal, the *Voice of the People*, and continued to put forward a broad black nationalist platform with African emigration as its centerpiece. But circulation of the new monthly remained small, and Turner's fiery appeals now met more apathy than hostility. Still, Bishop Turner remained a commanding presence. When black Georgia's political and intellectual leaders met in Macon in 1906 to form the Georgia Equal Rights Association, Turner was selected to head the group, which included such strident activists as Augusta editor William J. White and Atlanta University's W. E. B. Du Bois.

The Georgia Equal Rights Convention was something of a last hurrah for Bishop Turner. He would live on for nearly a decade, and his name would surface from time to time, usually at the center of some minor controversy. But age and infirmity—as well as American history—had taken their toll. A once herculean frame had grown portly, and his broad shoulders were drooped. Yet as he rose to address his colleagues assembled in Macon, he was again the Turner of old. In his deep booming voice he thundered his most famous lines: "I used to love what I thought was the grand old flag, and sing with ecstasy about the Stars and Stripes, but to the Negro in this country the

American flag is a dirty and contemptible rag. Not a star in it can the colored man claim, for it is no longer the symbol of our manhood rights and liberty. . . . Without multiplying words, I wish to say that hell is an improvement on the United States where the Negro is concerned." For Henry McNeal Turner the flag had always stood as a metaphor for the American dream. His remarks at Macon represented a final judgment upon a nation that had consistently disappointed him, along with millions of other black Americans.

Turner remained active in the church until the end. He died in Ontario, Canada, on April 8, 1915, at the age of 81, after suffering a heart attack. He had gone there against the advice of his physician to preside over the Quarterly Conference of the AME church.

The estimated 25,000 mourners who attended Bishop Turner's funeral in Atlanta represented a cross-section of black America, with a number of prominent figures leading the procession. The eulogies praised his church and missionary work, along with his contributions to black education, but made only passing reference to his early political career and his emigrationist activities. Most of those paying their respects were poor blacks. They were not asked to make speeches, but they recognized in Turner's life the embodiment of their spirit. Whether or not they shared in his African dream, they endorsed his appeals to racial pride and applauded his bold, incisive attacks on American society. Bishop Turner was, in Du Bois's words, a "charging bull," the "last of his clan: mighty men, physically and mentally, who started at the bottom and hammered their way to the top by brute strength."

Henry McNeal Turner was a leader who defies easy categorization. A deeply religious man with the political instincts of a street fighter, an intellectual whose natural constituency existed in the shacks of unlettered sharecroppers, Turner could be maddeningly inconsistent in his political behavior, but he was unswerving in his advocacy of black nationalism and African emigration as the only righteous road to freedom and dignity. He was an agitator and a prophet, who articulated the hopes and frustrations of three generations of Afro-Americans trapped along the color line.

A Primary Perspective

IDA B. WELLS AND THE ANTI-LYNCHING MOVEMENT

The late 19th century was the heyday of American lynching. The most frequent victims were southern blacks suspected of real and imaginary offenses that ranged from discourtesy to murder. During a period when white southern society evinced acute concern about matters of racial control, lynching became the most vicious

Source: Ida B. Wells, *Southern Horrors: Lynch Law in All Its Phases* (New York: The New York Age Print, 1892), pp. 22–24.

of the various means employed to keep African Americans in their place. Of those who sought to combat this horrific development, no one did more to keep the issue before the public than Ida B. Wells, a black writer, suffragist, and founding member of the National Association for the Advancement of Colored People (NAACP). After a Memphis mob lynched three of her friends in 1892—a year that witnessed 230 such killings—she used her position as editor of the Memphis *Free Speech* to launch what would be a lifelong crusade against this barbarous practice. In the extract that follows, Wells speaks of the incident that prompted her activism in the course of urging other African Americans to take a more aggressive stance against lynching.

Self-Help

To Northern capital and Afro-American labor the South owes its rehabilitation. If labor is withdrawn capital will not remain. The Afro-American is thus the backbone of the South. A thorough knowledge and judicious exercise of this power in lynching localities could many times effect a bloodless revolution. The white man's dollar is his god, and to stop this will be to stop outrages in many localities.

The Afro-Americans of Memphis denounced the lynching of three of their best citizens and urged and waited for the authorities to act in the matter and bring the lynchers to justice. No attempt was made to do so, and the black men left the city by thousands, bringing about great stagnation in every branch of business. Those who remained so injured the business of the street car company by staying off the cars, that the superintendent, manager, and treasurer called personally on the editor of the *Free Speech,* asked them to urge our people to give their patronage again. Other businessmen became alarmed over the situation and the *Free Speech* was run away that the colored people might be more easily controlled. A meeting of white citizens in June, three months after the lynching, passed resolutions for the first time condemning it. . . .

The appeal to the white man's pocket has ever been more effectual than all the appeals ever made to his conscience. Nothing, absolutely nothing, is to be gained by a further sacrifice of manhood and self-respect. By the right exercise of his power as the industrial factor of the South, the Afro-American can demand and secure his rights, the punishment of lynchers, and a fair trial for accused rapists.

Of the many inhuman outrages of the present year, the only case where the proposed lynching did *not* occur, was where the men armed themselves in Jacksonville, Florida, and Paducah, Kentucky, and prevented it. The only times an Afro-American who was assaulted got away has been when he had a gun and used it in self-defense.

The lesson this teaches and which every Afro-American should ponder well, is that a Winchester rifle should have a place of honor in every black home, and it should be used for that protection which the law refuses to give. When the white man who is always the aggressor knows he runs as great a risk of biting the dust every time his Afro-American victim does, he will have greater respect for Afro-American life. The more the Afro-American yields and cringes and begs, the more he has to do so, the more he is insulted, outraged and lynched. . . .

Nothing is more definitely settled than he must act for himself. I have shown how he may employ the boycott, emigration and the press, and I feel that by a combination of all these agencies can be effectually stamped out lynch law, that last relic of barbarism and slavery. "The gods help those who help themselves."

QUESTIONS

1. What place did the Civil War have in Turner's theological interpretation of history? Why did he support planter interests at Georgia's constitutional convention following the war? Why did his later initiatives as a Georgia state legislator differ so markedly from his performance at the convention?

2. Turner's career spanned a period of extraordinary change in African-American society. Identify a major turning point in his life and explain why you think it was significant.

3. How would you describe Turner's views on the relationship between religion and society? In what ways did his religious beliefs influence his actions as a politician and racial leader?

4. What were Turner's greatest strengths as a religious leader? Why did he get along so poorly with his fellow bishops within the African Methodist Episcopal church? Given the often troubled nature of these relations, how was Turner able to become such a powerful figure in the church?

5. What developments prompted Turner to become an outspoken proponent of African colonization? Why did middle-class African Americans tend to oppose African emigration? What was Ida B. Wells's likely reaction to emigration proposals?

6. What did Wells mean when she said that African Americans were "the backbone of the South"? What was the main theme of her statement? How do you think Turner reacted to her message? In what ways did the two black leaders' views of American life differ?

  ## ADDITIONAL RESOURCES

The standard modern biography of Turner is Stephen Ward Angell, *Bishop Henry McNeal Turner and African American Religion in the South* (1992), which can be supplemented with the source materials in Edwin S. Redkey, ed., *The Writings and Speeches of Henry McNeal Turner* (1971). Redkey has also provided a searching examination of Turner's emigrationist initiatives in *Black Exodus:*

Black Nationalist and Back-to-Africa Movements, 1890–1910 (1969). Those wishing to learn more about the controversial churchman might consult the relevant sections of the following studies: Leon F. Litwack, *Been in the Storm So Long: The Aftermath of Slavery* (1979); Edmund L. Drago, *Black Politicians and Reconstruction in Georgia: A Splendid Failure* (1982); Clarence E. Walker, *A Rock in a Weary Land: The African Methodist Church during the Civil War and Reconstruction* (1982); Henry J. Young, *Major Black Religious Leaders, 1775–1940* (1977); August Meier, *Negro Thought in America, 1880–1915* (1963); and John Dittmer, *Black Georgia in the Progressive Era, 1900–1920* (1977).

The film *Black Communities after the Civil War* (17 minutes) examines ex-slave migration to Oklahoma and their experiences through the 1920s and is available from Films for the Humanities and Sciences.

Chapter 5

John D. Rockefeller

*D*uring the last third of the 19th century, the U.S. economy grew by leaps and bounds. A major contributing factor was the extension of the railroad network. The construction and operation of railroads required vast quantities of steel, iron, coal, and other products. And as the railroads expanded, these industries also experienced substantial growth. Even more important, as rail lines gradually penetrated all regions of the country, a national market began to take shape. This in turn spurred the creation of ever larger productive units that combined organizational innovations with the newest technology to take advantage of economies of scale. In so doing, the new corporations established formidable market positions at the expense of smaller, less efficient firms.

One example was the Carnegie Steel Company, which by 1890 outpaced all other producers in that industry, and which in 1901 combined with its 10 largest competitors to form the U.S. Steel Corporation. Another was John D. Rockefeller's Standard Oil Company. As early as 1870, Standard controlled nearly 40 percent of the oil industry; by century's end, it owned most of the nation's pipelines and refined more than 80 percent of the oil produced in the United States. Had these firms achieved such dominance on the basis of efficiency alone, the enormous power they wielded would have excited alarm.

As it was, they often employed a variety of unscrupulous tactics to drive competitors to the wall. And where some observers lauded the new corporate chieftains as industrial statesmen and captains of industry who had imposed stability on a chaotic economic system, others viewed them as mean-spirited plunderers who wantonly destroyed peoples' lives in their single-minded pursuit of wealth. In the words of historian Hal Bridges, "They were a set of avaricious rascals who habitually cheated and robbed investors and consumers, corrupted government, fought ruthlessly among themselves, and in general carried on predatory activities comparable to those of the robber barons of medieval Europe."

In the essay that follows, Robert L. Heilbroner gives us an opportunity to assess the validity of these competing interpretations. His examination of the business career and private life of John D. Rockefeller reveals a complex and somewhat eccentric individual who is not easily categorized. Indeed, there is much in Heilbroner's portrait of the oil tycoon to support the contentions of both critics and defenders of the new corporate elite. Readers will thus have to draw their own conclusions as to whether Rockefeller was a robber baron, captain of industry, or something apart from the images suggested by these descriptive terms.

John D. Rockefeller: America's First Billionaire

Robert L. Heilbroner

The incredibly shrunken face of an animate mummy, grotesque behind enormous black-rimmed glasses; the old boy tottering around the golf course, benign and imperturbable, distributing his famous dimes; the huge foundation with its medical triumphs; the lingering memory of the great trust and the awed contemplation of the even greater company; and over all, the smell of oil, endlessly pumping out of the earth, each drop adding its bit to the largest exaction ever levied on any society by a private individual—with such associations it is no wonder that the name has sunk into the American mind to an extraordinary degree. From his earliest days the spendthrift schoolboy is brought to his senses with: "Who do you think you are, John D. Rockefeller?"

Yet for all the vivid associations, the man himself remains a shadowy presence. Carnegie, Morgan, or Ford may not have entered so decisively into the

Source: Reprinted by permission of American Heritage, Inc. Copyright © 1964.

American parlance, but they are full-blooded figures in our memory: Carnegie, brash, bustling, proselytizing; Morgan, imperious, choleric, aloof; Ford, shrewd, small town, thing-minded. But what is John D. Rockefeller, aside from the paper silhouettes of very old age and the aura of immense wealth?

Even his contemporaries did not seem to have a very clear impression of Rockefeller as a human being. For forty years of his active career, he was commonly regarded as an arch economic malefactor—La Follette called him the greatest criminal of the age—and for twenty years, as a great benefactor—John Singer Sargent, painting his portrait, declared himself in the presence of a medieval saint—but neither judgment tells us much about the man. Nor do Ida Tarbell or Henry Demarest Lloyd, both so skillful in portraying the company, succeed in bringing to life its central figure; he lurks in the background, the Captain Nemo of Standard Oil. Similarly, in the reminiscences of his associates we catch only the glimmer of a person—a polite, reserved man, mild in manner, a bit of a stickler for exactitude, totally unremarkable for anything he says or for any particular style of saying it. Surely there must be more to John D. than this! What sort of man was this greatest of all acquisitors? What was the secret of his incredible success?

His mother came of a prosperous Scottish farming family, devout, straitlaced, uncompromising. She springs out at us from her photographs: a tired, plain face, deep-set eyes, and a straight, severe mouth announce Eliza Davison Rockefeller's tired, straight, severe personality. Rockefeller later recalled an instance when he was being whipped by her and finally managed to convince her that he was innocent of a supposed misdemeanor. "Never mind," she said, "we have started in on this whipping and it will do for the next time." Her approach to life made an indelible impression—even in his old age Rockefeller could hear her voice enjoining: "Willful waste makes woeful want."

His father, William Avery Rockefeller, was cut from a different bolt of cloth. Big, robust, and roistering, he treated his sons with a curious mixture of affection and contempt. "I trade with the boys," he boasted to a neighbor, "and skin 'em and I just beat 'em every time I can. I want to make 'em sharp." Sharp himself, he was in and out of a dozen businesses in John's youth and, we have reason to suspect, as many beds. Later, when his son was already a prominent businessman, we can still follow his father's erratic career, now as "Doctor" William A. Rockefeller, "the Celebrated Cancer Specialist," peddling his cures on the circuit. Still later, when John D. had become a great eminence in New York, the father drops into obscurity—only to materialize from time to time in the city, where he is shown around by an embarrassed Standard Oil underling. At the very end he simply disappears. Joseph Pulitzer at one time offered a prize of $8,000 for news of his whereabouts, and the rumor spread that for thirty-five years old William had led a double life, with a second wife in Illinois. No one knows.

It was an unpleasantly polarized family situation, and it helps us understand the quiet, sober-sided boy who emerged. His schoolmates called John "Old pleased-because-I'm-sad," from the title of a school declamation that fitted him to perfection; typically, when the boys played baseball, he kept score.

Yet, if it was subdued, it was not an unhappy boyhood. At home he milked the cow and drove the horse and did the household chores that were expected of a boy in upstate New York, but after hours he indulged with his brothers, William and Frank, in the usual boyhood escapades and adventures. A favorite pastime, especially savored since it was forbidden, was to go skating at night on the Susquehanna. On one occasion William and John saved a neighbor's boy from drowning, whereupon their evening's sally had to be admitted. Eliza Rockefeller praised their courage—and whipped them soundly for their disobedience.

Always in the Rockefeller home there was the stress on gainful work. Their father may have worked to make them sharp, but their mother worked to make them industrious. John was encouraged to raise turkeys, and he kept the money from their sale in a little box on the mantel until he had accumulated the sum of $50. A neighboring farmer asked to borrow the amount at seven percent for a year, and his mother approved. During that summer John dug potatoes at thirty-seven and a half cents a day. When the farmer repaid the loan with $3.50 in interest, the lesson was not lost on John: the earning power of capital was much to be preferred to that of labor.

He was then only in his teens—he was born in 1839—but already, frugal ways, a deliberate manner, and a strong sense of planning and purposefulness were in evidence. As his sister Lucy said: "When it's raining porridge, you'll find John's dish right side up." But now the time for summer jobs was coming to an end. The family had moved from Moravia and Oswego, where John had grown up, to Cleveland, where he went to the local high school in his fifteenth and sixteenth years. For a few months he attended Folsom's Commercial College, where he learned the elements of bookkeeping—and then began the all-important search for the first real job.

That search was performed with a methodical thoroughness that became a hallmark of the Rockefeller style. A list of promising establishments was drawn up—nothing second-rate would do—and each firm was hopefully visited. Rebuffed on the first go-round, John went the rounds again undaunted, and then a third time. Eventually his perseverance was rewarded. He became a clerk in the office of Hewitt & Tuttle, commission merchants and produce shippers. Typically, he took the job without inquiring about salary, hung his coat on a peg, climbed onto the high bookkeeper's stool, and set to work. It was a red-letter day in his life; later, when he was a millionaire many times over, the flag was regularly hoisted before his house to commemorate September 26, 1855.

Work came naturally, even pleasurably to John Rockefeller. He was precise, punctual, diligent. "I had trained myself," he wrote in his memoirs, ". . . that my check on a bill was the executive act which released my employer's money from the till and was attended with more responsibility than the spending of my own funds."

With such model attitudes, Rockefeller quickly advanced. By 1858 his salary (which turned out to be $3.50 a week) had more than tripled, but when Hewitt & Tuttle were unable to meet a request for a further raise, he began to look elsewhere. A young English acquaintance named Maurice Clark, also a clerk, was similarly unhappy with his prospects, and the two decided to form a produce-shipping firm of their own. Clark had saved up $2,000, and John Rockefeller had saved $900; the question was, where to get the last necessary $1,000. John knew that at age twenty-one he was entitled to a patrimony of this amount under his father's will, and he turned to William Rockefeller for an advance. His father listened with mingled approval and suspicion, and finally consented to lend his son the money if John would pay interest until he was twenty-one. "And John," he added, "the rate is ten."

Rockefeller accepted the proposition, and Clark & Rockefeller opened its doors in 1859. The Cleveland *Leader* recommended the principals to its readers as "experienced, responsible, and prompt," and the venture succeeded from the start. In its first year the firm made a profit of $4,400; in the second year, $17,000; and when the Civil War began, profits soared. Rockefeller became known as an up-and-coming young businessman, a man to be watched. Even his father agreed. From time to time he would come around and ask for his loan back, just to be sure the money was really there, but then, unable to resist ten percent interest, he would lend it back again.

Meanwhile an adult personality begins to emerge. A picture taken just before he married Laura Spelman in 1864 shows a handsome man of twenty-five with a long, slightly mournful visage, a fine straight nose, a rather humorless mouth. Everyone who knew him testified to his virtues. He was industrious, even-tempered, generous, kind; and if it was not a sparkling personality, it was not a dour one. Yet there is something not quite attractive about the picture as a whole. Charitable from his earliest days, he itemized each contribution—even the tiniest—in his famous Ledger A, with the result that his generosity, of which there was never any doubt, is stained with self-observance and an over-nice persnicketiness. Extremely self-critical, he was given to intimate "pillow talks" at night in which he took himself to task for various faults, but the words he recalled and later repeated "Now a little success, soon you will fall down, soon you will be overthrown . . ." smack not so much of honest self-search as of the exorcising of admonitory parental voices. He was above all orderly and forethoughted, but there is a compulsive, and sometimes a faintly repellent quality about his self-control. He recounts that when he was travelling as a commission merchant, he would never grab a bite in the station and wolf it down, like the others on the train, but "if I could not finish eating properly, I filled my mouth with as much as it would hold, then went leisurely to the train and chewed it slowly before swallowing it."

Yet the faults, far from constituting major traits in themselves, were minor flaws in an essentially excellent character. Rockefeller forged ahead by his merits, not by meanness—and among his merits was a well-developed capacity to size up a business situation coolly and rationally. Living in Cleveland, he could scarcely fail to think about one such situation virtually under his nose. Less than a day's journey by train were the Oil Regions of Pennsylvania, one of the most fantastic locales in America. A shambles of mud, dying horses (their skins denuded by petroleum), derricks, walking beams, chugging donkey engines, and jerry-built towns, the Regions oozed oil, money, and dreams. Bits of land the size of a blanket sold on occasion for three and four hundred dollars, pastures jumped overnight into fortunes (one pasture rose from $25,000 to $1,600,000 in three months), whole villages bloomed into existence in a matter of months. Pithole, Pennsylvania, an aptly named pinprick on the map, became the third largest center for mail in Pennsylvania and boasted a $65,000 luxury hotel. Within a few years it was again a pinprick, and the hotel was sold for $50.

It is uncertain whether Rockefeller himself visited the Oil Regions in the halcyon early 1860s. What is certain is that he sniffed oil in Cleveland itself, where the crude product was transported by barge and barrel for distillation and refining. In any event, the hurly-burly, the disorganization, and above all the extreme riskiness of the Oil Regions would never have appealed to Rockefeller's temperament. Let someone else make a million or lose it by blindly drilling for an invisible reservoir—a surer and far steadier route to wealth was available to the refiner who bought the crude oil at thirty-one or thirty-two cents a gallon and then sold the refined product at eighty to eighty-five cents.

The chance to enter the refining business came to Clark and Rockefeller in the person of an enterprising and ingenious young engineer named Sam Andrews. Andrews, recently come from England (by coincidence, he was born in the same town as Clark), was restive in his job in a land refinery and eager to try his hand at oil refining. He talked with his fellow townsman and through Clark met Rockefeller. The three agreed to take a fling at the business. Andrews, together with Clark's brothers, took on the production side, and Maurice Clark and Rockefeller the financial side. Thus in 1863 Andrews, Clark & Company was born. Rockefeller, content behind the anonymity of the "Company," had contributed, together with his partner, half the total capital, but he retained his interest in the produce business. The investment in oil was meant to be no more than a side venture.

But the side venture prospered beyond all expectation. The demand for refined oil increased by leaps and bounds. As Allan Nevins has written: "A commodity that had been a curiosity when Lincoln was nominated, had become a necessity of civilization, the staple of a vast commerce, before he was murdered." And the supply of oil, despite a thousand warnings, auguries, and dire prophecies that the mysterious underground springs would dry up, always matched and overmatched demand.

As the business boomed, so did the number of refineries. One could go into the refinery business for no more capital than it took to open a well-equipped hardware store, and Cleveland's location with its favoring rivers and fortunately placed rail lines made it a natural center for the shipment of crude oil. Hence by 1866, only two years after Andrews, Clark & Company had opened its doors, there were over thirty refineries along the Cleveland Flats, and twenty more would be added before the year was out.

The Rockefeller refinery was among the largest of these. In Sam Andrews had been found the perfect plant superintendent; in Clark and Rockefeller, the perfect business management. From half-past six in the morning, when Andrews and Clark would burst in on their partner at breakfast, until they parted company just before supper, the three talked oil, oil, oil. Slowly, however, Andrews and Rockefeller found themselves at odds with Clark. They had become con-vinced that oil was to be a tremendous and permanent business enterprise; Clark was more cautious and less willing to borrow to expand facilities. Finally in 1865, it was decided to put the firm up for auction among themselves, the seller to retain the produce business. "It was the day that determined my career," Rock-efeller recalled long afterward. "I felt the bigness of it, but I was as calm as I am talking to you now." When at last Maurice Clark bid $72,000, Rockefeller topped him by $500. Clark threw up his hands. "The business is yours," he declared.

From the beginning Rockefeller & Andrews, as the new firm was called, was a model of efficiency. Even before acquiring the firm, Rockefeller had become interested in the economies of plant operation. When he found that plumbers were expensive by the hour, he and Sam Andrews hired one by the month, bought their own pipes and joints, and cut plumbing costs in half. When cooperage grew into a formidable item, they built their own shop where barrels cost them only forty percent of the market price, and soon costs were cut further by the acquisition of a stand of white oak, a kiln, and their own teams and wagons to haul the wood from kiln to plant. The emphasis on cost never ceased; when Rockefeller & Andrews had long since metamorphosed into the Standard Oil Company and profits had grown into the millions, cost figures were still carried to three decimal places. One day Rockefeller was watching the production line in one of his plants, where cans of finished oil were being soldered shut. "How many drops of solder do you use on each can?" he inquired. The answer was forty. "Have you ever tried thirty-eight? No? Would you mind having some sealed with thirty-eight and let me know?" A few cans leaked with thirty-eight, but with thirty-nine all were perfect. A couple of thousand dollars a year were saved.

The zeal for perfection of detail was from the beginning a factor in the growth of Rockefeller's firm. More important was his meeting in 1866 with Henry M. Flagler, the first of a half-dozen associates who would bring to the enterprise the vital impetus of talent, enthusiasm, and a hard determination to succeed. Flagler, a quick, ebullient, bold businessman who had fought his way up from the poverty of a small-town parsonage, was a commission merchant of considerable prominence when Rockefeller met him. The two quickly took a liking to one another, and Rockefeller soon induced Flagler to join the fast-expanding business. Flagler brought along his own funds and those of his father-in-law, Stephen Harkness, and this fresh influx of capital made possible even further expansion. Rockefeller, Andrews & Flagler—soon incorporated as the Standard Oil Company—rapidly became the biggest single refinery in Cleveland.

Flagler brought to the enterprise an immense energy and a playfulness that Rockefeller so egregiously lacked. The two main partners now had a code word in their telegrams—AMELIA—which meant "Everything is lovely and the goose hangs high." And everything *was* lovely. One of Flagler's first jobs was to turn his considerable bargaining skills to a crucial link in the chain of oil-processing costs. All the major refineries bought in the same market—the Oil Regions—and all sold in the same markets—the great cities—so that their costs of purchase and their prices at the point of sale were much alike. In between purchase and sale, however, lay two steps: the costs of refining and the costs of transportation. In the end it was the latter that was to prove decisive in the dog-eat-dog struggle among the refineries.

For the railroads needed a steady flow of shipments to make money, and they were willing to grant rebates to the refiners if they would level out their orders. Since there were a number of routes by which to ship oil, each refiner was in a position to play one road against another, and the Standard, as the biggest and strongest refiner in Cleveland, was naturally able to gain the biggest and most lucrative discounts on its freight. This was a game that Flagler played with consummate skill. Advantageous rebates soon became an important means by which the Standard pushed ahead of its competitors—and in later years, when there were no more competitors, an important source of revenue in themselves. By 1879, when the Rockefeller concern had become a giant, a government investigatory agency estimated that in a period of five months the firm had shipped some eighteen million barrels of oil, on which rebates ran from eleven percent on the B&O to *forty-seven* percent on the Pennsylvania Railroad. For the five months, rebates totalled over ten million dollars.

This is looking too far ahead, however. By 1869, a scant three years after Flagler had joined it, the company was worth about a million dollars, but it was very far from being an industrial giant or a monopoly. Indeed, the problem which constantly plagued Rockefeller and his associates was the extreme competition in the oil business. As soon as business took a downturn—as it did in 1871—the worst kind of cutthroat competition broke out; prices dropped until the Titusville *Herald* estimated that the average refiner lost seventy-five cents on each barrel he sold.

As the biggest refiner, Rockefeller naturally had the greatest stake in establishing some kind of stability in the industry. Hence he set about to devise a scheme—the so-called South Improvement Company—which would break the feast-and-famine pattern that threatened to overwhelm the industry. In its essence the South Improvement Company was a kind of cartel aimed at holding up oil prices—by arranging "reasonable" freight rates for its own members while levying far higher ones on "outsiders." Since the scheme was open to all, presumably there would soon be no outsiders, and once all were within the fold, the refiners could operate a single, powerful economic unit.

The plan might have worked but for the inability of such headstrong and individualistic groups as the railroads and the producers to cooperate for more than a passing moment. When the producers in the Oil Regions rose in wrath against a plan which they (quite rightly) saw as a powerful buying combination against them, the scheme simply collapsed.

The idea of eliminating competition did not, however, collapse with it. Instead, Rockefeller turned to a plan at once much simpler and much more audacious. If he could not eliminate competition, then perhaps he could eliminate his competitors by buying them up one by one—and this he set out to do. The plan was set in motion by a meeting with Colonel Oliver Payne, the chief stockholder in Rockefeller's biggest competitor. Briefly Rockefeller outlined the ruinous situation which impended if competition were permitted to continue unbridled; equally briefly, he proposed a solution. The Standard would increase its capitalization, the Payne plant would be appraised by impartial judges, and its owners would be given stock in proportion to their equity. As for Payne himself, Rockefeller suggested he should take an active part in the management of the new, bigger Standard Oil.

Payne quickly assented; so did Jabez Bostwick, the biggest refiner in New York, and one after another the remaining refiners sold out. According to Rockefeller, they were only too glad to rid themselves of their burdensome businesses at fair prices; according to many of the refiners, it was a question of taking Rockefeller's offer or facing sure ruin. We need not debate the point here; what is certain is that by the end of 1872 the Standard was the colossus of Cleveland. There remained only the United States to conquer.

Rockefeller himself was in his mid-thirties. The slightly melancholy visage of the younger man had altered; a thick mustache trimmed straight across the bottom hid his lips and gave to his face a commanding, even stern, aspect. In a family portrait we see him standing rather stiffly, carefully dressed as befits a man in his station. For he was already rich—even his non-oil investments, as he wrote to his wife, were enough to give him independence, and his style of life had changed as his fortune had grown. He and his wife now lived in Forest Hill, a large, gaunt house on eighty acres just east of Cleveland. He had begun to indulge himself with snappy trotters, and on a small scale commenced what was to become in time a Brobdingnagian pastime—moving landscape around.

In town, in his business pursuits, he was already the reserved, colorless, almost inscrutable personality who baffled his business contemporaries; at home, he came as close as he could to a goal he sought assiduously—relaxation. His children were his great delight: he taught them to swim and invented strange and wonderful contraptions to keep them afloat; he bicycled with them; he played daring games of blindman's bluff—so daring in fact that he once had to have stitches taken in his head after running full tilt into a doorpost.

It was, in a word, the very model of a Victorian home, affectionate, dutiful, and, of course, rich. An air of rectitude hung over the establishment, not so much as to smother it, but enough to give it a distinctive flavor. Concerts (aside from the performances of their children), literature, art, or theatre were not Rockefeller amusements; in entertaining, their tastes ran to Baptist ministers and business associates. An unpretentious and earnest atmosphere hid—or at least disguised—the wealth; until they were nearly grown up the children had no idea of "who they were."

And of course the beneficences continued and grew: $23,000 for various charities in 1878, nearly $33,000 in 1880, over $100,000 in 1884. But the nice preciseness of giving was maintained; a pledge card signed in 1883 for the Euclid Avenue Baptist Church reads:

Mrs. Rockefeller	$10.00 each week
Self	30.00 each week
Each of our four children	00.20 each week

How rich was Rockefeller by 1873, a mere ten years after Andrews, Clark & Company had opened its doors? We cannot make an accurate estimate, but it is certain that he was a millionaire several times over. In another ten years his Standard Oil holdings alone would be worth a phenomenal twenty million dollars—enough, with his other investments, to make him one of the half-dozen richest men in the country.

But now a legal problem began to obtrude. The Standard Oil Company was legally chartered in Ohio, and it had no right to own plants in other states. Not until 1889 would New Jersey amend its incorporation laws to allow a corporation chartered within the state to hold the stock of corporations chartered elsewhere. Hence the question: how was the Standard legally to control its expanding acquisitions in other states?

The problem was solved by one of Rockefeller's most astute lieutenants—Samuel Dodd, a round little butterball of a man with an extraordinarily clear-sighted legal mind and an unusually high and strict sense of personal integrity. Because he believed that he could render the best advice to the Standard if he was above any suspicion of personal aggrandizement, he repeatedly refused Rockefeller's offers to make him a director or to buy for him stock which would have made him a multimillionaire.

The sword which Dodd applied to the Gordian knot of interstate control was the device of the trust. In brief, he proposed a single group of nine trustees, with headquarters in New York, who would hold "in trust" the certificates of all Standard's operating companies, including the major company in Ohio itself. In 1882 the Standard Oil Trust was formally established, with John and his brother William Rockefeller, Flagler, Payne Bostwick, John D. Archbold, Charles Pratt, William G. Warden, and Benjamin Brewster as trustees. (Sam Andrews had sold the last of his stock to Rockefeller four years before, saying the business had grown too big.) In fact, though not in law, one enormous interstate corporation had been created.

Few people even at this time appreciated quite how great the company was. By the 1880s the Standard was the largest and richest of all American manufacturing organizations. It had eighty-five percent of a business which took the output of 20,000 wells and which employed 100,000 people. And all this before the advent of the automobile. The colossus of the Standard was built not on the internal combustion engine but on the kerosene lamp.

With the creation of the Trust the center of gravity of the concern moved to New York. Rockefeller himself bought a $600,000 brownstone on West Fifty-fourth Street, where the round of teas and dinners for temperance workers, church people, and Standard executives soon went on. The Trust itself occupied No. 26 Broadway, an eleven-story "skyscraper" with gay striped awnings shading its large windows. It was soon known as the most famous business address in the world. There Rockefeller appeared daily, usually in high silk hat, long coat, and gloves—the accepted costume for the big business executive of the time.

At 26 Broadway Rockefeller was the commanding figure. But his exercise of command, like his personality was notable for its lack of color, dash, and verve. Inquiring now of this one, now of that, what he thought of such and such a situation, putting his questions methodically and politely in carefully chosen words, never arguing, never raising his voice, Rockefeller seemed to govern his empire like a disembodied intelligence. He could be, as always, a stickler for detail; an accountant recalls him suddenly materializing one day, and with a polite "Permit me," turning over the ledger sheets, all the while murmuring, "Very well kept, very indeed," until he stopped at one page: "A little error here; will you correct it?" But he could also be decisive and absolutely determined. "He saw strategic points like a Napoleon, and he swooped down on them with the suddenness of a Napoleon," wrote Ida Tarbell. Yet even that gives too much of the impression of dash and daring. She was closer to the mark when she wrote: "If one attempts to analyse what may be called the legitimate greatness of Mr. Rockefeller's creation in distinction to its illegitimate greatness, he will find at the foundation the fact that it is as perfectly centralized as the Catholic Church or the Napoleonic government." It was true. By 1886 the Standard had evolved a system of committees, acting in advisory roles to the active management, which permitted an incalculably complex system to function with extraordinary ease. It is virtually the same system that is used today. Rockefeller had created the great Trust on which the eyes of the whole world were fastened, but behind the Trust, sustaining it, operating it, maintaining it, he had created an even greater Organization.

"It's many a day since I troubled you with a letter," wrote William Warden, a onetime independent Cleveland refiner who had been bought out and was now a trustee and major official in the Standard, "and I would not do so now could I justify myself in being silent. . . . We have met with a success unparalleled in commercial history, our name is known all over the world, and our public character is not one to be envied. We are quoted as representative of all that is evil, hard hearted, oppressive, cruel (we think unjustly), but men look askance at us, we are pointed at with contempt, and while some good men flatter us, it's only for our money. . . . This is not pleasant to write, for I had longed for an honored position in commercial life. None of us would choose such a reputation; we all desire a place in the honor & affection of honorable men."

It was a cry of anguish, but it was amply justified. By the 1880s the Standard was not only widely known—it was notorious. In part its increasingly bad business reputation originated in the business community itself. Stories began to circulate of the unfair advantage taken by the colossus when it bid for smaller properties: the case of the Widow Backus, whose deceased husband's refinery was supposedly bought for a pittance, was much talked about. Many of these tales—the Backus case in particular—were simply untrue. But as the Standard grew in size and visibility, other business practices came to light which *were* true, and which were hardly calculated to gain friends for the company.

Foremost among these practices was an evil device called the drawback. Not content with enjoying a large competitive advantage through its special rebates, Standard also forced the railroads to pay it a portion of the freight charges paid by non-Standard refiners! Thus Daniel O'Day, a particularly ruthless Standard official, used his local economic leverage to get a small railroad to carry Standard's oil at ten cents a barrel, to charge all independents thirty-five cents, *and to turn over the twenty-five cent differential to a Standard subsidiary.* Another Standard agent, finding that a competitor's car had slipped through without paying the Standard exaction, wrote the road to collect the amount owing, adding: "Please turn another screw."

Such incidents and practices—always denied by the company and never admitted by Rockefeller—plagued the Standard for years. And the impression of highhandedness was not much improved by the behavior of the Standard's officials when they went on public view. John D. Archbold, a key executive called to testify before New York State's Hepburn Committee in 1879, was a typical bland witness. When pressed hard, he finally admitted he was a stockholder of the Standard. What was his function there? "I am a clamorer for dividends. That is the only function I have in connection with the Standard Oil Company." Chairman Alonzo Hepburn asked how large dividends were. "I have no trouble transporting my share," answered Archbold. On matters of rebates he declined to answer. Finally Hepburn asked him to return for further questioning the next day. "I have given today to the matter," replied Archbold politely. "It will be impossible for me to be with you again."

Not least, there was the rising tide of public protest against the monopoly itself. In 1881 Henry Demarest Lloyd, a journalist of passionate reformist sentiments, wrote for the *Atlantic Monthly* an article called "The Story of a Great Monopoly." Editor William Dean Howells gave it the lead in the magazine, and overnight it was a sensation (that issue of the *Atlantic* went through seven printings). "The family that uses a gallon of kerosene a day pays a yearly tribute to the Standard of $32 . . . ," wrote Lloyd. "America has the proud satisfaction of having furnished the world with the greatest, wisest, and meanest monopoly known to history."

Standard's profits were nothing so great as described by Lloyd, but that hardly mattered. If the article was imprecise or even downright wrong in detail, it was right in its general thrust. What counted was Lloyd's incontrovertible demonstration that an individual concern had grown to a position of virtual impregnability, a position which made it in fact no longer subordinate to the states from which it drew its legal privilege of existence, but their very peer or better in financial strength and even political power. Before Lloyd wrote his article, the Standard was the source of rage or loss to scattered groups of producers, businessmen, or consumers. When he was through with his indictment, it was a national scandal.

That it should be a scandal was totally incomprehensible to John D. The mounting wave of protest and obloquy perplexed him more than it irritated him. Ida Tarbell's famous—and generally accurate—*History of the Standard Oil Company* he dismissed as "without foundation." The arrogance of an Archbold he merely chuckled at, recounting the Hepburn testimony in his *Random Reminiscences of Men and Events* with the comment that Archbold had a "well-developed sense of humor." With his own passion for order, he understood not a whit the passions of those whose demise was required that order might prevail. On one occasion when he was testifying in court, he spied in the courtroom George Rice, an old adversary (against whom, as a matter of fact, the famous screw had been turned, and whom Rockefeller had once offered to buy out). As he left the witness stand, Rockefeller walked over to Rice and, putting out his hand, said: "How do you do, Mr. Rice? You and I are getting to be old men, are we not?"

Rice ignored the hand. "Don't you think, Mr. Rice," pursued Rockefeller, "it might have been better if you had taken my advice years ago?"

"Perhaps it would," said Rice angrily. "You said you would ruin my business and you have done so."

"Pshaw! Pshaw!" rejoined Rockefeller.

"Don't you pooh-pooh me," said Rice in a fury. "I say that by the power of your great wealth you have ruined me."

"Not a word of truth in it," Rockefeller answered, turning and making his way through the crowd. "Not a word of truth in it."

He could not in fact bring himself to believe that there was a word of truth in any of it. There was nothing to argue about concerning the need for giant enterprise, or "industrial combinations" as they were called. They were simply a necessity, a potentially dangerous necessity admittedly, but a necessity nonetheless. All the rest was ignorance or willful misunderstanding. "You know," he wrote to a university president who offered to prepare a scholarly defense of Standard's policies, "that great prejudice exists against all successful business enterprise—the more successful, the greater the prejudice."

It was common, during the early 1900s, to read thunderous accusations against the Standard Oil Company and its sinister captain, but the fact was that John D. Rockefeller had severed all connection with the business as early as 1897. When news came to him, ten years later, that the great Trust had been heavily fined by the government, he read the telegram and without comment went on with his game of golf. At the actual dissolution of the Trust in 1911, he was equally unconcerned. For already his interests were turning away from business management toward another absorbing role—the disposition of the wealth which was now beginning to accumulate in truly awesome amounts.

Here enters the last of those indispensable subordinates through whom Rockefeller operated so effectively. Frederick T. Gates, onetime minister, now a kind of Baptist minister-executive, met Rockefeller when Gates played a crucial role in the studies that established the need for a great new university in Chicago. Shortly he became the catalytic figure in instituting the university with a Rockefeller gift of $600,000. (Before he was done, Rockefeller would give it 80 million dollars.) Then one morning in 1889, when the two were chatting, Rockefeller suddenly said: "I am in trouble, Mr. Gates." He told him of the flood of appeals which now came by the sackful, and of his inability to give away money with any satisfaction until he had made the most thorough investigation into the cause. Rockefeller continued: "I want you to come to New York and open an office here. You can aid me in my benefactions by taking interviews and inquiries and reporting the results for action. What do you say?"

Gates said yes, and it was under his guidance, together with that of Rockefeller's son, John D., Jr., that the great philanthropies took root: the General Education Board, which pioneered in the educational, social, and medical development of our own South; the Rockefeller Institute for Medical Research, quickly famous for its campaign against yellow fever; the Rockefeller Foundation with its far-ranging interests in the promotion of research. Not that the giving was done hastily. Gates had a meticulousness of approach which suited his employer perfectly. It was not until 1900 that more than 2 million dollars was given away, not until 1905 that the total of annual giving exceeded 10 million dollars, not until 1913 that the great climactic disbursements began to be made: 45 million dollars that year and 65 million the next, to establish the Rockefeller Foundation; finally 138 million dollars in 1919 to support the philanthropies already endowed.

Gates took his philanthropic duties with ministerial zeal and profound seriousness. Raymond Fosdick, president of the Rockefeller Foundation, recalls Gates' last meeting as a trustee. Shaking his fist at the startled board, he boomed: "When you die and come to approach the judgment of Almighty God, what do you think He will demand of you? Do you for an instant presume to believe He will inquire into your petty failures or your trivial virtues? No! He will ask just one question: *'What did you do as a Trustee of the Rockefeller Foundation?'*"

Gates was more than just a philanthropic guide. Rapidly he became a prime business agent for Rockefeller in the large business deals which inevitably continued to arise. When Rockefeller came into immense iron properties along the Mesabi Range, it was Gates who superintended their development and the creation of a giant fleet of ore carriers, and it was Gates who carried through their eventual sale to Morgan and Frick at the huge price of 88.5 million dollars. It was the only time in Gates' long association with John D. that he indicated the slightest desire to make money for himself. When the immense iron deal was complete and Gates had made his final report, Rockefeller, as usual, had no words of praise, but listened attentively and without objection and then said, with more emphasis than usual, "Thank you, Mr. Gates!" Gates looked at him with an unaccustomed glint in his eye. "Thank you is not enough, Mr. Rockefeller," he replied. Rockefeller understood and promptly saw to it that Gates was remunerated handsomely.

John D. was becoming an old man now. His face, sharper with age, took on a crinkled, masklike appearance, in the midst of which his small eyes twinkled. Golf had become a great passion and was performed in the deliberate Rockefeller manner. A boy was hired to chant: "Keep your head down," useless steps were saved by bicycling between shots, and even when he was playing alone, every stroke was remorselessly counted. (John D. was once asked to what he owed the secret of the success of Standard Oil; he answered: "To the fact that we never deceived ourselves.")

To the outside world the old man more and more presented a quaint and benevolent image. By the 1920s the antitrust passions of the 1890s and early 1900s had been transmuted into sycophancy of big business; there were no more cries of "tainted money," but only a hopeful queuing up at the portals of the great foundations. The man who had once been denounced by Theodore Roosevelt and Tolstoy and William Jennings Bryan was now voted, in a popular poll, one of the Greatest Americans. Cartoonists and feature writers made the most of his pith helmet and his paper vest, his monkishly plain food, his beaming, almost childlike expression. To the outside world he seemed to live in a serene and admirable simplicity, which indeed he did, in a purely personal sense. But the reporters who told of his afternoon drives did not report that the seventy miles of road over his estate at Pocantico Hills were built by himself, that the views he liked so well were arranged by moving hills around as an interior decorator moves chairs. The perfection of Pocantico became an obsession: some railway tracks that were in the way were relocated at the cost of $700,000, a small college that spoiled a view was induced to move for $1,500,000, a distant smokestack was camouflaged. It was, to repeat George Kaufman's famous line, an example of what God could have done if He'd only had the money.

In the midst of it all was the never-failingly polite, always slightly disengaged old man, somehow disappointing in close view, somehow smaller than we expect. There are mannerisms and eccentricities, of course, which, when viewed under the magnification of 900 million dollars, take on a certain prominence, but they are peccadilloes rather than great flaws. There is the enormous industrial generalship, to be sure, but it is a generalship of logic and plan, not of dash and daring. There is the generosity on a monumental scale, but then again, not on such a scale as to cut the Rockefeller fortune by ninety percent, as was the case with Carnegie. Rockefeller gave away over half a billion, but probably he kept at least that much for his family.

In short, the more we look into the life of John D. Rockefeller, the more we look into the life of an incredibly successful—and withal, very unremarkable—man. It is a curious verdict to pass on the greatest acquisitor of all time, and yet it is difficult to avoid the conclusion that John Flynn has perfectly phrased: "Rockefeller in his soul was a bookkeeper." We can see the bookkeeperishness in unexpected but telling places, such as in his *Random Reminiscences*, where he dilates on the importance of friendship, but cites as a dubious friend the man who protests, "I can't indorse your note, because I have an agreement with my partners not to . . ."; or again, when he expands on the nonmaterial pleasures of life, such as gardening, but adds as a clincher: "We make a small fortune out of ourselves, selling to our New Jersey place at $1.50 and $2.00 each, trees which originally cost us only five or ten cents at Pocantico." Whether he turns to friendship or to nature, money is the measure.

These are surely not the sentiments of greatness—but then John D. was not a great man. Neither was he, needless to say, a bad man. In most ways he was the very paragon of the business virtues of his day, and at the same time the perfect exemplar of the unvirtues as well. It is likely that he would have made his mark in any field, but unlikely that any commodity other than oil would have offered such staggering possibilities for industrial growth and personal aggrandizement. He personified in ideas the typical business thought of his day—very Christian, very conventional, very comfortable.

Yet as the image of John D. recedes, we realize the pointlessness of such personal appraisals. We study Rockefeller not so much as a person but as an agent—an agent for better and worse in the immense industrial transformation of America. Viewed against this stupendous process of change, even the largest lives take on a subordinate quality and personal praise and blame seem almost irrelevant. And Rockefeller was not one of the largest lives—only one of the luckiest.

In the end there was only the frail ghost of a man, stubbornly resisting the inevitable. His son, John D., Jr., whom he had fondly called "my greatest fortune," had long since taken over the reins of the great foundations and had begun to refashion the Rockefeller image in his own way: Rockefeller Center, The Cloisters, the restoration of Williamsburg. His grandsons, among them one who would one day aspire to the Presidency of the United States, were already young men, carefully imbued with the family style: determination, modesty on the grand scale, a prudent balance between self-interest and altruism. And the Standard itself, now split and resplit into a handful of carefully noncollusive (and equally carefully noncompetitive) companies, was bigger and more powerful than ever. All in all, it was an extraordinary achievement, and the old man must have enjoyed it to the hilt. For it had indeed rained porridge, and his dish had surely been kept right side up.

A Primary Perspective

AFFIDAVIT OF GEORGE O. BASLINGTON

John D. Rockefeller's philanthropic activities made little impression on the many people whom he drove out of business. Having experienced at firsthand the ruthless tactics used to establish the Standard Oil monopoly, they had little trouble deciding where they stood in the robber baron–captain of industry debate. One of these unfortunate businesspeople was George O. Baslington, the co-owner of Hanna, Baslington & Company, a Cleveland-based oil refinery founded in 1869. In the affidavit that follows, Baslington provided a revealing description of what happened to entrepreneurs who had something that Rockefeller wanted.

Some time in February, 1872, the firm received a message from the Standard Oil Company requesting said firm to have an interview as to the disposal of the refining works of said firm; that they were indisposed to enter into any arrangement for the disposition of said works because the investment of capital in said works had proved abundantly profitable to their satisfaction and they had no disposition whatever to part with the works; but upon investigation they were somewhat surprised to find that the Standard Oil Company had already obtained the substantial control of the different refineries in the City of Cleveland; that it had obtained such rates of transportation of crude and refined oil from the different railroads that it was impossible for them to compete with it, and upon an interview which was had by Mr. Hanna

Source: From "Affidavit of George O. Baslington" from *The History of the Standard Oil Company* by Ida M. Tarbell (1933).

and affiant with Mr. Rockefeller who was at the time president of the Standard Oil Company. Mr. Flagler, the secretary of the company, being present, Mr. Rockefeller in substance declared or said that the Standard Oil Company had such control of the refining business already in the City of Cleveland that he thought said firm of Hanna, Baslington & Company could not make any money; that there was no use for them to attempt to do business in competition with the Standard Oil Company.

Affiant further says that after having had an interview both with Mr. Watson, who was the president of a company called "The South Improvement Company," and Mr. Devereux, who was the general manager of the Lake Shore Road, he became satisfied that no arrangement whatever could be effected through which transportation could at least be obtained on the Lake Shore Road that would enable their firm to compete with the Standard Oil Company, the works of said Hanna, Baslington & Company, being so situated that they could only obtain their crude oil through the line of the Lake Shore Road. And finding that the Standard Oil Company had such special rates of transportation that unless the firm of Hanna, Baslington & Company were enabled to bring as much oil as the Standard Oil Company, that it was impossible for said firm of Hanna, Baslington & Company to obtain a fair competing rate with the Standard Oil Company. They at last came to the conclusion that it was better for them to take what they could get from the Standard Oil Company and let their works go.

And affiant further says that under these circumstances they sold their works to the Standard Oil Company, which were on the day of the sale worth at least $100,000, for $45,000 because that was all they could obtain from them, and works too which in cash cost them no less than $76,000, and which with a fair competition would have paid them an income of no less than 30 percent per annum on the investment.

Affiant further says that at the interviews which he had with Mr. Rockefeller, Mr. Rockefeller told him that the Standard Oil Company already had control of all the large refineries in the City of Cleveland and there was no use for them to undertake to compete against the Standard Oil Company, for it would only ultimate in their being wiped out, or language to that effect.

(November 1, 1880.)

QUESTIONS

1. What influence did Rockefeller's upbringing have on the development of his business views? In what ways did Rockefeller's subsequent business career reflect his internalization of the proverb that "willful waste makes woeful want"?

2. Why in his efforts to achieve a dominant position in the oil industry did Rockefeller concentrate on controlling the refineries rather than the oil fields? What economies did he institute to reduce costs? Why did railroad companies so readily agree to Standard Oil's business terms?

3. What steps did Rockefeller take to eliminate competition in the oil industry? To what extent were other oil refiners coerced to sell out to Standard Oil? What could someone like George Baslington do when confronted by Standard Oil? Were there any organizations or social movements to which he might have turned for support? What does Baslington's dilemma suggest about the state of public affairs in Gilded Age America?

4. Why was the trust device devised by Samuel Dodd so critical to Standard Oil's growth? Why did Standard Oil acquire such a poor business reputation?

5. To repeat a question raised by Heilbroner, "What was the secret of [Rockefeller's] incredible success?" What were his greatest strengths as a corporate manager? What did John T. Flynn mean when he wrote that "Rockefeller in his soul was a bookkeeper"? In what ways did Rockefeller's conduct of his personal life reflect his approach to business affairs?

6. Do you think that the robber-baron thesis provides an adequate conceptual framework for interpreting Rockefeller's business career? If not, can you suggest a more appropriate descriptive term?

7. What challenges does a biographer who has chosen to write about Rockefeller confront? How well did Heilbroner meet those challenges?

 ADDITIONAL RESOURCES

The most recent study of Rockefeller is Ron Chernow, *Titan: The Life of John D. Rockefeller* (1998), which replaces Allan Nevins, *A Study in Power: John D. Rockefeller, Industrialist and Philanthropist* (1953), as the standard biography. Those seeking a briefer treatment should see David Freeman Hawke, *John D.: The Founding Father of the Rockefellers* (1970). There are also a number of works on the Rockefeller family that interested readers might wish to consult. They include Peter Collier and David Horowitz, *The Rockefellers: An American Dynasty* (1976); William Manchester, *A Rockefeller Portrait: From John D. to Nelson* (1959); and John E. Harr and Peter J. Johnson, *The Rockefeller Century: Three Generations of America's Greatest Family* (1989). For more on the Gilded Age business world that Rockefeller did so much to shape, see Glenn Porter, *The Rise of Big Business, 1860–1910* (1973); Edward Kirkland, *Dream and Thought in the Business Community, 1860–1900* (1956); Matthew Josephson, *The Robber Barons: The Great American Capitalists, 1861–1901* (1934); Alfred D. Chandler, *The Visible Hand: The Managerial Revolution in America* (1977).

The PBS *American Experience* series provided a two-part installment entitled "The Rockefellers," which examines this family in its rise to power and prominence, envy and hatred.

Introduction

*I*f the main theme of American life during the first four and a half decades of the 20th century could be captured in one word, that word would be *struggle*. This was the case both at home and abroad. Not only did the United States play a major role in two international conflicts; on the domestic scene, movements for economic justice, women's rights, and racial equality posed unprecedented challenges to the status quo. Though the nation emerged from the period as the world's leading economic power, it did so only after experiencing the widespread social turmoil of the Great Depression.

One of the more significant political changes of these years was the growth of executive power. The administration of Theodore Roosevelt marked a major turning point. Unlike his Gilded Age counterparts, most of whom were little more than figureheads, Roosevelt brought a penchant for action to the White House that helped lay the foundation for the "Imperial Presidency" of later decades. His willingness to use the federal government as a vehicle for social and economic reform also made Roosevelt a leading figure in the progressive movement. In his essay on Roosevelt, Edmund Morris provides a lively portrait of this "over-engined" man whose expansive personality dominated the first decade of 20th-century American political life.

The social programs championed by progressive politicians like Roosevelt did not satisfy everyone. Where Roosevelt believed American society was fundamentally sound and needed only minor reform, others called for more sweeping changes. One such person was Eugene V. Debs, the best-known American socialist of the early 20th century. Outraged by corporate policies that impoverished and demeaned labor, Debs envisioned a world in which working people controlled their own destiny. And as Francis Russell notes in his essay, he possessed the oratorical skills needed to convey that vision to working-class audiences. Despite receiving nearly a million votes for president in 1912, Debs never achieved the state power that he sought for labor. Nevertheless, his tireless exertions on behalf of workers helped move the nation's political agenda to the left during a period of extensive social reform.

The group that benefited least from Progressive Era reforms were African Americans. In the South, social segregation and political disfranchisement placed sharp limitations on black achievement, while in many parts of the North, racism and discrimination made conditions only marginally better.

During the first half of the 20th century, few people worked harder than W. E. B. Du Bois to remove these barriers to racial equality. Moreover, as Elliott Rudwick relates in his essay, Du Bois did not confine his concerns to black Americans. A leading figure in the Pan-African movement, as well as a founding member of the National Association for the Advancement of Colored People (NAACP), he adopted a broad perspective that addressed the problems and prospects of people of color everywhere.

Whereas the struggle for racial equality faced formidable obstacles during the first half of the 20th century, the women's movement appeared, for a time at least, to be making significant headway. With ratification of the Nineteenth Amendment in 1920, women finally obtained the voting rights that had long been the movement's primary aim. Though a major accomplishment, some women insisted that much more remained to be done. Margaret Sanger, for example, believed women could hardly be said to have achieved true equality until they controlled their own bodies. Accordingly, she continued her campaign for female reproductive rights into the post–World War II period. In her essay on Sanger, Margaret Forster provides an insightful portrait of the nation's best-known birth control reformer.

Despite passage of the Nineteenth Amendment, it would be decades before large numbers of women would begin to hold elective office. Yet some women did exercise considerable political influence during the earlier period, perhaps none more so than Eleanor Roosevelt, who, in addition to being FDR's wife, was also one of his most trusted and able political advisors. As the conscience of the New Deal, she became a forceful advocate of women's equality, black rights, and a host of other noble causes; and as the leading voice of American liberalism, she remained a powerful presence in the Democratic party for decades afterward. In his essay on Roosevelt, William H. Chafe examines her sometimes troubled private life as well as her public achievements.

The broad-ranging New Deal reforms of the mid-thirties were not simply the work of compassionate insiders like Eleanor Roosevelt. They were also a response to a growing restiveness among the political left. When FDR's initial programs did little to relieve the widespread suffering of the Great Depression, a variety of individuals and groups proposed initiatives that went well beyond anything the president then had in mind. New Deal officials felt particularly threatened by Huey Long, whose Share Our Wealth plan promised every American a "household estate" of $5,000 and who appeared to have his own designs on the White House. Glen Jeansonne's portrait of the Louisiana "Kingfish" does much to explain why national political leaders considered Long such a serious threat.

In the end, it was not the New Deal but World War II that ended the Great Depression. As government war orders flooded U.S. factories following the Japanese attack at Pearl Harbor, labor shortages replaced unemployment as the nation's most pressing economic problem. Meanwhile, U.S. forces in Europe and Asia did their part to turn back the Axis onslaught. Among their commanding officers, few achieved greater renown than George Patton. In their essay on the colorful and hard-driving West Pointer, Stephen E. Ambrose and Judith D. Ambrose explore the complex personality of one of the war's most controversial generals.

Chapter 6

Theodore Roosevelt

T he first two decades of the 20th century are often called the Progressive Era. The term refers to a diverse group of reformers who sought to correct the accumulating social, economic, and political problems of Gilded Age America. The progressives were so diverse, in fact, that some historians have questioned whether they constituted a coherent movement. Not only were their concerns—which ranged from conservation to corporate regulation—as broad and variegated as the nation itself; they often disagreed about the best approach to specific issues. Yet, for all their differences, progressives did share several basic beliefs. These included an abiding faith in progress and a conviction that the laissez-faire attitudes of the previous century were no longer adequate. Government, they felt, could and should play a more positive role in American life.

The progressives operated at all levels of government. In major cities, the administrations of reform mayors such as Hazen S. Pingree of Detroit and Tom Johnson of Cleveland attacked political corruption and instituted a host of measures designed to improve urban life: opening parks and beaches, lowering utility rates, regulating transit systems, and improving various municipal services. At the same time, some progressive governors turned their states into virtual laboratories of reform. The

most notable example was Wisconsin, where Robert M. LaFollette often sought the counsel of social scientists in his efforts to reform electoral practices, curb corporate abuses, and protect state forests.

In 1901, when the assassination of William McKinley elevated Theodore Roosevelt to the presidency, progressivism also reached the White House. As president, Roosevelt made his mark in a number of areas important to progressives. In addition to being an ardent conservationist, he did as much as anyone of the period to increase the accountability of large corporations: by establishing the Bureau of Corporations, strengthening the Interstate Commerce Commission, and supporting the enactment of regulatory measures such as the Pure Food and Drug Act of 1906. Though primarily a domestic president, Roosevelt also exhibited a keen interest in international affairs, receiving the Nobel Peace Prize for mediating an end to the Russo-Japanese War of 1904–1905.

Despite all this, Roosevelt is remembered as much for his personality as for his accomplishments in office. An outspoken proponent of "the strenuous life" who projected an exuberant optimism, Roosevelt evoked strong feelings in people—not all of them positive. To some, he was an arrogant windbag; to others, he embodied all that was noble in American life. In the essay that follows, Edmund Morris provides a searching examination of Roosevelt's personality that explains much about the mixed reaction Americans had to this attention-seeking extrovert who restored the chief executive's role as a major player in U.S. government.

Theodore Roosevelt

Edmund Morris

Let us dispose, in short order, with Theodore Roosevelt's faults. He was an incorrigible preacher of platitudes; or to use Elting E. Morison's delicious phrase, he had "a recognition, too frequently and precisely stated, of the less recondite facts of life." He significantly reduced the wildlife population of some three continents. He piled his dessert plate with so many peaches that the cream spilled over the sides. And he used to make rude faces out of the presidential carriage at small boys in the streets of Washington.

Source: Reprinted by permission of American Heritage, Inc. Copyright © 1961.

Now those last two faults are forgivable if we accept British diplomat Cecil Spring-Rice's advice, "You must always remember the president is about six." The first fault—his preachiness—is excused by the fact that the American electorate dearly loves a moralist. As to the second and most significant fault—Theodore Roosevelt's genuine blood-lust and desire to destroy his adversaries, whether they be rhinoceroses or members of the United States Senate—it is paradoxically so much a part of his virtues, both as a man and a politician, that I will come back to it in more detail later.

One of the minor irritations I have to contend with as a biographer is that whenever I go to the library to look for books about Roosevelt, Theodore, they infallibly are mixed up with books about Roosevelt, Franklin—and I guess FDR scholars have the same problem in reverse. Time was when the single word "Roosevelt" meant only Theodore; FDR himself frequently had to insist, in the early thirties, that he was not TR's son. He was merely a fifth cousin, and what was even more distant, a Democrat to boot. In time, of course, Franklin succeeded in preempting the early meaning of the word "Roosevelt," to the point that TR's public image, which once loomed as large as Washington's and Lincoln's, began to fade like a Cheshire cat from popular memory. By the time of FDR's own death in 1945, little was left but the ghost of a toothy grin.

Only a few veterans of the earlier Roosevelt era survived to testify that if Franklin was the greater politician, it was only by a hairsbreadth, and as far as sheer personality was concerned, Theodore's superiority could be measured in spades. They pointed out that FDR himself declared, late in life, that his "cousin Ted" was the greatest man he ever knew.

Presently the veterans too died. But that ghostly grin continued to float in the national consciousness, as if to indicate that its owner was meditating a reappearance. I first became aware of the power behind the grin in Washington, in February of 1976. The National Theater was trying out an ill-fated musical by Alan Lerner and Leonard Bernstein, *1600 Pennsylvania Avenue*. For two and a half hours Ken Howard worked his way through a chronological series of impersonations of historic presidents. The audience sat on its hands, stiff with boredom, until the very end, when Mr. Howard clamped on a pair of pince-nez and a false mustache, and bared all his teeth in a grin. The entire theater burst into delighted applause.

What intrigued me was the fact that few people there could have known much about TR beyond the obvious cliches of San Juan Hill and the Big Stick. Yet somehow, subconsciously, they realized that here for once was a positive president, warm and tough and authoritative and funny, who believed in America and who, to quote Owen Wister, "grasped his optimism tight lest it escape him."

In the last year or so Theodore Roosevelt has made his long-promised comeback. He has been the subject of a *Newsweek* cover story on American heroes; Russell Baker has called him a cinch to carry all 50 states if he were running for the White House today; he's starring on Broadway in *Tintypes*, on television in *Bully*, and you'll soon see him on the big screen in *Ragtime*. Every season brings a new crop of reassessments in the university presses, and as for the pulp mills, he figures largely in the latest installment of John Jakes's *Kent Chronicles*. No time like the present, therefore, to study that giant personality in color and fine detail.

When referring to Theodore Roosevelt I do not use the word "giant" loosely. "Every inch of him," said William Allen White, "was over-engined." Lyman Gage likened him, mentally and physically, to two strong men combined; Gifford Pinchot said that his normal appetite was enough for four people; Charles J. Bonaparte estimated that his mind moved 10 times faster than average; and TR himself, not wanting to get into double figures, modestly remarked, "I have enjoyed as much of life as any nine men I know." John Morley made a famous comparison in 1904 between Theodore Roosevelt and the Niagara Falls, "both great wonders of nature." John Burroughs wrote that TR's mere proximity made him nervous. "There was always something imminent about him, like an avalanche that the sound of your voice might loosen." Ida Tarbell, sitting next to him at a musical, had a sudden hallucination that the president was about to burst. "I felt his clothes might not contain him, he was so steamed up, so ready to go, to attack anything, anywhere."

Reading all these remarks it comes as a surprise to discover that TR's chest measured a normal 42 inches, and that he stood only five feet nine in his size seven shoes. Yet unquestionably his initial impact was physical, and it was overwhelming. I have amused myself over the years with collecting the metaphors that contemporaries used to describe this Rooseveltian "presence." Here's a random selection. Edith Wharton thought him radioactive; Archie Butt and others used phrases to do with electricity, high-voltage wires, generators, and dynamos; Lawrence Abbott compared him to an electromagnetic nimbus; John Burroughs to "a kind of electric bombshell, if there can be such a thing"; James E. Watson was reminded of TNT; and Senator Joseph Foraker, in an excess of imagination, called TR "a steam-engine in trousers." There are countless other steam-engine metaphors, from Henry Adams's "swift and awful Chicago express" to Henry James's "verily, a wonderful little machine: destined to be overstrained, perhaps, but not as yet, truly, betraying the least creak." Lastly we have Owen Wister comparing TR to a solar conflagration that cast no shadow, only radiance.

These metaphors sound fulsome, but they refer only to TR's physical effect, which was felt with equal power by friends and enemies. People actually tingled in his company; there was something sensually stimulating about it. They came out of the presidential office flushed, short-breathed, energized, as if they had been treated to a sniff of white powder. He had, as Oscar Straus once said, "the quality of vitalizing things." His youthfulness (he was not yet 43 at the beginning of his first term, and barely 50 at the end of his second), his air of glossy good health, his powerful handshake—all these things combined to give an impression of irresistible force and personal impetus.

But TR was not just a physical phenomenon. In many ways the quality of his personality was more remarkable than its quantity. Here again, I have discovered recurrences of the same words in contemporary descriptions. One of the more frequent images is that of sweetness. "He was as sweet a man," wrote Henry Watterson, "as ever scuttled a ship or cut a throat." But most comments are kinder than that. "There is a sweetness about him that is very compelling," sighed Woodrow Wilson; "You can't resist the man." Robert Livingstone, a journalist, wrote after TR's death: "He had the double gifts of a sweet nature that came out in every hand-touch and tone . . . and a sincerely powerful personality that left the uneffaceable impression that whatever he said was right. Such a combination was simply irresistible." Livingstone's final verdict was that Theodore Roosevelt had "unquestionably the greatest gift of personal magnetism ever possessed by an American."

That may or may not be true, but certainly there are very few recorded examples of anybody, even TR's bitterest political critics, being able to resist him in person. Brand Whitlock, Mark Twain, John Jay Chapman, William Jennings Bryan, and Henry James were all seduced by his charm, if only temporarily. Peevish little Henry Adams spent much of the period from 1901 to 1909 penning a series of magnificent insults to the president's reputation. But this did not prevent him from accepting frequent invitations to dine at the White House and basking gloomily in TR's effulgence. By the time the Roosevelt era came to an end, Adams was inconsolable. "My last vision of fun and gaiety will vanish when my Theodore goes . . . never can we replace him."

It's a pity that the two men never had a public slanging match over the table, because when it came to personal invective, TR could give as good as he got. There was the rather slow British ambassador whom he accused of having "a mind that functions at six guinea-pig power." There was the state Supreme Court justice he called "an amiable old fuzzy-wuzzy with sweetbread brains." . . . Woodrow Wilson was "a Byzantine logothete" (even Wilson had to go to the dictionary for that one); John Wanamaker was "an ill-constitutioned creature, oily, with bristles sticking up through the oil"; and poor Senator Warren Pfeffer never quite recovered from being called "a pinheaded anarchistic crank, of hirsute and slabsided aspect." TR did not use bad language—the nearest to it I've found is his description of Charles Evans Hughes as "a psalm-singing son of a bitch," but then Charles Evans Hughes tended to invite such descriptions. Moreover, TR usually took the sting out of his insults by collapsing into laughter as he uttered them. Booth Tarkington detected "an undertone of Homeric chuckling" even when Roosevelt seemed to be seriously castigating someone—"as if, after all, he loved the fun of hating, rather than the hating itself."

Humor, indeed, was always TR's saving grace. A reporter who spent a week with him in the White House calculated that he laughed, on average, a hundred times a day—and what was more, laughed heartily. "He laughs like an irresponsible schoolboy on a lark, his face flushing ruddy, his eyes nearly closed, his utterance choked with merriment, his speech abandoned for a weird falsetto. . . . The president is a joker, and (what many jokers are not) a humorist as well."

If there were nothing more to Theodore Roosevelt's personality than physical exuberance, humor, and charm, he would indeed have been what he sometimes is misperceived to be: a simple-minded, amiable bully. Actually he was an exceedingly complex man, a polygon (to use Branden Matthews's word) of so many political, intellectual, and social facets that the closer one gets to him, the less one is able to see him in the round. Consider merely this random list of attributes and achievements:

He graduated magna cum laude from Harvard University. He was the author of a four-volume history of the winning of the West, which was considered definitive in his lifetime, and a history of the naval war of 1812, which remains definitive to this day. He also wrote biographies of Thomas Hart Benton, Gouverneur Morris, and Oliver Cromwell, and some 14 other volumes of history, natural history, literary criticism, autobiography, political philosophy, and military memoirs, not to mention countless articles and approximately 75,000 letters. He spent nearly three years of his life in Europe and the Levant, and had a wide circle of intellectual correspondents on both sides of the Atlantic. He habitually read one to three books a day, on subjects ranging from architecture to zoology, averaging two or three pages a minute and effortlessly memorizing the paragraphs that interested him. He could recite poetry by the hour in English, German, and French. He married two women and fathered six children. He was a boxing championship finalist, a Fifth Avenue socialite, a New York State assemblyman, a Dakota cowboy, a deputy sheriff, a president of the Little Missouri Stockmen's Association, United States civil service commissioner, police commissioner of New York City, assistant secretary of the Navy, colonel of the Rough Riders, governor of New York, vice president, and finally president of the United States. He was a founding member of the National Institute of Arts and Letters and a fellow of the American Historical Society. He was accepted by Washington's scientific community as a skilled ornithologist, paleontologist, and taxidermist (during the White House years, specimens that confused experts at the Smithsonian were occasionally sent to TR for identification), and he was recognized as the world authority on the big-game mammals of North America.

Now all these achievements *predate* his assumption of the presidency—in other words, he packed them into the first 43 years. I will spare you another list of the things he packed into his last 10, after leaving the White House in 1909, except to say that the total of books rose to 38, the total of letters to 150,000, and the catalogue of careers expanded to include world statesman, big-game collector for the Smithsonian, magazine columnist, and South American explorer.

If it were possible to take a cross section of TR's personality, as geologists, say, ponder a chunk of continent, you would be presented with a picture of seismic richness and confusion. The most order I have been able to make of it is to isolate four major character seams. They might be traced back to childhood. Each seam stood out bright and clear in youth and early middle age, but they began to merge about the time he was 40. Indeed the white heat of the presidency soon fused them all into solid metal. But so long as they were distinct they may be identified as aggression, righteousness, pride, and militarism. Before suggesting how they affected his performance as president, I'd like to explain how they originated.

The most fundamental characteristic of Theodore Roosevelt was his aggression—conquest being, to him, synonymous with growth. From the moment he first dragged breath into his asthmatic lungs, the sickly little boy fought for a larger share of the world. He could never get enough air; disease had to be destroyed; he had to fight his way through big, heavy books to gain a man's knowledge. Just as the struggle for wind made him stretch his chest, so did the difficulty of relating to abnormally contrasting parents extend his imagination. Theodore Senior was the epitome of hard, thrusting Northern manhood; Mittie Roosevelt was the quintessence of soft, yielding Southern femininity. The Civil War—the first political phenomenon little Teddie was ever aware of—symbolically opposed one to the other. There was no question as to which side, and which parent, the child preferred. He naughtily prayed God, in Mittie's presence, to "grind the Southern troops to powder," and the victory of Union arms reinforced his belief in the superiority of Strength over Weakness, Right over Wrong, Realism over Romance.

Teddie's youthful "ofserv-a-tions" in natural history gave him further proof of the laws of natural selection, long before he fully understood Darwin and Herbert Spencer. For weeks he watched in fascination while a tiny shrew successively devoured a mass of beetles, then a mouse twice her size, then a snake so large it whipped her from side to side of the cage as she was gnawing through its neck. From then on the rule of tooth and claw, aided by superior intelligence, was a persistent theme in Theodore Roosevelt's writings.

Blood sports, which he took up as a result of his shooting for specimens, enabled him to feel the "strong eager pleasure" of the shrew in vanquishing ever larger foes; his exuberant dancing and whooping after killing a particularly dangerous animal struck more than one observer as macabre. From among his own kind, at college, he selected the fairest and most unobtainable mate—"See that girl? I'm going to marry her. She won't have me, but I am going to have *her!*"—and he ferociously hunted her down. That was Alice Lee Roosevelt, mother of the late Alice Longworth.

During his first years in politics, in the New York State Assembly, he won power through constant attack. The death of Alice Lee, coming as it did just after the birth of his first child—at the moment of fruition of his manhood— only intensified his will to fight. He hurried West, to where the battle for life was fiercest. The West did not welcome him; it had to be won, like everything else he lusted for. Win it he did, by dint of the greatest physical and mental stretchings-out he had yet made. In doing so he built up the magnificent body that became such an inspiration to the American people (one frail little boy who vowed to follow the president's example was the future world heavyweight champion, Gene Tunney). And by living on equal terms with the likes of Hashknife Simpson, Bat Masterson, Modesty Carter, Bronco Charlie Miller, and Hell-Roaring Bill Jones, he added another mental frontier to those he already had inherited at birth. Theodore Roosevelt, Eastern son of a Northern father and a Southern mother, could now call himself a Westerner also.

TR's second governing impulse was his personal righteousness. As one reviewer of his books remarked, "He seems to have been born with his mind made up." No violent shocks disturbed his tranquil, prosperous childhood in New York City. Privately educated, he suffered none of the traumas of school. Thanks to the security of his home, the strong leadership of his father, and the adoration of his brother and sisters, Teddie entered adolescence with no sexual or psychological doubts whatsoever. Or if he had any, he simply reasoned them out, according to the Judeo-Christian principles Theodore Senior had taught him, reached the proper moral decision, and that was that. "Thank heaven!" he wrote in his diary after falling in love with Alice Lee, "I am perfectly pure."

His three great bereavements (the death of his father in 1878, and the deaths of his mother and wife in the same house and on the same day in 1884) came too late in his development to do him any permanent emotional damage. They only served to convince him more that he must be strong, honest, clean-living, and industrious. "At least I can live," he wrote, "so as not to dishonor the memory of the dead whom I so loved," and never was a cliché more heartfelt. Experiment after experiment proved the correctness of his instincts—in graduating magna cum laude from Harvard, in marrying successfully, in defying the doctors who ordered him to live a sedentary life, in winning international acclaim as writer and politician long before he was 30. (He received his first nomination for the presidency, by the Baltimore *American*, when he was only 28; it had to be pointed out to the newspaper's editors that he was constitutionally debarred from that honor for the next seven years.)

In wild Dakota Territory, he proceeded to knock down insolent cowboys, establish the foundations of federal government, pursue boat thieves in the name of the law, and preach the gospel of responsible citizenship. One of the first things he did after Benjamin Harrison appointed him civil service commissioner was call for the prosecution of Postmaster General William Wallace of Indianapolis—who just happened to be the president's best friend. "That young man," Harrison growled, "wants to put the whole world right between sunrise and sunset."

TR's egotistic moralizing as a reform police commissioner of New York City was so insufferable that the *Herald* published a transcript of one of his speeches with the personal pronoun emphasized in heavy type. The effect, in a column of gray newsprint, was of buckshot at close range. This did not stop TR from using the personal pronoun 13 times in the first four sentences of his account of the Spanish-American War. In fact, a story went around that halfway through the typesetting, Scribner's had to send for an extra supply of capital I's.

The third characteristic of Theodore Roosevelt's personality was his sense of pride, both as an aristocrat and as an American. From birth, servants and tradespeople deferred to him. Men and women of high quality came to visit his parents and treated him as one of their number. He accepted his status without question, as he did the charitable responsibilities it entailed. At a very early age he was required to accompany his father on Sunday excursions to a lodging house for Irish newsboys and a night school for little Italians. . . .

TR knew the value of an ethnic vote as well as the next man. There is a famous—alas, probably apocryphal—story of his appointment of Oscar Straus as the first Jewish cabinet officer in American history. At a banquet to celebrate the appointment, TR made a passionate speech full of phrases like "regardless of race, color, or creed" and then turned to Jacob Schiff, the New York Jewish leader, and said, "Isn't that so, Mr. Schiff?" But Schiff, who was very deaf and had heard little of the speech, replied, "Dot's right, Mr. President, you came to me and said, 'Chake, who is der best Choo I can put in de Cabinet?'"

TR realized, of course, that the gap between himself and Joe Murray—the Irish ward-heeler who got him into the New York Assembly—was unbridgeable outside of politics. But in America a low-born man had the opportunity—the *duty*—to fight his way up from the gutter, as Joe had done. He might then merit an invitation to lunch at Sagamore Hill, or at least tea, assuming he wore a clean shirt and observed decent proprieties.

Here I must emphasize that TR was not a snob in the trivial sense. He had nothing but contempt for the Newport set and the more languid members of the Four Hundred. When he said, at 21, that he wanted to be a member of "the governing class," he was aware that it was socially beneath his own. At Albany, and in the Bad Lands, and as colonel of the Rough Riders, he preferred to work with men who were coarse but efficient, rather than those who were polished and weak. He believed, he said, in "the aristocracy of worth," and cherished the revolution that had allowed such an elite to rise to the top in government. On the other hand (to use his favorite phrase), the historian John Blum has noted that he rarely appointed impoverished or unlettered men to responsible positions. He made great political capital, as president, of the fact that his sons attended the village school at Oyster Bay, along with the sons of his servants, of whom at least one was black; but as soon as the boys reached puberty he whisked them off to Groton.

Only the very young or very old dared call him "Teddie" to his face. Roosevelt was a patrician to the tips of his tapering fingers, yet he maintained till death what one correspondent called an "almost unnatural" identity with the masses. "I don't see how you understand the common people so well, Theodore," complained Henry Cabot Lodge. "No, Cabot, you never will," said TR, grinning triumphantly, "because I am one of them, and you are not." TR deluded himself. His plebian strength was due to understanding, not empathy.

The fourth and final major trait of Theodore Roosevelt's character was his militarism. I will not deal with it in much detail because it is a familiar aspect of him, and in any case did not manifest itself much during his presidency. There is no doubt that in youth, and again in old age, he was in love with war; but oddly enough, of all our great presidents, he remains the only one not primarily associated with war (indeed, he won the Nobel Peace Prize in 1906).

He did not lack for military influences as a child; four of his Georgian ancestors had been military men, and stories of their exploits were told him by his mother. Two of his uncles served with distinction in the Confederate navy—a fact of which he proudly boasts in his *Autobiography*, while making no reference to his father's civilian status. (The *Autobiography*, by the way, is one of history's great examples of literary amnesia. You would not guess, from its pages, that Theodore Senior ever hired a substitute soldier, that Alice Lee ever lived or died, that TR was blind in one eye as president, that anything called the **Brownsville Affair** ever occurred, or that Elihu Root ever sat at his cabinet table. As James Bryce once said, "Roosevelt wouldn't always *look* at a thing, you know.")

When TR learned to read, he reveled in stories "about the soldiers of Valley Forge, and Morgan's riflemen," and confessed, "I had a great desire to be like them." In his senior year at Harvard, he suddenly developed an interest in strategy and tactics and began to write *The Naval War of 1812;* within 18 months he was the world expert on that subject. As soon as he left college he joined the National Guard and quickly became a captain, which stood him in good stead when he was called upon to lead a cavalry regiment in 1898. Throughout his literary years he made a study of classical and modern campaigns, and he would wage the great battles of history with knives and forks and spoons on his tablecloth. No doubt much of this fascination with things military related to his natural aggression, but there was an intellectual attraction too: He read abstract tomes on armaments, navigation, ballistics, strategy, and service administration as greedily as swashbuckling memoirs. Nothing is more remarkable about *The Naval War of 1812* than its cold impartiality, its use of figures and diagrams to destroy patriotic myths. Roosevelt understood that great battles are fought by thinking men, that mental courage is superior to physical bravado. Nobody thrilled more to the tramp of marching boots than he, but he believed that men must march for honorable reasons, in obedience to the written orders of a democratically elected commander in chief. In that respect, at least, the pen was mightier than the sword.

Now how much did these four character traits—aggression, righteousness, pride, and militarism—affect TR's performance as president of the United States? The answer is, strongly, as befits a strong character and a strong chief executive. The way he arrived at this "personal equation" is interesting, because he was actually in a weak position at the beginning of his first administration.

When TR took the oath of office on September 14, 1901, he was the youngest man ever to do so—a vice president, elevated by assassination, confronted by a nervous cabinet and a hostile Senate. Yet from the moment he raised his hand in that little parlor in Buffalo, it was apparent that he intended to translate his personal power into presidential power. The hand did not stop at the shoulder; he raised it high above his head, and held it there, "steady as if carved out of marble." His right foot pawed the floor. *Aggression.* He repeated the words of the oath confidently,

Brownsville Affair A 1906 affair in which an African-American army regiment was unjustly accused of crimes which led to dishonorable discharges; these were changed to honorable discharges in 1972.

adding an extra phrase, not called for in the Constitution, at the end: "And so I swear." *Righteousness.* His two senior cabinet officers, John Hay and Lyman Gage, were not present at the ceremony, but TR announced that they had telegraphed promises of loyalty to him. Actually they had not; they were both considering resignation, but TR knew any such resignations would be construed as votes of no confidence in him, and he was determined to forestall them. By announcing that Hay and Gage would stay, out of loyalty to the memory of the dead president, he made it morally impossible for them to quit. *Pride.*

As for *militarism,* TR was seen much in the company of the New York State adjutant general the next few days, and an armed escort of cavalrymen accompanied him wherever he went. This was perhaps understandable, in view of the fact that a president had just been assassinated, but it is a matter of record that more and more uniforms were seen glittering around TR as the months and years went on. Toward the end of his second administration, *Harper's Weekly* complained that "there has been witnessed under President Roosevelt an exclusiveness, a rigor of etiquette, and a display of swords and gold braid such as none of his predecessors ever dreamed of."

As the theatrical gestures at TR's inauguration make plain, he was one of the most flagrant showmen ever to tread the Washington boards. He had a genius for dramatic entrances—and always was sure the spotlight was trained his way before he made one. The first thing he asked at Buffalo was, "Where are all the newspapermen?" Only three reporters were present. His secretary explained that there was no room for more. Ignoring him, TR sent out for the rest of the press corps. Two dozen scribes came joyfully crowding in, and the subsequent proceedings were reported to the nation with a wealth of detail.

Here again we see a pattern of presidential performance developing. The exaggerated concern for the rights of reporters, the carefully staged gestures (so easy to write up, such fun to read about!)—it was as if he sensed right away that a tame press, and an infatuated public, were his surest guarantees of political security. To win election in his own right in 1904—his overriding ambition for the next three years—he would have to awake these two sleeping giants and enlist their aid in moral warfare against his political opponents, notably Senator Mark Hanna. (Hanna was chairman of the Republican National Committee and the obvious choice to take over McKinley's government after "that damned cowboy," as he called TR, had filled in as interim caretaker.)

The new president accordingly took his case straight to the press and the public. Both instantly fell in love with him. Neither seemed to notice that administratively and legislatively he accomplished virtually nothing in his first year in office. As David S. Barry of the *Sun* wrote, "Roosevelt's personality was so fascinating, so appealing to the popular fancy, so overpowering, so alive, and altogether so unique that . . . it overshadowed his public acts; that is, the public was more interested in him, and the way he did things . . . than they were about what he did."

This does not mean that TR managed, or even tried, to please all the people all the time. He was quite ready to antagonize a large minority in order to win the approval of a small majority. The sods had hardly stopped rattling on the top of McKinley's coffin when the following press release was issued: "Mr. Booker T. Washington of Tuskegee, Alabama, dined with the president last evening." Now this release, arguably the shortest and most explosive ever put out by the White House, has always been assumed to be a reluctant confirmation of the discovery of a reporter combing TR's guest book. Actually the president himself issued it, at two o'clock in the morning—that is, just in time for maximum exposure in the first edition of the newspapers. By breakfast time white supremacists all over the South were gagging over their grits at such headlines as ROOSEVELT DINES A NIGGER, and PRESIDENT PROPOSES TO CODDLE THE SONS OF HAM. This was the first time that a president had ever entertained a black man in the first house of the land. The public outcry was deafening—horror in the South, acclamation in the North—but overnight nine million Negroes, hitherto loyal to Senator Hanna, trooped into the Rooseveltian camp. TR never felt the need to dine a black man again.

Although we may have no doubt he had the redistribution of Southern patronage in mind when he sent his invitation to Washington, another motive was simply to stamp a bright, clear, first impression of himself upon the public imagination. "I," he seemed to be saying, "am a man *aggressive* enough to challenge a 100-year prejudice, *righteous* enough to do so for moral reasons, and *proud* enough to advertise the fact."

Again and again during the next seven years, he reinforced these perceptions of his personality. He aggressively prosecuted J. P. Morgan, Edward H. Harriman, and John D. Rockefeller (the holy trinity of American capitalism) in the Northern Securities antitrust case, threw the Monroe Doctrine at Kaiser Wilhelm's feet like a token of war in the Caribbean, rooted out corruption in his own administration, and crushed Hanna's 1904 presidential challenge by publicly humiliating the senator when he was running for reelection in 1903. He righteously took the side of the American worker and the American consumer against big business in the great anthracite strike, proclaimed the vanity of muckrake journalists, forced higher ethical standards upon the food and drug industry, ordered the dishonorable discharge of 160 Negro soldiers after the Brownsville Affair (on his own willful reading of the evidence, or lack thereof), and to quote Mark Twain, "dug so many tunnels under the Constitution that the transportation facilities enjoyed by that document are rivalled only by the City of New York."

For example, when the anthracite strike began to drag into the freezing fall of 1902, TR's obvious sympathy for the miners, and for millions of Americans who could not afford the rise in fuel prices, began to worry conservative members of Congress. One day Representative James E. Watson was horrified to hear that the president had decided to send federal troops in to reopen the anthracite mines on grounds of general hardship. Watson rushed round to the White House. "What about the Constitution of the United States?" he pleaded.

"What about seizing private property for public purposes without the due processes of law?"

TR wheeled around, shook Watson by the shoulder, and roared, *"To hell with the Constitution when the people want coal!"* Remarks like that caused old Joe Cannon to sigh, "Roosevelt's got no more respect for the Constitution than a tomcat has for a marriage license."

Pride, both in himself and his office, was particularly noticeable in TR's second term, the so-called imperial years, when Henry James complained, "Theodore Rex is distinctly tending—or trying to make a court." But this accusation was not true. Although the Roosevelts entertained much more elaborately than any of their predecessors, they confined their pomp and protocol to occasions of state. At times, indeed, they were remarkable for the all-American variety of their guests. On any given day one might find a Rough Rider, a poet, a British viscount, a wolf hunter, and a Roman Catholic cardinal at the White House table, each being treated with the gentlemanly naturalness which was one of TR's most endearing traits. His pride manifested itself in things like his refusal to address foreign monarchs as "Your Majesty," in his offer to mediate the Russo-Japanese War (no American president had yet had such global presumptions), and, when he won the Nobel Peace Prize for successfully bringing the war to a conclusion, in refusing to keep a penny of the $40,000 prize money. This was by no means an easy decision, because TR could have used the funds: He spent all his presidential salary on official functions and was not himself a wealthy man. He confessed he was tempted to put the Nobel money into a trust for his children, but decided it belonged to the United States.

Pride and patriotism were inseparable in Theodore Roosevelt's character; indeed, if we accept Lord Morely's axiom that he "was" America, they may be considered as complementary characteristics. And neither of them was false. Just as he was always willing to lose a political battle in order to win a political war, so in diplomatic negotiations was he sedulous to allow his opponents the chance to save face—take all the glory of settlement if need be—as long as the essential victory was his.

As I have noted earlier, TR's militarism did not loom large during his presidency. The organizational structure of the U.S. Army was revamped in such a way as to strengthen the powers of the commander in chief, but Secretary of War Elihu Root takes credit for that. TR can certainly take the credit for expanding the American navy from fifth to second place in the world during his seven and a half years of power—an amazing achievement, but quite in keeping with his policy, inherited from Washington, that "to be prepared for war is the most effectual means to promote peace." The gunboat TR sent to Panama in 1903 was the only example of him shaking a naked mailed fist in the face of a weaker power; for the rest of the time he kept that fist sheathed in a velvet glove. The metaphor of velvet on iron, incidentally, was TR's own; it makes a refreshing change from the Big Stick.

If I may be permitted a final metaphor of my own, I would like to quote one from *The Rise of Theodore Roosevelt* in an attempt to explain why, on the whole, TR's character shows to better advantage as president than in his years out of power. "The man's personality was cyclonic, in that he tended to become unstable in times of low pressure. The slightest rise in the barometer outside, and his turbulence smoothed into a whir of coordinated activity, while a core of stillness developed within. Under maximum pressure Roosevelt was sunny, calm, and unnaturally clear." This explains why the first Roosevelt era was a period of fair weather. Power became Theodore Roosevelt, and absolute power became him best of all. He loved being president and was so good at his job that the American people loved him for loving it. TR genuinely dreaded having to leave the White House, and let us remember that a third term was his for the asking in 1908. But his knowledge that power corrupts even the man who most deserves it, his reverence for the Washingtonian principle that power must punctually revert to those whose gift it is, persuaded him to make this supreme sacrifice in his prime. The time would come, not many years hence, when fatal insolence tempted him to renege on his decision. That is another story. . . .

A Primary Perspective

CORPORATE REGULATION

Theodore Roosevelt assumed the presidency during the midst of one of the greatest corporate merger movements in American history. Unlike some progressives, who feared all forms of concentrated economic power, Roosevelt thought corporate consolidation was preferable to the cutthroat competition of the late 19th-century business world. Though often reluctant to dissolve major trusts, he strongly advocated corporate regulation, and federal oversight of economic affairs expanded markedly during his administration. In the following selection, taken from a 1910 speech, Roosevelt explains why he believed the federal government needed to take the lead in such matters.

Theodore Roosevelt's Natural Resources Speech

One of the most important Conservation questions of the moment relates to the control of the water power monopoly in the public interest. There is apparent to the judicious observer a distinct tendency on the part of our opponents to cloud the issue by raising the question of state as against federal jurisdiction. We are ready to meet this issue, if it is forced upon us. But there is no hope for the plain people in such conflicts of jurisdictions. The essential

Source: Theodore Roosevelt, "Natural Resources," speech at St. Paul, Minnesota, September 6, 1910.

question is not one of hair-splitting legal technicalities. It is not really a question of state against nation. It is really a question of special corporate interests against the popular interests of this nation. If it were not for those special corporate interests, you never would have heard of the question of state as against the nation. The question is simply this: Who can best regulate the special interests for the public good? Most of the great corporations, and almost all of those that can be legitimately called the great predatory corporations, have interstate affiliations. Therefore, they are out of reach of effective state control, and fall of necessity within the federal jurisdiction. One of the prime objects of those among them that are grasping and greedy is to avoid any effective control, either by state or nation; and they advocate at this time state control simply because they believe it to be the least effective. If it should prove effective, many of those now advocating it would themselves turn round and say that such control was unconstitutional. . . .

I want you to understand my position. I do not think that you will misunderstand it. I will do my utmost to secure the rights of every corporation. If a corporation is improperly attacked, I will stand up for it to the best of my ability. I would stand up for it even though I were sure that the bulk of the people were misguided enough for the moment to take the wrong side and be against it. I should fight hard to see that the people, through the national government, did full justice to the corporations; but I do not want the national government to depend upon their good will to get justice for the people. Most of these great corporations are in a large part financed and owned in the Atlantic states, and it is rather a comic fact that many of the chief and most serious upholders of states' rights in the present controversy are big business men who live in other states. The most effective weapon is federal laws and the federal executive. That is why I so strongly oppose the demand to turn these matters over to the states. It is fundamentally a demand against the interest of the plain people, of the people of small means, against the interest of our children and our children's children; and it is primarily in the interest of the great corporations which desire to escape effective government control.

QUESTIONS

1. Which of the four personality traits discussed in the essay do you think most influenced Roosevelt's behavior? Do you think Roosevelt would have exhibited the same lifelong preoccupation with "manliness" if he had enjoyed better health as a youth?
2. What influence did Roosevelt's class background have on the development of his personality? How was he able to get along so well with people from backgrounds different from his own?
3. What do the omissions in Roosevelt's autobiography tell us about his personality? What does the Booker T. Washington incident suggest about Roosevelt's character and approach to politics?

4. In light of the views expressed by Roosevelt in his speech on corporate regulation, how do you think he felt about John D. Rockefeller's Standard Oil Company? How would he have reacted to George O. Baslington's account of the way Rockefeller conducted business?
5. In the essay, Morris states that Roosevelt "intended to translate his personal power into presidential power." What evidence does Morris provide to support this observation? How effective a president do you think Roosevelt would be today?
6. What challenges does a biographer who has chosen to write about Roosevelt confront? Based on what you know about Roosevelt, would your assessment of him be positive or negative?

 ## ADDITIONAL RESOURCES

Those wishing to learn more about Roosevelt have a broad range of works from which to choose. Major biographies include Kathleen Dalton, *A Strenuous Life* (2002); Edmund Morris, *Theodore Rex* (2001); H. W. Brands, *T.R.: The Last Romantic* (1998); Nathan Miller, *Theodore Roosevelt: A Life* (1992); David McCullough, *Mornings on Horseback: The Story of an Extraordinary Family, a Vanished Way of Life and the Unique Child Who Became Theodore Roosevelt* (1981); and William H. Harbaugh, *Power and Responsibility: The Life and Times of Theodore Roosevelt* (1968). Studies that focus more narrowly on his political career include Lewis L. Gould, *The Presidency of Theodore Roosevelt* (1991); John Morton Blum, *The Republican Roosevelt* (1977); and George Mowry, *The Era of Theodore Roosevelt, 1900–1912* (1958). For a comparative analysis of Roosevelt and the leading Democratic politician of the Progressive Era, see John Milton Cooper, Jr., *The Warrior and the Priest: Woodrow Wilson and Theodore Roosevelt* (1983). On Roosevelt's approach to foreign affairs, Howard K. Beale, *Theodore Roosevelt and the Rise of America to World Power* (1956), remains required reading a half-century after its publication.

The most recent documentary treatment of Theodore Roosevelt can be found as part of *The American Experience* series on the U.S. Presidents. Specifically, the multipart "TR, The Story of Theodore Roosevelt" tells the story of America's youngest president to date. Roosevelt's exploits in the war that made his national reputation can be found in another PBS presentation, *The Crucible of Empire: The Spanish-American War.*

Chapter 7

Eugene V. Debs

*D*uring the late nineteenth century, the rise of massive corporations employing thousands of workers presented the American labor movement with both new opportunities and new problems. On one hand, the concentration of large numbers of people in a single workplace made organization potentially easier; moreover, the long hours, low wages, and substandard working conditions that most industrial workers endured gave them ample incentive to join unions. On the other hand, huge, multidivisional corporations were formidable adversaries, all too capable of mobilizing their vast material resources to crush labor's organizational campaigns. During strikes, manufacturers also could expect assistance from the government, as friendly judges issued injunctions that restricted picket-line activity and state

authorities called out the National Guard to protect corporate property. On some occasions, as at Pullman in 1894, striking workers had to contend with federal troops as well.

Given the hostile, antilabor climate of the period, some union leaders opted for a defensive strategy. This was the tack taken by Samuel Gompers and the American Federation of Labor (AFL). Rather than openly confronting the new corporations, where semiskilled operatives comprised the bulk of the workforce, the AFL chose instead to focus on the organization of skilled craftsmen, many of whom still labored in small shops. This same cautiousness can be seen in the AFL's reluctance to become actively involved in politics. Federation leaders believed labor could expect little aid from the capitalist-dominated major parties. They also wished to avoid the political controversies that long had been a source of factionalism among unionists.

Not all labor leaders accepted the AFL approach. Some continued to espouse a much broader vision of labor's role in American society. One of them was Eugene V. Debs, the founder of the American Railway Union and a leading figure in socialist politics for more than two decades. Although Debs had largely withdrawn from active trade union work by the late 1890s, he remained a staunch advocate of industrial unions that protected all workers, not simply skilled craftsmen. Debs further believed labor had to achieve state power in its own right. Only then could workers successfully challenge capitalist–government collusion and claim their fair share of America's expanding economic surplus.

Although Debs never realized his dream of a labor commonwealth, the first two decades of the twentieth century were a heady time when anything seemed possible for American socialists. And as Francis Russell contends in the essay that follows, party successes during the period owed much to the lanky railroad unionist from Terre Haute. With his manifest sincerity, extraordinary oratorical powers, and ability to cut through Marxist abstractions, Debs captivated American audiences in ways unmatched by any other major figure of the political left.

Eugene V. Debs

Francis Russell

In the decades before the First World War he was the most dynamic, persuasive, and at the same time the most lovable figure that American socialism had produced. He hated capitalism but could hate no man. Hoosier-born, he combined in his gangling person a rural nativist populism and the class-conscious zeal of the urban foreign-born worker. Now that the American Socialist movement, shattered by World War I and disintegrated by the Russian Revolution, has faded and the other Socialist leaders of that era are

Source: Reprinted by permission of American Heritage, Inc. Copyright © 1975.

forgotten or all but forgotten, Eugene Debs remains a vital memory. His Indiana friend James Whitcomb Riley wrote of him:

> And there's 'Gene Debs—a man 'at stands
> And jes' holds out in his two hands
> As warm a heart as ever beat
> Betwixt here and the Jedgement Seat.

On the platform, with his gymnastic delivery, he was the very **Billy Sunday** of socialism, carrying his audience along as much by his personality as by what he said. Once, facing a crowd of hostile Poles in Chicago, he completely captivated them by his presence, his voice, and the animation of his gestures, even though most of them could not understand his words. He was a man it was impossible to dislike. When, after his leadership in the great Pullman strike of 1894, he was sent to the McHenry County jail for six months for violating a court injunction, he formed a friendship with the sheriff and his family that lasted the rest of his life. Twenty-five years later he was sentenced to 10 years in prison under Wilson's Espionage Act for an antiwar speech he made at Canton, Ohio, in the summer of 1918. The first few months he spent in the West Virginia state prison at Moundsville. When he was transferred to the federal penitentiary at Atlanta, the Moundsville warden wrote to the Atlanta warden: "I never in my life met a kinder man. He is forever thinking of others, trying to serve them, and never thinking of himself." At Atlanta he charmed everyone he came in contact with, prisoners and guards alike. "While there is a lower-class, I am in it," he had written earlier. "While there is a criminal class, I am of it. While there is a soul in prison I am not free." He took pains to seek out the dregs among the prisoners, to encourage them by letting them know that he cared about them. Prisoners of all sorts came to him for advice. Whenever the men were allowed outside their cells, Debs always formed the center of a group, radiating warmth and fellowship. The warden came to feel deeply obligated to him for his tremendous influence in calming and often rehabilitating other prisoners. During his penitentiary term the Socialists in 1920 nominated him for the fifth time as their presidential candidate, and over 900,000 Americans voted for him. President Wilson, always relentless against anyone who opposed him, refused even to consider reducing Debs's sentence. It took the easygoing Harding, after his inaugural in March 1921, to release the Socialist leader as soon as it seemed politically propitious. Three weeks after the inauguration Debs was allowed to go on the train to Washington alone and unguarded for a three-hour interview with Harding's attorney general, Harry Daugherty. That scarred and cynical politician was, against all his instincts, captivated by his visitor. "He spent a large part of the day in my office," Daugherty later confided to Clarence Darrow, "and I never met a man I liked better."

On December 23 the White House announced that Debs and 23 other political prisoners would be released on Christmas Day. He could not go directly to his home in Terre Haute,

> **Billy Sunday** An evangelical preacher with a sensational style who preached a fundamentalist theology.

Indiana, however, for Harding had asked him to call at the White House in passing. As he walked through the penitentiary gates for the last time 2,300 convicts crowded against the prison's front wall—the warden having in his honor suspended the usual rules—to wave and cheer him on his way. Just outside the gates Debs turned to face them, the tears running down his cheeks.

Free after two years and eight months, he arrived at the White House to find the genial Harding his most genial self. "Well," said the president, bounding out of his chair to shake hands, "I have heard so damned much about you, Mr. Debs, that I am now very glad to meet you personally." What the two men discussed in their private interview they never said. But afterward Debs told the waiting reporters: "Mr. Harding appears to me to be a kind gentleman, one whom I believe possesses humane impulses. We understand each other perfectly."

When Eugene Victor Debs was born in Terre Haute in 1855, that roistering frontier town on the Wabash River had a population of 6,000. His bookish father, Daniel, an Alsatian millowner's son, had named his own son after his two literary heroes, Eugène Sue and Victor Hugo. Daniel had left Alsace in 1848 for what he considered the freer life of America, but bad luck had dogged him from the outset. On the 71-day voyage over he was fleeced of all his money by an American con man and arrived in New York penniless. Supporting himself by odd jobs, he nevertheless managed to save enough to send for his fiancée, Daisy Bettrich, one of his father's mill hands, whom he would have married in Alsace if his class-conscious family had not been so opposed. Marriage in New York did not change his luck. He found no permanent work, and Daisy's first child, a daughter, died a few days after birth. In their sadness and isolation the young couple struck out for the West, ending up in Terre Haute, where they heard there was a French colony. All their small possessions were accidentally shipped down the river to New Orleans and lost for good.

In Terre Haute, Daniel worked 14 hours a day in the fetid dampness of a packinghouse until his health gave out. Then he drifted from one casual job to another. Daisy gave birth to a second daughter, who did not live long enough to be named. But when life seemed at its lowest ebb for the Debses, the tide slowly shifted. Two more daughters were born, and both lived. The determined and practical-minded Daisy took $40 that she had somehow managed to save, bought a stock of groceries, and opened a store in the front room of their little frame house. The Debses were well liked, and against Daniel's gloomy predictions the store soon brought them a modest living.

The two Debs daughters had been baptized, but by the time Eugene Victor was born, the Protestant Daniel and the Catholic Daisy had drifted away from the church. Daniel became a freethinker. Whenever he could save a little money, he ordered books, filling his shelves with the French and German classics and even buying small busts of Rousseau and Voltaire for the mantel. At home the parents spoke French and German, and the children picked up a smattering of both languages.

Eugene was five when the Civil War broke out. Almost his first memories were of marching men, of troop trains moving slowly through the town. More garish were his memories of the frontier town itself on a Saturday night, the flaring lights of Wabash Street just west of the canal, with its saloons and gambling joints and sporting houses. But he found the most permanent fascination of his boyhood in the railroads: trains and the men who ran them.

School with its prosaic, didactic curriculum bored the growing boy. High school bored him still more. In 1870, when he was 14, thin, angular, and six feet tall, he quit. Gravitating to the railroad, he found his first job with the Vandalia line, cleaning grease from the trucks of freight engines at 50 cents a day. At the end of the long workday his hands would be raw and his knuckles bleeding from the potash he used to loosen the grease. The youngest and least in the roundhouse, he had to take orders from everyone. Railroading soon lost much of its glamour for the weary boy. Yet he stayed on, proud at least to bring home his pay on a Saturday night. The grocery business continued to prosper. Daniel moved to a larger house. There were five children in the family now.

Gene's shop torment ended when he was sent with a crew to paint switches on the 70-mile stretch of track between Terre Haute and Indianapolis. He soon showed himself deft at painting. Later he was assigned to paint stripes on car bodies, then to lettering locomotives. In his spare time he made signs for his friends. Always he showed a friendly readiness to do small favors for anyone, without any thought of ulterior reward. Children loved him. He made kites for them and brought them pocketfuls of candy from his father's store.

In December 1871, when a drunken fireman failed to show up for work, the gangling boy was pressed into service as a night fireman. There he remained, on the run between Terre Haute and Indianapolis. "As a locomotive fireman," Debs wrote in reminiscent bitterness, "I learned of the hardships of the rail in snow, sleet, and hail, of the ceaseless danger that lurks along the iron highway, the uncertainty of employment, scant wages, and altogether trying lot of the workingman, so that from my very boyhood I was made to feel the wrongs of labor. . . ." That feeling actually came later. For the present he was contentedly earning more than a dollar a night. With the extra money he went to business college every afternoon but found himself too drugged from lack of sleep to learn much. The scantiness of his education now began to trouble him, and he tried with only modest success to study at home. On the day his former high-school class graduated in 1873, he crept to his attic bed and cried.

The panic of that same year threw him out of a job, along with thousands of others. Since there was nothing for him in Terre Haute, he rode a freight to Evansville, where he found the prospects as bleak as at home. He moved on to St. Louis, and he was lucky enough to be hired as a fireman. But in St. Louis, for the first time in his life, he encountered large-scale urban misery: unemployed derelicts, homeless, wandering families, others living in shacks by the Mississippi, a world of desolation he had known before only in the pages of Victor Hugo's *Les Misérables*. What he as an individual could do about such conditions he did not know, but he burned with unfocused indignation.

Railroading was then a very hazardous trade, with accidents frequent and most of the lines callously indifferent to even elementary safety measures. Late in 1874, after one of Gene's friends slipped under a locomotive and was killed, his mother begged him to come home. At her insistence he gave up railroading and returned to Terre Haute to become a billing clerk with the wholesale grocers Hulman & Cox, the largest firm in the Midwest. Yet for all its hardships and dangers, railroad life continued to fascinate him. The wholesale grocery business did not. "There are too many things in business that I cannot tolerate," he wrote. "Business means grabbing for yourself." Evenings he used to like to walk down the tracks and watch the engines back and switch. Often he would drop in at one of the bars near the station to pass an hour or two with the trainmen. On one such evening he learned that Joshua Leach, the grand master of the Brotherhood of Locomotive Firemen, as he was entitled with Masonic grandeur, was coming to Terre Haute to organize a lodge. The idea of fraternal unity in a common cause, a railroad cause, appealed vastly and at once to the young billing clerk. He attended the meeting and at the end pushed forward and asked to join the newly founded Vigo Lodge. Leach—whose organizing efforts over two years had met only scanty success—concealed his surprise and asked the eager young man if he felt he could do his duty on being admitted. With no real idea as to what his duty might be, Debs answered, "Yes sir!"

In his enthusiasm Debs soon took over as secretary of Vigo Lodge No. 16. It was a job no one else would take. The brotherhood itself was a weak, benevolent organization concerned chiefly with group insurance plans at a time when the real issues for the railroad workers were pay, safety measures, and hours. Membership in the new lodge declined. Sometimes the young secretary would be the only one present at the fortnightly meeting. Undiscouraged, he turned to other town affairs, helping to found the Occidental Literary Club, a weekly debating society to which he invited such well-known speakers as Robert G. Ingersoll, Wendell Phillips, the women's-rights crusader Susan B. Anthony, and the then almost unknown rhymester James Whitcomb Riley. Everybody in Terre Haute had come to know and like the lanky, friendly Gene Debs by this time. In 1879, as a Democrat, he was elected city clerk. Two years later, in spite of a general Republican comeback, he was reelected.

In 1880, with the firemen's brotherhood almost bankrupt, the grand master persuaded the reluctant Debs to become secretary–treasurer of the moribund organization and editor of its paper, *The Magazine*. To accommodate Debs, union headquarters were moved to Terre Haute. The young secretary's determination and abounding effort soon brought an astonishing reversal in the brotherhood's fortunes. When he took over, assisted by his younger brother Theodore, he found himself working 18 hours a day on the firemen's problems. Suddenly the organization was alive. New members flooded in. The sprightly *Magazine* circulated far beyond the membership.

This success, however, hardly foreshadowed Debs's later career. Wrapped up as he was in his benevolent-association union, he did not think of himself as a socialist. The railroad brotherhoods were nonstriking unions, and in those early years Debs found even Samuel Gompers's American Federation of Labor too radical. The closed shop he considered an infringement on liberty, and he could even refer to the rapacious William H. Vanderbilt as "the great railroad president." In 1884, thinking he could help his union as a lawmaker, he ran successfully as a Democratic candidate for the state legislature. But after he saw a railroad safety bill that he had sponsored buried in the upper house, he lost faith in the two-party parliamentary system, with its inevitable jobbery; he did not run again.

With his customary drive and enthusiasm he now went on to organize the neglected brakemen, a task he found challenging but physically and finan-cially exhausting. Coming back to Terre Haute from week-long travels for the new Brotherhood of Railroad Brakemen, often with scanty results, he turned for consolation and encouragement to his sister's solemnly handsome friend Kate Metzel, stepdaughter of the town's most prominent druggist. Debs's social life had been confined more to saloons than to the dances and polite evenings of the increasingly prim upper-class Terre Haute, and until he met Kate, he had paid little attention to women. But she, drawn to him from the beginning, listened to him gravely, as women do when they are in love, her interest in him masking her basic lack of interest in his concerns. What she herself cared about most deeply was material success: elegance, a large house, membership in Terre Haute's emergent society. Why she chose him she prob-ably later wondered herself. They were married a few months before his 30th birthday in a formal wedding at Saint Stephen's Episcopal Church, of which Kate was a devout member. After a brief honeymoon they returned to house-keeping rooms. Kate found herself much alone in her rented quarters while her husband traveled from state to state drumming up membership for his union. Whatever his salary might be, money had a way of slipping through his fingers. Railroad men in their need habitually turned to him. Once when he learned that a fireman could not be promoted for lack of a good watch, he gave the man his own. At least once he gave away his overcoat. His wife never suffered actual want, but such casualness, such a hit-or-miss life, was not what she had dreamed of in her girlhood. She loved her husband and would con-tinue to love him, but she could not give her heart to his activities. On the death of an aunt she inherited enough money to build her dream house, a towered and gabled affair of her own design on an upper-class street.

The panic year 1893 marked Debs's break with his conservative past. Up until then he could still write that "we indulge in none of the current vagaries about a conflict between capital and labor." But after Chicago's 1886 Haymarket bombing he edged toward a more militant stance. The bombing was basic for him. There, in Haymarket Square during a pro-longed strike for an eight-hour day, a police captain advanced with a squad of bluecoats as a local anarchist was addressing a small but orderly crowd and ordered the meeting dispersed. When the police closed in, some unknown person threw a bomb. Seven policemen died. In the aftermath eight anarchists and union leaders were arrested and tried, and four of them were hanged for the crime—although only two of the convicted men had even been near the square. The outraged Debs, like many other labor leaders, came to regard the executed men as martyrs to the cause of industrial freedom. Following Haymarket, after Henry Frick of the Carnegie Steel Company had brutally broken the Homestead steelworkers' strike in 1892 and after federal troops had at about the same time put down a silver miners' strike in Coeur d'Alene, Idaho, Debs turned permanently to the radical left. During the depression of 1893 he denounced capitalists furiously in his *Magazine*, comparing them to tentacled devilfish dragging the workers down to degradation.

Such grim times, with over three million unemployed walking the streets, made Debs increasingly unhappy with the self-centered unionism of the railroad brotherhoods, who could not even be counted on to support one another in a strike. Engineers and conductors, the aristocrats of labor, held themselves aloof. Carmen, firemen, switchmen, raided each other's membership at will. Debs now set out to organize an American railway union that would take in *all* railroad employees, from engineer to engine wiper.

Even Debs was astonished at the immediate and overwhelming response to his union. Within three weeks 34 locals had been organized. Not only the unskilled and the unorganized joined, but many carmen, firemen, and even some of the engineers and conductors transferred their lodges *in toto*, braving the surly resentment of the brotherhood officers. The new union's first test of strength came when it launched a strike against James Hill's Great Northern Railroad. The autocratic Hill, who regarded unionism as an infringement on his God-given right to do as he pleased, had already cut wages twice on his line in that depression year. When, from his office in St. Paul, he announced a third cut, Debs called the strike. Within days the Great Northern was brought to a standstill. Seeking a solution to the impasse, the St. Paul Chamber of Commerce asked Debs to state his case. Generally Debs spoke in the florid McKinley-baroque manner of his day, but this time, facing a group of essentially hostile businessmen, he muted his rhetoric to tell them simply and directly what it was like to be a section hand or a brakeman, what it meant to raise a family on a dollar a day. So persuasive was he that he completely won over his audience. A delegation of chamber leaders visited Hill and told him he would have to arbitrate. The arbitrators granted the union almost all its demands. It was a handsome victory for Debs. When his train left St. Paul, after Hill had signed the agreement, the section men stood along the tracks at attention, bare-headed, shovels in hand.

On the heels of his victory over Hill, Debs found himself in an even more formidable confrontation with George M. Pullman, the president of the Pullman Palace Car Company, maker of dining and chair cars as well as the celebrated sleepers. Just outside Chicago, Pullman had built what he considered a model town. So it appeared, in green contrast to the industrial grime of Chicago, with neat brick homes, shaded streets, grassy yards, and even an artificial lake beside which the Pullman band gave summer concerts. But it was Pullman's town—houses, schools, churches, the luxurious new library, even the cemetery. With the onset of the depression Pullman discharged over a third of his workers and cut the wages of the others by up to half while refusing to lower rents at all. During the bleak and bitter winter of 1893–1894 destitution spread along Pullman's well-planned streets. Many of the tenants all but starved even as the company's dividends increased. Children lacked shoes to wear to school; some stayed in bed all day to keep warm in the heatless houses.

Because of a few miles of track operated by the Pullman company its workers were eligible for the American Railway Union. In the late spring of 1894 they rushed to join. Their first act was to call a strike, even before Debs had put in an appearance. Debs arrived in Pullman knowing little about conditions there. He was appalled at what he discovered. Yet he was at the same time cautious. His victory over Hill was the only success any union had scored that year. Strike after strike had been broken. Labor was in retreat. Debs knew he could expect little help from the railroad brotherhoods. Rather than risk defeat he preferred to arbitrate. But Pullman refused to sit down at any discussion table. "Nothing to arbitrate," was his stock reply. Pushed along by the indignation of the American Railway Union members and the Pullman workers, Debs finally proposed that switchmen refuse to switch Pullman cars onto trains. At the same time he warned against violence. In response to this the General Managers' Association, representing the 24 railroads running out of Chicago, announced that switchmen who balked at switching Pullman cars would be discharged.

Nevertheless, the boycott began on June 26, 1894, spreading quickly to 27 states and territories in the most extensive strike the country had yet known. More than a hundred thousand men walked out; 20 railroads were shut down. United States Attorney General Richard Olney, a former railroad lawyer and member of the General Managers' Association, then obtained an injunction against the union and the strikers that was one of the most sweeping and drastic ever issued. Workers who quit interstate jobs were to be considered criminals. Union leaders were forbidden to take part in or even to talk about the boycott.

For Debs to obey the injunction would be for him to lose the strike by default and probably destroy his union. To disregard it might send him and other leaders to jail. He felt he had no choice but to disregard it. Olney, by a process of maneuvering and misinformation, persuaded President Cleveland that the safety of the mails was endangered by the chaos in Chicago. The president, believing the situation critical, dispatched infantry, cavalry, and artillery. In spite of Debs's warning against violence, turbulent crowds had begun to hold up trains and detach the Pullman cars. With the arrival of the troops at Chicago—aided by over 3,000 floaters hastily sworn in as deputy federal marshals—violence exploded. Mobs smashed switches, halted trains, and burned hundreds of railroad cars. A mob finally attacked the troops. They in turn opened fire, and seven men lay dead in the street. The soldiers now took over the city. Two days later Debs and three colleagues were arrested, then tried and sentenced for contempt and for obstructing the mails. The strike was broken, and Debs was on his way to jail.

The Pullman strike became known as Debs's strike. On his release from jail six months later he was the most famous labor leader in the United States. While in jail he had been visited by Victor Berger and other Socialist leaders, who hoped to enlist him in their cause. Yet for all his increased radicalism Debs remained unconvinced. Populism attracted him more than socialism. In 1896 the Populists even considered running him as their presidential candidate, and a third of the delegates to their convention were pledged to him. He urged them instead to support the silver-tongued, silver-minded William Jennings Bryan. Bryan became the nominee of both the Populists and the Democrats. McKinley's defeat of Bryan was the weight thrown in the balance that finally convinced Debs that the old system of capitalism was not enough, that it must be superseded by a system of public ownership and public use. On New Year's 1897, in a lead article in the *Railway Times*, the journal of his now faltering American Railway Union, he announced that he was a Socialist.

Debs was a Socialist more of the heart than of the head, a utopian rather than a **dialectical materialist.** Though he later kept a framed picture of Karl Marx in his office, it is doubtful that he ever read **Das Kapital.** While in the Atlanta penitentiary he tacked on the wall of his cell a picture of Jesus Christ, whom he liked to consider the first socialist. To the small Socialist Labor party, founded in 1877 and appealing mostly to the eastern foreign-born, he brought a western nativism as homespun as that of his friend James Whitcomb Riley. Debs Americanized the Socialist party. In turn it became his final vision. "Promising indeed is the outlook for socialism in the United States," he wrote at the beginning of the new century. "The very contemplation of the prospect is a wellspring of inspiration."

In 1900 the Socialists looked to Debs as their logical and their most inspiring presidential candidate. At first he refused. But at the party convention the leaders finally persuaded him to put aside his personal reluctance for the sake of the cause. "With your united voices ringing in my ears, with your impassioned appeals burning and glowing in my breast," he told the delegates in his Sunday-best rhetoric, "I am brought to realize that in your voice is a supreme command of duty."

Renaming themselves the Social Democratic party, the Socialists put forward a socialist-reformist platform that they hoped would appeal to the Populists and draw many of the disaffected from Bryan. Debs proved himself a spectacular campaigner. An actor by instinct, he found that he loved the applause of crowds, the open platform, the tense moment of anticipation as men waited for his words. Yet for all his zeal and enthusiasm he polled fewer than a hundred thousand votes, while McKinley was reelected comfortably with 7,218,491 votes to 6,356,734 for Bryan. Swallowing

dialectical materialist A person who believes in the theory and practice of weighing and reconciling contradictory arguments for the purpose of arriving at the truth, especially through discussion and debate.

Das Kapital A monumental political-economic study written by Karl Marx that serves as the theoretical basis of communism.

his chagrin, Debs bravely predicted that "the next four years will witness the development of socialism to continental power and proportions."

During those four years Debs became a permanent propagandist for the Socialist cause, lecturing, speaking, organizing, exhausting his none-too-robust body on journeys up and down the land. Rarely did he get enough sleep; rarely did he eat properly. Though only in his mid-40s he looked much older: bald, gaunt, hollow-eyed. His evenings of speeches and discussions were often followed by drinking bouts that exhausted him still further. But socialism as a force was taking hold. He could see that in the crowds he met, in the tumultuous welcome he got from western logging camps and mining towns. The Socialist press was growing too. The party had high hopes in 1904 when the Social Democratic Convention chose him by acclamation as its presidential candidate. "I shall be heard in the coming campaign," he told the delegates, "as often, and as decidedly, and as emphatically, as revolutionarily, as uncompromisingly as my ability, my strength, and my fidelity to the movement will allow."

Under the dual banners of the Red Flag and the Stars and Stripes, the Socialists waged a presidential campaign with the customary paraphernalia of badges, buttons, ribbons, lithographs, and lantern slides, plus thousands of "little red stickers" and a catchy song, "The Dawning Day." Theodore Roosevelt, president by inheritance, easily defeated the conservative Democrat, Judge Alton B. Parker, by over two and a half million votes. But Debs's vote increased fourfold, to 402,895. One voter in 36 had voted for the Socialists, establishing them as a third party that, they were convinced, would in a decade or so become America's first party.

In 1901 the Social Democrats united with dissident socialists to form the Socialist party of the United States. During the next four years the party doubled its membership. Farmers of the West and Midwest, workers, scholars, intellectuals, liberal clergymen, suffragists, and social workers were drawn by their different roads to the Red Flag. Every state in the Union now had its Socialist locals. There were a hundred Socialist newspapers; there was the Rand School of Social Science in New York; there was the Intercollegiate Socialist Society, supported by Jack London's lusty presence. Debs was now recognized across America as the popular spokesman for socialism. In 1905 he helped "Big Bill" Haywood organize the lumberjacks and miners and other revolutionary-minded Westerners into the Industrial Workers of the World. Though himself inclined to the radicals, he managed to hold the radical and conservative wings of the party together. In 1908 he was nominated for the third time as presidential candidate, but not by acclamation and not unanimously. Conservative Socialists like Victor Berger—"Slowcialists," as some called them—were beginning to have reservations.

The Socialist campaign was made both widespread and spectacular by the Red Special, a train that Debs rented as his mobile headquarters. Decked out with red flags and banners, carrying a brass band, the Red Special's three cars started from Chicago at the end of August on a two-months' journey that would take Debs across the West to California and back to Boston and New York to end with a 10-mile-long triumphant parade in Chicago. Crowds packed Boston's Faneuil Hall and New York's Hippodrome to hear him. Crowds lined the tracks at whistle stops to watch him pass. In sections of Wisconsin the schools were closed to let the children see the Red Special. Debs spoke until his throat was raw. Sometimes his voice failed him completely, and his younger brother Theodore, who much resembled him, took over in his place. "The 'Red Special' is a trump," Debs wrote halfway across America. "The people are wild about it and the road will be lined with the cheering hosts of the proletarian revolution."

But for all the Red Special's sensational passage and the warm welcomes Debs received, the election results were coldly disillusioning. The Socialists increased their total of four years earlier by a mere 18,000 votes. Yet even as they were debating the discouraging results, in the months that followed they benefited from a sharp upturn in popular favor as a result of the Taft–Roosevelt split and the rise of progressivism. In 1910 the Socialists even elected a mayor of Milwaukee, and Victor Berger became the first Socialist congressman, representing the same bumptious city. By 1911 some 435 Socialists had been elected to office in various parts of the country. Yet the party's 1912 convention was marked by increasing dissent between the "Slowcialists" and the radicals. The conservatives finally forced through an amendment excluding those who, like Haywood's IWW Wobblies, favored industrial sabotage and violence over mere political agitation. Debs was in an anomalous position. He disliked any form of violence, and yet when he called for revolution he did not mean evolution. Never wholly trusting him, the conservatives put forward several other candidates to oppose him. Still, there could be no doubt about the outcome. Debs, like no other leader, had captured the imagination and the hearts of the rank-and-file party members. He was the inevitable candidate.

That election of 1912 was the most frenzied, the most viciously contested, since Bryan had run against McKinley in 1896. With Roosevelt and his Bull Moose party moving head-on against Taft and the embattled party regulars, the election of New Jersey's Governor Woodrow Wilson was predictable. As Debs admitted to Lincoln Steffens, he himself campaigned for Socialist propaganda purposes, with never the remotest hope of winning. His campaign was as lively as ever, though it lacked the flamboyance of the Red Special this time. Again he toured the country, and again he brought the crowds to their feet with his electrifying delivery, his evangelistic denunciations of capitalism. The more optimistic Socialists had predicted he would gather in at least two million votes. Though this was wide of the mark, Debs did manage to more than double his 1908 vote. Almost 1 voter in 16 had given the Socialists his allegiance. They seemed now a permanent force in American politics.

Kate Debs did not accompany her husband on his tours. His brother and his parents had followed him enthusiastically into socialism, but there was a rumor that Kate had fainted when he announced his conversion. Socialism was alien to her bourgeois heart. She remained nevertheless a loyal wife. In a short article, "How My Wife Has Helped Me," Debs wrote in 1922:

> She trudged through the snow to a cold office when I was on the road, lighted the fire, emptied the ashes, cleaned the office, answered the mail, shipped bundles of literature to me and to others, and then returned to cook her meals, set the house in order, and attend to the wants of the home.

But even at the time when he wrote this, Debs, from a health sanitarium, was writing perfervid letters to another woman.

Debs was never a philanderer. He cared deeply for his wife, who represented home for him, with all the connotations of the word. But passion, unstinted affection, and emotional release he found in a Terre Haute neighbor, Mabel Curry, the wife of a professor of literature at Indiana State Normal College. She and Debs first became intimate two decades after his marriage. A blond and rather buxom housewife, mother of three daughters, she was for Debs **"Juno the Divine,"** without whom, he told her over and over, he could not have endured his loneliness. During the Red Special's tour she sometimes traveled aboard or met him secretly at one of the cities where he stopped off. Although not a formal Socialist, she was much more sympathetic to socialist doctrine than Kate was. She was for him beautiful, lovable, irresistible, he repeats in letters cloying in their repetitiveness. At the same time a strong streak of religiosity runs through the letters. Though Debs adhered to no formal religion, he tells Mabel that he believes with all his heart and soul in a future life and is convinced that she will have her place in it with him. Love, he insists, defies reason and the limitations of the human senses because it is itself divine and akin to the creative soul of the universe. God still reigns, he assures her, and love holds the planets in their orbits and the stars in their courses.

The bright day that seemed to dawn for American socialism in 1912 soon clouded over. As Wilson captured the popular imagination with his New Freedom, interest in socialism waned. Then the fateful August of 1914 arrived. Debs and his American comrades were thunderstruck as the European Socialists declared for war and nationalism. "I am opposed to every war but one," Debs wrote; "I am for that war heart and soul, and that is the worldwide revolution." As American sentiment swung from neutrality to the side of the Allies, and even after the entry of the United States into the war, Debs never moved an inch from that early statement. He was certain that peace could come only by the destruction of capitalism, not by the victory of the Allies. All his innate anger had been aroused by Wilson's dispatch of American troops to Mexico in 1914 for what Debs maintained was merely a defense of Standard Oil interests. At the outbreak of the European war he called for unconditional neutrality; and when, after the sinking of the *Lusitania*, the preparedness tide rose higher, so that even Socialists like Upton Sinclair were carried along, Debs joined Bryan, Jane Addams, and Senator LaFollette in stern opposition to militarism in any form.

In 1916 he refused to consider running again for president, and the

Juno the Divine An ancient Roman goddess of womanhood.

Socialists named a competent but relatively obscure newspaperman as their candidate. Nevertheless, over Debs's protests, the Indiana comrades nominated him for Congress. Into this more limited role he put his best efforts, touring his district in a Model T and concluding the campaign with a boisterous torchlight parade through Terre Haute. Kate, nettled by reports and rumors that she was at odds with her husband, marched arm in arm with him at the parade's head.

Wilson won only narrowly over the Republicans' more war-minded Charles Evans Hughes. The Socialist vote dropped to almost half that of 1912. Debs ran ahead of the Democratic congressman, but the Republican candidate won easily. The United States war declaration, following on the heels of Wilson's second inauguration, split the Socialist party. Debs, aging and in ill health, remained as adamant as ever in his attitude toward the war. But much of the spark seemed to have gone out of him. Although the wartime hysteria of patriotism and the violations of civil liberties stirred him to angry protest, he did not publicly denounce the conscription act, the Liberty Loan drives, or the subsidies to the Allies.

Socialists proved themselves scarcely more immune to the war fever than the rest of the country. Some 100,000 of them made a public declaration of their support of the war. A bare 20,000 refused. Debs saw his own wife carried away in the surge of conforming patriotism. Kate became chairman of the women's division of the Liberty Bond drive, was active in the Red Cross, and knitted socks for our boys "over there."

Russia's October Revolution came as a breath of life to the more intransigent American radicals and Socialists. For the great majority of Americans, carried away by their war sentiments, it seemed a betrayal. All who were not for America were against America. To speak out against the war became dangerous. Pressure for conformity culminated in the Espionage Act, a law so draconian that one could be sent to jail merely for commenting adversely on a soldier's uniform or using language judged to aid the enemy's cause. That act reactivated Debs, and he determined to defy it. On June 16, 1918, at Nimisilla Park in Canton, on a platform bare of flags, he made a defiant two-hour speech that became a Socialist legend and that he knew would bring him to jail. "I would a thousand times rather be a free soul in jail than a sycophant and a coward in the streets," he told a crowd of 1,200. Government agents took down every word he spoke. A fortnight later he was arrested.

He had expected no other outcome. On leaving for prison he threw a kiss to Kate from the train, and he told a friend en route that "she has stood shoulder to shoulder with me through every storm that has beat upon us and she is still standing firm now." Yet in all the months he spent at the Atlanta penitentiary she never once visited him. Nor had she attended his trial. The reasons given by his biographers—her own ill health, the care of her aged mother, and the burden of running her Terre Haute house—seem hardly adequate. Debs's one constant visitor was Mabel Curry, who gave up her own homelife for months to see and be near him. She visited him daily, smuggled notes past the guards for him, and even took charge of the large correspondence that came to him from all over the world. He was 64 when he entered the penitentiary, an old man in failing health. Yet the letters he wrote her in those years are those of a young lover—eager, idealistic, and, it must be admitted, somewhat florid and sentimental. There are few actual letters from prison, partly because Mabel was there much of the time to see him, partly because the one letter a week he was allowed to send he generally wrote to Kate.

In 1920 the battered Socialist party, from which the Left Socialists had seceded the year before to form the Communist and the Communist Labor parties, met in convention in New York to choose a presidential candidate. After a ritual singing of the "Marseillaise" and the "Internationale" the delegates piled red roses around a portrait of the absent Debs, and he, Convict No. 9653, was nominated by acclaim. A delegation arrived at Atlanta to notify him formally, and he received them in his prison denims. He was allowed to issue statements of 500 words a week, and that was the extent of his campaigning. In the year that had expanded the electorate to include women, he received 919,977 votes, 3.5 percent of the total and about half his percentage of 1912. The victorious Harding had 16,152,200 votes. A few Socialists tried to take heart at almost a million votes, but the old-time Socialist leader Morris Hillquit sensed the election rightly as "the last flicker of the dying candle." Over the decades the two major parties would borrow much from the Socialist program as the United States stumbled toward the welfare state. But socialism as a third-party alternative was gone.

Following his release from Atlanta, Debs spent a half year with Kate in Terre Haute. At 67 his health was broken. He was suffering from heart trouble, kidney trouble, arthritis, and blinding headaches, and his digestion had still not recovered from his prison diet. After six months in Terre Haute he went to the Lindlahr Sanitarium, a "nature" health resort near Chicago.

There in his room night after night the faded Socialist leader bent his head over his desk—he claimed to have had only three hairs left—writing to his Juno with all the fervor of an adolescent. Rarely did he mention politics or his Socialist activities. But he let her see the underlying sadness beneath the equanimity of his painfully assumed cheerful exterior. Most of his life, he admitted, had been spent in the depths and very little on peaks.

Debs lived on for six more years in increasingly poor health and reduced activity. When he had entered the penitentiary, he was so sympathetic to Soviet Russia that he had declared himself a Bolshevik from the top of his head to the soles of his feet. Now, when fellow travelers like Lincoln Steffens and Communist stalwarts like Ella Reeve Bloor urged him to show his allegiance to the Soviet state, he replied that "when the people of Russia aspire toward freedom I'm all for them, but I detest the terror which the Bolsheviks imposed to wrest and hold power. I still have, and always will have, a profound faith in the efficacy of the ballot." Nor did he have any more sympathy for the American Communists, with their tactics of violence and underground activity. In 1923 he tried to resuscitate his dying party by a speaking tour of the major cities. Huge crowds came to listen to him, more out of curiosity and respect than conviction. Finally he collapsed and had to return to the sanitarium. He had stated that he would never run for president again. Nor, as 1924 approached, would his physical condition have allowed it. In that year the Socialists ran no candidate, but instead endorsed the candidate of the new Progressive party, Wisconsin's Senator Robert LaFollette.

In 1925 Debs was able to attend the banquet that the Socialist party of New York gave him on his 70th birthday. Yet it was almost beyond his strength. To the chance remark that socialism was dead he could still respond with the old fire. But he was a dying man. Some time in the spring of 1926 he went with Kate on a cruise to Bermuda and after a singularly rough return voyage came home worse than when he had started. Although he had hoped to attend a Socialist national convention in Pittsburgh on May 1, he was too ill to leave his bed. There he managed to write an appeal for Sacco and Vanzetti, his last published work. On September 20 he went back to the Lind-lahr Sanitarium for another cure and died there three weeks later, with Kate and Theodore at his bedside.

Debs is remembered as the brightest star of American socialism, yet more for his character and kindly spirit than for his doctrinaire beliefs. That man was naturally good was his simplistic conviction. In his own case it happened to be true.

A Primary Perspective

CHILD LABOR

The working people who listened most intently to Eugene Debs had no greater concern than their children's welfare. All too often, however, poverty-level wages placed sharp limitations on what they could do for their offspring. This was particularly so among the semiskilled, foreign-born machine tenders who formed the largest group in most early twentieth-century factories. The children of these workers frequently left school and filed into the mills alongside their parents shortly after their 14th birthday. As the youths interviewed below make clear, many had no alternative.

Statement of Charles Vasiersky, Fifteen-Year-Old Doffer at the Everett Mills, Lawrence, Massachusetts, 1912

MR. LENROOT: How much have you been to school?
MASTER VASIERSKY: I have been to school until I was 14 years old.
MR. LENROOT: What grade were you in when you left?
MASTER VASIERSKY: I was in the seventh grade when I left.
MR. LENROOT: Would you have liked to keep on there if you could?

Source: U.S. Congress, House of Representatives, *The Strike at Lawrence: Hearings before the Committee on Rules of the House of Representatives on Resolutions 409 and 433*, 62nd Cong., 2d sess. (Washington, D.C.: Government Printing Office, 1912), pp. 145, 153.

MASTER VASIERSKY: I would have kept on, but we did not have anything to eat, and so I had to go to work.

MR. LENROOT: Do you go hungry sometimes?

MASTER VASIERSKY: Not all the time; but when I come home we do not have much to eat; just a piece of bread; instead of butter we have molasses.

Statement of John Boldelar, Fourteen-Year-Old Bobbin Boy at the Arlington Mill, Lawrence, Massachusetts, 1912

MR. CAMPBELL: What school did you attend?

MASTER BOLDELAR: I went to Arlington school.

MR. CAMPBELL: What grade were you in when you quit?

MASTER BOLDELAR: I was in the fourth grade, naval, when I quit.

MR. CAMPBELL: Were you glad when you quit school?

MASTER BOLDELAR: No, sir.

MR. CAMPBELL: You would have been glad if the law had not permitted you to go to work until you were 16?

MASTER BOLDELAR: If we had had enough money, I would not have quit it.

MR. CAMPBELL: But you would like to have the law changed so that boys could not go into the mill until they were 16?

MASTER BOLDELAR: I would; but what would we eat if I go to school? We should live on bread and water all the time.

QUESTIONS

1. Why did Debs decide to form the American Railway Union? How would you assess his leadership of the Pullman strike? What influence did the strike have on the development of Debs's political beliefs?

2. Why did Debs give up active trade-union work to become a Socialist orator and politician? In what ways did Debs "Americanize" the Socialist movement?

3. What factors were most responsible for the electoral successes of the Socialist Party during the early 20th century? Do you think the general reform sentiment of the period increased or diminished the Socialist appeal? What effect did World War I have on the American Socialist movement?

4. How do you think Debs felt about Theodore Roosevelt? Would their views regarding child labor have been appreciably different? Can you think of any other issues on which Debs and Roosevelt might have adopted similar positions?

5. How did Debs respond to the growing factionalism within the Socialist movement during the 1910s? What was his reaction to the Russian Revolution and the rise of an American Communist movement?

6. What influence did Debs have on the times in which he lived? Would he have been any more successful if he had chosen to work within the mainstream of the labor movement?

ADDITIONAL RESOURCES

The best biography of the Socialist leader is Nick Salvatore, *Eugene V. Debs: Citizen and Socialist* (1982), although Ray Ginger, *The Bending Cross: A Biography of Eugene Victor Debs* (1949), is still worth consulting. Studies of the Socialist movement include Howard H. Quint, *The Forging of American Socialism: Origins of the Modern Movement* (1953); David A. Shannon, *The Socialist Party of America: A History* (1955); James Weinstein, *The Decline of Socialism in America, 1912–1925* (1967); and William M. Dick, *Labor and Socialism in America: The Gompers Era* (1972). Two important analyses of major developments in the world of labor during Debs's lifetime are David Montgomery, *The Fall of the House of Labor: The Workplace, the State, and American Labor Activism, 1865–1925* (1987), and the relevant chapters in Bruce Laurie, *Artisans into Workers: Labor in Nineteenth-Century America* (1989).

Cambridge Documentary Films presents *Eugene Debs and the American Movement: A Documentary Film of Worker Struggle* (43 min.), which uses Debs's own words to illustrate the American labor struggle in the decades surrounding the turn of the 20th century.

Chapter 8

W. E. B. Du Bois

*D*uring the late 19th century, assaults on the liberties and the well-being of nonwhite peoples increased everywhere. In the western world, it was an era of imperialism and scientific racism—a time when major European powers, marching beneath the banner of a Social Darwinism that decreed "superior races" had a right and duty to dominate the world's "lesser peoples," acquired colonies throughout the globe. By century's end, the United States also had entered the competition, staking its claim to possessions in both the Pacific and the Caribbean.

Meanwhile, the condition of African Americans continued to deteriorate. This was especially so in the South, where social segregation and political disfranchisement became the order of the day. To make matters worse, most northerners had by this time lost interest in what they euphemistically referred to as the "Southern Question," and regional blacks had limited means of resisting these developments. No one considered open rebellion a serious option, as this was the heyday of southern lynching, a period when white mobs needed little incitement to shoot, hang, or mutilate African Americans who violated regional racial norms. It was against this grim backdrop that the founder and president of the Tuskegee Institute in Alabama, Booker T. Washington, formulated an accommodationist program that urged

southern blacks to forgo political action, accept the constraints of segregation, and focus their energies on constructing an economic base within the South.

Washington's message found a ready audience among both southern whites and northern conservatives. By the early 20th century, extensive contacts in business and government had made the "Wizard of Tuskegee" the nation's most powerful black leader. But not everyone believed African Americans should follow his counsel. The most outspoken dissenter was a young college professor named W. E. B. Du Bois. Although Du Bois fully understood the oppression most blacks faced, it was not in his nature to submit. Addressing Washington in his 1903 classic, *The Souls of Black Folk,* Du Bois could barely conceal his contempt: "In the history of nearly all other races and peoples the doctrine preached at such crises has been that manly self-respect is worth more than lands and houses, and that a people who voluntarily surrender such respect, or cease striving for it, are not worth civilizing." For Du Bois, this was only the beginning. During the next half-century, no American—black or white—would write so eloquently or so discerningly about what he called "the problem of the color line."

For all his militancy, Du Bois was not one of those activists who unreservedly embraced a given policy and refused to adapt to changing conditions. A keen observer of world affairs, he knew that history does not stand still; and as the times changed, so did he. In the essay that follows, Elliott Rudwick examines the evolution of Du Bois's thought and explores the inner forces that drove this proud, contentious black leader who unfailingly exhibited the courage of his convictions.

W. E. B. Du Bois

Elliott Rudwick

During the nineteenth century and the early decades of the twentieth, when blacks were virtually powerless, propagandists like Frederick Douglass, Booker T. Washington, and W. E. B. Du Bois naturally loomed large in the **pantheon** of black leaders. The term propagandist—used here in its neutral meaning as denoting one who employs symbols to influence the feelings and behavior of an audience—is a particularly apt description of the role played by Du Bois, the leading black intellectual and the most important

---

pantheon A collective reference to the gods of a people.

---

black protest spokesman in the first half of the twentieth century. As platform lecturer and particularly as editor of several publications, Du Bois was a caustic and prophetic voice, telling whites that racist social institutions oppressed blacks and telling blacks that change in their subordinate status was impossible unless they demanded it insistently and continuously. Du Bois himself in his noted autobiographical work, *Dusk of Dawn*, aptly evaluated his principal contribution when he wrote of "my role as a master of propaganda."

Central to Du Bois's role as a propagandist were the ideologies that he articulated. And Du Bois's ideas reflected most of the diverse themes in black thinking about how to assault the bastions of prejudice and discrimination. Most important, he articulated the blacks' desire for full participation in the larger American society and demanded "the abolition of all caste distinctions based simply on race and color." On the other hand, he also exhibited a nationalist side—a strong sense of group pride, advocacy of racial unity, and a profound identification with blacks in other parts of the world. As he said in one of his oft-quoted statements,

> One ever feels his twoness—an American, a Negro; two souls, two thoughts, two unreconciled strivings; two warring ideals in one dark body, whose dogged strength alone keeps it from being torn asunder. The history of the American Negro is the history of this strife—this longing to attain self-conscious manhood, to merge his double self into a better and truer self. In this merging he wishes neither of the older selves to be lost. . . . He simply wishes to make it possible for a man to be both a Negro and an American, without being cursed and spit upon by his fellows, without having the doors of opportunity closed roughly in his face.

In addition Du Bois was both a pioneering advocate of black capitalism, and later was one of the country's most prominent black Marxists. Essentially a protest leader, he was also criticized at times for enunciating tactics of accommodation. An elitist who stressed the leadership role of a college-educated Talented Tenth, he articulated a fervent commitment to the welfare of the black masses.

Given the persistent and intransigent nature of the American race system, which proved quite impervious to black attacks, Du Bois in his speeches and writings moved from one proposed solution to another, and the salience of various parts of his philosophy changed as his perceptions of the needs and strategies of black America shifted over time. Aloof and autonomous in his personality, Du Bois did not hesitate to depart markedly from whatever was the current mainstream of black thinking when he perceived that the conventional wisdom being enunciated by black spokesmen was proving inadequate to the task of advancing the race. His willingness to seek different solutions often placed him well in advance of his contemporaries, and this, combined with a strong-willed, even arrogant personality made his career as black leader essentially a series of stormy conflicts.

Thus Du Bois first achieved his role as a major black leader in the controversy that arose over the program of Booker T. Washington, the most prominent and influential black leader at the opening of the twentieth century.

Amidst the wave of lynchings, disfranchisement, and segregation laws, Washington, seeking the good will of powerful whites, taught blacks not to protest against discrimination, but to elevate themselves through industrial education, hard work, and property accumulation; then, they would ultimately obtain recognition of their citizenship rights. At first Du Bois agreed with this gradualist strategy, but in 1903 with the publication of his most influential book, *Souls of Black Folk,* he became the chief leader of the onslaught against Washington that polarized the black community into two wings—the "conservative" supporters of Washington and his "radical" critics. For Du Bois, the blacks' only effective way to open the doors of opportunity was to adopt tactics of militant protest and agitation; by employing this style of propaganda, he made a key contribution to the evolution of black protest in the twentieth century—and to the civil rights movement.

Du Bois's background helps explain his divergence from the Washingtonian philosophy. From a young age, Du Bois saw himself as a future race leader, part of an elite corps of black college graduates dedicated to advancing the welfare of black people. The Tuskegean deprecated Du Bois's perspective, and although other factors were involved in the disagreement between the two men, a central issue in what became a titanic leadership struggle was Washington's denigration of the Du Boisian commitment to higher education.

Du Bois was born in Great Barrington, Massachusetts in 1868, and his sense of special mission to free black America had appeared even before his graduation at twenty from Fisk University, one of the leading black institutions of higher education. Committed to a platform of racial unity, Du Bois, while still an undergraduate, was earnestly lecturing fellow students that as "destined leaders of a noble people," they must dedicate themselves to the black masses. He declared to his classmates: "I am a Negro; and I glory in the name! . . . From all the recollections dear to my boyhood have I come here [to Fisk], . . . to join hands with this, my people." Du Bois felt that a college degree was important because it equipped black youth with knowledge and wisdom essential to serve the race.

The first application of Du Bois's ideas about the role of an educated elite took the form of scientific investigations that were intended to advance the cause of social reform. In 1895 Du Bois became the first black to receive a Ph.D. from Harvard University, and utilizing his broad training in the social sciences, he published *The Philadelphia Negro* in 1899, the first in-depth case study of a black community in the United States. By then as a professor at Atlanta University, he had begun to publish annual sociological investigations about living conditions among blacks. Du Bois at this point in his career passionately believed that social science would provide white America's leaders with the knowledge necessary to eliminate discrimination and solve the race problem. At the same time he had seen much value in Washington's program. But with his sociological publications virtually ignored by influential reformers, and with the Negroes' status deteriorating under Washington's ascendancy, Du Bois gradually came to the conclusion that only through agitation and protest could social change ever come.

The unbridgeable differences that thus appeared between Washington's accommodating stance and Du Bois's advocacy of militant protest were rooted in personality incompatibility as well as irreconcilable emphases regarding the solution of the race problem. Du Bois felt awkward and uneasy with Washington, who, in turn, considered him haughty and arrogant and who appeared jealous of highly educated blacks with Ivy League degrees and cultural advantages. But the more serious barrier to a trusting relationship lay beyond personality. Where the heart of Du Bois's solution to the race problem lay in the hopes for the Talented Tenth—the college-trained leadership cadre responsible for elevating blacks economically and culturally—Washington was the preeminent black advocate of industrial education. Beyond this and other ideological concerns lay certain very practical conflicts: that because of the popularity of industrial education the needy black colleges were slighted by the philanthropists, and that the Tuskegean—while decrying black political participation—acted as a White House broker for black appointees. Increasingly, Du Bois became incensed that Washington was using connections with the powerful to build up his own Tuskegee Machine while doing little to disturb the caste barriers that were causing devastating problems for blacks.

In 1903 Du Bois took the crucial step that led to his command of a movement dedicated to reducing Washington's influence and to raising black consciousness against the caste system. For the very first time, the Atlanta professor publicly denounced the Tuskegean for condoning white racism and for shifting to blacks the major blame for their deprivation. Charging that the accommodationist Tuskegean had brought together the South, the North, and the blacks in a monumental compromise that "practically accepted the alleged inferiority of the Negro," Du Bois declared that social justice could not be achieved through flattering racist whites; that blacks could not gain their rights by voluntarily tossing them away or by constantly belittling themselves; and that what was needed was a clamorous protest against oppression. Du Bois's critical analysis of Washington's leadership was later credited by James Weldon Johnson with effecting "a coalescence of the more radical elements . . . thereby creating a split of the race into two contending camps." Yet the camps were not evenly matched; Washington had the support of most articulate blacks and among most of those whites who displayed any interest in black advancement, and in successive battles the Du Bois forces were outmaneuvered by the wily Tuskegean.

Nevertheless Du Bois initiated a frontal assault on this Tuskegee Machine in 1905, publicly charging that Washington was imposing thought control inside black America through payments of "hush money" to certain editors. More important, Du Bois was already meeting privately with fellow "radicals" in several cities, exploring the extent of potential support for a militant anti-Washington movement dedicated to protesting this accommodation to white supremacy and segregation. Yet Du Bois had to ponder the chances of survival for an organization that challenged Washington. Could it accomplish anything constructive if nearly all influential whites and the most powerful among the blacks opposed its ideas? Might a militant protest prove counterproductive by arousing a white backlash? And could Du Bois answer Washington's charge that black intellectuals were merely status-hungry elitists far removed from the black masses?

Responding to Du Bois's call, twenty-nine delegates, who had been carefully screened to eliminate "bought" and "hidebound" Washingtonians, met on the Canadian side of Niagara Falls in July 1905. The Niagara Movement, whose tiny membership was drawn chiefly from the ranks of northern college-educated professional men, held annual meetings for the next five years. The chief function of these gatherings was to issue declarations of protest to white America. On every basic issue the Niagara men stood in direct contrast to Washington—denouncing the inequities of the separate-but-equal doctrine, the unfairness of the disfranchisement laws, and the notion that blacks were contentedly climbing from slavery by "natural and gradual processes." Niagara platforms—in whose formulation Du Bois played the most prominent role—were sharp and vigorous, clearly telling whites that they had caused the "Negro problem" and insisting that blacks should unequivocally protest. The Niagara men declared in 1905: "We repudiate the monstrous doctrine that the oppressor should be the sole authority as to the rights of the oppressed. . . . The Negro race in America, stolen, ravished, and degraded, struggling up through difficulties and oppression, needs sympathy and receives criticism, needs help and is given hindrance, needs protection and is given mob-violence, needs justice and is given charity, needs leadership and is given cowardice and apology, needs bread and is given a stone. . . . We do not hesitate to complain and to complain loudly and insistently. To ignore, overlook, or apologize for these wrongs is to prove ourselves unworthy of freedom. Persistent manly agitation is the way to liberty."

While articulating the anger of a small group of black intellectuals, the leaders of the Niagara Movement like Du Bois said they wanted to be "in close touch with the people and with intimate knowledge of their thoughts and feelings." Clearly the Atlanta professor hoped that his propaganda would both raise the consciousness of the black millions and awaken the complacent whites. And in view of the Tuskegee Machine's influence with the mass media, both black and white, not surprisingly two basic Niagara principles were "freedom of speech and criticism" and "an unfettered and unsubsidized press." As it turned out, Du Bois was very proficient at composing annual Addresses to the Nation, but powerless at removing the barriers that prevented the messages from being widely heard.

From the day of its inception Washington plotted the destruction of the Niagara Movement. He and his associates used political patronage to strengthen their hand, and they even considered the idea of having leading Niagara men fired from their federal jobs. The public speeches of key Niagara people like Du Bois were regularly monitored, and Washington, acting through his private secretary Emmett Scott, even planted spies to report what was transpiring at the organization's conventions. Yet these cloak-and-dagger operations could hardly have produced enough significant information to justify all the trouble, and the Washingtonians were far more effective in stymying the movement through their influence over the black press. Usually black editors were counseled to ignore Niagara, but for a period Scott decided that it would be more damaging if the race press would "hammer" the movement. The Tuskegean himself justified these maneuvers on the grounds that Niagara's leaders were not honest "gentlemen," and he even went so far as to subsidize key black journals in cities where his opponents were especially active.

In the large northern centers Washington had considerable contacts among white editors who easily concluded that the Niagara Movement was potentially damaging to harmonious race relations. Thus they followed the strong suggestions of Washington and his agents to ignore the activities of Du Bois and his group. Since the Tuskegean was assumed to be the blacks' only "real leader," white editors found nothing incongruous about giving the Niagara Movement the silent treatment. Indeed with the saintly image that Washington cultivated in the white media, the Niagara Movement's anti-Washington stance was beyond their comprehension. In 1906 the editor of the prominent white weekly the *Outlook* contrasted the pronouncements of the Tuskegean's National Negro Business League with the recent Niagara manifesto, and Washington's "pacific" group was praised because it demanded more of blacks themselves, while Du Bois's "assertive" group unreasonably demanded more of whites on behalf of blacks—to the latter's moral detriment. The Business League was lauded for focusing on achieving an "inch of progress" rather than strangling itself in a "yard of faultfinding" as the Niagara Movement was doing. Washington's supporters in the black press made even more invidious contrasts. Thus the New York *Age* asserted that blacks needed "something cheerful," which the Tuskegean offered the masses, rather than the "lugubrious" and "bitter" commentary of Niagara's jealous "aggregation of soreheads."

Despite these highly personal attacks, the Tuskegeans were correct about the lack of accomplishments of the Niagara Movement, whose local branches were usually inactive or ineffective. The Illinois unit futilely tried to mobilize when the **Negrophobic** *Clansman* opened at a Chicago theater, while the Massachusetts branch lobbied unsuccessfully to prevent the state legislature from appropriating tax dollars for Virginia's segregated exposition celebrating the three hundredth anniversary of the founding of Jamestown. The Niagara Movement's weakness existed less because of its leaders than because of the nation's racist social climate. Epitomizing the steady deterioration in race relations and the Niagara Movement's inability to do anything about it were the eruption in 1906 of a race riot in Atlanta, the city where Du Bois lived and worked, and later in the same year the serious miscarriage of justice at Brownsville, Texas, where despite inadequate evidence, three companies of black soldiers were dishonorably discharged on unproven charges of "shooting up" the Texas town. Helplessly the Niagara Movement issued an "Address to the World" attacking President Theodore Roosevelt (to whom enfranchised blacks had long given political allegiance) for his unfair treatment of the soldiers.

> **Negrophobic** Fear or hatred of black people.

The 1907 Niagara conference was very depressing, with Du Bois himself conceding his own "inexperience" as a leader and admitting that the movement was now operating with "less momentum" and with considerable "internal strain." Indeed during the conclave he had a serious falling-out with Boston *Guardian* editor William Monroe Trotter, one of the earliest and most prominent critics of Washington. With this controversy further damaging the Movement's morale, the organization limped along; most of its 400 members even declined to pay the modest annual dues. When the fourth annual conference opened in 1908 soon after the Springfield, Illinois, race riot, the small band of black militants faced its own impotence and the powerlessness of a race that could not count on the authorities for protection even in the North. The leaders could only curse the "Negro haters of America" and remind blacks that they possessed the right to use guns against white mobs.

While the Niagara Movement was thus falling apart, Du Bois, undoubtedly to compensate for the organization's inability to obtain publicity, managed to implement his long-held dream of editing a militant "national Negro magazine" that would be a vehicle for his agitation. Although an earlier effort to publish a periodical of "new race consciousness," the *Moon*, had failed after a brief existence, Du Bois and two associates (F. H. M. Murray and L. M. Hershaw, both civil servants in Washington) had in 1907 started publishing *Horizon*, the Niagara Movement's unofficial organ. As Du Bois informed the *Horizon*'s early subscribers, "We need a journal, not as a matter of business, but as a matter of spiritual life and death." The journal enunciated the Niagara Movement's philosophy and sought to convert the slight voting power of northern Negroes into a racial asset. Preaching that blacks owed nothing to the Republicans, it condemned the GOP and hammered away at the theme that Secretary of War William Howard Taft (associated with Roosevelt in the Brownsville injustice and a veteran apologist for the southern caste system as well as a denigrator of higher education for blacks) had to be prevented from reaching the White House in 1908 as Roosevelt's successor. But the Tuskegee Machine, operating on the Republicans' behalf, flailed away at Du Bois's political defection to the Democrats; to the disappointment of the editors of *Horizon*, on election day most black voters made Washington's choice their own. Not surprisingly, Du Bois's two colleagues on the *Horizon* had placed their government jobs in jeopardy because of their service to the race. Charles W. Anderson, who as collector of Internal Revenue in New York was a prominent Republican politician in the Tuskegee Machine, tried to persuade the president to fire the pair.

With the Niagara Movement hovering near death, it was clear that the resources to make the black protest movement viable would have to be found elsewhere. Du Bois and other leading "radicals" had been in touch with the small number of prominent whites who were becoming disillusioned with Washington's accommodationist platform. Du Bois concluded that an interracial protest movement was essential, considering the devastating problems that his black movement had experienced and the increased resources and legitimization that prominent whites could provide. It was the mob violence at Springfield in

1908 that finally convinced this group of whites of the absolute necessity of form-ing an interracial protest organization possessing the aims or goals of the Niagara Movement. Through publicity directed at the whole nation, through litigation in the courts and lobbying in the legislature, this new organization, called the National Association for the Advancement of Colored People, hoped to topple the walls of race discrimination. Du Bois became the principal black founder and the most prominent Niagara veteran connected with the NAACP.

Although the membership was overwhelmingly black, for nearly a decade the NAACP was largely white-funded and white-dominated, and Du Bois was the only black in its inner circle. He performed a very significant role in the organization—serving as the embodiment of militant protest, the link to the small band of black "radicals," and the symbol to the public of demonstrably successful interracial cooperation. Beyond these contributions lay his more significant asset to the NAACP as its chief propagandist. As director of Pub-licity and Research, he founded the *Crisis* in 1910 and edited this influential NAACP official organ for a quarter-century.

In many ways Du Bois was all that the white founders had hoped for. It is true that he was not intimately involved in the administrative work of the NAACP, and only on rare occasions did he even attempt to influence policy. He quite consciously confined himself to his work as *Crisis* editor and saw his role as being a molder of public opinion—chiefly among blacks. As *Crisis* editor he recorded and supported the NAACP program for constitutional rights; he stirred up intellectual controversies, commented on current events related to the race problem, and provided arguments for racial equalitarian-ism. His expressions of protest were clearly, sharply, and often dramatically written, in sentences sometimes so **aphoristic** that black readers cherished them: "*I am resolved to be quiet and law abiding, but to refuse to cringe in body or in soul, to resent deliberate insult, and to assert my just rights in the face of wanton aggression.*" "Oppression costs the oppressor too much if the oppressed stand up and protest." "Agitate, then, brother; protest, reveal the truth and refuse to be silenced." "A moment's let up, a moment's acquiescence, means a chance for the wolves of prejudice to get at our necks." The reverence that many black families had for the magazine was described by the writer J. Saunders Redding, who recollected that in his boyhood home the only periodical that the children could not touch was the *Crisis*, which "was strictly inviolate until my father himself had unwrapped and read it—often . . . aloud" to the family.

At last Du Bois had fulfilled the vision that had inspired him for so many years. The *Crisis* was his opportunity to edit a national black journal of opin-ion to which people would listen. As early as 1913, when the NAACP could scarcely attract 3,000 members, the circulation of the *Crisis*—chiefly among blacks—reached 30,000. Clearly Du Bois was making a considerable impact. Yet given his personality and his deep-seated desire for autonomy, the public image of harmony within the NAACP was belied by the battling that erupted between Du Bois and certain key board members.

---

aphoristic A concise, pointed statement of a principle.

The basic problem involved how much independence Du Bois as the only board member who was also a paid NAACP executive would have in operating the organization's official magazine, and what contributions to other NAACP activities were required of him. Du Bois, who was frequently unavailable for organizational chores like writing pamphlets, regarded the *Crisis* as "the only work" in the NAACP "which attracts me." In fact, he believed that the *Crisis*, rather than serving the NAACP as its interpreter to the public, was the one vehicle—through raising the consciousness of thousands of blacks—that could "make the NAACP *possible*." Demanding "independence of action" in running the *Crisis*, Du Bois was determined "to prove the possibilities of a Negro magazine," and he clashed with two successive white board chairmen—Oswald Garrison Villard (who was dictatorial and seemed at times subtly prejudiced) and Joel Spingarn (whom Du Bois described as a "knight" untarnished by any racist tendencies). To these board chairmen, faced with the problem of stretching limited funds to cover such vital activities as branch development and legal redress, the *Crisis* did not have the same priority that it had for Du Bois. And when the *Crisis* editor published materials that the other NAACP leaders felt were tactically ill advised and even harmful to the organization, open conflict resulted.

Villard was determined that the *Crisis* editor, like other paid executives, should be subordinated to the board chairman. Moreover, he resented that although the magazine was the property of the NAACP, and despite its large circulation not self-supporting, Du Bois wanted to "carry it around in his pocket." In protest Villard resigned as chairman in late 1913, being replaced by Spingarn—but the board struggle with the editor continued. Spingarn was more understanding than Villard and wanted to see a black editor like Du Bois exercise maximum influence, but he also believed that Du Bois's difficult personality produced situations that damaged the organization. Indeed there were even times when the NAACP, in its drive for black support, was acutely embarrassed by the editor's attacks on black ministers, journalists, and educators. For example, in 1912 Du Bois had indicted the Negro churches: "the paths and the higher places are choked with pretentious ill-trained men . . . in far too many cases with men dishonest and otherwise immoral." Two years later at a time when the NAACP desperately needed support from the black press, Du Bois fired a volley against these weeklies, claiming that many were not "worth reprinting or even reading" because their editors were venal, empty-headed, or ungrammatical. The barrage did not go unanswered, and Du Bois created a serious public relations problem for the NAACP.

Du Bois's original indiscretion had been precipitated by his acute sensitivity to a black newspaper's comment that the *Crisis* was financially dependent on an NAACP subsidy. Moreover the subsidy was one that the NAACP found it hard to afford, especially with a recent recession sharply reducing the organization's income. Nonetheless, Spingarn and the board reluctantly acceded to Du Bois's demands for more staff and office space—at a time when the national administrative office with fund-raising responsibilities shouldered by a small staff was forced to accept budgetary cuts. Because of such incidents,

Spingarn, although having the highest respect for Du Bois, like Villard, eventually concluded that the *Crisis* editor was exercising too much autonomy and reluctantly announced his own intention to resign as chairman. Yet in the end Spingarn had too much admiration for Du Bois's contributions to make more than a gentle rebuke. In 1916 he and the board agreed that the *Crisis* under Du Bois could not simply be a house organ and that its editorials must be permitted to represent Du Bois's opinions within the framework of broad NAACP policy.

By 1916 in the wake of Washington's death, Du Bois became the nation's most prominent black leader, freed now from the heavy burden of competing with the Tuskegean. To the end, the *Crisis* editor had remained Washington's most implacable foe among NAACP leaders. Even before Washington's death, a noticeable shift in sentiment had begun among leading blacks, which was reflected in the successful attempts to organize NAACP branches. This shift reflected not only the growing stature of Du Bois and the NAACP, but changing social conditions as well. With increasing urbanization and educational attainment and with more migration to the North, growing numbers of blacks by World War I were embracing Du Bois's doctrine of agitation and protest.

Ironically, with the passing of Washington from the scene and the decline of Tuskegee's influence, Du Bois and the NAACP now occupied a centrist rather than a "radical" role in the black community, and the editor of the *Crisis* even found himself on occasion attacked for conservatism and lack of militancy. To some extent Du Bois made himself vulnerable on this score, since during World War I he muted his criticism. Hopeful that with the return of peace blacks would be rewarded for their contributions to the war that was supposed "to make the world safe for democracy," he had urged blacks to "forget our special grievances" and "close ranks" with fellow white Americans in the battle against the country's European enemies. Not only did a number of black editors openly criticize Du Bois for this stand, but during the war and postwar years the young socialist A. Philip Randolph stridently condemned the NAACP spokesman as a "hand-picked, me-too-boss, hat-in-hand, sycophant, lick spittling" Negro.

For his part, Du Bois, disillusioned by the new spurt in racism and the resurgence of mob violence that followed the war, composed some of the most ringingly militant editorials of his career. Enraged when he discovered evidence that black soldiers who had risked their lives in Europe were discriminated against by the American military establishment there, Du Bois documented these facts in a special *Crisis* issue that also featured an editorial, "Returning Soldiers": "By the God of Heaven, we are cowards and jackasses if now that the war is over, we do not marshal every ounce of our brain and brawn to fight a sterner, longer, more unbending battle against the forces of hell in our own land. *We return. We return from fighting. We return fighting.* Make way for Democracy! We saved it in France, and by the Great Jehovah, we will save it in the United States of America, or know the reason why."

This particular number of the *Crisis*, which sold 100,000 copies, was not only widely discussed among blacks but created a furor outside the race. To say that certain U.S. government officials were alarmed is putting it mildly. The Post Office Department held up the copies while debating whether to allow them through the mails. Representative James Byrnes of South Carolina, epitomizing the sentiment of many in Congress, delivered a speech charging that Du Bois and other black newsmen had precipitated the postwar rioting. Although white mobs had caused most of the bloodshed, Byrnes singled out "Returning Soldiers" as the inspiration for black violence, holding that Du Bois should be indicted for having encouraged resistance to the government. Du Bois's fury continued unabated, and he warned blacks again to arm themselves against white mobs. The Justice Department, also anxious about "Returning Soldiers," investigated the *Crisis*, Randolph's *Messenger*, and other black periodicals. Noting that blacks like Du Bois had counseled retaliatory violence against white attackers, the department reported that black newsmen were actually "antagonistic to the white race and openly defiantly assertive of [their] own equality and even superiority."

As noted earlier, there had always been a strong nationalist strain in Du Bois's thinking, and in the postwar era this aspect of his propaganda became the focus of another controversy—his acrimonious struggle with the famous black separatist leader **Marcus Garvey.** The most influential aspect of Du Bois's nationalism had been his pioneering advocacy of Pan-Africanism, the belief that all people of African descent had common interests and should unite in the struggle for their freedom. Moreover, he articulated both a cultural nationalism encouraging the development of black literature and art and an economic nationalism urging blacks to create a separate "group economy."

All of these themes had been expressed much earlier. Thus in an 1897 paper aptly entitled "The Conservation of Races," Du Bois enunciated the doctrine of "Pan-Negroism"—that regardless of what nation they lived in, Africans and their descendants had a common identity and should feel an emotional commitment to one another. American blacks, the vanguard of blacks the world over, should have a special attachment to Africa as the race's "greater fatherland." Arguing that "the Negro people as a race have a contribution to make to civilization and humanity, which no other race can make," he maintained that blacks possessed "a distinct mission as a race . . . to soften the whiteness" of an uninspiring materialistic Teutonic culture that seemed to dominate the world. Accordingly, Du Bois argued that Afro-Americans should maintain their group identity and institutions; for them salvation would come only from an educated elite who would chart the way to cultural and economic elevation, teaching the doctrine that blacks "MUST DO FOR THEMSELVES," by developing their own businesses, newspapers, schools, and welfare institutions.

Later Du Bois used the *Crisis* as a vehicle for cultural nationalism. Calling for the systematic cultivation of all kinds of black art forms, he proudly presented works by young black novelists, essayists, painters,

Marcus Garvey Black nationalist leader of the 1910s and 1920s, who advocated racial separatism and founded the Universal Negro Improvement Association.

and poets, and in the early 1920s he proposed an Institute of Negro Literature and Art. Determined to harness the race's creative strivings, he told
defeatists, "Off with these thought-chains and inchoate soul-shrinkings, and
let us train ourselves to see beauty in black." Blacks were "a different kind"
of people, possessing the spirit and power to build a "new and great Negro
ethos." The race, armed with "group ideals," could bring forth a flood of artis-
tic and literary creation based on themes in black life and black history. Above
all, blacks could enrich themselves and America only by defining their own
standards of beauty, rather than permitting whites to define them.

The *Crisis* also taught lessons in *economic nationalism*. Early in his life
Du Bois had made bourgeois pleas for black capitalist enterprises based on
the Negro market, but after coming under Socialist influences during his leadership of the Niagara Movement, he began advocating black consumers' and
producers' cooperatives as a basic weapon for fighting discrimination and
poverty. Du Bois devoted considerable space in the *Crisis* to stimulate readers
to open cooperative stores, and in 1918 he helped form the Negro Cooperative Guild, which hoped to set up retail stores, cooperative warehouses, and
even banks. Du Bois believed that white racism, by reducing the range of
black incomes, had unintentionally made a socialized black economy feasible.
Blacks, rather than aspiring to be rapacious millionaires, would find it satisfying to be "consecrated" workers devoted to "social service" for the race. Du
Bois saw no reason why this "closed economic circle" could not encompass a
complex racial manufacturing-distributive system, with profits reinvested in
useful race projects like large housing developments. Moreover, a black cooperative system could be extended to race members in far off places like Africa.

Du Bois's cultural nationalism was intimately related to the stirrings
among black intellectuals and artists known as the Harlem Renaissance,
but his quasi-socialistic brand of economic nationalism was never widely
accepted. Even his more influential Pan-Africanism was really not a central
element in Afro-American thinking at that period. Du Bois had probably
been the first black American to develop explicitly the concept of Pan-
Africanism; certainly of all the black American intellectuals, he was the one
most deeply identified with Africa itself—at a time when most Afro-Americans
were embarrassed by the "primitiveness" of their ancestral societies. In 1900
Du Bois had been a leader in the first Pan-African Conference, and as chairman of its "Committee on the Address to the Nations of the World," he
called for the creation of "a great central Negro State of the World" in Africa,
which would raise the status of blacks wherever they lived. No sooner had
World War I ended when, amidst the discussion of European imperialism
and the disposition of the German colonies in Africa, Du Bois again took up
the Pan-African theme and convened four Pan-African congresses in Europe
and the United States between 1919 and 1927. Urging the recognition of the
"absolute equality of races" and the end of imperialist exploitation of blacks
everywhere, these conclaves focused on racial developments in Africa and
were, in fact, a concrete application of his notion that black intellectuals
should lead the race into the future.

His nationalist Pan-African Movement shared several parallels with the integrationist Niagara Movement: it was dominated by Du Bois's towering personality; it attracted only a very small segment of the Talented Tenth; it suffered from serious internal schisms; it exemplified his strength as a propagandist leader and his weakness as an organizational leader; it clashed sharply with a popular black spokesman of the period; and yet it was important as an ideological forerunner of very significant future developments among Afro-Americans.

When Du Bois revived the Pan-African Movement in 1919, he had hoped that the NAACP would be a base of grass-roots support. But neither the black middle and upper classes who were the readers of the *Crisis* and the backbone of the NAACP's supporters nor the masses of the black poor rallied to it. The NAACP contributed only token funds and considered the movement incompatible with its basic thrust. Since Du Bois largely isolated himself from the machinery of the NAACP and was not essentially an organizational leader, he did almost nothing to convince the board to adopt his cause as their own. Certainly Du Bois did not try to alter the thinking of the leadership in conferences with key officials or in board meetings. Nor did he seek to organize NAACP branch officials behind the Pan-African Movement. Characteristically, he attempted to **proselytize** through *Crisis* editorials and seemed satisfied to persuade the NAACP to make occasional official statements (which he wrote) supporting his views on Africa.

Regardless of his differences with the NAACP on Pan-Africa and other matters, Du Bois usually could be counted upon to defend the organization publicly. Thus in 1921 when the *Crisis* exonerated the board of charges of undemocratic domination, its editor declared, "It is foolish for us to give up this practical program." But behind the scenes, however, the potential for serious disruption was inherent in the ongoing problem of competition for scarce resources. Money difficulties became even more acute during the 1920s because the circulation of the *Crisis* fell drastically, from over 100,000 in 1919 to about 30,000 in 1930. Du Bois expected the board to cover the deficit, and the board did so, although his colleagues would undoubtedly have been more agreeable to providing additional money had Du Bois been willing to make the *Crisis* more decidedly the house organ of the NAACP and to devote more pages to the organization's national projects as well as branch activities. But Du Bois found that route unpalatable—he still insisted that he must "blaze a trail" and perform "a work of education and ideal beyond the practical steps of the NAACP."

At the end of the 1920s the financial crunch facing the *Crisis* set the stage for a serious, in one sense fatal, conflict between Du Bois and new NAACP Executive Secretary Walter White. White disliked Du Bois intensely and believed that the *Crisis* had become the NAACP's rather superfluous tail; for Du Bois, of course, it was still the other way around. In 1929, White protested that Du Bois's requests for ever-larger subsidies were being granted only at the expense of a weakened administrative office and

---

proselytize To make converts.

were becoming a luxury that could be afforded no longer. But the board managed to find the money until the Great Depression set in, when its members paid more attention to White's admonitions that scarce dollars could be better spent on anti-lynching campaigns, court cases, and legislative lobbying.

Du Bois's problem was that as the Depression deepened, White's powers grew not only in the administrative office but also in matters directly affecting the *Crisis*. Thus in 1931, after the magazine lost another several thousand dollars (although the NAACP was paying Du Bois's entire salary), the Crisis Publishing Company was organized (with White on the board of directors) as a legal maneuver to limit the NAACP's liability for the obligations of the *Crisis*. Du Bois fought back, ostensibly to overhaul the NAACP's structure but actually to strip White of much of his power. First the *Crisis* editor informed the board that its members were undemocratically chosen since the rank-and-file throughout the country had no voice in the selection process. Then in 1932 he went public with his charges and called for transferring the central office's power to the branches; simultaneously he urged that the NAACP adopt a program that would replace the "mere negative attempt to avoid segregation and discrimination." In his solution to the many problems posed by the Depression, Du Bois went beyond the NAACP's official program of protecting constitutional rights and revived his old dream for systematic "voluntary segregation" in the form of a separate black cooperative economy. "That race pride and race loyalty, Negro ideals and Negro unity have a place and function today, the NAACP never has denied and never can deny!" Refusing to accept Du Bois's distinction between enforced and voluntary separation, White and Spingarn challenged the *Crisis* editor, contending that he was undermining the decades-long struggle against segregation. White declared that blacks "must, without yielding, continue the grim struggle *for* integration" and stop the damage that Du Bois was inflicting on the organization. The whole debate degenerated into bitter personal recriminations between White and the *Crisis* editor. Defeated, Du Bois resigned in 1934 and returned to his old professorship at Atlanta University.

Neither inside nor outside the NAACP had there been any groundswell of support for Du Bois's position. The Talented Tenth by and large was marching to a different drummer. Black intellectuals like the sociologist E. Franklin Frazier, the political scientist Ralph Bunche, and the former NAACP Executive Secretary James Weldon Johnson all repudiated his separatism, arguing that an all-black economy in an era of black powerlessness could easily be destroyed by "the legal and police forces of the state [which] would inevitably be aligned against them." Most critics actually viewed Du Bois's call as retrogression, a return to Washington's accommodationist apologia for segregation.

Thus Du Bois had created serious problems for himself. His "voluntary segregation" campaign put him outside the mainstream of the civil rights movement in the mid-1930s, and in severing his *Crisis* ties he had given up the platform that was essential for his role as propagandist. Although he remained a venerated symbol, he had lost his position of effective leadership.

No longer was he the molder and shaper of Negro opinion that he had been since the early part of the century.

During the 1940s Du Bois downplayed the plan for a separate economy, but he gradually identified himself with pro-Russian causes, thus drifting further from the main currents of black thinking at the time. In 1951 he was tried in federal court on charges of being an unregistered agent of a foreign power, and although the judge directed an acquittal, Du Bois became so thoroughly disillusioned about the United States that in 1961 he officially joined the Communist party and moved to Ghana.

Du Bois continued to write and lecture until the end of his life, but the output of his last three decades had slight impact among his black American contemporaries. Then, ironically, shortly after his departure from the United States, Du Bois's reputation soared, and he was transformed into a prophet. In the early 1960s the militant integrationist phase of the black direct-action protest movement was building toward its climax, and his enormous contributions became widely recognized and revered among young activists. Du Bois died on the very day that one-quarter of a million people gathered at the March on Washington—August 27, 1963. Moments before the mammoth march departed from the Washington Monument, the vast assemblage stood bowed in silent tribute at the announcement of his death. Later at the Lincoln Memorial Roy Wilkins, now executive secretary of the NAACP, referred to Du Bois's vast contributions to the long struggle for black freedom. Then a few years afterward, with the decline of militant integrationism and the ascendancy of the Black Power Era with its separatist thrust, the relevance of his nationalist writings became widely appreciated.

W. E. B. Du Bois, the propagandist, had now become symbol and prophet, and events both in the United States and abroad vindicated the celebrated words he had used in *Souls of Black Folk* in 1903: "The problem of the Twentieth Century is the problem of the color line."

A Primary Perspective

BOOKER T. WASHINGTON

During the early part of his career, Du Bois's main ideological adversary within black America was the politically powerful president of Tuskegee Institute, Booker T. Washington. A complex man who surreptitiously aided efforts to achieve full racial equality, Washington publicly counseled black southerners to accept segregationist policies and concentrate on achieving the kinds of economic advances that would win the approval of regional whites. The most famous expression of this

Source: Louis R. Harlan, Stuart B. Kaufman, and Raymond W. Smock, eds., *The Booker T. Washington Papers: Volume 3, 1889–1895* (Urbana: University of Illinois Press, 1974), pp. 584–86.

accommodationist philosophy was Washington's Atlanta Compromise address of 1895, from which excerpts appear below.

Atlanta Compromise Address, September 1895

. . . Our greatest danger is that in the great leap from slavery to freedom we may overlook the fact that the masses of us are to live by the productions of our hands, and fail to keep in mind that we shall prosper in proportion as we learn to dignify and glorify common labour, and put brains and skill into the common occupations of life; shall prosper in proportion as we learn to draw the line between the superficial and the substantial, the ornamental gewgaws of life and the useful. No race can prosper till it learns that there is as much dignity in tilling a field as in writing a poem. It is at the bottom of life we must begin, and not at the top. Nor should we permit our grievances to over-shadow our opportunities.

To those of the white race who look to the incoming of those of foreign birth and strange tongue and habits for the prosperity of the South, were I permitted I would repeat what I say to my own race, "Cast down your bucket where you are." Cast it down among the eight millions of Negroes whose habits you know, whose fidelity and love you have tested in days when to have proved treacherous meant the ruin of your firesides. Cast down your bucket among these people who have, without strikes and labour wars, tilled your fields, cleared your forests, builded your railroads and cities, and brought forth treasures from the bowels of the earth, and helped make possible this magnificent representation of the progress of the South. Casting down your bucket among my people, helping and encouraging them as you are doing on these grounds, and to education of head, hand, and heart, you will find that they will buy your surplus land, make blossom the waste places in your fields, and run your factories. While doing this, you can be sure in the future, as in the past, that you and your families will be surrounded by the most patient, faithful, law-abiding, and unresentful people that the world has seen. As we have proved our loyalty to you in the past, in nursing your children, watching by the sick-bed of your mothers and fathers, and often following them with tear-dimmed eyes to their graves, so in the future, in our humble way, we shall stand by you with a devotion that no foreigner can approach, ready to lay down our lives, if need be, in defense of yours, interlacing our industrial, commercial, civil, and religious life with yours in a way that shall make the interests of both races one. In all things that are purely social we can be as separate as the fingers, yet one as the hand in all things essential to mutual progress. . . .

The wisest among my race understand that the agitation of questions of social equality is the extremest folly, and that progress in the enjoyment of all the privileges that will come to us must be the result of severe and constant struggle rather than of artificial forcing. No race that has anything to contribute to the markets of the world is long in any degree ostracized. It is important and right that all privileges of the law be ours, but it is vastly more important that we be prepared for the exercise of these privileges. The opportunity to earn a dollar in a factory just now is worth infinitely more than the opportunity to spend a dollar in an opera-house.

QUESTIONS

1. What were the practical and philosophical differences between Du Bois and Booker T. Washington? Are there any parts of Washington's Atlanta Compromise speech with which Du Bois might have agreed? Why did white editors side with Washington in his struggle with the Niagara Movement? Why, as editor of the *Horizon*, did Du Bois single out Republicans for criticism?
2. Why did Du Bois believe an organization like the NAACP was necessary? Why was he constantly at odds with prominent NAACP board members? Do you think the *Crisis* was as indispensable to the struggle for black rights as Du Bois believed?
3. In what ways did Du Bois's later views on the race question differ from the approach he had championed during the early 20th century? Why did Du Bois identify so closely with Africa and Africans? What do you think Du Bois meant when he said that black people had a mission to "soften the whiteness" of Teutonic culture? Why did so few African Americans support his Pan-African campaign of the 1920s?
4. Why did Du Bois sever his longtime relationship with the NAACP during the 1930s? In what ways did the civil rights movement of the 1960s reflect Du Bois's thinking on racial matters?
5. Do you see any similarities between Du Bois and Henry McNeal Turner? What were they? In what ways did Du Bois differ from Turner? In what ways did Du Bois's writings and organizational initiatives parallel the activism of Ida B. Wells?
6. Which aspects of Du Bois's life do you find most interesting? If asked to write about Du Bois, in what ways would your profile differ from Rudwick's portrait?

 ADDITIONAL RESOURCES

David Levering Lewis's two-volume treatment, *W. E. B. Du Bois: Biography of a Race, 1868–1919* (1993) and *W. E. B. Du Bois: The Fight for Equality and the American Century* (2000), should be the standard biography of Du Bois for decades to come. Older studies include Elliott M. Rudwick, *W. E. B. Du Bois: Propangandist of the Negro Protest* (1960), and Francis L. Broderick, *W. E. B. Du Bois: Negro Leader in a Time of Crisis* (1959). Du Bois provided his own account of major episodes in his life in *Dusk of Dawn: An Essay Toward an Autobiography of a Race Concept*, intro. by Martin Luther King, Jr. (1968). For more on the NAACP during the Du Bois era, see Charles F. Kellogg, *NAACP: A History of the National Association for the Advancement of Colored People* (1970). The best biography of Du Bois's main African-American adversary is Louis R. Harlan's excellent two-volume work, *Booker T. Washington: The Making of a Black Leader, 1856–1901* (1972) and *Booker T. Washington: The Wizard of Tuskegee, 1901–1915* (1983). August Meier, *Negro Thought in America, 1880–1920: Racial Ideologies in the Age of Booker T. Washington* (1970), is an able examination of African-American social thought during an important period of Du Bois's life.

"America: 1900" (PBS: *The American Experience*) supplies a look at American race relations in 1900 in Part 3, "A Great Civilized Power" (50 minutes). The film examines the Jim Crow system in the South and the debate between Du Bois and Booker T. Washington. *Marcus Garvey: Look for Me in the Whirlwind* from PBS explores the life of one of Du Bois's contemporaries, and rivals, when it looks at the life of Marcus Garvey, who advocated black self-help and nationalism.

Chapter 9

Margaret Sanger

*A*mong the more significant social developments in 19th-century America was a dramatic drop in the national birthrate. Whereas married women bore an average of seven children in 1800, that figure had declined by half a century later. Despite this drop, women concerned about family limitation still faced major obstacles. One was the limited knowledge available. Not only did most women know little about the process of conception, but most members of the medical profession refused to aid them. Many doctors believed that, as one prominent Gilded Age physician put it, females had a special "aptitude for impregnation." Where women could expect little help from physicians of this sort, those doctors who did provide counsel on birth control frequently offered conflicting advice.

When women sought other sources of assistance, they confronted additional barriers. Beginning in 1868, a series of states passed laws forbidding the dissemination of birth control information; and in 1873 Congress enacted a statute providing for the "suppression of trade in and circulation of obscene literature and articles of immoral use"—a ban that included materials related to family limitation. To enforce the measure, postal authorities hired the New York vice crusader Anthony Comstock as a special agent, and for the next half-century he would carry out his duties with a zealousness that bordered on fanaticism.

The feminist response to these developments was mixed. On one hand, sexual radicals such as Victoria Woodhull openly denounced the moral tyranny of Comstock. Believing that women would never achieve full independence until they separated sexuality from reproduction, Woodhull viewed all restrictions on the distribution of birth control information as an assault on women's autonomy. But the sexual radicals were a distinct minority. Most feminists adopted a more cautious stance. Unlike Woodhull, who equated birth control with sexual freedom, the majority of women's rights activists called for "voluntary motherhood." This emphasis on family limitation rather than sexual autonomy both reflected their concerns about preserving women's respectability and underscored their main objective: the attainment of female self-control within the marriage relationship.

These legal restraints and ideological differences provided the context for Margaret Sanger's efforts on behalf of birth control. Like Victoria Woodhull, Sanger equated reproductive control with the free expression of women's sexuality. And as Margaret Forster shows in the essay that follows, her crusade encountered opposition from conservative feminists as well as Anthony Comstock and other Victorian moralists. In relating Sanger's story, Forster provides a fascinating portrait of a headstrong individual who had a well-earned reputation for outspoken aggressiveness.

Margaret Sanger

Margaret Forster

Margaret Higgins was one of the few feminist activist leaders to come from a working-class background. She was born on September 14th, 1879 (a date carefully concealed as she always made herself four years younger), in Corning, a factory town in upstate New York. She was the 6th of 11 children and realized very early what being part of a large, poor family meant: going without. Yet, in spite of the material deprivation she suffered, she valued the love she had been given by her parents and remembered with gratitude the closeness of her family. There was respect and affection among them in the midst of all the hardship. The family was dominated by the father, Michael Higgins, born in Ireland and once a drummer boy in Lincoln's army. He was a large, redheaded, free-thinking man, a stonemason by trade, and his one rule in life was that people should "say what they mean." He was a member of the **Knights of Labour** and organized visits from other free-thinkers which often ended in fights. Margaret was, she said, neither ashamed nor frightened on these occasions and was in fact quite proud of being called, with her brothers and sisters, "children of the devil." Her father represented power to her. Her mother, Anne (also of Irish descent), worked hard to keep the family and the house clean and tidy even though she was not physically strong. She always had a cough and was always recovering from or about to undergo childbirth. But there was no friction between these parents—"no quarreling or bickering"—and they each idolized the other. Michael Higgins was a great believer in women's rights, supporting female suffrage and even the wearing of the bloomer costume, but this "never evidenced itself in practical ways." He would sit "when he had nothing on hand" laughing and joking while Anne worked incessantly around him.

Outside her home, the young Margaret was conscious of different lives going on. Corning was an unattractive place and the poor, like the Higgins family, lived in the most unattractive part, on the crowded river banks near the factories. The rich lived literally above them, on the hill tops above all the noise, dirt, and overcrowding. Margaret envied them. She noticed in particular the contrast between her mother's way of life and that of the women who lived up there: "mothers . . . played croquet and tennis with their husbands in the evening . . . (they were) young looking . . . with pretty, clean dresses and they smelled of perfume." Margaret's own mother usually smelled of milk as she produced and fed baby after baby, all delivered by Michael Higgins himself. He would never allow a doctor anywhere near his wife, not even to attend to her cough. After every birth she was weaker and coughed more but he dosed her with whisky and eventually she would be on her feet again. None of this put Margaret off childbirth. She loved the babies and looked forward to having her own. She liked to look at pictures of the Virgin Mary and fantasized herself looking like that after she had had a baby. "Sex knowledge," she wrote, "was a natural part of my life." She always knew how babies were made and how they arrived and there seemed nothing repugnant or scarring about either process. Babies were always welcome in the overcrowded Higgins household and if one died the grief was real. Margaret remembered vividly the death of Henry, aged four, and her mother's inconsolable distress which her father tried to soothe. He took Margaret with him in the night to the cemetery where he dug up Henry's coffin, opened it, took a plaster cast of his face and next day made a bust of the dead child for his wife. She was greatly comforted.

Knights of Labour An industrial union founded in Philadelphia in 1869 and headed by a general assembly to which workers belonged regardless of sex or race.

But if she loved her family, Margaret hated Corning. She wanted to get out. Her two older sisters, Mary and Nan, recognizing that she had talent and ambition deserving something better than they had had, saved up to send her away to school.

Both of them had worked from the age of 14 as companions and maids to sup-plement the family income and they wanted Margaret to escape this likely fate. Entirely through their self-sacrifice, Margaret was sent to Claverack, one of the first coeducational schools in the East, at the age of 13, supplementing her board by helping as a domestic assistant. At home, she had had no background of learning although her father was an intelligent man and a great reader of political tracts. . . . She had a great deal of background to make up but did well, although causing some problems as the ringleader in various escapades.

When her schooldays ended, she found a job in a new public school in southern Jersey as a student teacher, but she was called home after a few months. Her mother was dying. The TB from which she had clearly suffered for a decade at least, even if it did go undiagnosed, had flared up after the birth of her 11th child and not even Michael Higgins's all-purpose whisky cure worked. Her death was a long drawn-out affair during which she tried des-perately to protect her children from witnessing the full horror of it. One by one they were sent off on "holidays" to stay with friends and relatives in the surrounding area while she battled to prepare her husband for the inevitable end. But he remained willfully blind and unprepared. When Anne Higgins died, aged only 48, Michael Higgins became an embittered, unpleasant, bel-ligerent man. Grief made him violent and tyrannical. Margaret began to hate him. She was expected to look after the smaller children and require no life of her own. If she went out with her sister Ethel to a dance, they were quite likely to come back and find the door bolted against them. Margaret stood this for a year but then she had had enough. She managed to find a place for herself at White Plains Hospital, near New York, where she could train as a nurse. It was not what she wanted, which was to be a doctor so that she could save people like her mother, but it was the best escape route she could find.

White Plains, which she entered in 1898 aged 18, was not a modern hospi-tal run on any kind of Nightingale lines. The building was old, a three-story manor house set in overgrown grounds which gave it a "spooky" air to the young nurses. There was no resident intern. The probationers not only made and fixed dressings but also did a great deal of heavy domestic work. They also assisted at operations and Margaret was pleased to find she could do so with-out feeling squeamish. The hardest part of her job was night-duty, which she hated. All sorts of emergencies, with which she was not equipped to deal, tended to happen at night and she found it frightening to have to cope with them. . . .

Most of these were maternity cases. They would arrive to find neither qualified midwife nor doctor present and would just have to go ahead and deliver the baby themselves. Naturally, this gave Margaret valuable practical obstetric experience, which she found exciting, but it also plunged her into a world she had never encountered before. Most of the mothers were not ecstatic with joy at giving birth, and new babies were not greeted with the rapture which had awaited them in the Higgins household. The circumstances in which they arrived were often not just poor but desperate. The most common question Margaret was asked by the mothers whose confinements she attended was "Miss, what should I do not to have another baby straight away?" She did not know. When she referred the question to the doctor on the case, if there was one, he would brush it aside and remonstrate with the mother for asking it of a young nurse. She grew used to seeing not just women but men, too, driven nearly insane with worry about having more children. Something, clearly, was wrong. . . .

The last six months of Margaret's three-year training were spent at the Manhattan Eye and Ear Hospital. While there, she met a young architect called William Sanger at one of the hospital dances. He was eight years older than Margaret and the first serious suitor she had had. His mother was German and his father had been a wealthy sheep farmer in Australia. He was, wrote Margaret, "a dark young man with intense, fiery eyes" who was very romantic and ardent. He proposed marriage very quickly, but Margaret says she was adamant she did not want to marry. It was, she said, "a kind of suicide." But Bill Sanger was "impatient of conventionalities, intense in his new love" and she was deeply attracted to him. He admired her tremendously, writing that he thought her "really heroic" for putting up with the hours she did and he didn't know how she could stand it—"I must have at least six hours sleep," he wrote, "and you have none at all at night!" He wanted her to "give up this strenuous life" and promised he would soon be able to provide her with "a real home . . . a little house nestling under the trees—we shall build it, of course we shall. . . ."

In the last week of her training, she capitulated and married him. Bill whisked her off to a secret wedding ceremony. "That beast of a man William," she wrote to her sister Mary, "took me for a drive last Monday and drove me to a minister's residence and married me. I wept with anger and wouldn't look at him for it was so unexpected. . . . I had on an old blue dress and looked horrid. . . . He was afraid this precious article would be lost to him. . . . I am very, very sorry to have the thing occur but yet I am very, very happy." To her sister Nan she gave a simpler explanation. Bill was, she wrote, "beastly, insanely jealous." He insisted on marriage and, since she did not want to lose him and he would not wait, she married him. But even then Margaret was a strong character. She would never have married Bill Sanger if she had not thought she loved him and certainly not out of fear of losing him alone. The fact was, she was not just attracted to him but irresistibly drawn to the way of life he could offer her.

The marriage was at first happy, in spite of Margaret's poor health. She had been ill off and on throughout her nurse's training with "gland trouble" and when she became pregnant soon after her marriage this flared into TB. She was sent to a sanatorium outside New York where she was acutely miserable and determined to leave. In November 1903 she returned home to her apartment in New York and gave birth to her first son, Stuart. It was, she commented, "agonizing" and made worse by the inexperience of the doctor who attended her. She was sent back to the hated sanatorium but quickly rebelled against the régime imposed there. Deciding that if she was going to die she'd rather do it at home, she discharged herself and once more returned to New York. There she doctored herself and against all expectations the

outbreak of TB began to subside (although she was never free from such outbreaks for the rest of her long life). Meanwhile, intent on fulfilling his wife's
dream and also moving her to somewhere healthier, Bill had designed and
begun to build a house at Hastings-on-Hudson, a pleasant suburb outside
New York. It took a long time to complete, but in 1907 the Sangers moved in
and early the next year Margaret gave birth to her second son, Grant. She then
found herself happily in the position she had always wanted to be. . . . In
1910, when a daughter, Peggy, was born, everything seemed perfect.

But it was not. Margaret was far too honest to pretend her dream life satisfied her. She became restless and critical not just of the life she was living
but of the people among whom she was living it. She saw that "this quiet
withdrawal into the tame domesticity of the pretty hillside suburb was bordering on stagnation." It bored her. She had no great love for cooking or dress-
making or any of the other hobbies with which her neighbors filled their time,
and although she maintained she had "a passion for motherhood" it did not
prove an all-consuming one. If Bill was disappointed he did not show it. He
said he did not particularly like Hastings-on-Hudson either and was perfectly
agreeable to moving. So the Sangers sold their dream house and moved back
into New York, into Greenwich Village. There, they joined the local Socialist
party, Labour Five, and instantly became involved in recruiting new members
from the clubs of working women in the area. It beat genteel games of tennis
any day. . . . Among the wives of Hastings-on-Hudson careers were rare and
frowned upon, but in Greenwich Village any self-respecting Socialist wife
wished to justify her existence. Bill's mother came to stay to look after Peggy
and Grant while Stuart was enrolled in a progressive local school and
Margaret took on obstetric cases (because these were short term).

Her work took her more and more frequently to the lower East Side of
New York, where she came across misery far worse than any she had found
during her training. She was called to cases in tenements where families were
living 10 to a small room, where women had neither the food nor the money
to support the babies she was delivering, where both men and women alike
were prematurely aged by the struggle to survive. But what was even more of
a shock to her was her involvement in botched abortions. She would be called
out to what she thought was a birth and arrive to find some terrified woman
bleeding to death. She passed queues on Saturday nights outside well-known
(but not to the authorities) abortionists and found herself the next morning
dealing with the effects of what the women had been given to take. What disturbed her most was that the women who tried to abort their babies were so
very often "good" mothers. They were not the feckless or wanton type, nor
were their husbands blackguards or brutes. It was simply cause and effect.
Marriage meant sex, sex meant babies, babies meant increased poverty. The
only solution was abstinence, but even having sexual intercourse only once a
year produced a baby a year. To Margaret's disgust she heard doctors tell one
distraught husband to "go and sleep on the roof" if he wanted to avoid his
wife becoming pregnant again. It was this brutal indifference to genuine
suffering that made Margaret determined to do something to help.

She was by this time not the inexperienced young girl of the White Plains days. As a married woman, who after the birth of her third child had been advised not to have any more children, she had practiced contraception herself. But when she came to pass on to her patients the "secret" of not having any more babies, she found that her wonderful information was virtually useless to them. "I resolved," she wrote, ". . . to do something to change the destiny of the mothers whose miseries were as vast as the sky." She discovered that explaining about **coitus interruptus** and condoms changed no destinies among the mothers of the lower East Side. What they needed was *female* contraception which was efficient and above all easy to use. They wanted the responsibility in their own hands. They also wanted to understand more about the workings of their own bodies, and it was this demand for knowledge that led Margaret to give health talks for the Women's Commission of the Socialist party and to write short articles on health matters for the New York paper *Call*. Out of all this came a series of articles in 1912 originally entitled *What Every Mother Should Know* then changed to *What Every Girl Should Know*. These at first simply gave information about sex and facts about reproduction which mothers were advised to tell their daughters, but then the articles became bolder, including more detailed notes on human physiology and also trying to stress that the sex act was normal and healthy and not something to be feared or shunned by women. Finally, the last article touched on venereal disease, its causes and effects, and how to avoid it. The Post Office immediately banned *Call* under the 1873 Comstock Law which made it illegal to send obscene matter through the U.S. mail.

As far as Margaret Sanger was concerned, this was flinging down the gauntlet. She determined to pick it up. Bill encouraged her, urging her to write up her articles into a pamphlet for distribution by hand. "You go ahead and finish your writing," she quotes him as saying, "and I'll get the dinner and wash the dishes." This he would then do, "drawing the shades so no one would see him." The children were not so cooperative. She describes her sons hating to come home and find her writing. But a sense of mission had begun to inspire her, and she began trying to find out all she could about every form of contraception available. Her quest took her to various libraries, where she missed a lot of valuable information apparently through not knowing how to look for it, and to talk with Socialists like Bill Haywood who had a great interest in the subject of limiting families through judicious use of contraception. Emma Goldman, whom Margaret also met, had already included the subject in her lectures. But as she went about her enquiries, interrupted by helping to organize picket lines during the Paterson silk-workers' strike of February 1913, Margaret began to doubt whether even those advocating contraception were doing so for the reasons which inspired her. Were any of them really thinking about the women, or were they just influenced by political and economic considerations? "I was enough of a feminist," she wrote, "to

---

coitus interruptus Sexual intercourse which is purposely interrupted in order to prevent the ejaculation of semen into the vagina.

resent the fact that woman and her requirements were not being taken into account in reconstructing this new world about which all were talking. They were failing to consider the quality of life itself." This, she became convinced, was for women intimately bound up with being able not only to *choose* to have babies but also to enjoy the act which produced them. But where was the simple, safe contraceptive which even an illiterate woman could use? She might find it, Bill Haywood said, in France.

There was really no sense in going to France in person (and perhaps no real need at all if only Margaret could have tapped existing American sources), but both the Sangers became wildly enthusiastic about such a venture. . . . They ended up on the Left Bank in Paris. Bill immediately plunged himself into the art world, where he met **Matisse** and was "aglow" with pleasure, while Margaret followed up Bill Haywood's introductions to people who would help her find out about contraception. What she discovered was that although there was no actual movement, there was a large body of individual knowledge about family limitation in existence. "I went into shops and bookstalls," she wrote, "and purchased all the devices of contraception available." She was shown pamphlets which were in circulation and talked to women who possessed "recipes" for suppositories passed down from generation to generation. It amazed her that in a Catholic country it should prove easier to learn about contraception for women than in New York, where the Comstock Law had made the circulation of information impossible.

When the three-month trip was at an end, it was Margaret and not Bill Sanger who was ready to go home. She was full of enthusiasm for her cause, eager to return to New York with samples of all kinds of contraceptives and ready to put into practice what she had learned. Beside the thought of this mission, the fun of being in Paris was nothing. But Bill did not agree. He loved Paris, felt he was making progress as an artist, and had no desire at all to return. Far from causing conflict in the Sanger marriage, this difference of opinion was faced by both Bill and Margaret with equanimity. He would stay, she would go. In fact, Margaret was glad to go back just with the children. She wanted a return to America "to stir up a national campaign" and Bill would just get in the way. But of course there was more to it than that. After 12 years of marriage Margaret was beginning once more to view the institution as "a kind of suicide." She felt stifled by being married. Although Bill was the most understanding and accommodating of husbands, she still wanted to be on her own and free of the emotional obligation under which he placed her. Nobody mentioned the phrase "trial separation," but it is clear Margaret thought that was what she was embarking on when in December 1913 she sailed for home.

As soon as she arrived she rented an apartment in upper Manhattan and set about planning the production of her own newspaper in order to spread contraceptive advice. At once she came up against those laws with which she was already familiar, the Comstock laws. These proved far

Matisse Brilliant French painter of the era.

more all-embracing and obstructive than she had ever realized, especially since Anthony Comstock himself was still in office as special inspector of the Post Office. He had been responsible personally for 700 arrests, 333 sentences, and the seizure of 34,836 articles classed as "for immoral use." Margaret raged against him—"his stunted, neurotic nature and savage methods of attack had ruined thousands of women's lives"—but she was not quite so silly as to doubt that any direct challenge to Comstock would invite certain prosecution and probable imprisonment.

For a while, she cast about trying to find ways of getting round the Comstock laws, as many had done before her, and seeking help for her general mission. Naturally, she approached influential feminists, among them Charlotte Perkins Gilman. They advised her (so she said) to join them in helping to win the vote and then all would be well—women would vote for the right to information on contraception. Margaret did not believe them, nor did she have any intention of waiting until the millennium dawned. It made her angry that the avowed feminists were not giving priority to the release of woman from her biological subservience, which in her opinion was a far greater obstacle to progress than not having the vote. The Socialists were of more use to her (and of course a great many of them were also feminists) because they gave her hints on how to set about publishing a clandestine newspaper, which they had great experience in doing. But Margaret was determined to accept only advice from her political friends and nothing more: Her newspaper would not be part of any general political propaganda but specifically feminist in purpose. She said she wished to make it "as red and flaming as possible" in order to bring to everyone's notice the problems affecting women.

She called her newspaper *The Woman Rebel*. The first issue, on eight pages of cheap paper, came out in March 1914 and was a very serious-looking publication. Bill Sanger had sent over some cartoons to enliven the pages, but Margaret scorned them—she *was* serious and was not going to dress up what she had to offer. The whole tone of her paper was strident and belligerent, full of startling statements like "The marriage bed is the most degenerating influence of the social order." It was sent by mail to a list of 2,000 subscribers obtained from Socialist friends. There was no precise contraceptive advice given, but it was made clear that contraception was approved of and known about. Meanwhile, Margaret was working hard to provide this very information. A pamphlet she was writing called *Family Limitation* was going to be absolutely explicit.

Family Limitation was written in plain, strong, fearless language. It was outspokenly feminist, stating women's right to enjoy sex as much as men and even asserting that if they did not it was usually because men were "clumsy fools." It tried to rouse women to help themselves, speaking scornfully of women who were lazy or sentimental—"of course it is troublesome to get up to douche, it is also a nuisance to have to trouble about the date of the menstrual period . . . it seems inartistic and sordid to insert a **pessary** or a suppository . . . but it is far more

---

pessary An instrument or device worn in the vagina to prevent conception.

sordid to find yourself several years later burdened down with half-a-dozen unwanted children . . . yourself a dragged out shadow of a woman. . . ." What to do to prevent yourself becoming a shadow was starkly set out. The importance of keeping a calendar of monthly periods was stressed, the existence of any "safe" period emphatically denied, coitus interruptus condemned as well as all douches labeled as cleansing but no preventative in themselves. Advice on condoms was thorough (what they were made of, which were best, where to buy them, how to make sure they were used properly) but the real emphasis was on female contraceptives.

Crude, and rather alarming, diagrams (Marie Stopes found them "prurient") illustrated how to use a pessary and fears about the use of it were banished—it was "silly" to think this object might "go up too far" and mysteriously get lost—"It cannot get into the womb nor can it get lost." Nor was there any need to worry about it spoiling a man's pleasure (though the pamphlet made it quite clear what it thought on *that* subject). Sponges, if used with the right chemical solution, were recommended and if all else failed suppositories were better than nothing. A recipe was given for a vaginal suppository for those quite unable to get them—"take 1 ounce of cocoa butter, 60 grains quinine, melt the cocoa butter, mix the quinine with it, form it into suppositories by letting the mixture harden into a cake and then cutting it up into ten pieces—insert one into the vagina 3 minutes before the act." An address was given for mail-order goods in case anybody lived far from a chemist. At the end of the pamphlet 14 of the most common queries about contraception were printed (e.g., "Does nursing a baby prevent pregnancy?") and dealt with. Women were urged to tell other women how to avoid pregnancy—"spread this important knowledge!"—and to help the movement towards birth control (a term she had coined and now used for the first time) which it was prophesied "will shortly win full acceptance and sanction by public morality as well."

Naturally, once Margaret finished her pamphlet she then found it difficult to get it printed. She touted it round various Socialist printers, who all "turned deadly pale" and told her the risks were too great, until she found Russian-born Bill Shatoff, who was prepared to do the job on his own after hours so that it could be kept completely secret and nobody else would risk imprisonment. But, as soon as the printing of 100,000 copies had been arranged in the summer of 1914, events began to move too fast. Within days of the first issue of *Woman Rebel* coming out in March, letters started to arrive asking for specific information, but by that time the Post Office had sent word to say the newspaper was breaking the Comstock Law. Margaret ignored the communication and went ahead with the April issue. There were no objections to that one. In May, July, August, other issues appeared and then at the end of August Margaret received a visit from two officials. They told her the last three issues broke the law on nine counts. They refused to say how but announced they had orders to arrest her. She received the news calmly, but was instantly aware that she must move very fast to exploit her arrest as much as possible.

Margaret was told she would have plenty of time to prepare her case, but in October she was "suddenly informed" that it would be in two days' time. Considering she had had six weeks since August 25th when she was told a trial would take place, she was perhaps unreasonable to find this "sudden" but she seems to have been genuinely startled. In any case, although thrilled at the thought of hearing the words "The People vs. Margaret Sanger," and longing to stand up to open court and proclaim her beliefs, she had no intention of going to battle over the *Woman Rebel*. She wanted to do so over *Family Limitation*. It seemed to her foolish to risk losing the chance to fight over this much more important document, so she decided to take the drastic step of leaving the country, having *Family Limitation* released as soon as she was safely away, then returning after an interval with a case prepared specifically on the birth control issue. In one way, this made obvious sense, but it was fraught with problems. The most important one was the fate of her children. Stuart, then 10, was at camp and could stay there until he returned to his boarding school where he had been for some years, but Grant was only five and Peggy three. . . .

What Margaret then decided to do is very difficult to understand. Grant and Peggy were sent on holiday to the Catskills with a friend and extremely precarious arrangements made for their return. . . . She seems to have convinced herself that she had made the "supreme sacrifice" a mother could make. She claimed to be "passionately maternal" and yet thought sending children away, to school or anywhere else, "the most unselfish act . . . because it shows a selfless consideration for the child's good rather than an egoistic self-indulgence in sentimentality." Any consideration for her own children's good seems nevertheless to have been entirely lacking when she decided, the day before she was due to appear in court, to take the train for Montreal. This can either be seen as heroic or as incomprehensible, but either way it puts Margaret Sanger's attitude to motherhood in a different category from most women's.

In Montreal, Margaret was put up by some friends until a place was found for her on the RMS *Virginian*, sailing for Liverpool on November 1st, 1914. She selected the pseudonym "Bertha Watson," which she said was a name so "atrociously ugly" that it robbed her of her femininity every time she answered to it. Unable to produce a passport, she had no idea how she would get herself into England, especially in wartime conditions, but she says she made friends with an official on board who managed to arrange her entry. She stayed in Liverpool for a few "dreadful bleak weeks," suddenly feeling not quite so brave and noble and miserably conscious that her children, especially Peggy whom she had left with a sore leg, might be missing her as much as she was missing them. Then she went to London where she rented a room in Torrington Square. From there, she went every day to the British Museum to do research on birth control methods.

She was not friendless, arriving in London with several useful introductions to leading exponents of birth control in England. The Drysdales asked her to tea and through them she received an invitation to visit **Havelock Ellis,** whose books she had just read and admired. She took a bus to Dover Mansions in Brixton and had tea and toast with him in front of the fire. Afterwards, they met in the British Museum, where Ellis showed himself keen to direct the studies of this young and attractive student. Very soon they were close friends, though never lovers technically if Ellis is to be relied upon. "On me this first meeting simply left a pleasant impression," he wrote, "aided by sympathy with her lonely situation in a strange city," and after the second he found himself brought into "a relationship of friendship, I may say of affectionate friendship. . . ." Within two weeks they were on kissing terms which for Ellis, says his biographer, counted as "near rape by anyone else." Even if, as Ellis maintained, the friendship with Margaret merely had a touch of "sweet intimacy" about it, he records himself, after a kiss on New Year's Eve, as "like a drunken man . . . all of a rapture . . . I was aching and beaten and sore." Perhaps in kissing as in all else Margaret Sanger was a powerful lady. But for her part, although pleased with Ellis's attention, she was hardly swept off her feet. Her relationship with her husband she now regarded as finished and was about to write him "an epoch making letter" telling him so. Starting another such relationship was no part of her plan. She had work to do.

It was Ellis who suggested to her a visit to Holland where, he had been told, birth control clinics were in existence teaching the use of the comparatively newly invented diaphragm. England was of course at war and the idea of going to Holland a dangerous one, but Margaret set off in January 1915 with introductions to Dr. Rutgers of The Hague. Dr. Rutgers was elderly and harassed and his English was poor but he was very welcoming. He took Margaret to his clinic, showed her the Mensinga diaphragm and demonstrated with several of his patients how to use it. . . . The diaphragm was *not* a cervical cap of the type Margaret Sanger and others had publicized but a much simpler and more efficient cap which fitted longitudinally in the vagina, secured by the pubic bone. It amounted to the greatest advance since the condom and had the additional advantage of being for women. At his clinic Dr. Rutgers showed his fascinated visitors 14 different sizes of the German diaphragm which, since its use in Holland, had become known as the Dutch cap, and he emphasized that accurate fitting was vital. It was, he stressed, a medical matter and decidedly not something women could do for themselves, although once fitted and taught they could certainly manage to use it much more easily than a pessary. Margaret was at first disappointed. Her vision had been of women taking matters into their own hands and helping each other until a chain of self-help existed everywhere. But she accepted Dr. Rutgers's verdict quickly and turned to examining how his clinics worked.

A network of birth control clinics was already in existence in Holland under the direction of Dr. Aletta Jacobs, a great feminist as well as the country's first qualified woman

> **Havelock Ellis** A British physician noted for his investigation of human sexual behavior and author of the seven volume *Studies in the Psychology of Sex.*

doctor. Unfortunately, Dr. Jacobs was not as friendly or helpful as Dr. Rutgers. She was deeply suspicious of this young, nonmedical American woman and refused either to meet her or to take her round her clinics. Brusquely, she said birth control was not a matter for laypeople. Offended and annoyed, Margaret had to make do with visiting other doctors. She also discovered that, in spite of the insistence by them that this was a medical matter, women could actually go into shops throughout Holland and be fitted up. She went into several herself and found ". . . there was a small, adjoining room, containing a reclining chair and a wash basin. The woman, if she so desired, was taken into this room, examined, and fitted by the shop attendant." It seemed to her that this being so there must be room for some sort of compromise. Nurses, for example, like herself, were surely medical—perhaps it would be possible to run clinics with specially trained nurses in charge. What she wanted was a system whereby women went to places specifically designed for this one purpose and where they would find other women specifically catering for this purpose without doctors necessarily being in control as Dr. Jacobs insisted they must be. Beside that, pamphlets paled into insignificance. What she wanted to do now was return to New York, face her trial, then put her energies into opening clinics. . . . For a while, she hesitated. In her autobiography she goes over the alternatives: Should she bring Grant and Peggy over to join her, leaving Stuart at school, and take them to Paris to write a book? But that was as risky as returning herself. Which risk ought she to take?

While all this agonizing was going on, Bill Sanger, back in New York, had been arrested by Comstock's agents for possessing one of Margaret's *Family Limitation* pamphlets. He wrote telling her what had happened and assuring her that he was proud to be standing trial for her sake. Offered a free pardon by Comstock if he revealed where his wife was, Bill boasted that he had replied he would "Let hell freeze over first." If he expected Margaret to be impressed or touched, he was greatly mistaken. She was extremely angry, commenting "Bill had to get mixed up in my work after all and of course it made it harder for me." She saw his stand as showing off and an attempt to ingratiate himself with her. But at least it brought her to a rapid decision: She must return at once before Bill grabbed any more of the limelight. In September 1915 she sailed, via Bordeaux, through the torpedo-threatened Atlantic to New York, arriving safely only to find Bill had already been released after serving a nominal jail sentence and that, ironically, his trial had been the occasion of Anthony Comstock catching a chill which had killed him. She also found that in other ways the birth control scene had significantly changed. Other people were now interested and trying to take control of a movement she had regarded as hers to head and lead. One of these "other people" was **Mary Ware Dennet,** who infuriated Margaret by explaining that she envisaged, now that Comstock was dead, an orderly campaign staying strictly within the law aimed at repealing those statutes blocking the advance of birth control. This Margaret rejected. What *she* wanted was direct

> **Mary Ware Dennet** Suffragist, pacifist, and birth control and sex education advocate of the early 20th century.

action, challenging the law flamboyantly, and starting with her own deferred court case, for which she desired maximum publicity. As far as she was concerned ". . . the whole issue is not one of a mistake, whereby getting into jail or keeping out of jail is important, but the issue is to raise . . . birth control out of the gutter of obscenity and into the light of understanding." To attract even more "light," she intended to conduct her own defense at her trial.

Before this was to take place, Margaret Sanger had a trial of a different sort to go through. On November 6th, 1915, five-year-old Peggy died of pneumonia. Margaret was never able to write about it, as Josephine Butler later managed to, nor was this normally expressive woman able to express her grief. "The joy in the fullness of life went out of it on that morning," she wrote, "and has never returned." As well as grief there was also guilt to confront— guilt that of Peggy's short life she had robbed herself of almost a quarter by leaving her to go to England and that during the remainder she had very often indeed put her second to work. But there was no breakdown. The horror of Peggy's death seemed to freeze all emotion in her. Her only way of dealing with it was to block it out by redoubling her efforts for the birth control cause. She longed passionately for her trial to begin and was bitterly upset when told that instead the case against her was to be dropped. She *needed* that trial, needed to make it the focus of her damaged life, needed to stand up and show she had left Peggy for something that mattered. But pressure had been brought to bear upon the government to prevent it making a fool of itself. As George Bernard Shaw put it, "Comstockery is a world joke at the expense of the U.S." and the laughter was growing uncomfortably loud. The New York *Sun* commented accurately, "The Sanger case presents the anomaly of a prosecutor loath to prosecute and a defendant anxious to be tried." But on February 18th, 1916, the government finally entered a *nolle prosequi.*

Margaret's immediate reaction was to go off on a speaking tour for three months. She made the same speech 119 times, first practicing it from the roof of her hotel in Lexington Avenue. In it, she went over seven sets of circumstances in which birth control should be used, including the first two years of any young couple's marriage "to give them a chance to grow together." She began in New Rochelle by reading her speech but by Pittsburgh she had memorized it and become less nervous. She presented a curious spectacle wherever she went because of her apparent fragility. For a while, conscious that she might not look "serious," she wore "severe suits" but soon gave up because they made her feel constrained and uncomfortable. In any case, she quickly realized that there was in fact an advantage in looking frail and feminine—it made audiences protective and that was an asset. . . . Wherever she went she was a great success. People packed the halls in which she spoke and supporters marched the streets with banners proclaiming such slogans as "Poverty and large families go hand-in-hand." The atmosphere everywhere on this issue was

nolle prosequi An entry on the records of a legal action denoting that the prosecutor or plaintiff will proceed no further in his or her actions or suit.

highly charged and Margaret delighted in inflaming passions. She wrote that "my flaming Feminist speeches . . . scared some . . . out of their wits." When the opposition took action by arresting her or locking her out of halls, she was pleased and said, "I see immense advantages in being gagged. It silences me but it makes millions of others talk about me and the cause in which I live."

But Margaret Sanger's avowed purpose in returning to America had been to open clinics, and once her tour was over she began to consider how and where she could start. She had already been quoted in [the] *Tribune* as saying, "I have the word of four prominent physicians that they will support me in the work. . . . There will be nurses in attendance at the clinic and doctors who will instruct women in the things they need to know. All married women, or women about to be married, will be assisted free and without question." As she herself added, "A splendid promise but difficult to fulfill." For a start, which "prominent physician" when it came to the bit would put his professional head on the legal block? The answer, as she found, was not one of them. Carefully, she went over and over the two sections of the 1873 Comstock Law, under which she would be prosecuted if she opened a clinic, looking for a loophole. Section 1142, the one most often cited, said *no one* could give information to prevent conception to *anyone* for *any* reason, but Section 1145 did say that doctors could give advice "to cure or prevent" sexual diseases. This had been squeezed in to cover venereal disease, but Margaret saw how it might be used if the prevention of disease was interpreted as covering lives endangered through too many pregnancies. But she did not, of course, really imagine that such a specious line of argument would be accepted. Obviously, as soon as she opened a clinic it would be closed and she would then face arrest and trial. She knew this, and accepted her fate not just with resignation but with positive relish.

This decided, she set about finding premises and helpers. "I preferred a Jewish landlord," she wrote later, "and a Mr. Rabinowitz was the answer." The point of him being Jewish was that she had the idea "Jewish people were more interested in health." The obliging Mr. Rabinowitz lived in Brownsville, a poor but perfectly respectable immigrant district of New York. "He was willing to let us have No. 46, Amboy St. at $50 a month, a reduction from the regular rent because he realized what we were trying to do." He spent hours cleaning the rooms they were going to use and even insisted on white-washing the walls so that the atmosphere would be "more hospital looking." . . .

On the morning the clinic was due to open, October 16th, 1916, there was a long queue outside—"halfway to the corner they were standing in line, at least 150, some shawled, some hatless, their red hands clasping the cold, chapped, smaller ones of their children." It was a pathetic and moving sight. By seven in the evening, they were still arriving, standing patiently and hopefully in line, many of them accompanied by men. It was impossible to see them all. When the doors were regretfully closed at the end of that first exhausting day a hundred women had been seen—but not one by a doctor. Margaret had failed to recruit a single qualified doctor. She had to run the clinic herself with the help of her sister Ethel, also a nurse.

Another friend, Fania Mindell, helped by keeping the records and looking after the children while Ethel and Margaret lectured batches of 7 to 10 women each, in separate rooms, on contraception in general. It had not escaped Margaret's notice that in Holland no records were kept. She had rightly concluded that if there had been records, which could be collated and published, they might be of great value for research purposes and so she was determined from the beginning to adopt this businesslike approach—it was all part of her greater design and indicated the scope of her ambition. She knew quite well that her Brownsville clinic would in itself be insignificant, but that was not the point. The point was to make a positive beginning from which all else would flow.

And it did, remarkably rapidly. The clinic was only open nine days, packed to bursting all the time, before it was raided in a gratifyingly spectacular fashion. Black Marias, screeching sirens, fully armed policemen, and all to herd three perfectly willing women to the local police station. If the authorities had been trying to attract sympathy for Margaret Sanger and publicity for her cause, they could not have managed it better. By the time the first case was called, against Ethel, a committee of a hundred prominent women had been formed to work for the reform of the Comstock Law. On the day of Ethel's trial, 50 of them took Margaret to breakfast at the Vanderbilt Hotel before proceeding with her to the courtroom. Ethel, sentenced under Section 1142, as expected, was given 30 days' imprisonment. She went on hunger strike, refusing liquid as well as food. Margaret, still awaiting her own trial, was genuinely concerned for her sister's health but determined to exploit the situation, as indeed Ethel wished her to do. She kept Ethel's suffering in the public eye, in spite of attempts by the authorities first to keep it secret and then to play it down. By the time she herself went on trial, a month later, public opinion was widely alerted to what was going on. When she took the stand, she was impressive. Every allegation the prosecution made was fiercely contested, especially that of wishing "to do away" with Jewish people by preventing them breeding. Birth control, she said, was nothing to do with doing away of any sort, nor was it a way of making money as was also alleged. She itemized the cost of her clinic and invited those in court to do their own sums.

After half of the 50 Brownsville mothers who had attended the clinic had given evidence, Judge Freschi said, "I can't stand this any longer," and adjourned the court—he was overwhelmed by the endless recitation of miscarriages, illnesses, and childbirths. When it met again, a compromise was quickly offered: If Mrs. Sanger would promise to agree not to break the law again she would get a free pardon this time. She refused, standing up and saying, "I cannot respect the law as it stands today." She was sentenced to 30 days, like Ethel. This was more of a shock than she had thought. Whenever she had thought of going to prison, she said, she had somehow always imagined that at the last minute she would be saved—"I believed fully and firmly that some miracle would happen and that I should not go to jail." But no miracle happened, and she went to jail, quite amazed to find the indignities

of which she had heard actually coming to pass. Even so, she was given pref-
erential treatment (not, for example, being strip-searched) and knew she had
an easy time compared to others. Nobody stopped her giving birth control
talks to the other prisoners and she enjoyed herself. What she enjoyed even
more was coming out to the strains of the Marseillaise being sung at the gates
by a crowd of her friends. "No other experience in my life has been more
thrilling," she wrote triumphantly.

Yet when she took stock of what opening a clinic and going to prison
had gained her, she was depressed to conclude very little indeed. She was
particularly disappointed at the response from the women of New York
whom she described as sitting "with folded hands" and keeping "aloof from
the struggle for women's freedom." She had, she felt, sounded the call to
action but "American women were not going to use direct action." The next
few years, 1917 to 1921, were "leaden years." She had resolved, after prison,
on a four-part campaign: agitation, education, organization, and legislation,
but it was hard to be the driving force behind all four. Most of her energies
went into launching a magazine again, the *Birth Control Review*, which she
herself helped to sell on street corners. "Street selling was torture for me,"
she said, "but I sometimes did it for self-discipline and because only in this
way could I have complete knowledge of what I was asking others to do."
She soon found that selling the magazine was an unsatisfactory business anyway. Those who bought it were aggrieved and disappointed when they found
it contained no practical contraceptive advice. However hard she tried, it
seemed impossible to give people what they undoubtedly wanted without
promptly landing back in prison again and again. Not only did her work
make her unhappy at this time but so did her personal life. She had been a
woman on her own since her return in 1915. Her two sons were at boarding
school, and she was lonely. She had always thought she liked to be on her
own, but the reality of "not a cat, dog, or bird to greet this homecoming, the
fire dead in the grate" was too much. Work was not, after all, enough. Her
health was poor again in the winter of 1917–18, so she went to California,
uprooting Grant and taking him with her for company. There, she spent three
months recuperating and writing a book.

The book was *Woman and the New Race*, finally published in 1920. In it,
Margaret Sanger expounded with great fervour and passion her belief that
the most important force in the remaking of the world was "a free motherhood." Legal and suffrage rights were utterly unimportant beside birth control because "these don't affect the most vital factors of her existence." But
"free motherhood" was not going to be given to women—she stressed
repeatedly it was something they had to claim for themselves. Women had
to stop accepting their inferior status. They had to realize they had power
of their own, because it was only through them that the future generations
could be born. The "new woman" so in vogue thought the ability to earn
her own living a great victory, and perhaps it was, but "it is of little account
beside the untramelled choice of mating or not mating." Only by using contraception could women make the most of this "untramelled choice." The

"new woman" must look after herself and not be stupid enough to leave it to men. As for any idea that using birth control was immoral—that was absurd. All that was immoral was having unwanted babies, or leading oneself to believe that governments were right to encourage large families. This was "the most serious evil of our times" especially as the modern woman was not as suited as other generations to motherhood because of the tension of modern life. . . .

When she returned from California (and put Grant back into school as quickly as she had snatched him out), she felt rejuvenated. She had also decided to try new tactics to get clinics opened. Aware that certain prominent medical men, such as Dr. Robert Dickinson (who was one of America's most eminent gynecologists), were beginning to feel uneasy about their profession's attitude to birth control, Margaret Sanger decided to set about suggesting her movement could be put into the hands of doctors. In 1923 she opened a Clinical Research Bureau on Fifth Avenue in New York and then asked Dickinson if he and his newly formed Committee on Maternal Health (composed of New York obstetricians and gynecologists and privately financed) would like to take the bureau over and develop it. She herself, of course, would still control it, but she would be more than happy to involve Dickinson and his colleagues in the running of it. If they wanted to, they could man it completely. For seven years of constant argument Dickinson tried to get doctors to do this but he failed. The stumbling block was always Mrs. Sanger herself. The doctors neither liked nor trusted her. They suspected her motives, doubted her competence, and feared her interference. Yet in spite of this setback, Margaret was more hopeful and buoyant than she had been since her imprisonment. She had failed to get any "doctors only" legislation through state legislatures and failed to get medical cooperation for her research bureau, but everywhere she saw her movement making headway. . . .

It seemed, in the twenties and thirties, that Margaret Sanger was everywhere, endlessly traveling and lecturing and preaching for her cause. Her personal life was also happier. In 1920 she had been quietly divorced from Bill Sanger, for whom she still felt affection but nothing more. He irritated her, he was in the way. In the way of what, she did not quite know, and when she got her official freedom she describes in her autobiography how she went through a period of slight panic during which she attempted to form closer relationships with her sons, then 17 and 12. Grant, the younger one, was easier for her to woo. He was always the more original and still young enough for her to dominate. In 1921 she once more took him out of school, against the advice of the headmaster, who strenuously objected on the grounds that Grant's studies were continually interrupted to serve as his mother's companion, and took him with her to Japan. He was "a tall, dark, rather gawky youth," very affectionate and demonstrative. Margaret was extremely proud of him, referring to him as "Exhibit A." She was rather hurt when, during the last part of this Far Eastern tour, he announced he was fed up and wished he could get to see some decent tennis. She let him go home ahead of her but missed him dreadfully.

When she arrived home herself, she amazed her friends by marrying again, in 1922. Noah Slee, her new husband, was a businessman 20 years older than she who had courted her with presents of filing cabinets and date stamps. Hearing that although she was a formidable career lady she was frivolous enough to enjoy dancing, he had also taken 10 lessons at Arthur Murray's Dancing School so that he could partner her. Once again, Margaret succumbed to the prospect of a way of life put before her. Noah Slee was a rich widower. He was only too willing to put considerable amounts of money and his business organization at the service of birth control. So, at the age of 43, Margaret married him, on the understanding that she would not be tied down by the marriage. . . .

The same year that she married Noah Slee, Margaret had also published another book—*The Pivot of Civilization*. In it she had a great deal to say about the importance of sex. "Woman," she wrote, "must elevate sex into another sphere." To do so, she must reject the present teaching that sex was merely a means of procreating children. This was "a superficial and shameful view of the sexual instinct." Birth control carried with it, she argued, "a thorough training in bodily cleanliness and physiology, and a definitive knowledge of the physiology and function of sex." She attacked the Catholic church for saying birth control was "unnatural" when what was in fact unnatural was being forced to thwart or subdue the sexual instinct. Mankind had gone forward to "capture and control the forces of nature" and this should be a matter of rejoicing. No longer need fear inhibit women—"women can attain freedom only by concrete, definite knowledge of themselves, a knowledge based on biology, physiology, and psychology." Using birth control was the means to all this, she claimed. Margaret Sanger called this book her "head" book, full of reasoned argument she hoped, while her earlier one, *Woman and the New Race*, was her "heart" book, full of passion and emotion. In fact, they were both similar, setting out the same arguments and only differing in the emphasis on sex and in the examples she chose to illustrate her points. They both sold well and established her more firmly as a figure on the international birth control scene. But she was not a secure figure in her own country. From the day she founded the American Birth Control League (in 1921) Margaret Sanger was involved in internal power struggles and in 1928 she resigned as its president. She also gave up the *Birth Control Review*, and Noah withdrew his financial support. From then onwards, she confined herself to the research bureau and to a new organization she set up, the National Committee on Federal Legislation for Birth Control.

In 1937, the Committee on Contraception of the American Medical Association agreed that physicians now had the right to give contraceptive advice and that the subject should be taught in medical schools. By then, the anti-contraception laws had been side-stepped for nearly a decade anyway and the birth control movement had become respectable. But Margaret Sanger saw this victory as only the first official one of the many more needed. The next battle was to get the government to make birth control a public health program. "Birth control must seep down until it reaches the strata where the need is greatest; until it has been democratized there can be no rest." A visit to India in 1936 had made her see the true evils of overpopulation and she was haunted by the sight of the "unspeakable poverty . . . the poorest women of Bombay, sober faced and dull looking . . . lived in the grubby and deadly 'chawls,' huts of corrugated iron, no windows, no lights, no lamps, just three walls and sometimes old pieces of rag or paper hung up in front in a pitiful attempt at privacy." It made her determined not just to establish a whole, worldwide system of birth control clinics but to continue to seek a better, simpler, cheaper female contraceptive. The rest of her life remained devoted to this quest. From her winter home in Tucson, Arizona, and her New York estate, Willow Lake in Dutchess County, she sallied forth agitating for more money to spend on research and contributing a good share of her own from the inheritance Noah left her on his death in 1943. It was her research bureau which financed Dr. Ernst Graefenberg, pioneer of the IUD [intrauterine device], and began work on hormonal contraceptives which led to the development of the Pill. In 1959, Dr. Gregory Pincus inscribed the report on oral contraceptives: "To Margaret Sanger with affectionate greetings—this product of her pioneering resoluteness." By then, she was living full-time in Arizona, on her own, feeling very much out of contact with what was going on in the movement to which she had dedicated her life. "I would hesitate to go anywhere to speak on birth control these days," she said. There was no need to do so. By the time she died in 1966, it looked as though the Pill had solved the whole birth control problem, at least in the Western world, and with it many of the problems feminism had been unable to overcome.

A Primary Perspective

LETTERS TO MARGARET SANGER

Although middle-class women dominated the leadership ranks of the campaign to distribute birth control information, the movement also drew support from working-class mothers. For many of the latter, reproductive control often meant the difference between destitution and making ends meet. As the letters below indicate, these women were deeply appreciative of Sanger's efforts.

I am the mother of four little ones, the oldest only six years old. They are all puny little things, and need so much care and I am not strong enough to care for them, although I try, as we are not able to hire help. The baby is five weeks old. I am so nervous and weak I can hardly stand, yet I have all the care of the children, cooking, washing to do. My husband is a hired man on a farm. His pay is $50.00 per month. What can we do for our children? We can't even dress them comfortably and feed them as they should be fed, although we try

Source: From Margaret Sanger, *Motherhood in Bondage.* Copyright © 1928. Reprinted by permission of Alexander C. Sanger, Executive of the Estate of Margaret Sanger.

so hard. My man goes to work at six in the morning and comes back at seven in the evening so he can't help me any. He isn't strong, only weighs 125 pounds, while I weigh 100 pounds. It is an awful thing for us to bring more children, little weak things like ourselves, with no way to make a living only their two hands, into the world to be knocked and brow-beat all their lives. I cry and pray and be careful and it all does no good. I have one of your books and don't see why there isn't more people like you in this world. I am only 26 years old, my husband the same, so we have a long time yet ahead, although we both have lots of gray hair already, we are old at 26. What a burning shame when I think of how rearing children has brought us down from what we were. I can't see why I should be denied the information I ask for.

• • • • •

I am 35. In 17 years of married life have brought eight children into the world and went down in the grave after three I failed to get. We bought us a little home to start with and oh, the struggle! Have both worked like slaves, I with my own efforts have kept the family in what we had to buy, have sold $300.00 worth of butter, eggs, and chickens. He raises what he can for us to eat and saves a little and in this way we have managed to pay for our little home, but have no conveniences whatever. Sometimes I've had only my husband to wait on me when the children came and in every instance have been on the job, slinging pots and pans when my baby was two weeks old and strange to say am still well. I have six children in school and two under my feet, am milking five cows, sell from 75 to 100 pounds of butter a month, fit a package for parcel post every day.

I have milked six cows at six o'clock and brought a baby into the world at nine.

My baby is nine months old and the thoughts of another almost kills me.

Oh! tell me how to keep from having another. Don't open the door of heaven to me and then shut it in my face.

Oh! please tell me, I feel like it's more important to raise what I have than to bring more.

QUESTIONS

1. In what ways, if any, did Sanger's childhood and adolescent experiences shape her later activities as a birth control reformer? What influence did working as a nurse have on Sanger's developing views about family limitation?
2. What did Sanger mean when she described marriage as "a kind of suicide"? How would you characterize her attitudes toward motherhood? Did her first husband help or hinder her work?
3. Why do you think someone like Anthony Comstock was able to acquire the power that he did? What does this suggest about popular attitudes toward women and sexuality during the late 19th and early 20th centuries?

4. Why did Sanger have such a negative opinion of physicians? Why were doctors so reluctant to cooperate with her?
5. What advice do you think Sanger offered to working-class mothers who wrote to her? How would you have responded to these letters?
6. Why was Sanger so often at odds with most voting-rights feminists? Do you think Sanger's personality traits strengthened or weakened her campaign for birth control reform? In what ways did Sanger's achievements influence the development of the contemporary women's rights movement?

ADDITIONAL RESOURCES

The most recent biography of Sanger is Ellen Chesler, *Woman of Valor: Margaret Sanger and the Birth Control Movement in America* (1992), though readers also might consult *An Autobiography* (1938), in which the famous reformer relates her own story. All major examinations of the birth control movement provide additional information on Sanger. Three especially noteworthy works are Linda Gordon, *Woman's Body, Woman's Right: A Social History of Birth Control in America* (1977); James Reed, *From Private Vice to Public Virtue: The Birth Control Movement in America Since 1830* (1978); and David M. Kennedy, *Birth Control in America: The Career of Margaret Sanger* (1970). For a comprehensive historical overview of American attitudes toward sexuality, see John D'Emilio and Estelle Freedman, *Intimate Matters: A History of Sexuality in America* (1988). A more specialized study of the subject is G. J. Barker-Benfield, *Horrors of the Half-Known Life: Male Attitudes Toward Women and Sexuality in Nineteenth Century America* (1976), which focuses on the opinions and activities of physicians.

For Margaret Sanger, *A Public Nuisance*, a 1992 film, treats the controversial advocate of birth control in a 28-minute representation by Terese Svoboda and Steve Bull. *Century of Women* (1994) provides a look at women's lives over the course of the 20th century.

Chapter 10

Eleanor Roosevelt

*A*s the man who led the country through the Great Depression and World War II, Franklin D. Roosevelt (FDR) is one of the most esteemed figures in American political history. This was especially so among working people, one of whom remarked that FDR was "the first man in the White House to understand that my boss is a son of a bitch." Yet little in Roosevelt's background suggested that he would become a champion of the common man. Born into one of the nation's most famous families, he grew up on the family's vast estate in Hyde Park, New York. Mindful of his quasi-aristocratic origins, historians later referred to him as the Lord of the Manor and the Squire of Hyde Park.

How, then, did FDR manage to achieve such rapport with America's working masses? According to one interpretation, a major turning point occurred during the early 1920s when he was paralyzed with polio. Never able to walk again without support, Roosevelt struggled desperately to come to grips with this awful disease, so that he could resume his political career. It was during this period, some have suggested, that FDR developed those qualities that as president enabled him to win the love and admiration of the nation's dispossessed. This is all speculation, though there is no reason to doubt that Roosevelt's battle against polio made him better able to sympathize with the personal misfortune of others.

More certain is the influence that his wife, Eleanor (ER), had on both FDR and his presidency. Although she came from a background just as privileged as that of her husband, ER exhibited a lifelong concern with the plight of those less fortunate than herself. After FDR was stricken with polio, she also demonstrated a political acumen that made her indispensable to her ailing husband during this critical period of his career. By 1928, when FDR won election as governor of New York, ER had become a major player in state politics; and when FDR secured the presidency four years later, ER became a powerful national advocate for a broad range of liberal causes. She would remain so for the last three decades of her life.

In the public sphere, that life was one of enormous self-fulfillment. But in other areas, it contained a good deal of disappointment. Though ER and her husband functioned well together as political partners, their marital relationship often left much to be desired. In the essay that follows, William H. Chafe not only discusses her influence on Democratic party politics during the New Deal years and beyond, he also examines her efforts to compensate for a marriage that had lost much of its lustre while she was still a young woman. The result is a compelling portrait of a compassionate but tough-minded individual who never stopped believing that the world could be made a better place in which to live.

Eleanor Roosevelt

William H. Chafe

Anna Eleanor Roosevelt was born in New York City on October 11, 1884, the first child and only daughter of Elliott Roosevelt and Anna (Hall) Roosevelt. Descended on both sides from distinguished colonial families active in commerce, banking, and politics, she seemed destined to enjoy all the benefits of class and privilege. Yet by the time she was 10, both her parents had died, as had a younger brother, Elliott, leaving her and her second brother, Hall, as the only survivors.

As a youngster, Eleanor experienced emotional rejection almost from the time she could remember. "I was a solemn child," she recalled, "without beauty. I seemed like a little old woman entirely lacking in the spontaneous

Source: From *Without Precedent: The Life and Career of Eleanor Roosevelt*, edited by Joan Hoff-Wilson and Marjorie Lightman. Indiana University Press © 1984. Reprinted by permission of the author from *Biographical Sketch*.

joy and mirth of youth." Her mother called her "Granny" and, at least in Eleanor's memory, treated her daughter differently than her son, warmly embracing the boy while being only "kindly and indifferent" to her little girl. From most of her family, young Eleanor received the message that she was "very plain," almost ugly, and certainly "old fashioned." When her parents died, she went to live with her grandmother, who was equally without warmth. As Eleanor's cousin Corinne later remarked, "it was the grimmest childhood I had ever known. Who did she have? Nobody."

In fact, Eleanor had one person—her father. "He was the one great love of my life as a child," she later wrote, "and . . . like many children, I have lived a dream life with him." Described by his friends as "charming, impetuous, high-spirited, big-hearted, generous, [and] friendly," Elliott exhibited ease and grace in his social interactions. With Eleanor, he developed an intimacy that seemed almost magical. "As soon as I could talk," she recalled, "I went into his dressing room every morning and chattered to him . . . I even danced with him, intoxicated by the pure joy of motion . . . until he would pick me up and throw me into the air." She dreamed of the time when they would go off together—"always he and I . . . and someday [we] would have a life of our own together."

But Elliott's capacity for ebullient play and love also contained the seeds of self-destruction—alcoholism, irresponsibility, cruelty. He never found an anchor, either in public life or business, to provide stability for himself and his family. Elliott's emotional imbalance quickly produced problems in his marriage and banishment from the household. The last four years of his life were like a roller coaster. Elliott nourished the emotional relationship with Eleanor through letters to "father's own little Nell," writing of "the wonderful long rides . . . through the grand snow-clad forests, over the white hills" that he wanted them to enjoy together. But when his long-awaited visits occurred, they often ended in disaster, as when Elliott left Eleanor with the doorman at New York's Knickerbocker Club, promising to return but going off on a drunken spree instead. The pain of betrayal was exceeded only by Eleanor's depth of love for the man she believed was "the only person who really cared." Looking back later in life for an explanation of her inability to express emotions spontaneously, she concluded that the trauma of her childhood was the main cause. "Something locked me up," she wrote.

After her father's death, an emotional void pervaded Eleanor's life until, at age 14, she enrolled in Allenswood, a girls' school outside London presided over by Marie Souvestre, daughter of a well-known French philosopher and radical. At Allenswood, the girl found a circle of warmth and support. "She was beloved by everybody," her cousin remarked. "Saturdays we were allowed a sortie in Putney which has stores where you could buy books, [and] flowers. Young girls had crushes and you left [gifts] in the room with the girl you were idolizing. Eleanor's room every Saturday would be full of flowers because she was so admired." Allenswood also provided educational inspiration. Souvestre passionately embraced unpopular causes, staunchly defending

Dreyfus in France and the cause of the Boers in South Africa. "I consider the three years which I spent with her as the beginning of an entirely new outlook on life," Eleanor wrote. Marie Souvestre toured the continent with the girl, confiding in her and expressing the affection that made it possible for Eleanor to flower. Describing her stay at Allenswood as "the happiest years of my life," Eleanor noted that "whatever I have become since had its seeds in those three years of contact with a liberal mind and strong personality." The love and admiration were mutual. "I miss you every day of my life," Souvestre wrote her in 1902.

The imprint of Marie Souvestre was not lost when Eleanor returned to the United States at age 17 to "come out" in New York society. Even in the rush of parties and dances, she kept her eye on the more serious world of ideas and social service. Souvestre had written her in 1901: "Even when success comes, as I'm sure it will, bear in mind that there are more quiet and enviable joys than to be among the most sought-after women at a ball." Heeding the injunction, Eleanor plunged into settlement-house work and social activism.

Much of Eleanor Roosevelt's subsequent political life can be traced to this early involvement with social reform. At age 18 she joined the National Consumers' League, headed by Florence Kelley. The league was committed to securing health and safety for workers—especially women—in clothing factories and sweatshops. On visits to these workplaces, Eleanor learned firsthand the misery of the working poor and developed a lifelong commitment to their needs. At the same time, she joined the **Junior League** and commenced work at the Rivington Street Settlement House, where she taught calisthenics and dancing and witnessed both the deprivation of the poor and the courage of slum dwellers who sought to improve their lot. Eleanor discovered that she preferred social work to debutante parties. More and more, she came to be recognized as a key member of a network of social reformers in New York City.

At the same time, however, Eleanor was secretly planning to marry her cousin Franklin Roosevelt, an event that would be followed by a 15-year hiatus in her public activities. Like his godfather (Eleanor's father), Franklin was "a gay cavalier," spontaneous, warm, and gregarious. But unlike Elliott, Franklin also possessed good sense and singleness of purpose. Eleanor saw in him the spark of life that she remembered from her father. After their engagement, she even sent to Franklin a letter signed "little Nell," her father's favorite name for her. Franklin, in turn, saw in Eleanor the discipline that would curb his own instincts toward excess.

After their marriage on March 17, 1905, the young Roosevelts settled in New York City while Franklin finished his law studies at Columbia. Franklin's mother Sara had warned Eleanor that

> **Dreyfus** French army officer of Jewish descent who was convicted of treason in 1894, sentenced to life imprisonment, and ultimately acquitted when the evidence against him was shown to have been forged.
>
> **Junior League** A voluntary organization in which members are engaged in volunteer charity or civic affairs.

she should not continue her work at the settlement house because she might bring home the diseases of the slum, but soon Eleanor was preoccupied with other concerns. Within a year, Anna was born (1906), then the next year James (1907), and two years later Franklin. Although Eleanor cherished her children, it was not a happy time. Sara dominated the household and imposed her will on almost all issues, including the raising of the children. As Eleanor later recalled, her mother-in-law "wanted . . . to hold onto Franklin and his children; she wanted them to grow up as she wished. As it turned out, Franklin's children were more my mother-in-law's children than they were mine." Nor was Sara's possessiveness limited to the children. At the family estate at Hyde Park, she was in total control. At dinner, Franklin sat at one end of the table, his mother at the other, and Eleanor in the middle. Before the fireplace there were two wing chairs, one for the mother, the other for the son. Eleanor was like an uninvited guest.

Fearing that she would hurt Franklin and lose his affection, Eleanor did not rebel. But she did experience a profound sense of inadequacy about her abilities as a wife and mother. Daughter Anna described her mother as unpredictable and inconsistent with the children, sweet one moment, critical and demanding the next. "Mother was always stiff, never relaxed enough to romp. . . . Mother loved all mankind, but she did not know how to let her children love her." Eleanor herself recognized the problem. "It did not come naturally to me to understand little children or to enjoy them," she later said. "Playing with children was difficult for me because play had not been an important part of my own childhood." Instead of comforting the children when they experienced pain, she urged upon them an attitude of stoicism and endurance, as if to say that expressing emotion was a sign of bad character. The death of her third child, Franklin, a few months after his birth only reinforced Eleanor's unhappiness and feeling of inadequacy. Three additional children were born in the next six years—Elliott in 1910, Franklin in 1914, and John in 1916. Eleanor was devoted to each, yet motherhood could not be fulfilling in a household ruled by a grandmother who referred to the children as "my children . . . your mother only bore you."

In the years between 1910 and the beginning of World War I, Eleanor Roosevelt's activities revolved more and more around Franklin's growing political career. Elected as the Democratic assemblyman from Dutchess County in 1910, he rapidly became a leader of insurgent **anti-Tammany forces** in Albany. In 1913 Franklin was appointed assistant secretary of the Navy, and Eleanor, in addition to managing a large household, became expert at hosting the multiple social events required of a subcabinet member, as well as moving the entire household at least twice each year—to Campobello in New Brunswick during the summer, then to Hyde Park and back to Washington. During these years, she fulfilled the many traditionally female social activities expected of her.

America's entry into World War I in 1917 provided the occasion for Eleanor to reassert the public side of

---

anti-Tammany forces Opponents of the often corrupt political machine of New York City.

her personality. As her biographer Joseph Lash has noted, "the war gave her a reason acceptable to her conscience to free herself of the social duties that she hated, to concentrate less on her household, and to plunge into work that fitted her aptitude." She rose at 5 A.M. to coordinate activities at the Union Station canteen for soldiers on their way to training camps, took charge of Red Cross activities, supervised the knitting rooms at the Navy department, and spoke at patriotic rallies. Her interest in social welfare led to her drive to improve conditions at St. Elizabeth's mental hospital, while her sensitivity to suffering came forth in the visits she paid to wounded soldiers. "[My son] always loved to see you come in," one mother wrote. "You always brought a ray of sunshine."

The war served as a transition for Eleanor's reemergence as a public personality during the 1920s. After Franklin's unsuccessful campaign for the vice presidency on James Cox's ticket in 1920, the Roosevelts returned to New York where Eleanor became active in the League of Women Voters. At the time of her marriage, she had opposed suffrage, thinking it inconsistent with women's proper role; now, as coordinator of the league's legislative program, she kept track of bills that came before the Albany legislature, drafted laws providing for equal representation for men and women, and worked with Esther Lape and Elizabeth Read on the league's lobbying activities. In 1921 she also joined the Women's Trade Union League—then viewed as "left-leaning"—and found friends there as well as political allies. In addition to working for programs such as the regulation of maximum hours and minimum wages for women, Eleanor helped raise funds for the WTUL headquarters in New York City. Her warm ties to first- and second-generation immigrants like Rose Schneiderman and Maud Swartz highlighted how far Eleanor had moved from the upperclass provincialism of her early years.

When Franklin was paralyzed by polio in 1922, Eleanor's public life expanded still further: She now became her husband's personal representative in the political arena. With the aid of Louis Howe, Franklin's political mentor and her own close friend, Eleanor first mobilized Dutchess County women, then moved on to the state Democratic party, organizing all but five counties by 1924. "Organization," she noted, "is something to which [the men] are always ready to take off their hats." No one did the job better. Leading a delegation to the Democratic convention in 1924, she fought (unsuccessfully) for equal pay legislation, the child labor amendment, and other planks endorsed by women reformers.

By 1928, Eleanor Roosevelt had clearly become a political leader in her own right. Once just a "political wife," she gradually extended that role and used it as a vehicle for asserting her own personality and agenda. In 1928, as head of the national women's campaign for the Democratic party, she made sure that the party appealed to independent voters, to minorities, and to women. She was also instrumental in securing the appointment of Frances Perkins as commissioner of industrial relations in New York after Franklin had been elected governor there. Dictating as many as one hundred letters a day, speaking to countless groups, acting as an advocate of social reform and women's issues, she had become a political personality of the first rank.

Eleanor Roosevelt's talent for combining partisan political activity with devotion to social welfare causes made her the center of an ever-growing female reform network. Her associates included Marion Dickerman and Nancy Cook, former suffragists and Democratic party loyalists; Mary (Molly) Dewson, a longtime research secretary of the National Consumers' League; and Mary Dreier of the Women's Trade Union League. She walked on picket lines with Rose Schneiderman, edited the *Women's Democratic News*, and advised the League of Women Voters on political tactics. Her political sophistication grew. "To many women, and I am one of them," she noted, "it is difficult to care enough [about an issue] to cause disagreement or unpleasant feelings, but I have come to the conclusion that this must be done for a time so we can prove our strength and demand respect for our wishes." By standing up for women in politics, ER provided a model for others to follow. In the process, she also earned the admiring, if grudging, respect of men who recognized a superb organizer when they saw one.

During the 1932 campaign, which led to Franklin's election to the presidency, Eleanor coordinated the activities of the Women's Division of the Democratic National Committee. Working with Mary (Molly) W. Dewson, she mobilized thousands of women precinct workers to carry the party's program to local voters; for example, the women distributed hundreds of thousands of "rainbow fliers," colorful sheets containing facts on the party's approach to various issues. After the election, Mary (Molly) W. Dewson took charge of the Women's Division, corresponding daily with Eleanor both about appointing women to office and securing action on issues that would appeal to minorities, women, and such professional groups as educators and social workers. The two friends were instrumental in bringing to Washington an unprecedented number of dynamic women activists. Ellen Woodward, Hilda Worthington Smith, and Florence Kerr all held executive offices in the Works Progress Administration, while Lorena Hickok acted as eyes and ears for WPA Director Harry Hopkins as she traveled across the country to observe the impact of the New Deal's relief program. Mary Anderson, director of the Women's Bureau, recalled that women government officials had formerly dined together in a small university club. "Now," she said, "there are so many of them that we need a hall."

Eleanor Roosevelt not only provided the impetus for appointing these women but also offered a forum for transmitting their views and concerns across the country. Soon after she entered the White House, she began a series of regular press conferences to which *only* women reporters were admitted, and where the first lady insisted on making "hard" news as well as providing social tidbits for the "women's page." She introduced such women as Mary McLeod Bethune and Hilda Worthington Smith to talk about their work with the New Deal. These sessions provided new status and prestige for the female press corps and they also underlined the importance of women's issues to the first lady. Her efforts helped create a community of women reporters and government workers. When the all-male Gridiron Club held its annual dinner to spoof the president and his male colleagues, the first lady initiated a Gridiron Widows' Club where the women in Washington could engage in their own satire.

Largely as a result of ER's activities, women achieved a strong voice in the New Deal. The proportion of women appointed as postmasters shot up from 17.6 percent in 1930 to 26 percent between 1932 and 1938. More important, the social welfare policies of the administration reflected a reform perspective that women like Ellen Woodward and Florence Kerr shared with men like Harry Hopkins and Aubrey Williams. When a particularly difficult issue involving women came up, the first lady would invite Mary (Molly) Dewson to the White House and seat her next to the president, where she could persuade him of her point of view. ER's own political role appears most clearly in her work on the reelection drive of 1936, when she coordinated the efforts of both men and women and used the "educational" approach developed by the Women's Division in 1932 as a major campaign weapon. More than 60,000 women precinct workers canvassed the electorate, handing out "rainbow fliers" as the party's principal literature. For the first time women received equal representation on the Democratic Platform Committee, an event described by the *New York Times* as "the biggest coup for women in years."

Eleanor Roosevelt's fear that she would have no active role as a presidential wife had been unfounded. She toured the country repeatedly, surveying conditions in the coal mines, visiting relief projects, and speaking out for the human rights of the disadvantaged. Through her newspaper column, "My Day," she entered the homes of millions. Her radio programs, her lectures, and her writings communicated to the country her deep compassion for those who suffered. At the White House, in turn, she acted as advocate of the poor and disenfranchised. "No one who ever saw Eleanor Roosevelt sit down facing her husband," Rexford Tugwell wrote, "and holding his eyes firmly, [and saying] to him 'Franklin, I think you should' . . . or, 'Franklin surely you will not' . . . will ever forget the experience. . . . It would be impossible to say how often and to what extent American governmental processes have been turned in a new direction because of her determination." She had become, in the words of columnist Raymond Clapper, a "cabinet minister without portfolio—the most influential woman of our times."

But if Eleanor had achieved an unparalleled measure of political influence, it was in place of, rather than because of, an intimate personal relationship with Franklin. In 1932 Eleanor described a perfect couple as one where two people did not even need to tell each other how they felt, but cared so much that a look and the sound of a voice would tell all. Probably at no time after their first few years together did Franklin and Eleanor achieve that degree of intimacy. Not only was Sara still a dominant presence, but Franklin had embarked on his own interests and enthusiasms, often different from Eleanor's. The differences in their temperaments became a permanent barrier that tormented their relationship. He loved to party; she held back and frowned on his willingness to "let go." . . .

During the years he was assistant secretary of the Navy, Franklin acted more frequently on his fun-loving instincts. "He deserved a good time," Eleanor's cousin Alice Roosevelt acidly noted, "he was married to Eleanor." A frequent companion on Franklin's pleasurable excursions was Lucy Mercer,

Eleanor's social secretary. Over time, the relationship between Lucy and Franklin became intimate, particularly during the summers when Eleanor was absent at Campobello. After Franklin was stricken with pneumonia in the fall of 1918, Eleanor discovered the letters between Franklin and Lucy describing their affair. Although Franklin refused Eleanor's offer of divorce, and Sara engineered an agreement for them to stay together if Franklin stopped seeing Lucy, their marriage would never again achieve the magical possibility of being "for life, for death," one where a word or look would communicate everything. In the wake of the Mercer affair, James Roosevelt later wrote, his parents "agreed to go on for the sake of appearances, the children and the future, but as business partners, not as husband and wife. . . . After that, father and mother had an armed truce that endured until the day he died."

In the eyes of some, Eleanor Roosevelt's emergence as a public figure seemed a direct consequence of profound anger at her husband's betrayal. Yet Eleanor's activism predated her discovery of the Mercer affair. World War I provided the occasion for expressing long-suppressed talents and energies that could be traced back to her early involvement with the National Consumers' League and the settlement house and were rooted, ultimately, in her relationship with Marie Souvestre. The Lucy Mercer affair, like Franklin's polio, reinforced the move toward public self-assertion, but did not itself cause a transformation.

What the Mercer affair did cause was a gradual reallocation of emotional energy away from Franklin and toward others. Through the polio episode and afterward, Eleanor remained devoted to Franklin's care and career. During the 1920s a warmth of tone and feeling continued in her letters to and about him. Yet gradually their lives became separate. Franklin went off on his houseboat in Florida or to Warm Springs, Georgia, with his secretary Missy LeHand. Eleanor stayed away, as if intentionally ceding to others any emotional involvement with her husband. . . .

Increasingly, Eleanor appeared to draw on her own family experience when offering advice to others. When a woman wrote her in 1930 about a marital problem, Eleanor replied: "All men who make successes of their work go through exactly the same kind of thing which you describe, and their wives, one way or another, have to adjust themselves. If it is possible to enter into his work in some way, that is the ideal solution. If not, they must develop something of their own and if possible make it such a success they will have something to interest their husbands." In a poignant piece entitled "On Being Forty-five," which she wrote for *Vogue* in 1930, Eleanor elaborated

> Life is a school in which we live all our days, and by middle-age, we should know that happiness . . . is never ours by right, but we earn it through giving of ourselves. You must have learned self-control. No matter how much you care, how much you may feel that if you knew certain things you could help, you must not ask questions or offer help, you must wait until the confidence is freely given, and you must learn to love without criticism. . . . If you have learned these things by 45, if you have ceased to consider yourself as in anyway important, but understand well the place that must be filled in the family, the role will be easy.

Above all, Eleanor concluded, the 45-year-old woman must

> keep an open and speculative mind . . . and [then] she will be ready to go out and try new adventures, create new work for others as well as herself, and strike deep roots in some community where her presence will make a difference in the lives of others. . . . One can no longer be interested in one's self, but one is thereby freed for greater interest in others and the lives of others become as engrossing as a fairy story of our childhood days.

Taking her own advice, Eleanor increasingly transferred the emotional focus of her life away from Franklin. The political network of women reformers of which she was the center provided intimate friendship as well as political camaraderie. During the 1920s she spent one night a week with Esther Lape and Elizabeth Read, reading books together and talking about common interests. She also became close friends with Women's Trade Union League women like Rose Schneiderman, inviting them to Hyde Park for picnics. Mary (Molly) Dewson became an especially close friend, and Eleanor wrote in 1932 that "the nicest thing about politics is lunching with you on Mondays." In a revealing comment made in 1927, Eleanor observed that "more than anything else, politics may serve to guard against the emptiness and loneliness that enter some women's lives after their children have grown."

Many of Eleanor's friendships during the 1920s and 1930s were with women who lived with other women. She had become particularly close to Nancy Cook and Marion Dickerman, who lived together in New York City. In 1926 she moved with them into Val-Kill, a newly constructed cottage at Hyde Park, an event that accurately symbolized her growing detachment from Franklin and his mother. Although she returned to the "Big House" at Hyde Park when Franklin was present, it was never without resentment and regret. She and Dickerman purchased Todhundter, a private school in New York, where Eleanor taught three days a week even after Franklin was elected governor of New York. The three women also jointly managed a furniture crafts factory at Val-Kill. The linen and towels at Val-Kill were monogrammed "EMN," and the three women together constituted as much a "family" for Eleanor during those years as Franklin and her children.

There were always "special" relationships, however, and during the 1930s these acquired an intensity and depth that were new to Eleanor's life. One of these was with her daughter Anna and Anna's new love, John Boettiger, a reporter whom Anna had met during the 1932 presidential campaign. Eleanor shared a special bond with her daughter, different from the one she had with her sons. Although the two women had had a difficult relationship during Anna's adolescence and early adulthood, caused partly by Anna's resentment of her mother's "distance" and preference for other, competing personalities like Louis Howe, the two women rekindled their affection during Anna's romance with John. Eleanor seemed to be reliving her early days with Franklin by investing enormous energy and love in Anna and wanting her daughter to find the kind of happiness she felt she had lost forever with her own husband. . . .

Perhaps Eleanor's most carefree relationship during these years occurred with Earl Miller, a former state trooper who had been Governor Al Smith's bodyguard and who subsequently provided the same service to the Roosevelt family. He encouraged Eleanor to drive her own car, take up horseback riding again, and develop confidence in her own personality. He was strikingly different from her other friends—tall, handsome, a "man's man." Although they talked about ideas and politics, the relationship was more that of "boon companions." With Earl Miller, Eleanor found a way to escape the pressures of her political and social status. She went frequently to his home for visits, had him stay at Val-Kill or her New York apartment, and accompanied him whenever possible for long walks and late-evening suppers. Although some of her friends disliked his tendency to "manhandle" Eleanor, all understood the importance of the relationship, and Marion Dickerman even said that "Eleanor played with the idea of marriage with Earl." Miller himself denied that the subject had ever been raised. "You don't sleep with someone you call Mrs. Roosevelt," he said. But without question, the two had an extraordinarily close relationship, and James Roosevelt later observed that his mother's tie to Miller "may have been the one real romance in [her] life outside of marriage. . . . She seemed to draw strength from him when he was by her side, and she came to rely on him. . . . Above all, he made her feel like she was a woman."

It was Eleanor Roosevelt's relationship with Lorena Hickok, however, that proved most intense during the 1930s and that subsequently has caused the most controversy. The two women became close during the 1932 campaign, when Hickok was covering the prospective first lady in her role as a reporter for the Associated Press. "That woman is unhappy about something," Hickok noted. Eleanor had not wanted Franklin to become president and feared that life in the White House would destroy her independence and cast her in an empty role as hostess and figurehead. As the two women talked about their respective lives, they developed an intimacy and affection so close that Hickok felt compelled to resign her position as a reporter because she no longer could write "objectively" about the Roosevelts.

Within a short time, the two women were exchanging daily letters and phone calls, the contents of which suggested that each woman was deeply infatuated with the other. "Hick darling," Eleanor wrote on March 6, "how good it was to hear your voice. It was so inadequate to try to tell you what it meant. Jimmy was near and I could not say, **je t'aime et je t'adore** as I long to do but always remember I am saying it and I go to sleep thinking of you and repeating our little saying." The next night, Eleanor was writing again. "All day," she said, "I thought of you, and another birthday I *will* be with you and yet tonight you sounded so far away and formal. Oh! I want to put my arms around you. I ache to hold you close. Your ring is a great comfort. I look at it and think she does love me, or I wouldn't be wearing it!" The two women plotted ways to be together, to steal a few

---

je t'aime et je t'adore I love and adore you.

days in the country, to bridge the gap of physical separation that so often stood between them.

> Only eight more days [Hickok wrote]. Twenty-four hours from now it will be only seven more—just a week! I've been trying today to bring back your face—to remember just *how* you looked. . . . Most clearly I remember your eyes, with the kind of teasing smile in them, and the feeling of that soft spot just northeast of the corner of your mouth against my lips. I wonder what we will do when we meet—what we will say when we meet. Well—I'm rather proud of us, aren't you? I think we have done rather well.

Over time, the relationship cooled somewhat under the pressure of Hickok's demands on Eleanor's time and Eleanor's reluctance to give herself totally to her new friend. Hickok was jealous of Eleanor's other friends, even her children. "Darling," Eleanor wrote, "the love one has for one's children is different, and not even Anna could be to me what you are." From Eleanor's point of view, the two were like a married couple whose relationship had to "flower." "Dearest," she wrote, "strong relationships have to grow deep roots. We are growing them now, partly because we are separated. The foliage and the flowers will come somehow, I'm sure of it. . . ." But an impatient Hickok was jealous of Eleanor's other friends and unable to limit the ardor of her affection.

In time, the situation became too much for Eleanor. In an attempt to explain herself to Hickok, she wrote: "I know you often have a feeling for me which for one reason or another I may not return in kind, but I feel I love you just the same and so often we entirely satisfy each other that I feel there is a fundamental basis on which our relationship stands." "Hick" had to understand, Eleanor wrote, "that I love other people the same way or differently, but each one has their place and one cannot compare them." But in the end, Eleanor could not explain herself sufficiently to satisfy Hickok and concluded that she had failed her friend. . . .

Many observers have speculated on the sexual significance of Roosevelt's relationship with Hickok. Hickok herself appears to have had numerous lesbian involvements, and the intimacy of her correspondence with Roosevelt has suggested to some that the love the two women shared must, inevitably, have had a sexual component as well. Many of Eleanor's other women friends lived together in what were called, at the time, "Boston marriages," and some of these associates undoubtedly found fulfillment through sexual relationships with other women. In all likelihood, Marie Souvestre was one of these. Nor has speculation about Eleanor's sexual life been limited to women. Her son James believed that she had an affair with Earl Miller, and later in her life some believed that she had sexual relationships with other men.

Although the accuracy of such speculation may ultimately be irrelevant, the preponderance of evidence suggests that Eleanor Roosevelt was unable to express her deep emotional needs in a sexual manner. Her friend Esther Lape has recalled the distaste and repugnance with which Eleanor responded to the issue of homosexuality when they discussed a French novel dealing with the topic in the 1920s. Eleanor herself told her daughter that sex was something to be "borne," not enjoyed. Eleanor's own reference to Hickok having "a feeling for me which for one reason or another I may not return in kind" may be an allusion to a sexual component of Hickok's desire that Roosevelt could not reciprocate. Earl Miller, and other men with whom Eleanor was rumored to have had a sexual relationship, have all denied—persuasively—the truth of such conjecture. Moreover, we must never forget that Eleanor was raised in a Victorian culture that attempted to repress the sexual drive. She tied her daughter's hands to the top bars of her crib in order to prevent her from masturbating. "The indication was clearly," Anna recalled, "that I had had a bad habit which had to be cured and about which one didn't talk!"

All of this conforms to Eleanor's own repeated declarations that she could never "let herself go" or express freely and spontaneously her full emotions. A person who had been raised to believe that self-control was all-important was unlikely to consider sexual expression of love—especially outside of marriage—a real option. She might sublimate her sexual drives and seek fulfillment of them through a series of deeply committed, even passionate, ties to a variety of people. But it is unlikely that she was ever able to fulfill these drives through actual sexual intimacy with those she cared most about. She was imprisoned in the cage of her culture, and her own bitter experiences through childhood and marriage reinforced her impulse toward self-control and repression. . . .

In this context, it is not surprising that Eleanor Roosevelt derived some of her emotional gratification from public life and by giving herself emotionally even to distant correspondents who somehow sensed her willingness to listen to their needs. Such expression of concern constituted the intersection of her public and private lives. Over and over again she answered pleas for help with either a sensitive letter, an admonition to a federal agency to take action, or even a personal check. When a policeman she knew suffered a paralyzing injury, she helped pay for his treatment, visited him repeatedly and, to encourage his rehabilitation, even asked him to help type a book she was composing about her father. The indigent wrote to her because they knew she cared, and in caring she found an outlet for her own powerful emotional needs.

The same compassion was manifested in Eleanor Roosevelt's advocacy of the oppressed. It was almost as though she could fully express her feelings only through externalizing them on political issues. Visiting the poverty-stricken countryside of West Virginia and hearing about the struggle of Appalachian farmers to reclaim land, she became a champion of the Arthurdale Resettlement Administration Project, devoting her lecture fees as well as influence to help the community regain autonomy. Poor textile workers in the South and garment union members in the North found her equally willing to embrace their cause. She invited their representatives to the White House and seated them next to the president at dinner so that he might hear of their plight. She and Franklin had worked out a tacit understanding that permitted her to bring the cause of the oppressed to his attention and allowed him, in turn, to use her activism as a means of building alliances with groups to his left. The game had clear rules: Franklin was the politician, Eleanor the agitator, and frequently he refused to act as she wished. But at least the dispossessed had someone advocating their interests.

Largely because of Eleanor Roosevelt, the issue of civil rights for black Americans received a hearing at the White House. Although Roosevelt, like most white Americans, grew up in an environment suffused with racist and nativist attitudes, by the time she reached the White House she was one of the few voices in the administration insisting that racial discrimination had no place in American life. As always, she led by example. At a 1939 Birmingham meeting inaugurating the Southern Conference on Human Welfare, she insisted on placing her chair so that it straddled both the black and white sides of the aisle, thereby confounding local authorities who insisted that segregation must prevail. Her civil-rights sympathies became most famous when in 1939 she resigned from the Daughters of the American Revolution after the organization denied Marian Anderson permission to perform at Constitution Hall. Instead, the great black artist sang to 75,000 people from the Lincoln Memorial—an idea moved toward reality owing to support from the first lady.

Roosevelt also acted as behind-the-scenes lobbyist for civil rights legislation. She had an extensive correspondence with Walter White, executive secretary of the NAACP [National Association for the Advancement of Colored People], who wished to secure her support for legislation defining lynching as a federal crime. She immediately accepted the role of intermediary and argued that the president should make such a bill an urgent national priority. She served as the primary advocate for the anti-lynching bill within the White House, and she and White became fast friends as they worked toward a common objective. When the NAACP sponsored a New York City exhibit of paintings and drawings dealing with lynching, Roosevelt agreed to be a patron and attended the showing along with her secretary. After White House Press Secretary Steve Early protested about White, she responded: "If I were colored, I think I should have about the same obsession [with lynching] that he has." To the president ER communicated her anger that "one could get nothing done." "I'm deeply troubled," she wrote, "by the whole situation, as it seems to me a terrible thing to stand by and let it continue and feel that one cannot speak out as to his feelings."

Although Eleanor lost out in her campaign for Franklin's strong endorsement of an anti-lynching bill, she continued to speak forthrightly for the cause of civil rights. In June 1939, in an address before the NAACP's annual meeting, she presented the organization's Spingarn Medal to Marian Anderson. A few weeks later, she formally joined the black protest organization.

As the threat of war increased, Roosevelt joined her black friends in arguing that America could not fight racism abroad yet tolerate it at home. Together with Walter White, Aubrey Williams, and others, she pressed the administration to act vigorously to eliminate discrimination in the Armed Forces and defense employment. Although civil-rights forces were not satisfied with the administration's actions, especially the enforcement proceedings of the Fair Employment Practices Commission created to forestall A. Philip Randolph's 1941 March on Washington, the positive changes that did occur arose from the alliance of the first lady and civil-rights forces. She would not give up the battle, nor would they, despite the national administration's evident reluctance to act.

Roosevelt brought the same fervor to her identification with young people. Fearing that democracy might lose a whole generation because of the Depression, she reached out to make contact with the young. Despite warnings from White House aides that her young friends could not be trusted, between 1936 and 1940 she became deeply involved in the activities of the American Student Union and the American Youth Congress, groups committed to a democratic socialist program of massively expanded social-welfare programs. She advanced their point of view in White House circles and invited them to meet the president so that they might have the opportunity to persuade him of their point of view. To those who criticized her naiveté, she responded: "I wonder if it does us much harm. There is nothing as harmful as the knowledge in our hearts that we are afraid to face any group of young people." She was later betrayed by some of her young allies, who insisted on following the Communist party line and denouncing the European war as imperialistic after the Nazi-Soviet Non-Aggression Pact in 1940. Nonetheless, Roosevelt continued to believe in the importance of remaining open to dissent. . . .

With the onset of World War II, the first lady persisted in her efforts for the disadvantaged. When it appeared that women would be left out of the planning and staffing of wartime operations, she insisted that administration officials consult women activists and incorporate roles for women as a major part of their planning. Over and over again, she intervened with war-production agencies as well as the military to advocate fairer treatment for black Americans. After it seemed that many New Deal social-welfare programs would be threatened by war, she acted to protect and preserve measures directed at the young, tenant farmers, and blacks. Increasingly, she devoted herself to the dream of international cooperation, perceiving, more than most, the revolution rising in Africa and Asia, and the dangers posed by the threat of postwar conflict.

When Jewish refugees seeking a haven from Nazi persecution received less than an enthusiastic response from the State Department, it was Eleanor Roosevelt who intervened repeatedly, trying to improve the situation. Parents, wives, or children separated from loved ones always found an ally when they sought help from the first lady. Nowhere was Roosevelt's concern more poignantly expressed than in her visits to wounded veterans in army hospitals overseas. When the world of hot dogs and baseball seemed millions of miles away, suddenly Eleanor Roosevelt would appear, spending time at each bedside, taking names and addresses to write letters to home, bringing the cherished message that someone cared.

Perhaps inevitably, given the stresses of the times, the worlds of Franklin and Eleanor became ever more separate in these years. As early as the 1936 reelection campaign, she confessed to feeling "indifferent" about Franklin's chances. "I realize more and more," she wrote Hickok, "that FDR's a great man, and he is nice, but as a person, I'm a stranger, and I don't want to be anything else!" As the war proceeded, Eleanor and Franklin more often became adversaries. He was less able to tolerate Eleanor's advocacy of unpopular causes, or her insistence on calling attention to areas of conflict within the administration. "She was invariably frank in her criticism of him," one of his speechwriters recalled, "[and] sometimes I thought she picked inappropriate times . . . perhaps a social and entertaining dinner." In search of release from the unbearable pressures of the war, Franklin came more and more to rely on the gaiety and laughter of his daughter Anna and other women companions. One of these was Lucy Mercer Rutherfurd, who began to come to White House dinners when Eleanor was away (with Anna's complicity) and who, unbeknownst to Eleanor, was with the president in Warm Springs when he was stricken by a cerebral hemorrhage and died in April 1945.

With great discipline and dignity, Eleanor bore both the pain of Franklin's death and the circumstances surrounding it. Her first concern was to carry forward the policies that she and Franklin had believed in and worked for despite their disagreements. Writing later about her relationship with Franklin, she said: "He might have been happier with a wife who had been completely uncritical. That I was never able to be and he had to find it in some other people. Nevertheless, I think that I sometimes acted as a spur, even though the spurring was not always wanted nor welcome. I was one of those who served his purposes." What she did not say was that Franklin had served her purposes as well. Though the two never retrieved the intimacy of their early relationship, they had created an unparalleled partnership to respond to the needs of a nation in crisis.

Not long after her husband's death, she told an inquiring reporter, "The story is over." But no one who cared so much for so many causes, and was so effective as a leader, could long remain on the sidelines. Twenty years earlier, ER had told her students at Todhunter: "Don't dry up by inaction, but go out and do new things. Learn new things and see new things with your own eyes." Her own instincts, as well as the demands of others, reaffirmed that advice. Over the next decade and a half, Roosevelt remained the most effective woman in American politics. She felt a responsibility not only to carry forward the politics of the New Deal, but also to further causes that frequently had gone beyond New Deal liberalism. In long letters to President Truman, she implored the administration to push forward with civil rights, maintain the Fair Employment Practices Committee, develop a foreign policy able to cope with the needs of other nations, and work toward a world system where atom bombs would cease to be negotiating chips in international relations.

Appropriately, President Truman nominated the former first lady to be one of America's delegates to the United Nations. At the UN, her name became synonymous with the effort to compose a declaration of human rights embodying standards that civilized humankind would accept as sacred and inalienable. For three years, she argued, debated, lobbied, and compromised until finally on December 10, 1948, the document she had fundamentally shaped passed the General Assembly. Delegates rose in a standing ovation to the woman who more than anyone else had come to symbolize the cause of human rights throughout the world. Even those in the United States who had most opposed her nomination to the delegation applauded her efforts. . . .

Although Roosevelt disagreed profoundly with some of the military aspects of U.S. foreign policy, she supported the broad outlines of America's response to Russia in the developing Cold War. In debates at the UN, she learned quickly that Soviet delegates could be hypocritical, and on more than one occasion she responded to Russian charges of injustice in America by proposing that each country submit to investigation of its social conditions—a suggestion the Soviets refused. When Henry Wallace and other liberal Americans formed the Progressive party in 1947 with a platform of accommodation toward the Soviet Union, Roosevelt demurred. Instead, she spearheaded the drive by other liberals to build Americans for Democratic Action, a group that espoused social reform at home and support of Truman's stance toward Russia.

Through public speeches and her newspaper column, as well as her position at the UN, Roosevelt remained a singular public figure, able to galvanize the attention of millions by her statements. She became one of the staunchest advocates of a Jewish nation in Israel, argued vigorously for civil rights, and spoke forcefully against the witch-hunts of McCarthyism, attacking General Dwight Eisenhower when he failed to defend his friend George Marshall from Senator McCarthy's smears. Although Eisenhower did not reappoint her to the United Nations when he became president in 1953, she continued to work tirelessly through the American Association for the United Nations to mobilize public support for international cooperation. She also gave unstintingly of her time to the election campaigns in 1952 and 1956 of her dear friend Adlai Stevenson, a man who brought to politics a wit and sophistication Roosevelt always admired. . . .

As she entered her eighth decade, Eleanor Roosevelt was applauded as the first lady of the world. Traveling to India, Japan, and the Soviet Union, she spoke for the best that was in America. Although she did not initially approve of John Kennedy and would have much preferred to see Adlai Stevenson nominated again, she lived to see the spirit of impatience and reform return to Washington. As if to prove that the fire of protest was still alive in herself, in 1962 Roosevelt sponsored hearings in Washington, D.C., where young civil-rights workers testified about the judicial and police harassment of black protestors in the South.

It was fitting that Eleanor Roosevelt's last major official office should be to chair President Kennedy's Commission on the Status of Women. More than anyone else of her generation, her life came to exemplify the political expertise and personal autonomy that were abiding themes of the first women's rights movement. Eleanor Roosevelt had not been a militant feminist. Like most social reformers, she publicly rejected the Equal Rights Amendment of the National Woman's Party until the early 1950s, believing that it would jeopardize protective labor legislation for women then on the statute books. Never an enthusiastic supporter of the ERA, neither she nor JFK's commission recommended the amendment. In addition, she accepted the popular argument during the Great Depression that, at least temporarily, some married women would have to leave the labor force in order to give the unemployed a better chance. At times, she also accepted male-oriented definitions of fulfillment. "You are successful," she wrote in a 1931 article, "when your husband feels that he has been a success and that life has been worthwhile."

But on the issue of women's equality, as in so many other areas, Eleanor Roosevelt most often affirmed the inalienable right of the human spirit to grow and seek fulfillment. Brought up amid anti-Semitic and antiblack attitudes, she had transcended her past to become one of the strongest champions of minority rights. Once opposed to suffrage, she grew to exemplify women's aspirations for a full life in politics. Throughout, she demonstrated a capacity for change grounded in a compassion for those who were victims.

There was, in fact, a direct line from Marie Souvestre's advocacy of intellectual independence to Eleanor Roosevelt's involvement in the settlement house, to her subsequent embrace of women's political activism in the 1920s and 1930s, and to her final role as leader of the Commission on the Status of Women. She had personified not only the right of women to act as equals with men in the political sphere, but the passion of social activists to ease pain, alleviate suffering, and affirm solidarity with the unequal and disenfranchised of the world.

On November 7, 1962, Eleanor Roosevelt died at home from a rare form of bone-marrow tuberculosis. Just 20 years earlier, she had written that all individuals must discover for themselves who they are and what they want from life. "You can never really live anyone else's life," she wrote, "not even your child's. The influence you exert is through your own life and what you've become yourself." Despite disappointment and tragedy, Eleanor Roosevelt had followed her own advice and because of it had affected the lives of millions. Although her daughter Anna concluded that Eleanor, throughout her life, suffered from depression, she had surely tried—and often succeeded—through her public advocacy of the oppressed and her private relationships with friends to find some measure of fulfillment and satisfaction.

"What other single human being," Adlai Stevenson asked at Eleanor Roosevelt's memorial service, "has touched and transformed the existence of so many? . . . She walked in the slums and ghettos of the world, not on a tour of inspection . . . but as one who could not feel contentment when others were hungry." Because of her life, millions of others experienced a new sense of possibility. It would be difficult to envision a more enduring or important legacy.

A Primary Perspective

AFRICAN AMERICANS AND THE NEW DEAL

Although African Americans overwhelmingly supported Franklin Roosevelt, his administration's record on racial issues was decidedly mixed. Blacks certainly benefited from New Deal policies, but never to the degree that they might have. Whereas some programs were segregated, others functioned in ways that harmed African Americans. Black leaders had no illusions about what was happening. They

Source: Obtained from papers of Eleanor Roosevelt (1986), published by LexisNexis, a division of Reed Elsevier, Inc. Letter, Roy Wilkins to Eleanor Roosevelt, May 20, 1935, reel 19, Papers of Eleanor Roosevelt, Microfilm Edition (1986).

also knew that, more so than most administration figures, Eleanor Roosevelt shared their concerns. In the letter below, Roy Wilkins informs ER that her attendance at the NAACP annual convention would do much to allay black misgivings about the New Deal.

Roy Wilkins to Eleanor Roosevelt, May 20, 1935

I want to add a personal note to the official invitation extended to you, and say what had better be left unsaid in our official letter.

There is great restlessness, doubt, and even some hostility among the colored people because of some things which the administration has, or has not, done. I think it extremely important that at this conference, which comes just prior to the election year, that the administration have a good will spokesman. . . .

There is hardly a phase of the New Deal program which has not brought some hardship and disillusionment to colored people. The N[ational] R[ecovery] A[dministration] benefited them little, if at all; from the P[ublic] W[orks] A[dministration] they secured a very small amount of employment; from the A[gricultural] A[djustment] A[ct] the black tenants and sharecroppers have thus far received little consideration; the F[ederal] E[mergency] R[elief] A[ct] has benefited them some, but there has been a great deal of discrimination in its administration. Now that the new $5 billion work relief program is announced, colored people are viewing their prospects with greater and greater cynicism.

It has not helped any of these matters that the anti-lynching bill, despite all the support it had, was not able to get a hearing and a vote in the Senate.

It is my feeling that it would be good strategy from the administration's standpoint, and good Americanism from the standpoint of our people, for some emissary to give a sincere word of reassurance to the colored population through their oldest civil rights organization. We hope that you will consent to be that ambassador.

QUESTIONS

1. In what ways did ER's later activities reflect the influence of Marie Souvestre? In what ways did World War I mark a period of transition in ER's life?
2. How did ER's life change after her husband was paralyzed by polio? How would you characterize her personal relationship with FDR? How did ER attempt to compensate for the emotional barrenness of the relationship?
3. What were ER's greatest strengths as a political activist? In what policy areas did ER have the greatest influence on her husband? Why was she increasingly at odds with FDR over political matters during World War II? In what ways would the New Deal have been different if she had not attempted to influence her husband's actions?

4. What does Roy Wilkins's letter tell us about ER's role as a political operative? Why did Wilkins communicate his misgivings to ER personally rather than include them in the NAACP's official letter? Would he have been better advised to make a public statement? What would W. E. B. Du Bois have done in this situation?

5. Do you see any similarities between ER and Margaret Sanger? In what ways did the two women differ? Do you think they would have worked well together?

6. What was ER's greatest contribution to the struggle for women's equality? Of the first ladies who have since followed her in the White House, which one do you think has been most similar to ER?

ADDITIONAL RESOURCES

When completed, Blanche Wiesen Cook's multivolume treatment should be the most authoritative biography of Roosevelt. To date, Cook has finished the first two volumes, *Eleanor Roosevelt, 1884–1933: A Life: Mysteries of the Heart* (1992) and *Eleanor Roosevelt, 1933–1938* (1999). Interested readers should also consult Joseph Lash's excellent two-volume work, *Eleanor and Franklin: The Story of Their Relationship Based on Eleanor Roosevelt's Private Papers* (1971) and *Eleanor: The Years Alone* (1972). Other studies include Lois Scharf, *Eleanor Roosevelt: First Lady of American Liberalism* (1987), Doris Kearns Goodwin, *No Ordinary Time: Franklin and Eleanor Roosevelt: The Home Front in World War II* (1994), and the collection of articles from which the essay above is taken: Joan Hoff-Wilson and Marjorie Lightman, eds., *Without Precedent: The Life and Career of Eleanor Roosevelt* (1984). For more on the New Deal women's network, see two works by Susan Ware: *Beyond Suffrage: Women in the New Deal* (1981) and *Partner and I: Molly Dewson, Feminism, and New Deal Politics* (1987). Ware has also written a fine survey of women in the Great Depression, *Holding Their Own: American Women in the 1930s* (1982).

Again the PBS program, *The American Experience*, delivers with a film entitled, "Eleanor Roosevelt." The film is 2 hours and 30 minutes long and includes rare footage from home movies and recollections by surviving friends and relatives.

Chapter 11

Huey Long

*B*y late 1934 Franklin Roosevelt's New Deal appeared to have lost its way. Despite the unprecedented wave of reform legislation that had marked Roosevelt's first 18 months in office, unemployment remained unacceptably high. Meanwhile, there was growing criticism of the president's policies. Some of it came from the Right—from groups like the Liberty League, an organization of conservative Democrats backed by some of the nation's wealthiest businesspeople and dedicated to laissez-faire principles of government. Because so many Americans were then living in poverty or worse, Roosevelt could safely ignore these attacks. In fact, he soon found that such criticism added to his popularity. After five years of depression, many people believed that corporate remedies would more likely worsen than cure the country's economic ills.

More worrisome was the growing restiveness on the Left. In Minnesota, the Farmer-Labor party had drafted a platform that was considerably more progressive than that of the national Democrats. And in California, Upton Sinclair had recently received nearly a million votes for governor in a campaign that proposed doing away with the profit system: by establishing land colonies that would produce food to feed the jobless and creating state-run factories to meet their remaining needs.

Because they were state-based, these developments did not pose an immediate threat to Roosevelt. Of much greater concern were three other move-ments: Dr. Francis E. Townsend's campaign for old-age security; Father Charles Coughlin's radio crusade for monetary reform; and Huey Long's Share Our Wealth initiative, which promised every American family a "household estate" of $5,000. All three movements had national followings, and if they had ever joined forces—as it appeared for a time they might—the Roosevelt administration would have been in for the fight of its life.

New Deal strategists particularly feared Huey P. Long. To Franklin Roosevelt, he was one of the two most dangerous men in America. (General Douglas McArthur was the other.) It is easy to understand why the president felt as he did. In addition to being one of the most talented politicians of the era, Long was also one of the most ruthless. During the 1930s, he established a virtual dictatorship in Louisiana, and by the time of his assassination in 1935, he had become a viable contender for the presidency. In the essay that follows, Glen Jeansonne explores the complex personality of this brilliant but flawed politician.

Huey P. Long

Glen Jeansonne

Huey P. Long is Louisiana's most controversial citizen. Some believe that he was Louisiana's greatest governor. Others claim that he was a thief and a Fascist dictator. Thousands of pages have been written to substantiate both sides of the question and more than fifty years after his death politicians, his-torians, and ordinary citizens continue to debate the issue. Former governor Sam Jones wrote: "More bunkum has been written about Huey Long and his place in history than any man in this region I know of." He has been hailed as the first Southerner since John C. Calhoun to have an original idea and con-demned as a man obsessed with personal power. John Kingston Fineran, who entitled his book about Long *The Career of a Tinpot Napoleon*, terms him, "that most extraordinary **mountebank,** that most mendacious liar, that eminent blackguard and distinguished sneak-thief, Huey P. Long." On the other hand, the late Professor T. Harry Williams argues that "the politician who wishes to do good may have to do some evil to achieve his goal."

No one questions Long's bril-liance. James A. Farley believed Long

> **mountebank** A boastful and false pretender.

Source: "Huey P. Long: A Political Contradiction" by Glen Jeansonne. *Louisiana History* 31 (Winter 1990): 373, 378–385. Reprinted with permission.

had the best mind he had ever known, but had squandered it. Long himself quipped, "There may be smarter men than me, but they ain't in Louisiana." Perhaps the writer put it best who said of Long: "He did more good and more evil than any other man in the history of his state." This statement captures the paradox of Huey Long and the complexity of Louisiana. . . .

There were reform governors both before and after Huey Long. William W. Heard, Newton C. Blanchard, J. Y. Sanders, and Luther Hall all initiated limited reforms. John M. Parker, elected in 1920, had a reform program that rivals Long's except that he would not resort to deficit financing, which has proven in our own time a dubious device at best. Sam Jones, Robert Kennon, Earl Long, John J. McKeithan, and even Edwin Edwards are all governors who followed Long and have substantial claims to reforms. In reality Long's predecessors and successors did more than is generally recognized.

How then, did Huey Long differ? Why does he seem to tower over other Louisiana politicians? For one thing, he had precisely what almost all of them lacked: charisma. His program differed from theirs not so much in substance as in style, oratory, and notoriety. No one can deny that Long knew how to attract and hold attention. A child prodigy, he grew up in a middle-class family in Winnfield. He married at nineteen and was a lawyer at twenty-one, a public official at twenty-five, governor at thirty-five. He was dead at forty-two. No one else packed so much drama into so brief a political career.

Furthermore, Long was ambitious, aggressive, and uninhibited. On the night of his election as governor, in the midst of celebrating, he announced he would someday be president. He relished power. He enjoyed humiliating enemies. He excelled at oratory. And he recruited lieutenants who deferred to his judgement and never questioned his decisions. He was an overpowering personality.

As governor, Long set out to bring his version of a Great Society to Louisiana. When he tried to tax heavily the powerful Standard Oil Company, it proved a rallying issue to his opponents. They voted to impeach him for violation of almost every impeachable offense cited in Louisiana's constitution. He escaped impeachment by a technicality, but it made him bitter. He vowed that he would no longer say "please" but would "dynamite" opponents out of his path.

Long fulfilled enough of his promises to make credible his claim to be a champion of the poor. He provided free schoolbooks, expanded adult education, and made Louisiana State University a showcase of his administration. But in both public works and education he seemed more concerned with publicity than with substance. His activities at LSU centered on the football team and the band more than on mundane academics. He made the band the largest in the nation. In fact, during one year the university expended more money on the band than on the law school and graduate school combined.

Long hired the best football coaches money could buy and then told them how to run the team, although he had never played football himself. He housed gifted players in the Governor's Mansion, where he fattened them up on milkshakes and sirloin steaks. He bought an airplane to use on recruiting trips and offered state jobs to athletes and their families. He even appointed a star halfback to the state legislature. When editors of the LSU student newspaper condemned the act, he had them expelled. After LSU lost one game 7-6 he had a follower introduce a bill outlawing the point after touchdown.

It is not that Long did not do some good, but that his priorities were misplaced. He built roads, which were needed, but left the problem of paying for them to future governors. His attention to LSU was salutary; the state needed a first-class university. But LSU was not the only college in the state and appropriations for other colleges declined. Salaries for elementary and secondary teachers also declined, and blacks were paid much less than whites. True, the country was in the midst of the Great Depression. But if Long could find money for roads, for LSU, and for a new capitol, why could he not find money for teachers, for other colleges, and for stipends for the unemployed?

The reason Long was so interested in making improvements that showed was that he intended to use them as a stepping-stone to higher offices. In 1930, two years before his term as governor ended, he ran for the United States Senate. He defeated the incumbent but did not take his seat until his term as governor expired because he distrusted his lieutenant governor. After 1932 he continued to control Louisiana through an amiable puppet, O. K. Allen, a Winnfield friend whom he rewarded with the governorship for having financed his first political campaign. But Huey, not Allen ran the state. When Long came down from Washington to the capitol in Baton Rouge, he took over Allen's office. Governor Allen moved out into the receptionist's office and she moved out into the hall. Someone joked that Allen was so accustomed to following Huey's orders that once when a leaf flew in his window he instinctively signed it, assuming that it was one of Long's bills.

Long was popular with his Louisiana constituents, but he was not a popular senator in Washington. He delivered long speeches, but introduced few bills. He had few personal friends in the Senate.

In 1932 Huey supported Franklin Roosevelt for president. However, soon after the inauguration, they broke. Many people thought that Roosevelt's bevy of bills to mitigate the Depression during his first hundred days in office, was too much, too soon. Long thought it was too little, too late, and he had an alternative. His alternative to the New Deal was something he called the Share Our Wealth plan.

Long attributed the Depression to an unequal distribution of wealth. He promised, if his plan were enacted, to give to every American family a home, a car, a radio, a guaranteed job and income, and a free college education for their children. He would finance this simply by confiscating the fortunes of millionaires. No one but millionaires would pay any taxes at all.

The plan was a politician's dream and its appeal to the public was astounding. Long created a club he called the Share Our Wealth Society for people who supported his scheme. Within a month of its founding in 1934 it had 200,000 members; within a year, 3 million. By the early months of 1935 there were 7.5 million. Huey's mail increased enormously. He received more mail than the president and as much as all the other senators combined. Mail was delivered to the Senate in two trucks: one for Huey and one for all the other senators. Long hired a former Shreveport preacher named Gerald L. K. Smith to travel around the country signing up members for the Share Our Wealth Society.

Long frankly admitted that he wanted to be the next president. He said he could defeat Franklin Roosevelt because he could out-promise him. Huey even wrote a book entitled *My First Days in the White House*. In it he talked about millionaires surrendering their fortunes to President Long without a whimper. John D. Rockefeller signed away his entire fortune. Andrew Mellon praised Long for relieving him of a fortune he considered a burden.

It seemed unlikely that the Democratic party would deny the presidential nomination to President Roosevelt in 1936; therefore Long began to think about a third party. By mid-1935 Long had discussed a third party with such potential allies as Father Charles E. Coughlin, the influential radio priest, and Georgia governor Eugene Talmadge. He sent Gerald Smith to talk with Republican leaders. Smith reported that the Republicans would help finance Long's candidacy because he would take votes away from Roosevelt, the likely Democratic nominee.

Long thought he could take enough votes away from the Democrats to cause a Republican victory in 1936. But he had selfish reasons of his own for desiring a Republican victory. He thought the Republicans would be thoroughly ineffectual in office and that the Depression would worsen. By 1940 the public would be tired of them. This would set the stage for Huey. He would threaten the Democrats with another third-party candidacy and, likely, another Republican victory. To prevent that they would offer Huey the nomination. He would accept, and proceed to defeat the Republicans. By 1940 Huey Long would be president.

The plan, of course, had flaws. For one thing, Franklin Roosevelt was a popular president, a charismatic speaker, and a manipulator of no mean ability. It was not clear that any Republican would defeat him, even with Long in the race. For another, some doubted the sincerity of Long's advocacy of sharing the wealth. For example, they said, Long did not practice in Louisiana what he preached in Washington. Louisiana did not have a system of sharing the wealth; it did not even have an income tax until 1934. When asked why he did not push for ratification by his compliant Louisiana legislature of a constitutional amendment to limit child labor, Long remarked that picking cotton was fun for kids. When questioned by labor leaders about the absence of a minimum wage law in Louisiana, Long bristled. He told them that the minimum wage on state projects was as low as he could get men to work, adding that they should be happy to get work at any salary.

Furthermore, Long's Share Our Wealth program was transparently impractical and was labelled so by every qualified economist who examined it. There was not enough money to go around. Confiscating millionaire fortunes would have yielded only one dollar and fifty cents for every poor family. There were not many millionaires in the Depression year, 1935. Furthermore, there would be no incentives for industrialists to continue production, and enforcement would require a police state. Long gave no explanation as to how he could liquidate tangible wealth such as factories, ships, and mines into a form that could be distributed equally. How could the Ford Motor Company's assets be converted to provide homes, radios, and college educations? A family might find itself the owner of two gears from an assembly line, a car door, a two-ton cornerstone from an office building, or the mast of a millionaire's yacht. The only things that could be distributed were profits, and these represented only a small fraction of the total value of any great fortune. And how would Long get his plan enacted by a Congress that considered it ridiculous? He had introduced it several times and it never got more than fourteen votes from among the ninety-six senators.

Long's Share Our Wealth plan, however, cannot be judged solely upon its feasibility and it cannot be understood in economic terms alone. It is comprehensible only if we understand that Long was a consummate politician and an ambitious individual. The economic feasibility of the plan was not important to Long. What was important was the degree to which it could bring him to national power.

The plan had undeniable appeal to people who were standing in line for bread and jobs, shivering on park benches, or being turned away from factories. His plan exploited the discontent of his constituents. Any proposal for change seemed worth a chance to them. Moreover, it appealed to the sense of justice for the underdog. Long wanted to turn the world upside down: to exchange the places of the ins and outs, the rich and poor, the powerful and powerless.

But the problems of the nation did not arise solely from materialistic causes. Long overlooked entirely problems arising from relationships between persons of different skin pigments, educational attainments, religious views, and cultural traditions. Moral questions were telescoped into a single issue; moral questions apart from material distribution were ignored.

Real economic levelling requires meticulous planning as well as vivid imagination. But it is to the imaginations and fantasies of the American people in the Great Depression that Long appealed. That is why he could practice the politics of hope, because in a hopeless situation any change seems a change for the better. Long had keen insights into the needs of his constituents. He knew their fears, their aspirations, and their jealousy of the wealthy. Hope was in short supply, and Long provided it. No logical argument could refute the simple desires of millions of hungry, discouraged Americans. Long could promise more than Roosevelt. Maybe Long was better than Roosevelt.

Long never got the chance to test his theories or to demonstrate his vote-getting ability in the nation at large. In the fall of 1935, a little over a year before the election, Long was assassinated in Baton Rouge. He was killed by a lone gunman, Dr. Carl Austin Weiss. The coroner found one bullet in Huey and sixty-one bullet holes in Dr. Weiss, whose body was shredded by bullets from Long's bodyguards.

But what if Huey Long had lived? Would the world have been a better place? Was it better because he lived? Was Louisiana? In some respects it was. Louisiana needed the roads and bridges he built; it even needed the new state capitol and the governor's mansion he built. It needed the free schoolbooks. If it also got a bigger band and better football team at LSU, and a politicized educational system, perhaps that was a part of the bargain. He gave Louisiana something to be proud of even if he gave it much to be ashamed of.

His soaring oratory was not entirely misplaced; his simple eloquence sometimes rang true. The words that mark his grave on the grounds of the capitol he built are his own:

> My voice will be the same as it has been. Patronage will not change it. It cannot be changed while people suffer. The only way it can be changed is to make the lives of these people decent and respectable. No one will ever hear political opposition out of me when that is done.

Gerald Smith lamented that Long did not live to complete his work. Smith said in his funeral oration over Long's grave:

> This tragedy fires the souls of us who adored him. . . . He has been the wounded victim of the green goddess; to use the figure, he was the Stradivarius whose notes rose in competition with jealous drums, envious tomtoms. He was the unfinished symphony.

On the other hand, there were some who believed Long got exactly what he deserved. Those who live by the sword die by the sword. Long's gravesite on the capitol grounds was for many years protected by an armed guard. Most people thought the guard was hired to keep vandals out, but some wisecracked that it was to keep Huey in. . . .

Exactly what type of person was Huey Long? That is no easier to answer than someone who asks: What type of state is Louisiana? Long had within his own personality the complexity of the state he represented; he practiced the politics of hope and the politics of hate. He was cheerful, but moody; generous, yet vindictive; ambitious, but neurotic; verbally aggressive, but physically cowardly. He was superficially assertive, yet pathetically wanted to be liked and accepted. He was Louisiana in microcosm.

A Primary Perspective

ADDRESS BY FATHER CHARLES E. COUGHLIN, 1936

After Huey Long's assassination in 1935, Father Charles E. Coughlin replaced the Louisiana "Kingfish" as the main threat from the Left. Known as the "Radio Priest," Coughlin was the Canadian-born pastor of a Roman Catholic parish in

Source: From Charles E. Coughlin, "A Third Party," *Vital Speeches of the Day,* 2 (July 1, 1936), pp. 614–15. Reprinted by permission of Vital Speeches of the Day.

Royal Oak, Michigan, whose radio sermons reached an estimated 30 to 40 million people by the mid-1930s, and whose small army of secretaries and clerks answered about 80,000 letters each week. Although Coughlin's message initially drew on Catholic social teachings, as the Depression deepened it became increasingly radical; and as it did, his relations with Roosevelt soured. By late 1934 he was charging that the administration was "wedded basically to the philosophy of the money changers." The following excerpt is from a 1936 speech condemning New Deal policy in which Coughlin announced the creation of a Union party to challenge Roosevelt—a party that Huey Long may well have headed had he lived.

A Third Party

March 4, 1933! I shall never forget the inaugural address, which seemed to re-echo the very words employed by Christ Himself as He actually drove the money changers from the temple.

The thrill that was mine was yours. Through dim clouds of the Depression this man Roosevelt was, as it were, a new savior of the people!

Oh, just a little longer shall there be needless poverty! Just another year shall there be naked backs! Just another moment shall there be thoughts of revolution! Never again will the chains of economic poverty bite into the hearts of simple folks, as they did in the past days of the Old Deal!

Such were our hopes in the springtime of 1933.

My friends, what have we witnessed as the finger of time turned the pages of the calendar? 1933 and the National Recovery Act which multiplied profits for the monopolists; and 1934 and the A[gricultural] A[djustment] A[ct] which raised the price of foodstuffs by throwing back God's best gifts into His face; 1935 and the Banking Act which rewarded the exploiters of the poor, the Federal Reserve bankers and their associates, by handing over to them the temple from which they were to have been cast! . . .

Neither Old Dealer nor New Dealer, it appears, has courage to assail the international bankers, the Federal Reserve bankers. In common, both the leaders of the Republicans and the Democrats uphold the old money philosophy. Today in America there is only one political party—the banker's party. In common, both old parties are determined to sham battle their way through this November election with the hope that millions of American citizens will be driven into the no-man's land of financial bondage.

My friends, there is a way out, a way to freedom! There is an escape from the dole standard of Roosevelt, the gold standard of Landon. No longer need you be targets in no-man's land for the financial crossfire of the sham-battlers!

Six hours ago the birth of "the Union party" was officially announced to the newspapers of the nation, thereby confirming information which hitherto was mine officially. The new candidate for president, together with his sponsors, formally requested my support, as they handed to me his platform. I have studied it carefully. I find that it is in harmony substantially with the principles of social justice.

QUESTIONS

1. To what extent was Long, as governor of Louisiana, motivated by a genuine desire to improve the lives of common people in the state? Given the extent of political corruption in state government during the Long era, why was he such a popular political figure in Louisiana? Do you think his programs had a positive or negative effect on the state?
2. How would you characterize Long's governing style as chief executive of Louisiana? In what ways did Long's personality prevent him from becoming an effective U.S. senator? In answering the question, relate Jeansonne's observations on Long's character and personal idiosyncrasies to what you know about how the Senate functions.
3. What does the popularity of Long's Share Our Wealth plan reveal about American politics in the mid-1930s? Do you think Long gave much thought to the economic feasibility of the plan? What does the proposal tell us about Long and his approach to politics?
4. Do you agree with Roosevelt's remark that Long was one of the most dangerous men in America? Give reasons for your answer.
5. How do you think Roosevelt reacted to Father Coughlin's speech on the New Deal? Do you think Coughlin and Long would have been able to work together as leaders of the same political party?
6. Was Long's presidential plan realistic? If he had managed to become president, what kind of a chief executive do you think he would have been? To repeat a question of Jeansonne's, "Would the world have been a better place" if Long had lived?

 ## ADDITIONAL RESOURCES

The most recent biographies of Long are William Ivy Hair, *The Kingfish and His Realm: The Life and Times of Huey Long* (1991), and Glen Jeansonne, *Messiah of the Masses: Huey P. Long and the Great Depression* (1997). For an immensely readable earlier treatment, see T. Harry Williams, *Huey Long* (1969). Long's place in Depression-era politics is ably examined in Alan Brinkley, *Voices of Protest: Huey Long, Father Coughlin and the Great Depression* (1982). For more on Louisiana politics during the Long era, see Allen P. Sindler, *Huey Long's Louisiana: State Politics, 1920–1952* (1956). The most comprehensive survey of the South during the period is George Brown Tindall, *The Emergence of the New South, 1913–1945* (1967). Major studies of the New Deal and Great Depression include Robert S. McElvaine, *The Great Depression: America, 1929–1941* (1984);

Anthony Badger, *The New Deal: The Depression Years, 1933–1940* (1989); David M. Kennedy, *Freedom from Fear: The American People in Depression and War, 1929–1945* (1999); and William E. Leuchtenberg's still valuable older work, *Franklin D. Roosevelt and the New Deal, 1932–1940* (1963).

All the King's Men adapted to film Robert Penn Warren's novel of the same name about a charismatic Southern politician, Willie Stark, a character inspired by the real-life Huey Long. Filmmaker Ken Burns provides a look at one of the fascinating political characters of the twentieth century in "Huey Long," which he made for the *American Experience* series on PBS.

Chapter 12

George Patton

On December 7, 1941, Japanese planes attacked the U.S. naval base at Pearl Harbor. Although the assault caught American forces in Hawaii by surprise, Washington responded immediately and in the week that followed events moved quickly both there and in other parts of the world. On December 8, the United States and Britain declared war on Japan. Three days later, Hitler recognized his obligations to the Japanese under the Tripartite Pact and declared war on the United States. Meanwhile, Japanese armies invaded Thailand, Malaysia, the Philippines, and Java. The Second World War had truly become a global conflict.

American troops contributed much to the fighting of that war, in Europe as well as the Pacific. In fact, U.S. policymakers had decided months earlier that if

the nation did go to war, its first aim would be to defeat Hitler. They had several reasons for doing so. One was geographical: Access to the Atlantic made Germany a more direct threat to the Western Hemisphere, particularly if it knocked Britain out of the war. American planners further felt that Germany was more likely than Japan to achieve some revolutionary breakthrough in military technology. Lastly, Great Britain and Russia had already made a full commitment to stopping the Axis powers (Germany, Italy, and Japan). By contrast, Chinese resistance to Japan was considerably less active; and given

China's internal political problems, no informed observer looked for much improvement anytime soon.

In its initial deployment of U.S. forces, Washington followed Britain's lead and adopted a Mediterranean strategy. This entailed pushing the Axis armies out of North Africa, invading Sicily, and moving up the boot of Italy. In June 1944, American and British armies finally crossed the English Channel and stormed the beaches of Normandy. Although this was a chancy operation—in that the Germans knew an invasion was coming—the Allies held on and established a second front in Europe. Hitler's days were now numbered. He did launch a major counteroffensive that winter, but it proved to be too little, too late. In the Battle of the Bulge, Allied forces not only managed to maintain several key positions; they afterward regrouped, closed the gap in their lines, and on January 3, 1945, retook the offensive. Although several months of hard fighting lay ahead, the war in Europe was effectively over.

From the invasion of North Africa in November 1942 to the Battle of the Bulge and beyond, George Patton seldom ventured far from the action. A strong proponent of mobility, Patton had, in Dwight Eisenhower's words, "more 'drive' on the battlefield than any other man I know." At the same time, Patton's arbitrary actions and undiplomatic assertions made him one of the most controversial generals of the war. In the essay that follows, Stephen E. Ambrose and Judith D. Ambrose analyze Patton's complex personality and sometimes contradictory behavior, examine his relations with Eisenhower, and assess his strengths and weaknesses as a military leader.

George Patton

Stephen E. Ambrose and Judith D. Ambrose

Shortly after the end of World War II elements of the U.S. Seventh Army were in a little village in Czechoslovakia west of Prague. It was a hot spring day, and the men and officers were concerned with the usual problems of occupation duty, enlivened only by the possibility of conflict with the nearby Russians. Suddenly the quiet of the main street gave way to a blast of noise.

Source: This article is reproduced from the July 1966 issue of *American History Illustrated* with the permission of PRIMEDIA (History Group), copyright © American History Illustrated.

Armored cars, jeeps, and wagons began to pour into the village. Horns blared and flags waved from all the cars. There was even a soldier blowing a trumpet. A cloud of dust rose everywhere. As it settled, the Seventh Army men saw sitting in a jeep in the middle of the convoy a general of the United States Army, wearing high, brightly polished boots, two ivory-handled revolvers, and a huge grin. George Patton had arrived.

The members of the Seventh Army were not happy with this development. In the first place, Patton usually meant trouble. More important, they did not like him. His Third Army had stolen the headlines since the preceding August; Patton's men felt they were something special, and they let everyone know it. As Patton bounded out of his jeep he was greeted with formal handshakes and cold stares.

Patton just smiled and asked the local commander to call his men together for a review in the village square. When they were all assembled, he went up on a bandstand, looked them over, and said, "So this is the Seventh Army! By God, I've heard a lot about you men. I'm sorry as hell I didn't have a chance to lead you in battle." Patton had a notorious reputation for saying what he thought and the men accepted his flattery as sincerely as he had apparently given it. When he stepped down from the stand, they cheered madly.

That night the officers arranged a banquet. The mayor and other local officials and dignitaries attended. Patton spent the evening talking to the Czechs in French about opera, central European history and geography, and philosophy. As the general left, his caravan again stirring up a cloud of dust, an English-speaking Czech turned to one of the Seventh Army officers and said, "But, monsieur, you did not tell us he was a man of culture."

They had just seen one aspect of the most complicated man of World War II. George Patton was many things, not only to others but to himself. He was a consummate actor always conscious of the role he was playing. Blond and brawny, he carried himself with dignity and poise, usually dressed to the hilt. He saw people as individuals and reacted accordingly. When he wanted to pull out the stops and impress a bunch of tough GIs, he would curse with some of the foulest language ever heard in any army. When he wanted to stir his staff to greater activity he would throw fits of rage that outdid **Caligula.** Then, as the chastised staff left his office, he would turn to his orderly, smile, and say softly, "That ought to get them going." If he were among intellectuals, he would draw on his amazing knowledge of history to impress them. But always, in these and other situations, he was conscious of playing a role, and he kept the real man submerged.

Patton was a man of diverse and often contradictory moods. He was ambivalent in his attitude toward the Germans, extending them grudging respect for their technical abilities while being utterly contemptuous of their strategical mistakes and horrified at their criminal actions. When the Third Army liberated a Nazi concentration camp Patton called the

Caligula Emperor of Rome whose ruthlessness, extravagance, and megalomania led to his assassination.

supreme commander, Dwight D. Eisenhower, and insisted that he bring a
touring congressional delegation, plus all the attached reporters, to the camp
immediately. Patton did not want anyone saying after this war that the
German atrocities were all propaganda. As the group toured the camp Patton
had to excuse himself and go to a bathroom where he was violently ill. Yet a
couple of months later he could tell reporters that "this Nazi business" was
just like the Republicans and Democrats back home.

He was also capable of making contradictory statements and sticking with
them in the face of all logic. During the summer campaign in Sicily in 1943,
Patton paid a visit to some combat-zone hospitals. He saw a great many seriously wounded men and tried to say a kind word to each of them. As he was
about to leave the tent he saw a boy in his mid-twenties sitting on a box near
the dressing station. There was nothing obviously wrong with the soldier,
Private Charles H. Kuhl, so Patton went over and asked what was the matter. Kuhl gave Patton a fearful look, then muttered, "I guess I can't take it."

Patton completely lost his temper, slapped Kuhl, kicked him in the pants,
swore at him, called him a loathsome coward, and told the doctor, "Don't
admit this sonuvabitch. I don't want yellow-bellied bastards like him hiding
in their lousy cowardice around here, stinking up this place of honor." Turning again to Kuhl, he shrieked, "You gutless bastard, you're going back to the
front, *at once!*"

Later that day, August 10, 1943, Patton visited another hospital and
repeated the scene, this time knocking the patient's helmet off. When the shell-
shocked soldier told Patton it was his nerves and began to sob, the general
screamed at him, "Your nerves, hell, you are just a goddamn coward, you
yellow son of a bitch." He again slapped the man, shouting, "Shut up that
goddamned crying," and again ordered the doctors not to admit the soldier.
On the same day, incidentally, Patton had had a long argument with one division commander, another with Omar Bradley, and relieved General Terry
Allen of 1st Division. The war in Sicily was not going well at the time.

The story of the slapping, despite Eisenhower's best efforts, leaked, and
Patton had a lot of explaining to do. His cause was weak because it was
learned that Kuhl suffered from chronic diarrhea, had a temperature of 102.2°,
and had malaria. The second soldier also had a high fever. Patton gave out
two separate and distinct explanations, sometimes simultaneously. The first
was that he was so upset by seeing apparently healthy men in a hospital with
the seriously wounded that he simply lost his temper. He did not believe there
was such a thing as shell-shock; it was simply cowardice. The second was that
he had had a friend in World War I who suffered from shell-shock and eventually committed suicide. Patton maintained that if someone had slapped his
friend at the beginning, he would have been all right. In short, Patton felt he
was playing psychiatrist and that his treatment would cure the soldiers. He
stuck with both stories until the day he died.

In contrast to the slapping incidents, but illuminating the emotional nature
of Patton, there is the story of another visit he made to a hospital shortly after
VE-Day. During the war his daughter had gone to Walter Reed Hospital in

Washington and asked to be assigned as a nurse's aide in the multiple amputee ward. The superintendent of nurses agreed, not knowing who she was. When her father came to Washington for a short visit, Ruth Ellen asked him to visit her ward. Patton was greatly affected. He tried to make a little speech to the soldier patients but broke down and wept. Finally he gained control of himself and said, "If I had been a better general you wouldn't be here."

There were contradictions in his relationships with his friends, too, most notably with Dwight Eisenhower. Patton and Eisenhower knew each other well, since both had been in armor in World War I. Eisenhower looked up to Patton, who was his senior both in years and in combat experience, and shortly before America entered World War II told Patton he would like to fight under him, perhaps as commander of a regimental combat team. When Eisenhower began his climb Patton adjusted to it easily and was delighted to have a role to play under his old friend in the November 1942 invasion of North Africa. For his part Eisenhower, well aware of Patton's reputation as a troublemaker and generally embarrassing person to have around, believed that the U.S. Army had available no finer leader of troops in battle and was willing to put up with almost anything to keep Patton in the field.

From the first Patton put Eisenhower's faith to the test. In North Africa he hobnobbed with **Vichy** Frenchmen and various sultans. In Sicily he slapped soldiers. He frequently muttered threats about resigning and going home to tell the "real truth" unless he was given this or that assignment. Withal, Eisenhower stuck with him, absorbing a volume of criticism that Patton never knew about. And for his part Patton too delivered, as in his lightning campaign through Sicily, where he ran the Germans and Italians ragged and showed his heels to Bernard Montgomery and the British Eighth Army.

When Franklin Roosevelt designated Eisenhower as the supreme commander for operation OVERLORD, the invasion of France, Chief of Staff George Marshall gave Eisenhower a free hand in picking his subordinates. Eisenhower's first choice was Omar Bradley. His second was George Patton. At the time, December of 1943, Patton was under tremendous criticism in the United States for the slapping incidents, and Eisenhower along with him for shielding him. The easy thing would have been to pick Mark Clark. But Eisenhower wanted Patton and got him. He told Patton he would have to behave, and Patton was grateful for the opportunity—but resentful because of the lecture. Later, in England training for the invasion, Patton made some ill-considered remarks in a public gathering about how England, the United States, and Russia would have to run the world after the war. Again Eisenhower lectured him but refused to consider dropping him. Again Patton was both grateful and resentful.

In preparing the Third Army for the invasion Patton used many personal touches. Most of his men had not yet participated in combat and he had a favorite story he liked to tell them. Later, like most Patton stories, it became famous. "There is a hill in Sicily," he said, "where several score of soldiers lay down to sleep under

---

Vichy The capital of unoccupied France during the Second World War.

the olive trees. They had had a lot of fighting during the day, and were tired and sleepy. They put out a few sentries. But the sentries, too, went to sleep. The corporals didn't make the rounds to see that the sentries were awake, and the sergeants didn't check on the corporals. No officer inspected the sentries, either. Late that night the enemy crept into that olive grove and silently cut the throats of all the sleeping men, who today are buried on that hillside."

Patton had made his point. But then he grinned wolfishly, and added, "There is only one good thing about it. The men whose throats were cut were Germans. The enemy who did the cutting were our men." The men of Third Army had unbounded confidence in their commander from then on.

On the eve of Third Army's crossing of the Channel, Patton delivered to the assembled throng his greatest speech. Unfortunately, to my knowledge, no verbatim copy exists. It was by all odds the most stirring and the most scurrilous, the most inspiring and the most indecent, eve-of-battle talk ever given. Dwight MacDonald reprinted parts of it in an article called "My Favorite General," but no chopped-up version can do it justice and no complete version could go through the U.S. mails.

The deterioration of the Patton–Eisenhower relationship continued after the invasion. Third Army was not in on the initial landings and did not become operational until the breakout from the beachhead, early in August 1944. Patton and his staff began to feel that Eisenhower and **SHAEF** [Supreme Headquarters Allied Expeditionary Forces] were against them. When Third Army was unleashed, SHAEF tried to keep its presence on the battlefield a secret, so Patton's boys did not get the credit they deserved. It was in those first weeks of August that Third Army did its best work, overrunning France in a campaign unmatched in all history. Patton's staff began to feed him the idea that SHAEF—and Eisenhower—were jealous and would not give him the credit he deserved. The situation became worse in September, as the Allied armies outstripped their supplies, and there was not enough for anyone. Patton was convinced he could go right through the German West Wall and into Berlin if only SHAEF would give his tanks the gas they needed. Montgomery, to the north, was equally convinced that his 21st Army Group could do the same thing. Eisenhower could not satisfy either one, but he did tend to favor Montgomery, since the port of Antwerp was within Montgomery's boundary and its capture would ease the supply problem. Patton began to mutter that Eisenhower was the best general the British had.

Other incidents piled up. They got worse after the war, when Patton assumed the duties of military governor of Bavaria. He refused to follow Eisenhower's—really, the Allied—policy of a hard line toward the Germans and consistently employed or refused to fire former SS men and Nazis. A climax came at a press conference when Patton asserted that the military government "would get better results if it employed more former members of the Nazi party in administrative jobs and as skilled workmen." He then made his statement that joining

> **SHAEF** Supreme Headquarters Allied Expeditionary Forces, led by Dwight Eisenhower.

the Nazi party was just like joining the Republicans or the Democrats back home. Eisenhower was furious. He ordered Patton to call another press conference and take back everything he had said. Patton called the conference, read Eisenhower's general orders on de-Nazification, and then claimed that he had been carrying out the official policy and would continue to act as he had in the past. Eisenhower was dissatisfied. He made Patton come to his headquarters, where he relieved him of his duties. Even at this moment Eisenhower tried to ease the blow, allowing Patton to select his successor. Patton, however, left the meeting murmuring that he now saw the truth of Henry Adams's phrase that a friend in power is a friend lost.

But ingratitude, if that is what it was, was only one of the many facets of Patton's personality. He came from a very rich family that had roots in Boston, old Virginia, and California. Until he entered West Point he followed no formalized schooling program, and was in fact a spoiled boy who did about what he wanted to. His three great loves were horses, history, and shocking people. He cultivated swearing with such a persistence that he soon became a recognized expert, and he employed his profanity whenever and wherever he felt like it. As it happened, he often felt like it. He liked to show off his ability to carry out his favorite maxim, which was that any true gentleman should be able to curse for two minutes steady without repeating a single word. However, a long-time cavalry friend of his said recently, "Sure, he was an *artiste* with profanity but I was never conscious of his being obnoxious around ladies. After all, he was brought up to be a gentleman, and he was one."

Only "Georgie's" love of horses and history exceeded his fondness for profanity. He could ride with the best, was an outstanding polo player, and probably would have been happiest as a cavalry officer under J. E. B. Stuart. He had authentic connections, through his ancestors, with the Army of Northern Virginia, and studied thoroughly the campaigns of the Civil War. He spent most of the twenties and thirties in the cavalry, which he recognized as a defunct branch of the army—he had been in armor in World War I and was enthusiastic about its possibilities—but which allowed him to ride, socialize, and study history. Unlike most army officers of the period, however, his knowledge went far beyond the American Civil War. He was well versed in all branches of military history, from Alexander the Great to the present. When his troops captured a historic fortress in World War II, such as Metz, he could recount not only how many times Metz had fallen before, not only to whom, but exactly how it had happened. He was also well, if not thoroughly, acquainted with all aspects of European and American history in general.

"He had the damnedest library you ever saw," said the contemporary quoted above. "I remember commenting on this and he told me he had every book obtainable on Napoleon."

Patton was a warm and compassionate family man. To his children he seemed a god, but a god who often descended to earth to play with them. His wife, Beatrice Ayer Patton, of a wealthy Boston family, was a lovely woman whom he loved deeply and who shared and enjoyed his life fully. Because her husband liked horses, she became an avid horsewoman; because he was a deep ocean yachtsman, she became an accomplished sailorwoman, winning many championships in small racing sloops. Her husband liked history, so she, too, studied it. One thing she did not do: she refused to adopt her husband's practice of spelling the same word in several different ways.

Patton could be fatherly to his enlisted men, too. Before the war he was commanding officer at Fort Myer, Virginia, across the river from Washington, D.C. One Sunday a practical joker among the soldiers on the post told two recruits, "You men go at once to call on the post commander. It is the custom in the army." Never suspecting that the custom applied only to officers and their ladies, the recruits put on their ill-fitting blouses, brushed their hair, and presented themselves at the door of the commanding officer's quarters. Those who knew Patton, as the practical joker did, expected that when the recruits told him what they had come for he would make an immediate and noisy ascension.

Instead, Patton politely invited them in, ushered them into the drawing room, presented them to Mrs. Patton, and began a pleasant and amiable chat. Mrs. Patton served tea. The men back at the barracks never believed this story, but Patton loved to tell it on himself.

Enlisted men did not always fare so well with Patton. During the war he began to take violent objection to the characters in Bill Mauldin's cartoons, especially Willie and Joe. Patton thought Mauldin was disrespectful toward the army and under no circumstances did he want his men looking like, or admiring, soldiers who were as sloppy as Willie and Joe. By 1944 Patton could stand it no longer, and he ordered that the *Stars and Stripes*, the enlisted men's newspaper in which Mauldin's cartoons appeared, should no longer circulate in the Third Army.

Eisenhower felt at least as strongly about censorship as Patton did about sloppy soldiers, and he immediately ordered Patton to back down. Patton refused. Eisenhower's personal aide, Harry Butcher, then arranged for a meeting between Patton and Mauldin. Mauldin, who wore three stripes on his arm as compared to the three stars on Patton's shoulders, was scared to death, but at Butcher's urging he went. Patton gave Mauldin the full treatment, appealing to his patriotism and his pride in the army. It didn't work— Mauldin defended his rights as an artist. Patton went into a rage, but although his profanity turned Mauldin's face white it didn't change his mind.

A few weeks later Butcher saw Patton and showed him a *Time* magazine story on the meeting, a story which concluded with a statement from Mauldin to the effect that Patton had not convinced him and he was fairly sure he had not convinced Patton. Patton, in his high-pitched voice, said to Butcher, "Why, if that little s.o.b. ever comes in the Third Army area again, I'll throw him in jail." But Eisenhower overruled Patton, the *Stars and Stripes* did circulate in the Third Army, and the sergeant won the battle with the three-star general.

Yet none of these facets of Patton's personality—the polo playboy, the spewer of profanity, the historian, the psychiatrist, the family man, or the actor—represented the true Patton. At heart he was a man with a fierce inner compulsion to excel at whatever he did. It did not much matter if it was at cursing, making war, or studying history—Patton had to be the best. It was the compulsion that helped create the near-eccentric personality; it was also the compulsion that helped create America's greatest combat soldier.

What George Patton did best of all, better than anyone else, was make a certain type of war. He was not a brilliant strategist nor was he exceptional in launching an attack. But in the pursuit he was the best America or anyone else ever had. His theory of war was simple: "Go like hell." In Sicily he told his men, "We must retain this advantage [the initiative] by always attacking rapidly, ruthlessly, viciously, without rest. However tired and hungry you may be, the enemy will be more tired, more hungry." Once Patton got the enemy started, he never let him stop. If his own superiors began to worry and tried to slow him down, he just cut his communications with the rear and drove right on. He pushed, pulled, cajoled, threatened, screamed at his men, in order to get superhuman efforts out of them, to keep them moving, to grind down and destroy the enemy before he had a chance to rest and regroup and rearm. Like Ulysses Grant he thought not about what the enemy might do to him, but about what he might do to the enemy. In the pursuit he never worried about his flanks, for he was sure—and events proved him right—that an off-balance enemy could never mount a serious counterattack. He used his tanks with audacity and intelligence, and he showed the world mobile armored warfare that no one had previously dreamed possible.

Patton's Third Army went across France in August and September of 1944 faster than the Germans had come through in their much more famous blitzkrieg of 1940, and Patton did it against a stronger and better led opponent. He beat the Germans worse than the Russians, or anyone else, ever did. And they knew it. Hitler and his generals feared Patton more than any other opposing general, as both Heinz Guderian and Gerd von Rundstedt told American officers after the war. Patton moved so fast the Germans simply could not believe it.

Neither could anyone else. No supply service in the world could have kept up with Patton's tanks, much less one depending on a couple of small, damaged ports and required to serve two entire army groups. Patton, in turn, could never understand why they could not keep up, and harbored thoughts of persecution. He did what he could to keep the advance going—hoarding captured gasoline and oil and not telling SHAEF about the capture, so that he received his pittance from supply headquarters in addition to the German materials—but it was not enough. And so he ran out of gas, and a war which he firmly believed he could have ended before Christmas of 1944 dragged on until May of 1945.

No one really knows if Patton could have fought on the defensive. He never had the test, as he never fought a truly set battle—Montgomery's favorite kind—and he quickly turned every defensive-looking situation into a counteroffensive. On December 16, 1944, the Germans began the Battle of the Bulge. On December 19 Eisenhower held a meeting at Verdun. Bradley, Patton, and others were present. Everyone was gloomy, for none had believed that the Germans were capable of launching an attack of this size and scope.

Eisenhower looked at his subordinates and declared, "There will only be cheerful faces at this conference table." Patton looked at him, grinned, and said, "Hell, let's have the guts to let the—go all the way to Paris. Then we'll really cut 'em off and chew 'em up." Eisenhower then asked Patton, in the middle of planning an offensive of his own, how long it would take him to change direction and hit the southern flank of the German breakthrough. It was a difficult request. To change direction in the middle of an operation involving a half-dozen divisions, with all the administrative, supply, organizational, and human problems involved, is extremely difficult. Montgomery would have taken three weeks or a month.

Patton said he would do it in four days. He did it in three.

Patton's abilities, according to his most ardent admirers, were never fully tested. According to them he should have been given at least an army group to command. Actually, he had probably reached his limit with the Third Army. He lacked the tact and breadth of vision to command an army group, with its huge staff system and personality problems with army, corps, and division commanders. Similarly, his tactical maxims do not reveal a particularly brilliant or original mind. Rather, they point up his one-sidedness, a one-sidedness that showed to tremendous advantage with the Third Army but might not have done so elsewhere.

Some of Patton's combat principles, as he called them, were: "There is no approved solution to any tactical situation." "In battle, casualties vary directly with the time you are exposed to effective fire. Your own fire reduces the effectiveness and volume of the enemy's fire, while rapidity of attack shortens the time of exposure. A pint of sweat will save a gallon of blood!" "Battles are won by frightening the enemy. Fear is induced by inflicting death and wounds on him. Death and wounds are produced by fire. Fire from the rear is more deadly and three times more effective than fire from the front, but to get fire behind the enemy, you must hold him by frontal fire and move rapidly around his flank." "Catch the enemy by the nose with fire and kick him in the pants with fire emplaced through movement." "Use roads to march on, fields to fight on." "Troops should not deploy into line until forced to do so by enemy fire." "The larger the force and the more violence you use in the attack, whether it be men, tanks, or ammunition, the smaller will be your proportional losses."

It was not long after World War I that Lawrence of Arabia decided that he had played out his role on the world stage. For himself, he had done what he wanted to do, and after a disastrous venture into occupation politics in the areas he had liberated he actively sought oblivion. He found it first as an enlisted man in the air force, then in death.

George Patton blazed his way through World War II and onto the world stage in much the same way as Lawrence had done earlier. And like Lawrence, his role ended when the shooting stopped. He did not actively seek death, but when it came, in a senseless and minor automobile accident in December 1945, it reminded some observers of Lawrence's death on his motorcycle years earlier. Both men had located and climbed their mountains; there was nothing left for them to conquer.

A Primary Perspective

D-DAY

At daybreak on June 6, 1944, an Allied invasion of nearly 200,000 troops began hitting the beaches along the Normandy coast of France. It was the largest amphibious landing in history. Despite heavy aerial and naval bombardment of German defensive positions, Axis forces put up a fierce resistance and it was not immediately clear whether the operation would succeed. One of the men who went ashore that morning was Ernie Pyle, a combat journalist famous for his firsthand reporting on the lives of frontline soldiers. In the selection that follows, Pyle provides a gripping account of what it was like during those first critical days in Normandy.

Brave Men

Our men simply could not get past the beach. They were pinned down right on the water's edge by an inhuman wall of fire from the bluff. Our first waves were on that beach for hours, instead of a few minutes, before they could begin working inland.

The foxholes were still there—dug at the very edge of the water, in the sand and the small jumbled rocks that formed parts of the beach.

Medical corpsmen attended the wounded as best they could. Men were killed as they stepped out of landing craft. An officer whom I knew got a bullet through the head just as the door of his landing craft was let down. Some men were drowned.

The first crack in the beach defenses was finally accomplished by terrific and wonderful naval gunfire, which knocked out the big emplacements. Epic stories have been told of destroyers that ran right up into shallow water and had it out point-blank with the big guns in those concrete emplacements ashore.

When the heavy fire stopped, our men were organized by their officers and pushed on inland, circling machine-gun nests and taking them from the rear.

As one officer said, the only way to take a beach is to face it and keep going. It is costly at first, but it's the only way. If the men are pinned down on the beach, dug in and out of action, they might as well not be there at all. They hold up the waves behind them, and nothing is being gained.

Our men were pinned down for a while, but finally they stood up and went through, and so we took that beach and accomplished our landing. In the light of a couple of days of retrospection, we sat and talked and called it a miracle that our men ever got on at all or were able to stay on.

Source: "D-Day" from *Brave Men*, p. 248. Copyright © 1944. Reprinted by permission of Scripps Howard Foundation and Indiana University Press.

They suffered casualties. And yet considering the entire beachhead assault, including other units that had a much easier time, our total casualties in driving that wedge into the Continent of Europe were remarkably low—only a fraction, in fact, of what our commanders had been prepared to accept.

And those units that were so battered and went through such hell pushed on inland without rest, their spirits high, their egotism in victory almost reaching the smart-alecky stage.

Their tails were up. "We've done it again," they said. They figured that the rest of the army wasn't needed at all. Which proves that, while their judgment in this respect was bad, they certainly had the spirit that wins battles, and eventually wars.

QUESTIONS

1. In what ways did Patton's study of history contribute to his development as a military leader? What influence did Patton's experience as a cavalry officer have on the tactics he later employed in World War II?
2. As a former cavalry officer, Patton had much in common with Philip Sheridan. Do you see any similarities between the two men? How do you think Sheridan would have responded to the challenges of World War II? How do you think Patton would have conducted the Indian wars of the late 19th century?
3. How would you characterize Patton's relationship with Eisenhower? In that Patton was a more experienced field commander than Eisenhower, why was the latter chosen as the supreme commander for the invasion of France? Do you think Patton could have followed Eisenhower's example and made a successful transition to political life after the war?
4. What do the Mauldin incident and Patton's abuse of shell-shocked soldiers tell us about the general's personality? How was Patton able to command such loyalty from his own troops?
5. What were Patton's greatest strengths as a military leader? What were his shortcomings? Do you agree with the authors' observation that Patton had probably reached his limit as commander of the Third Army?
6. Which of the historical figures profiled in Part Two would you most like to write about? What questions would you ask in a study of that person? What types of sources would you consult to answer those questions?

 ## ADDITIONAL RESOURCES

Three of the better biographies of the colorful general are Carlo D'Este, *Patton: A Genius for War* (1995); Ladislas Farago, *Patton: Ordeal and Triumph* (1963), and Martin Blumenson, *Patton: The Man and the Legend, 1884–1945* (1985). Blumenson has also edited *The Patton Papers*, 2 vols. (1972–1974). The military career of Patton's wartime commander in Europe is examined in Stephen E. Ambrose, *Eisenhower: Soldier, General of the Army, President-Elect, 1890–1952* (1983). For more on the broader context in which Patton operated during the war, see Geoffrey Perret, *There's a War to Be Won: The United States Army in World War II* (1991); Robert Leckie, *Delivered from Evil: A Saga of World War II* (1987); and B. H. Liddell Hart, *History of the Second World War* (1970). Domestic as well as military developments during the period are ably surveyed in William L. O'Neill, *A Democracy at War: America's Fight at Home and Abroad in World War II* (1993).

The monumental 1970 film *Patton* is the best film source for understanding the character of this complex leader. The film is nearly three hours in length but is one of the best biographies ever produced for the screen. The 1986 sequel, *The Last Days of Patton*, which also starred George C. Scott, is less satisfying but completes the story of the colorful general's life and career.

Introduction

The quarter-century after World War II was a period of unprecedented prosperity in the United States. It all began with the release of personal savings accumulated during the war. As consumer goods became increasingly available, Americans went on an incredible spending spree. They later benefited from the sorry condition of the world's leading industrial nations immediately after the war. Of the major combatants, only the United States came out of the conflict with its manufacturing base intact. By contrast, major production centers in the Soviet Union, Japan, Germany, and other parts of Europe had been devastated by wartime bombing. Because recovery took time, most U.S. corporations faced no serious foreign competition for years afterward. Meanwhile, steady increases in real income made American wage earners the world's most affluent working people.

Although the postwar economy's performance exceeded all expectations, there were a few dark spots on the horizon, none more ominous than the growing estrangement between the United States and its wartime ally, the Soviet Union. The resulting Cold War, during which the United States assumed the unaccustomed role of world policeman, had its domestic counterpart in the investigations of Red-hunting politicians who believed Communist subversives threatened major national institutions. The best known and most feared of these politicians was Joseph R. McCarthy. In his essay on the Wisconsin senator, Fred Cook examines the events that made McCarthy's name a byword for the public slandering of innocent citizens.

The postwar economic boom touched nearly all Americans. Not everyone, however, benefited equally. In most parts of the nation, particularly the South, discrimination and segregation still placed severe limits on what African Americans could do. Throughout the first half of the century, the struggle for black rights had focused on the courts, where National Association for the Advancement of Colored People (NAACP) lawyers had obtained a series of favorable rulings. The most notable of these was *Brown v. Board of Education of Topeka*, a 1954 decision in which the Supreme Court cleared the way for school integration by overturning the "separate but equal" doctrine that it had earlier enunciated in *Plessy v. Ferguson* (1896). Although *Brown* remains the NAACP's greatest triumph, the massive resistance provoked by the ruling revealed the limits of legalism. With the subsequent rise of mass action, the Civil Rights movement entered a new phase that increasingly centered on the streets rather than the courts. In his essay on Martin Luther King, Jr., Stephen B. Oates profiles the individual who best personified this phase of the movement.

The postwar period also witnessed the rebirth of the women's movement. There had been an earlier movement, whose most enduring legacy was the woman's suffrage amendment. But the movement itself did not survive the 1920s, and the postwar "cult of domesticity" that decreed woman's place was in the home had erased most memories of those earlier initiatives. Few people did more to revive the struggle for women's rights than Betty Friedan, who authored *The Feminine Mystique* (1963), a path-breaking work that prompted countless women to begin searching outside the household for a sense of fulfillment their domestic lives too often denied them. In his essay on Friedan, David Halberstam examines the developments that made *The Feminine Mystique* so important to the modern women's movement.

The campaign for gender equality that Friedan helped set in motion was one of several 1960s movements that drew inspiration from the achievements of civil rights activists. Another was Cesar Chavez's effort to organize California's farmworkers. The latter had long been among the nation's most exploited wage earners, and, as Cletus Daniel notes in his essay, Chavez confronted formidable obstacles then unknown to most labor leaders. Daniel further relates how, in the course of overcoming them, the charismatic organizer established a union that reflected his own dual personality as a social activist and a trade unionist.

One source of those problems was the changes that occurred in the nation's political climate following the 1960s. Not only did major elements of the Democratic coalition find it harder to work together as a result of intraparty disputes over issues such as affirmative action and the Vietnam War, but these differences surfaced at a time when American conservatives were overcoming long-standing divisions in their own ranks and becoming a major political force within the Republican party. Nothing better symbolized the conservative resurgence than the 1980 elevation of a one-time actor named Ronald Reagan to the presidency. Although something of a mystery to all who knew him, the former California governor had clear ideas about the direction in which he wanted to take the country. Whether Reagan's administration actually inaugurated a political revolution is one of several important questions that James T. Patterson addresses in an essay that looks at the man, his presidency, and his legacy.

The closing decades of the 20th century also witnessed continuing advances in communications technology. Perhaps the most significant development was the creation of the personal computer. Its widespread adoption after 1980 transformed workplaces and changed the ways people gather information, compose their thoughts, and interact with each other. PC usage expanded so quickly that in 1983 *Time* magazine chose the personal computer as its "Man of the Year." Were a publication to put a human face on the computer revolution today, it would probably select a picture of Bill Gates, whose Microsoft Corporation provides the operating systems for a substantial proportion of the world's personal computers. How Gates's firm achieved this place in the industry is the subject of H. W. Brands's essay on the Seattle entrepreneur.

Chapter 13

Joseph R. McCarthy

*D*uring the immediate postwar period, as tensions between the United States and the Soviet Union escalated, the two superpowers became locked in a Cold War that would last for more than 40 years. Internationally, the conflict involved struggles for dominance in such farflung locales as Poland, Czechoslovakia, China, Korea, and Vietnam. There also was a domestic Cold War. It took the form of security checks, congressional investigations of Communist subversion, and the harassment of dissident political groups. This domestic Cold War affected a broad range of American institutions: schools, unions, and the media, as well as the federal government, which was the initial target of Red-hunting politicians. Before it ended, the crusade destroyed the careers of numerous individuals in both the private and public sectors.

The 1948 presidential contest marked a major turning point in the emergence of the domestic Cold War. Republicans had not held the White House since Herbert Hoover's administration, and nearly everyone believed that this was their year. When Thomas Dewey unexpectedly lost the election, disappointed party leaders began looking for an issue with which to bring down the Truman presidency. A series of events the following year seemed to provide it. The first occurred in September, when Soviet officials announced the successful detonation of an atomic bomb. Coming a half-dozen years sooner than most people expected, the Soviet breakthrough prompted assertions that the activities of spies operating within the United States had made the Soviet accomplishment possible. The second event was the fall

of China a month later, which Republican leaders blamed on the actions of administration critics of Chiang K'ai-shek's nationalist government. Meanwhile, month after month throughout the year, an attentive national audience raptly followed the various twists and turns of the Alger Hiss espionage case. A former State Department official, Hiss had played a secondary but important role in a number of diplomatic initiatives during the Roosevelt era. He also was the walking embodiment of the eastern establishment: a cultured, well-educated, Ivy League type whom conservative Republicans from the nation's heartland instinctively distrusted and hated.

With these developments, the stage was set for the appearance of one of the most extraordinary demagogues in American history, Joseph R. McCarthy. The Wisconsin senator's public career as a Red hunter began on February 9, 1950, when he told startled members of the Women's Republican Club of West Virginia: "I have here in my hands a list of 205 [employees] made known to the secretary of state as being members of the Communist party and who nonetheless are still working and shaping policy." McCarthy never showed this list to anyone; indeed, he later forgot how many names were supposed to be on it. But this didn't matter to McCarthy, for he had accomplished his primary aim: to capture the country's attention. He remained in the national limelight for another four years.

During this period, McCarthy became the most feared politician in America. In the end, though, he overplayed his hand by deciding to take on the U.S. Army. This foolhardy act placed him at odds with President Eisenhower, the nation's most revered military figure. It was a serious mistake. Over the years McCarthy had made numerous enemies. When Ike turned on him, rival politicians and media critics sensed that it was open season and began firing from all sides. In the essay that follows, Fred Cook reviews significant features of the Wisconsin senator's colorful and destructive career, while providing a thorough examination of the Army–McCarthy hearings.

Joseph R. McCarthy

Fred Cook

Joe McCarthy, as he became known to millions of Americans, was a contradictory figure, two men in one. The first was a likable, backslapping boon companion who wanted to be loved by everyone. The second—the man who emerged under opposition or threat—was a savage, scowling battler who stopped at nothing.

McCarthy was born November 14, 1908, on a worn-out farm in upper Wisconsin about a hundred miles north of Milwaukee. He worked his way through college and law school. In college, he was an amateur boxer, a crude and unskilled one who threw all science to the winds and charged headlong, with swinging, wild, windmill blows. As a young lawyer, his earnings were small, and he played poker more than he worked at the law. He became known as a poker player who would bluff outrageously on every hand. Opponents never knew quite how to figure him. Just when they thought he must be bluffing again, he would come up with a pat hand and rake in a huge pot. These traits told much about Joe McCarthy; he was to remain all his life the reckless headlong battler—and master of the art of the colossal bluff.

In 1939 when he was 31 McCarthy joined the Republican party in Wisconsin and got himself elected as a circuit court judge. Just two years later the United States became involved in World War II, and he enlisted in the marines, was commissioned a lieutenant, and went off to the South Pacific. He was an intelligence officer, assigned to secure rear bases, but sometimes, just for the fun of it, he rode in the tail-gunner's seat of a bomber on routine missions and blasted away at coconut trees. Ever a master at publicizing himself, he had his picture taken in combat uniform; copies flooded the Wisconsin newspapers and, almost overnight, he became "Tail Gunner Joe"—a war hero.

The legend helped in 1946 when he ran for the U.S. Senate seat long held by Robert M. La Follette, Jr. La Follette was the son of Wisconsin's most famous politician, "Fighting Bob" La Follette. The La Follette name was a household word in the state, and few gave upstart young Joe McCarthy a fighting chance.

But times were changing. Even so soon after the war, the jitters were setting in. Russia had become a menace. Things had obviously gone wrong. Republicans throughout the 1946 campaign raised a great hue and cry against Communists and fellow travelers in the Democratic administration in Washington. La Follette, though running in the Republican primary in Wisconsin, had a liberal voting record, having sided on critical issues with the Democratic administration. The result was that La Follette found he had enemies on all sides. Conservative Republicans detested him for his liberalism. And Communists, then strong in some of Wisconsin's labor unions, hated him even more viciously because he had delivered one of the first Cold War speeches in the Senate, denouncing Russia as a menace to world peace. The situation was tailor-made for Joe McCarthy. He attacked La Follette sometimes as a pro-Fascist type; at other times, in utter contradiction, as a Communist fellow traveler. Enough of the wild charges stuck so that La Follette lost his usual strong backing in the big-city labor wards; and brash Joe McCarthy, scoring an upset of upsets, went to Washington as the new U.S. senator from Wisconsin.

As a freshman senator, McCarthy built a record of dubious value. He became known as the lobbyists' best friend. He accepted a $10,000 check from a manufacturer of prefabricated homes for trumpeting the virtues of such housing at the same time he was supposed, in his official capacity, to be investigating housing. He developed a close relationship with a Pepsi-Cola lobbyist who signed a $20,000 note for him—and he battled in the Senate to get postwar sugar rationing relaxed so that Pepsi-Cola could get more sugar. Even worse, he injected himself into a Senate investigation of the World War II Malmedy massacre. It was at Christmastime 1944 that Nazi storm troopers machine-gunned 100 helpless Belgian civilians and 150 captured American soldiers in the little crossroads Belgian town of Malmedy. After the war, several of the Nazi murderers were arrested, tried, and convicted. Then a publicity campaign began in Germany in an effort to save their lives. Back home in Wisconsin, McCarthy had had heavy backing among neo-Nazi elements; and so, though he was not a member of the Senate committee investigating the Malmedy atrocity, he took an active hand in the probe. And he wound up attacking American army officers, contending they had tortured the Nazis to obtain forced confessions. His tactics disrupted the hearings; and, in Germany, the Communist press had a field day slandering America and Americans. The death sentences of the condemned Nazis were finally commuted.

Up to 1950, then, the McCarthy record was hardly admirable. He had become the bosom pal of lobbyists. He had defended the Nazi murderers of Malmedy—and played into the hands of German Communists in doing so. It was not a record with which a politician could go back before his constituents, seeking reelection in 1952. McCarthy needed an issue.

He was hunting for one that would put his name in headlines. And in January 1950, at dinner with some friends in Washington's swank Colony Restaurant, several ideas were batted around unenthusiastically until finally someone suggested the Communist issue. McCarthy seized upon the idea at once and asked the Republican National Committee to arrange some speaking dates for him during the annual Lincoln Day party rallies taking place across the nation.

McCarthy was not well enough known at the time to rate major speaking engagements, and so the committee sent him off to Wheeling, West Virginia. It was there on February 9, 1950, at a Republican rally, that he delivered the speech that was to make him known in every household in America. One paragraph, one gesture stood out. McCarthy was quoted as saying:

> While I cannot take time to name all the men in the State Department who have been named as members of the Communist party and members of a spy ring, *I have here in my hand* a list of 205 that were known to the secretary of state as being members of the Communist party and who, nevertheless, are still working and shaping policy in the State Department.

It was a statement that touched off a frenzy. It was the charge that launched the worst witch hunt this nation has ever known.

Why should those few lines of type, why should that gesture of a paper waved aloft in clenched hand, have sent an entire nation down the road of a kind of mass insanity, hunting for Communists under every bed? The timing of the charge helps to explain the mass explosion.

Republicans had been trying for years to tar the liberal regimes of Presidents Franklin D. Roosevelt and Harry S. Truman with a Communist affiliation. They had struggled desperately to make the propaganda stick in the presidential campaign of 1948—and had failed by an eyelash. They had concentrated most of their fire on Alger Hiss, a brilliant young aide in the State Department; Whittaker Chambers, a confessed former Communist, charged that Hiss had passed him official papers to send to Russia. It was an infinitely complicated, mysterious case; but, finally, after two trials, Alger Hiss had been convicted of perjury on January 25, 1950, just 15 days before McCarthy spoke at Wheeling. And this was not all.

Even as McCarthy was speaking, the British press was announcing the arrest of Klaus Fuchs. Fuchs, a refugee scientist who had been cleared by British security, had been sent here during wartime to work on the development of the atom bomb. And now Fuchs confessed that he had been spying for Russia and had passed along information through a Communist spy ring operating in this country. Spies. Subversion. The "secret" of the atom bomb gone to Russia. Here was tinder waiting to set off a conflagration; and, at exactly the right minute, Joe McCarthy came along and applied the torch.

He did not realize at once what a good thing he had. There are even some indications he may have been a bit scared himself at first, for as he continued West on his Lincoln Day tour, reporters began to ask him about that 205 figure he had used at Wheeling, and McCarthy at first tried to back off. He didn't think he had used such a figure, he said, but it didn't matter really, he was certain there were enough Communists in the State Department to betray the nation.

In Salt Lake City two days after Wheeling, the 205 Communists had shrunk to 57, a figure that was still startling enough. And McCarthy was positive—oh, so positive—about these. He told a radio interviewer (his words were preserved on tape) that, if Secretary of State Dean Acheson "wants to call me tonight at the Utah Hotel, I will be glad to give him the names of those 57 card-carrying Communists." He added: "I don't want to indicate there are only 57, I say I have the names of 57."

As it became more and more evident that he had touched a quaking nerve in the nation, he became incredibly brash. He fired off a telegram to President Truman, challenging him to a duel of truth about those 57 Communists he said were making policy in the State Department. And, on his return to Washington, he took the Senate floor late in the afternoon of February 20, 1950, and in a long, rambling speech, he indicted the Truman administration for having permitted wholesale penetration and subversion of executive departments by Communists. But the figures had changed again. The number of Communists boring from within was no longer 205 or 57; it was now 81.

Even this new and revised tally would not stand close examination. Although McCarthy claimed to be citing specific cases, an analysis of the speech shows that McCarthy couldn't add. He didn't have 81 cases. He skipped some case numbers completely. He dragged in others even though he admitted himself that they did *not* involve Communist activities.

Sometimes he duplicated, and once he even caught himself in the act, confessing: "I believe I have covered this case before, and what I have just said seems to be a repetition. . . ."

When McCarthy had finished, even Senator Robert A. Taft, the conservative "Mr. Republican" of his party, admitted: "It was a perfectly reckless performance." But the Democrats, amazingly, had sat on their hands throughout those long hours while McCarthy ranted and raved and exposed himself as a perfect target for their fire. They badgered him about the 205 figure he had used at Wheeling, but they made no serious attack on his shot-full-of-holes recital. Why? Political observers speculated then and later that the Democrats' faith in themselves and their party had been destroyed by the Hiss case—a case which McCarthy and Republican orators repeatedly cited as the proof of everything—and so they hesitated to challenge McCarthy's thesis that there were any number of other Hisses running loose in the State Department. . . .

The presidential election of 1952 saw Joe McCarthy reaching a pinnacle of power. He had aroused such passions, he had gathered such a following that he became his party's ultimate weapon. General-hero Dwight D. Eisenhower was running for the presidency on the high road, bathed in the sunshine of popular adoration—and there on the low road was Joe McCarthy, the unrivaled hatchetman, slashing away at the Democratic nominee, Governor Adlai Stevenson, of Illinois.

In speech after speech, McCarthy referred to Stevenson as "little Ad-lie." He suggested sometimes that he could "teach patriotism to little Ad-lie" if someone would only smuggle him aboard the Democratic campaign special with a baseball bat in his hands. Sometimes he would pretend to have made a slip, referring to Governor Stevenson as "Alger—I mean Ad-lie," his coy way of reminding his audiences of the Alger Hiss case.

In his attacks on various candidates that year he always flourished aloft his trademark—a sheaf of paper—and proclaimed that "I have here in my hand" proof of one kind or another. The "proof" might consist simply of the charge that the candidate he was attacking had belonged during the 1930s, in an entirely different era with entirely different problems, to some organization that had been adjudged some 10 or 15 years later to have been a "Communist front." Sometimes it wasn't even necessary for a man to have belonged himself; he might just have been a friend of someone who had belonged, or was said to have belonged—and so he was considered guilty by this association. However remote the tie might be, it was enough to give McCarthy the chance to flourish aloft his papers and rave about his proof that the candidate was a traitor or, at least, a tainted fellow traveler.

When Eisenhower was elected in a landslide, Joe McCarthy bestrode Capitol Hill, a figure of menace, the author of a nightmare. Before the election, many had reasoned that Eisenhower would be able to contain and restrain McCarthy as the Democrats could not. But it soon became obvious that the very opposite was true. McCarthy had been reelected to the Senate in Wisconsin in the Eisenhower landslide; and when the Republicans took control of Congress, McCarthy was given power such as he had never had before. He was made chairman of the Senate Committee on Government Operations, with broad powers to investigate and with the command of an investigative staff. . . .

Some of President Eisenhower's supporters advised him repeatedly to confront McCarthy, to put an end to the frenzy and the witch hunt. But the president refused, insisting: "I just will not—*I refuse*—to get into the gutter with that guy." It was clear that Eisenhower did not want to fight, and it was just as clear that McCarthy was on a collision course, that a battle to the political death would be inevitable in the end.

The showdown came suddenly at a time when McCarthy seemed to be riding the crest of the wave of suspicion and frenzy he had created. It was largely the result of the antics of two young assistants on McCarthy's staff—Roy M. Cohn, whom McCarthy had named counsel of his investigating committee, and G. David Schine, a staff investigator and close friend of Cohn. These two brought McCarthy into direct conflict with one of the true power complexes of the nation—the U.S. Army.

Cohn and Schine were both 26. Cohn was so brilliant he had whipped through college and Columbia University Law School by the time he was 19, and he had to wait two years to become of age before he could take his bar examination. He was then appointed an assistant U.S. attorney in New York, and he began to investigate narcotics traffickers, counterfeiters, and, finally, spies.

Schine was a tall, sleepily handsome young man, the heir to a great hotel fortune. He had written a sketchy treatise on communism, which he had placed beside the Bibles in his family's hotels; and so he had come to the attention of Cohn and McCarthy and had been made a specialist in Communist investigations.

These two young men touched off the first wave of unfavorable publicity McCarthy had encountered. They toured Europe together at Easter time, 1953. Their purpose was to investigate the contents of U.S. overseas libraries, and they went to the kind of extremes that reminded many of the book purges in Germany during Hitler's time. . . .

The European tour of Cohn and Schine was followed by events that disgraced the United States as had nothing yet. Books that might offend the McCarthy witch hunters, including the detective stories of Dashiell Hammett, were removed from overseas library shelves. And in some cases books were actually burned. The number of volumes consigned to bonfires was minute, only a half-dozen or so, but it was the symbolism of the act that counted. Here were official agents of this supposedly great and free democracy doing just what the Nazis had done—destroying the works of authors they hated. Even President Eisenhower, who had gone to extremes to avoid a break with McCarthy, felt compelled to denounce book-burning as un-American, and Hammett's harmless detective stories and some other volumes that had been banned were brought out again into the light of day.

For the moment, it seemed, the showdown had been avoided; but all the time, behind the scenes, another drama was being enacted. In mid-July 1953, the U.S. Army began threatening G. David Schine with induction into military service. Roy Cohn, according to the army, began a series of frantic maneuvers designed to get his friend favored treatment. Not only the army but every other branch of the armed services was badgered to obtain a commission for Schine, but none would give him officer status. Cohn, according to the army, was wildly furious, and on one occasion threatened to "get" the army.

Dovetailing with this secret struggle was a succession of public events. There would be much dispute later about whether the Cohn–Schine rumpus was to blame, but the fact remained that it was just at this time that McCarthy began a series of attacks on the army. His first target was the great Signal Corps laboratory complex at Fort Monmouth, New Jersey, where much of the advanced radar for World War II had been developed.

McCarthy bellowed his way into headlines day after day, charging that the Fort Monmouth installations were riddled with spies. He conducted a series of secret hearings in New York, beginning on October 3, 1953; and, after each hearing, he would come out and tell reporters what he had discovered. Since the press could not know what had actually taken place behind the closed doors of the hearing room, it had to take McCarthy's word for it—and McCarthy's words were always alarming and sometimes horrifying. Over and over again, he claimed that he had uncovered evidence of spy rings that were still active at Fort Monmouth.

None of it was true. It took months—in some cases, years—for his charges to be sifted, but in the end they collapsed utterly, every one of them. The commanding general of Fort Monmouth, looking back in 1969, reported that only seven employees had been suspended as "security risks," a designation that is much broader than a charge of espionage. A man may be a security risk if he is a drunk or a homosexual, or if he is chronically head-over-heels in debt. What was truly startling in the Fort Monmouth case, however, was that not even the security risk firings could be sustained. According to Maj. Gen. William B. Latta in 1969, all seven employees suspended as security risks "were reinstated eventually"—and this under a system in which the government needed only to establish that there was enough evidence against a man to create "a doubt" about the advisability of his continued employment. Even under these one-sided circumstances, with all the dice loaded against the accused employees, there had been absolutely nothing to support McCarthy's sensational charges.

This, of course, could not have been apparent at the time, and McCarthy, as was typical of him, went on to a new sensation before the public had a chance to catch its breath. He discovered finally, perhaps for the only time in his career, a man who apparently had been a Communist.

The suspect was Irving Peress, a New York City dentist who had been drafted on October 15, 1952, and had been stationed at Camp Kilmer, New Jersey, outside New Brunswick. In filling out his personnel forms, Peress had claimed the privilege of the Fifth Amendment against possible self-incrimination in answering questions about possible subversive activities and associations. This telltale stain went undetected for months in the flood of paperwork that engulfed the Pentagon, and so on October 23, 1953, Peress was promoted to major. The promotion was not a personal reward; some 7,000 other doctors and dentists also received automatic promotions as provided by newly adopted regulations. But McCarthy, tipped to the possibilities of the Peress case, immediately summoned Peress to testify before him. Peress took the Fifth Amendment to 32 questions dealing with possible Communist affiliations, and McCarthy uttered a scream that made headlines across the nation: "Who promoted Peress?"

In an effort to answer the question, he summoned before him the commanding general of Camp Kilmer, Brig. Gen. Ralph W. Zwicker. Zwicker was a much-decorated hero of World War II. He had led a scouting force ashore in the early hours of the D-Day landing in Normandy. He had commanded a regiment of the Second Infantry Division in the Battle of the Bulge. There could be no question about his patriotism, but McCarthy treated him with contempt.

General Zwicker tried to explain that he had had nothing to say about the promotion of Peress. He had nothing to say about any case involving possible subversion. All such cases were referred to higher echelons in the Pentagon, where army intelligence specialists sifted the evidence and decisions were made as to what action should be taken. These decisions were relayed to General Zwicker through First Army Headquarters in New York. He was only the last man on the conveyor belt. None of this made any impression on McCarthy. He browbeat Zwicker unmercifully and finally denounced him as "unfit to wear that uniform."

This brazen slandering of a heroic general was too much. The Eisenhower administration, which had sat still while the State Department was trampled underfoot, now was faced with an issue it could not dodge; if McCarthy was to be allowed to rage on unchecked in this fashion, the morale of the army also would be destroyed.

The first Republican to see and seize the issue was a much-respected senator from Vermont, Ralph W. Flanders. On March 9, Flanders took the floor of the Senate and flayed McCarthy unmercifully. He accused McCarthy of trying to set up "a one-man party, McCarthyism," and then he launched into this description of McCarthy in action:

> He dons his warpaint. He goes into his war dance. He emits his warwhoops. He goes forth to battle and proudly returns with the scalp of a pink army dentist. We may assume that this represents the depth and seriousness of the Communist penetration at this time.

Secretary of the Army Robert T. Stevens, a mild-mannered former textile manufacturer, had also become enraged. Stevens may have been no army expert, but he knew one thing: He could not permit his officers to be kicked around and insulted by McCarthy and still retain their respect or, more important, have any morale left in the army. And so he denounced McCarthy's methods and announced he would not permit army personnel to appear before McCarthy again and be subjected to such abuse.

The feud grew hotter with every uttered word. The army now leaked to the press the details of the way in which, it said, Cohn had badgered it to get a commission for Schine. It implied that McCarthy's investigations of the army were motivated by spite aroused by the Schine affair. McCarthy roared that Stevens was "a liar," and he accused the army of trying to "blackmail" him to call off his investigations. The conflict now was out in the open. It was so bitter there could be no compromise, and an investigation would have to be held to determine who was telling the truth.

A reluctant U.S. Senate ordered hearings, and these began in the full glare of television lights on April 22, 1954. It was a show that captured the attention of the entire nation. For the next several weeks, millions of Americans would eat their evening meals from television trays in their living rooms, their eyes glued to the evening newscasts, anxious not to miss a single act of the proceedings.

The setting, the personalities, the showdown nature of the issues—all were made to order for the kind of drama one usually sees only on the stage. The hearings were held in the plush Senate Caucus Room, its high ceiling supported by majestic columns, the scene of many stormy McCarthy hearings in the past. Senator Karl Mundt, a Republican from South Dakota, a longtime supporter of McCarthy, presided. The committee members sat in comfortable chairs on a raised dais behind a long, continuous judge's bench, the American flag draped in the background.

Before this row of judges, behind a long low counsel table, sat the contending parties. At one end was Joe McCarthy, dark-browed, sharp-nosed, a scowl on his swarthy features as he leaned his head sidewise to listen to the whispered words of Roy Cohn, who was serving as his personal counsel. Farther down the table was Ray H. Jenkins, 57, a rugged, square-jawed six-footer from Knoxville, Tennessee, the committee counsel.

Toward the other end of the table sat Secretary Stevens, stocky, solid-faced, unemotional; and beside him sat the man who was to become the star of the show—Joseph Nye Welch, a 63-year-old Boston lawyer who specialized in trial work. Welch was a chunky man with a deceptively pixie-like look about him. He had wide lips, a long face, a large broad nose, and high-arched quizzical eyebrows. He dressed like the proper Bostonian in conservative suits, little bow ties, and vest. He seemed at times almost asleep, and he spoke in the softest tones. But his wit was rapier-sharp, and many a startled witness was to find that this mild-seeming man could skewer him with the harshest of harsh questions.

The hearing had hardly begun before Joe McCarthy propelled himself before the eyes of the watching television cameras.

"A point of order, Mr. Chairman, may I raise a point of order?" he cried in his shrill voice.

His objection was a highly technical one. Welch, he said, had represented himself as counsel for the army, and McCarthy contended Welch did not represent the army, but Stevens personally. The whole point seemed a bit silly, but McCarthy argued it as if the fate of the nation were at stake. Mundt finally cut him off and ordered Jenkins to call his first witness.

The brief flareup had served, however, to put Joe McCarthy immediately in the spotlight. It had given the public the first glimpse of McCarthy in action, and his cry—"Point of order, Mr. Chairman"—was one that was to be raised so incessantly in the coming days that it became in time a phrase of ridicule.

The hearings lasted for 36 days and amassed two million words of testimony. And, though many impressions were created, one came to dominate them all—the picture of Joe McCarthy snarling, ramping, raging, injecting himself into every scene, trying any dirty trick that he thought might work, and crying over and over again, "Point of order, Mr. Chairman." . . .

The hearings went on and on, it seemed almost endlessly. McCarthy hounded Secretary Stevens for 14 days. Though every question that could possibly be asked had been asked and answered, McCarthy insisted, when his turn for questioning came, on going over the same old ground again and again. The strain upon the secretary was evident. He became gray-faced under the glaring television lights; his right eye sometimes blinked uncontrollably; and his right cheek twitched.

Through it all, there was another major furor when McCarthy, in cross-examining Stevens, flashed what purported to be an FBI report, dated October 26, 1951, warning of possible espionage dangers at Fort Monmouth. How had McCarthy obtained an FBI "top secret" report? Was it genuine?

These questions occupied the committee for days. It finally developed that the McCarthy report was not a copy of the FBI original. It was a digest of a longer FBI document. And there was one striking difference between the two. The FBI report had not attempted to judge; it had merely recited what information had been obtained about various employees. McCarthy's version, however, had the word "derogatory" printed after some of the names. . . .

The dispute over the purloined and abbreviated FBI report led to the final, climactic scene. The hearings would drag on after it, twitching in a kind of final dying agony, but after this one unforgettable moment, nothing else really mattered.

This highlight came on June 9, 1954, while Welch was cross-examining Roy Cohn. Welch established that Cohn and McCarthy had had their version of the FBI report in their possession for months, yet they hadn't informed Secretary Stevens in their own Republican administration about it. . . .

Welch wanted to know if Cohn had any doubts about Stevens's fidelity. "No, sir." Or his honor? "No, sir." Or his patriotism? "No, sir." Welch drove home his point. "And yet, Mr. Cohn, you didn't tell him what you knew?" Cohn could only repeat helplessly that he did not know.

Then Welch, in his most puckish manner, suggested that when one had such information one should move "before sundown" to do something about it. "May I add my small voice, sir," he said in his gently sarcastic way, "and say whenever you know about a subversive or a Communist or a spy, please hurry. Will you remember those words?"

Ridicule is the deadliest weapon, and Joe McCarthy could no longer restrain himself.

"Point of order," he cried, and he charged one last fatal time before the television cameras.

"In view of Mr. Welch's request that information be given," he began, "I think we should tell him that he has in his law firm a young man named [Frederick H.] Fisher whom he recommended, incidentally, to do the work on this committee, who has been for a number of years a member of an organization which was named . . . as the legal bulwark of the Communist party . . ."

Roy Cohn sat slumped in the witness chair, shaking his head in silent protest, but McCarthy charged recklessly on. He explained that Fisher had belonged to the National Lawyers' Guild, an organization that had been labeled subversive by the House Un-American Activities Committee, and he accused Welch of having tried to get Fisher named, despite this, "as the assistant counsel for this committee."

"Now I have hesitated bringing that up," McCarthy said, adopting his pose as the fairest of men, "but I have been bored with your phony request to Mr. Cohn here that he personally get every Communist out of government before sundown. Therefore we will give you the information about the young man in your own organization.

"Now I'm not asking you at this time why you tried to force him on this committee. That you did, the committee knows . . ."

It instantly became apparent that the committee knew nothing of the sort. Senator Mundt, who in the past had supported McCarthy, broke into McCarthy's tirade, saying:

"The Chair wishes to say that he has no recognition or no memory of Mr. Welch recommending Mr. Fisher or anybody else as counsel for this committee."

Welch was staring at McCarthy. He no longer resembled the puckish actor. His face had gone white with anger.

"Senator McCarthy," he began in a voice that shook, "I did not know, Senator—Senator, sometimes you say, 'May I have your attention.' May I have yours, Senator?"

McCarthy turned his back . . . , calling loudly for a newspaper clipping about Fisher.

"I'm listening to someone in one ear and you in the other," he told Welch.

"Now this time, sir, I want you to listen with both," Welch snapped.

"Yes, sir."

McCarthy, boldly indifferent, went right on giving instructions about material he wanted to place in the record.

"Senator, you won't need anything in the record when I finish telling you this," Welch said, his voice still shaking with emotion, tears glistening in his eyes. "Until this moment, Senator, I think I never really gauged your cruelty or your recklessness.

"Fred Fisher is a young man who went to Harvard Law School and came into my firm and is starting what looks to be a brilliant career with us. When I decided to work for this committee I asked Jim St. Clair, who sits on my right, to be my first assistant. I said to him, 'Jim, pick somebody in the firm to work under you that you would like.'

"He chose Fred Fisher and they came down on an afternoon plane. That night when we had taken a little stab at trying to see what the case was about, Fred Fisher and Jim St. Clair and I went to dinner together.

"I then said to these young men: 'Boys, I don't know anything about you except I've always liked you, but if there's anything funny in the life of either one of you that would hurt anybody in this case, you had better speak up quick.'

"And Fred Fisher said: 'Mr. Welch, when I was in law school and for a period of months after, I belonged to the Lawyers' Guild,' as you have suggested, Senator.

"He went on to say, 'I am the secretary of the Young Republicans' League with the son of the Massachusetts governor and I have the respect and admiration of the 25 lawyers or so in Hale and Dorr [Welch's law firm].'

"And I said, 'Fred, I just don't think I'm going to ask you to work on the case. If I do, one of these days that will come out and go over national television and it will hurt like the dickens.'

"So, Senator, I asked him to go back to Boston. Little did I dream you could be so reckless and so cruel as to do an injury to that lad. It is true he is still with Hale and Dorr. It is true he will continue to be with Hale and Dorr.

"It is, I regret to say, equally true that I fear he shall always bear a scar, needlessly inflicted by you. If it were in my power to forgive you for your reckless cruelty, I would do so. I like to think I'm a gentle man, but your forgiveness will have to come from someone other than me."

The Senate Caucus Room was hushed, its audience spellbound. Few there probably realized how thoroughly McCarthy had exposed himself. Far from trying to get the committee to hire Fisher, Welch had sent him back to Boston as he had said; and in trying to anticipate McCarthy's moves and lessen the damage he might do, he had disclosed the action and the reasons for it at the time. The *New York Times* had carried the story and had used Fisher's picture; but, despite all this, McCarthy had not been able to resist the savage lunge and the unprincipled accusation before a nationwide television audience.

Having made the gamble, even McCarthy could now feel the force of Welch's anger and contempt. He fumbled with some papers before him, and then he tried to bluster his way through the gathering storm, rumbling that Welch "has been baiting Mr. Cohn here for hours" and "I just want to give him this man's record . . ."

Welch, the tears gone from his eyes, now had full control of himself. His eyes were cold and hard, his voice icy as he said: "Senator, may we not drop this? We know he belonged to the Lawyers' Guild."

"Let me finish this," cried McCarthy.

"And Mr. Cohn nods his head at me. I did you, I think, no personal injury, Mr. Cohn."

"No, sir."

"I meant to do you no personal injury, and if I did, I beg your pardon. Let us not assassinate this lad further, Senator. You've done enough. Have you no sense of decency, sir? At long last, have you left no sense of decency?"

"I know this hurts you, Mr. Welch," snarled McCarthy.

"I'll say it hurts."

"May I say, Mr. Chairman, as a point of personal privilege, that I'd like to finish this."

"Senator, I think it hurts you, too, sir," said Welch.

McCarthy rumbled on, trying to show that Welch had attempted to force Fisher upon the committee, a charge whose truth Mundt again denied. McCarthy then attempted to ask Welch a question, but Welch froze him with this final rejoinder:

"Mr. McCarthy, I will not discuss this further with you. You have sat within six feet of me and could ask, could have asked me about Fred Fisher. You have seen fit to bring it out, and if there is a God in Heaven it will do neither you nor your cause any good.

"I will not discuss it further. I will not ask Mr. Cohn any more questions. You, Mr. Chairman, may, if you will, call the next witness." . . .

Joe McCarthy was destroyed in that one, dramatic scene. He had been exposed to millions as a low, unprincipled battler. He would never recover.

The Senate, so long cowed by him, was now prodded by Senator Flanders to censure him. Senators always hate to take action against one of their exclusive club, and it was perhaps a measure of McCarthy's offenses against decency that the Senate was finally impelled to investigate him.

There were more hearings, more wild flailing about by McCarthy. In typical McCarthy fashion, he denounced mild-mannered Senator Arthur V. Watkins, a Utah Republican and chairman of the investigating committee. Watkins, he charged, was "cowardly" and "stupid"; the Watkins committee was serving as the "unwitting handmaiden," the "involuntary agent," and "attorneys in fact" of the Communist party.

It was too much to be borne. The Senate voted 67–22 to "condemn" McCarthy, not to "censure" him. His followers attempted to find some hope in that fact, but the effect was the same. McCarthy had been discredited and repudiated.

His collapse, both politically and physically, was incredibly swift. He wandered the halls of the Senate like some pale ghost of his former self. Where the press had hung on his every word in the glory days of the witch hunt, his speeches were now almost automatically consigned to the wastebasket. Always a heavy drinker, he drank more and more heavily—and carried it less well. Finally, on April 28, 1957, he was taken to the Bethesda Naval Hospital, where he had been treated several times previously, and there at 6:02 P.M. on May 2, he died. The cause of death was described as "peripheral neuritis," an affliction of the nervous system often associated with the disease of alcoholism.

Even in death, he was not forgotten, not without influence. There were still millions of Americans who believed that he really had been leading a great "crusade" against communism. A Gallup poll taken in August 1954, after his damaging self-exposure at the Army–McCarthy hearings, showed that 51 percent of all Americans opposed McCarthy, but—what was truly surprising— 36 percent, an enormous number, still had unshaken faith in him. They still believed—and much evidence indicates that many still do—that there were Communists everywhere and that all our troubles had been caused by conspiracy and betrayal.

Yet the facts were undeniable. Beginning in the Truman administration, every government employee, no matter how low his position, was investigated by departmental security agencies and the FBI. If there was *anything* in his record to cause a doubt or a suspicion, the employee was automatically suspended. He could appeal, but he was always at a disadvantage. He was not permitted to face his accusers; he could not cross-examine them. He was not permitted even to know who they were. In a reversal of all American tradition, the government did not have to prove an employee's guilt; it did not really have to prove anything. He had to prove—and prove beyond a shadow of a doubt—his complete innocence and trustworthiness.

This evidence, taken at appeal hearings, was passed on by loyalty boards composed of conservative Democrats and Republicans. President Truman, in an effort to avoid just the kind of demagogic hue and cry McCarthy had raised, had placed conservative and lifelong Republicans in charge of the State Department's Loyalty Board and the top Loyalty Review Board. Under these circumstances it is hardly enough to say the dice were loaded; they were double-loaded.

Yet out of nearly 5 million federal employees screened during the Truman administration, only 560—about one-hundredth of 1 percent—were dismissed "on grounds relating to loyalty." McCarthy and the Republicans, of course, clamored that the Truman system was too lax; they would tighten the net so that not even a gnat could get through. Yet the Eisenhower administration found it practically impossible to justify this pet theory. On February 18, 1954, it reported there had been some 2,200 "security risk" firings, but only 29 involved disloyalty. This figure was so small it was ridiculous, and so repeated and transparent efforts were made to revise it upward. In the next month, the figures were changed again and again until the administration finally proclaimed in March 1954 that out of 2,429 dismissals, 422 involved "subversives." Even if one discounts the constant shifting of the figures, even if one accepts this 422 tally as genuine, it didn't spell out the presence of a menace. There were then some 2.5 million federal employees; and even if 422 had finally rested under the shadow of a "doubt," this still represented less than two-hundredths of 1 percent of all government workers.

Those were the facts, but a demagogue does not deal in facts. He deals in fear, in blind unreasoning emotion, in hate and prejudice. Joe McCarthy knew and practiced the art as has no other demagogue in American history. He turned the nonexistent into a menace. He trampled on justice and fair play. He disgraced his country at home and abroad—and made millions believe they were following him in a holy crusade. Such is the power of the supreme demagogue; such, the lesson of Joe McCarthy.

A Primary Perspective

U.S. COLD WAR POLICY

The events that gave rise to McCarthyism also prompted important changes in U.S. foreign policy. At about the same time that McCarthy was making his Wheeling address, President Truman authorized a comprehensive reassessment of the nation's international commitments. The resulting study, NSC/68, was one of the most important policy statements of the entire Cold War era. In it, administration advisors urged that the United States accept the role of world policeman and develop free-world military capabilities on an international scale. The following excerpts from the report state its underlying assumptions and main recommendations.

NSC/68

The fundamental design of those who control the Soviet Union and the international Communist movement is to retain and solidify their absolute power, first in the Soviet Union and second in the areas now under their control. In the minds of the Soviet leaders, however, achievement of this design requires the dynamic extension of their authority and the ultimate elimination of any effective opposition to their authority.

The design, therefore, calls for the complete subversion or forcible destruction of the machinery of government and structure of society in the countries of the non-Soviet world and their replacement by an apparatus and structure subservient to and controlled from the Kremlin. To that end Soviet efforts are now directed toward the domination of the Eurasian land mass. The United States, as the principal center of power in the non-Soviet world and the bulwark of opposition to Soviet expansion, is the principal enemy whose integrity and vitality must be subverted or destroyed by one means or another if the Kremlin is to achieve its fundamental design. . . .

A more rapid buildup of political, economic, and military strength and thereby of confidence in the free world than is now contemplated is the only course which is consistent with progress toward achieving our fundamental purpose. The frustration of the Kremlin design requires the free world to develop a successfully functioning political and economic system and a vigorous political offensive against the Soviet Union. These, in turn, require an adequate military shield under which they can develop. It is necessary to have the military power to deter, if possible, Soviet expansion, and to defeat, if necessary, aggressive Soviet or Soviet-directed actions of a limited or total character. The potential strength of the free world is great; its ability to

Source: NSC/68.

develop these military capabilities and its will to resist Soviet expansion will be determined by the wisdom and will with which it undertakes to meet its political and economic problems. . . .

A comprehensive and decisive program to win the peace and frustrate the Kremlin design should be so designed that it can be sustained for as long as necessary to achieve our national objectives. It would probably involve:

1. The development of an adequate political and economic framework for the achievement of our long-range objectives.
2. A substantial increase in expenditures for military purposes adequate to meet the requirements. . . .
3. A substantial increase in military assistance programs, designed to foster cooperative efforts, which will adequately and efficiently meet the requirements of our allies. . . .
4. Some increase in economic assistance programs and recognition of the need to continue these programs until their purposes have been accomplished.
5. A concerted attack on the problem of the United States balance of payments. . . .
6. Development of programs designed to build and maintain confidence among other peoples in our strength and resolution, and to wage overt psychological warfare calculated to encourage mass defections from Soviet allegiance and to frustrate the Kremlin design in other ways.
7. Intensification of affirmative and timely measures and operations by covert means in the fields of economic warfare and political and psycho- logical warfare with a view to fomenting and supporting unrest and revolt in selected strategic satellite countries.
8. Development of internal security and civilian defense programs.
9. Improvement and intensification of intelligence activities.
10. Reduction of federal expenditures for purposes other than defense and foreign assistance, if necessary by the deferment of certain desirable programs.
11. Increased taxes.

QUESTIONS

1. Why did McCarthy wait until 1950 before focusing attention on the "Communists in government" issue? What do the tactics that McCarthy used to spotlight the issue tell us about the Wisconsin senator? Do you think he genuinely believed the State Department was riddled with Communists?
2. How was McCarthy able to become so powerful during the early 1950s? Was his rise to power simply a reflection of Cold War fears? To what extent was partisan politics a factor? Why didn't the Democrats respond more forcefully to McCarthy's charges?

3. What effect did the 1952 elections have on McCarthy's stature as a national political figure? How would you characterize McCarthy's relationship with the Eisenhower administration?
4. Why were U.S. allies so appalled by McCarthy's actions? What effect do you think McCarthyism had on the operation of the U.S. government? How did the Army–McCarthy hearings contribute to the Wisconsin senator's downfall?
5. What influence did McCarthy have on the times in which he lived? Was the threat that McCarthy posed to democracy as grave as Cook implies in the essay?
6. What challenges does a biographer who has chosen to write about McCarthy confront? How well do you think Cook met those challenges?
7. Implementation of the proposals contained in NSC/68 marked an important turning point in the evolution of the Cold War. If you were asked to prepare a major reassessment of contemporary U.S. foreign policy, what recommendations would you make?

 ADDITIONAL RESOURCES

Recent biographies of the Wisconsin senator include David M. Oshinsky, *A Conspiracy So Immense: The World of Joe McCarthy* (1983), and Thomas C. Reeves, *The Life and Times of Joe McCarthy: A Biography* (1982). A particularly insightful older work is Richard H. Rovere, *Senator Joe McCarthy* (1959), which contains a shrewd analysis of McCarthy's tactics. Important aspects of McCarthy's career are examined in Edwin R. Bayley, *McCarthy and the Press* (1981), and Robert Griffith, *The Politics of Fear: Joseph R. McCarthy and the Senate*, 2nd ed. (1987). Those wishing to learn more about the social and political consequences of McCarthyism and the postwar Red Scare should consult David Caute, *The Great Fear: The Anti-Communist Purge under Truman and Eisenhower* (1978); Earl Latham, *The Communist Conspiracy in Washington: From the New Deal to McCarthy* (1966); and Stanley I. Kutler, *The American Inquisition: Justice and Injustice in the Cold War* (1982).

Point of Order is a 1964 documentary by Emile de Antonio that examines the downfall of Senator McCarthy using footage from the Army–McCarthy hearings. It is available on video, as is the 1988 *Hollywood on Trial*, directed by David Halpern, which covers the investigations into communist influence in Hollywood. The Arts & Entertainment channel included "Senator Joseph McCarthy" as part of its *Biography* series and offers the program in VHS format.

Chapter 14

Martin Luther King, Jr.

*D*uring the mid-1950s, Montgomery, Alabama, the former capital of the Confederacy, differed little from other southern cities of the time. The majority of its African-American residents worked as laborers or domestics and had a median income that was about half that of local whites. It was also a place where local authorities rigidly enforced regional racial codes. Regardless of their personal accomplishments, all blacks were expected to behave deferentially toward whites. No African American could register at a white hotel, dine at a white restaurant, play on a white playground, or drink from a white water fountain. On the city's buses, blacks paid at the front, then stepped back off and reentered through the rear door. Once on the bus, black riders sat from back to front; and as the bus filled, they abandoned their seats from front to back. Moreover, they had to do so row by row, so that no white would be forced to sit in the same row as a black.

That was the situation on the Montgomery bus lines when, on December 1, 1955, a black seamstress named Rosa Parks refused to give up her seat in a half-filled row. She had been working all day and said her feet were tired. This made no impression on Montgomery authorities, who immediately arrested Parks for violating municipal segregation laws. As word of her arrest spread, the city's black leaders began mobilizing for action. Many had been waiting

for just such an opportunity, and by the following afternoon, local activists had distributed 40,000 leaflets calling for a bus boycott. The first major battle of the mass action phase of the Civil Rights movement had begun.

It was here that Martin Luther King, Jr., first captured widespread attention. After the boycott began, he quickly emerged as one of the movement's leaders. He did so in the same way that he would time and again in the future: through his unmatched ability to give expression to the most deeply felt aspirations of southern blacks. "My friends," he told local boycotters in his first political address, "I want it to be known— that we are going to work with grim and bold determination—to gain justice on the buses in this city." "And we are not wrong," he continued, employing the rhythmic cadences that were a hallmark of his oratorical genius:

> If we are wrong—the Supreme Court of this nation is wrong. If we are wrong—God Almighty is wrong! If we are wrong—Jesus of Nazareth was merely a utopian dreamer and never came down to earth! If we are wrong—justice is a lie. And we are determined here in Montgomery—to work and fight until justice runs down like water, and righteousness like a mighty stream!

It was an electrifying performance. And this was just the beginning for the 26-year-old minister. He would be dead in another 13 years, the victim of an assassin's bullet, but much would change before then.

Although King played a major role in bringing about those changes, he was in many respects an unlikely candidate to head a movement that would transform American social relations. By the standards of black southern society, he came from an extremely privileged background; and whatever plans his profoundly conservative father had for Martin, Jr., they did not include his leading a mass protest movement. In the essay that follows, Stephen B. Oates examines the forces that impelled King to choose the path that he did and discusses his changing conceptions regarding the movement's objectives.

Martin Luther King, Jr.

Stephen B. Oates

He was M.L. to his parents, Martin to his wife and friends, Doc to his aides, Reverend to his male parishioners, Little Lord Jesus to adoring churchwomen, De Lawd to his young critics in the Student Nonviolent Coordinating

Committee, and Martin Luther King, Jr., to the world. At his pulpit or a public rostrum, he seemed too small for his incomparable oratory and international fame as a civil rights leader and spokesman for world peace. He stood only five feet seven, and had round cheeks, a trim mustache, and sad, glistening eyes—eyes that revealed both his inner strength and his vulnerability.

He was born in Atlanta on January 15, 1929, and grew up in the relative comfort of the black middle class. Thus he never suffered the want and privation that plagued the majority of American blacks of his time. His father, a gruff, self-made man, was pastor of Ebenezer Baptist Church and an outspoken member of Atlanta's black leadership. M.L. joined his father's church when he was five and came to regard it as his second home. The church defined his world, gave it order and balance, taught him how to "get along with people." Here M.L. knew who he was—"Reverend King's boy," somebody special.

At home, his parents and maternal grandmother reinforced his self-esteem, praising him for his precocious ways, telling him repeatedly that he was *somebody*. By age five, he spoke like an adult and had such a prodigious memory that he could recite whole Biblical passages and entire hymns without a mistake. He was acutely sensitive, too, so much so that he worried about all the blacks he saw in Atlanta's breadlines during the Depression, fearful that their children did not have enough to eat. When his maternal grandmother died, 12-year-old M.L. thought it was his fault. Without telling anyone, he had slipped away from home to watch a parade, only to find out when he returned that she had died. He was terrified that God had taken her away as punishment for his "sin." Guilt-stricken, he tried to kill himself by leaping out of his second-story window.

He had a great deal of anger in him. Growing up a black in segregated Atlanta, he felt the full range of southern racial discrimination. He discovered that he had to attend separate, inferior schools, which he sailed through with a modicum of effort, skipping grades as he went. He found out that he—a preacher's boy—could not sit at lunch counters in Atlanta's downtown stores. He had to drink from a "colored" water fountain, relieve himself in a rancid "colored" restroom, and ride a rickety "colored" elevator. If he rode a city bus, he had to sit in the back as though he were contaminated. If he wanted to see a movie in a downtown theater, he had to enter through a side door and sit in the "colored" section in the balcony. He discovered that whites referred to blacks as "boys" and "girls" regardless of age. He saw "WHITES ONLY" signs staring back at him in the windows of barber shops and all the good restaurants and hotels, at the YMCA, the city parks, golf courses, swimming pools, and in the waiting rooms of the train and bus stations. He learned that there were even white and black sections of the city and that he resided in "nigger town."

Segregation caused a tension in the boy, a tension between his parents' injunction ("Remember, you are *somebody*") and a system that constantly demeaned and insulted him. He struggled with the pain and rage he felt when a white woman in a downtown store slapped him and called him "a little nigger" . . . when a bus driver called him "a black son-of-a-bitch" and made him surrender his seat to a white . . . when he stood on the very spot in Atlanta where whites had lynched a black man . . . when he witnessed nightriding

Klansmen beating blacks in the streets. How, he asked defiantly, could he heed the Christian injunction and love a race of people who hated him? In retaliation, he determined "to hate every white person."

Yes, he was angry. In sandlot games, he competed so fiercely that friends could not tell whether he was playing or fighting. He had his share of playground combat, too, and could outwrestle any of his peers. He even rebelled against his father, vowing never to become a preacher like him. Yet he liked the way Daddy King stood up to whites: He told them never to call him a boy and vowed to fight this system until he died.

Still, there was another side to M.L., a calmer, sensuous side. He played the violin, enjoyed opera, and relished soul food—fried chicken, cornbread, and collard greens with ham hocks and bacon drippings. By his mid-teens, his voice was the most memorable thing about him. It had changed into a rich and resonant baritone that commanded attention whenever he held forth. A natty dresser, nicknamed "Tweed" because of his fondness for tweed suits, he became a connoisseur of lovely young women. His little brother A.D. remembered how Martin "kept flitting from chick to chick" and was "just about the best jitterbug in town."

At 15, he entered Morehouse College in Atlanta, wanting somehow to help his people. He thought about becoming a lawyer and even practiced giving trial speeches before a mirror in his room. But thanks largely to Morehouse President Benjamin Mays, who showed him that the ministry could be a respectable forum for ideas, even for social protest, King decided to become a Baptist preacher after all. By the time he was ordained in 1947, his resentment toward whites had softened some, thanks to positive contact with white students on an intercollegiate council. But he hated his segregated world more than ever.

Once he had his bachelor's degree, he went north to study at Crozer Seminary near Philadelphia. In this mostly white school, with its polished corridors and quiet solemnity, King continued to ponder the plight of blacks in America. How, by what method and means, were blacks to improve their lot in a white-dominated country? His study of history, especially of Nat Turner's slave insurrection, convinced him that it was suicidal for a minority to strike back against a heavily armed majority. For him, voluntary segregation was equally unacceptable, as was accommodation to the status quo. King shuddered at such negative approaches to the race problem. How indeed were blacks to combat discrimination in a country ruled by the white majority?

As some other blacks had done, he found his answer in the teachings of Mohandas Gandhi—for young King, the discovery had the force of a conversion experience. Nonviolent resistance, Gandhi taught, meant noncooperation with evil, an idea he got from Henry David Thoreau's essay "On Civil Disobedience." In India, Gandhi gave Thoreau's theory practical application in the form of strikes, boycotts, and protest marches, all conducted nonviolently and all predicated on love for the oppressor and a belief in divine justice. In gaining Indian independence, Gandhi sought not to defeat the British, but to redeem them through love, so as to avoid a legacy of bitterness. Gandhi's term for this—*Satyagraha*—reconciled love and force in a single, powerful concept.

As King discovered from his studies, Gandhi had embraced nonviolence in part to subdue his own violent nature. This was a profound revelation for King, who had felt much hatred in his life, especially toward whites. Now Gandhi showed him a means of harnessing his anger and channeling it into a positive and creative force for social change.

At this juncture, King found mostly theoretical satisfaction in Gandhian nonviolence; he had no plans to become a radical activist in the segregated South. Indeed, he seemed destined to a life of the mind, not of social protest. In 1951, he graduated from Crozer and went on to earn a Ph.D. in theology from Boston University, where his advisor pronounced him "a scholar's scholar" of great intellectual potential. By 1955, a year after the school deseg-regation decision, King had married comely Coretta Scott and assumed the pastorship of Dexter Avenue Baptist Church in Montgomery, Alabama. Immensely happy in the world of ideas, he hoped eventually to teach theology at a major university or seminary.

But, as King liked to say, the *Zeitgeist,* or spirit of the age, had other plans for him. In December 1955, Montgomery blacks launched a boycott of the city's segregated buses and chose the articulate 26-year-old minister as their spokesman. As it turned out, he was unusually well prepared to assume the kind of leadership thrust on him. Drawing on Gandhi's teachings and exam-ple, plus the tenets of his own Christian faith, King directed a nonviolent boy-cott designed both to end an injustice and redeem his white adversaries through love. When he exhorted blacks to love their enemies, King did not mean to love them as friends or intimates. No, he said, he meant a disinter-ested love in all humankind, a love that saw the neighbor in everyone it met, a love that sought to restore the beloved community. Such love not only avoided the internal violence of the spirit, but severed the external chain of hatred that only produced more hatred in an endless spiral. If American blacks could break the chain of hatred, King said, true brotherhood could begin. Then posterity would have to say that there had lived a race of people, of black peo-ple, who "injected a new meaning into the veins of history and civilization."

During the boycott King imparted his philosophy at twice-weekly mass meetings in the black churches, where overflow crowds clapped and cried as his mellifluous voice swept over them. In these mass meetings King discovered his extraordinary power as an orator. His rich religious imagery reached deep into the black psyche, for religion had been the black people's main source of strength and survival since slavery days. His delivery was "like a narrative poem," said a woman journalist who heard him. His voice had such depths of sincerity and empathy that it could "charm your heart right out of your body." Because he appealed to the best in his people, articulating their deepest hurts and aspirations, black folk began to idolize him; he was their Gandhi.

Under his leadership, they stood up to white Montgomery in a remarkable display of solidarity. Pitted against an obdurate city government that blamed the boycott on Communist agitation and resorted to psychological and legal warfare to break it, the blacks stayed off the buses month after month, and walked or rode in a black-operated carpool. When an elderly woman refused the offer of a ride, King asked her, "But don't your feet hurt?" "Yes," she replied, "my feet is tired but my soul is rested." For King, her irrepressible spirit was proof that "a new Negro" was emerging in the South, a Negro with "a new sense of dignity and destiny."

That "new Negro" menaced white supremacists, especially the Ku Klux Klan, and they persecuted King with a vengeance. They made obscene phone calls to his home, sent him abusive, sickening letters, and once even dynamited the front of his house. Nobody was hurt, but King, fearing a race war, had to dissuade angry blacks from violent retaliation. Finally, on November 13, 1956, the U.S. Supreme Court nullified the Alabama laws that enforced segregated buses and handed King and his boycotters a resounding moral victory. Their protest had captured the imagination of progressive people all over the world and marked the beginning of a southern black movement that would shake the segregated South to its foundations. At the forefront of that movement was a new organization, the Southern Christian Leadership Conference (SCLC), which King and other black ministers formed in 1957, with King serving as its president and guiding spirit. Operating through the southern black church, SCLC sought to enlist the black masses in the freedom struggle by expanding "the Montgomery way" across the South.

The "Miracle of Montgomery" changed King's life, catapulting him into international prominence as an inspiring new moral voice for civil rights. Across the country, blacks and whites alike wrote him letters of encouragement; *Time* magazine pictured him on its cover; the National Association for the Advancement of Colored People (NAACP) and scores of church and civic organizations vied for his services as a speaker. "I am really disturbed how fast all this has happened to me," King told his wife. "People will expect me to perform miracles for the rest of my life."

But fame had its evil side, too. When King visited New York in 1958, a deranged black woman stabbed him in the chest with a letter opener. The weapon was lodged so close to King's aorta, the main artery from the heart, that he would have died had he sneezed. To extract the blade, an interracial surgical team had to remove a rib and part of his breastbone; in a burst of inspiration, the lead surgeon made the incision over King's heart in the shape of a cross.

That he had not died convinced King that God was preparing him for some larger work in the segregated South. To gain perspective on what was happening there, he made a pilgrimage to India to visit Gandhi's shrine and the sites of his "War for Independence." He returned home with an even deeper commitment to nonviolence and a vow to be more humble and ascetic like Gandhi. Yet he was a man of manifold contradictions, this American Gandhi. While renouncing material things and giving nearly all of his extensive honorariums to SCLC, he liked posh hotels and zesty meals with wine, and he was always immaculately dressed in a gray or black suit, white shirt, and tie. While caring passionately for the poor, the downtrodden, and the disinherited, he had a fascination with men of affluence and enjoyed the company of wealthy SCLC benefactors. While trumpeting the glories of nonviolence and redemptive love, he could feel the most terrible anger when whites murdered a black or bombed a black church; he could contemplate giving up, turning America over to the haters of both races, only to dedicate himself anew to his nonviolent faith and his determination to redeem his country.

In 1960, he moved his family to Atlanta so that he could devote himself full time to SCLC, which was trying to register black voters for the upcoming federal elections. That same year, southern black students launched the sit-in movement against segregated lunch counters, and King not only helped them form the Student Nonviolent Coordinating Committee (SNCC) but raised money on their behalf. In October he even joined a sit-in protest at an Atlanta department store and went to jail with several students on a trespassing charge. Like Thoreau, King considered jail "a badge of honor." To redeem the nation and arouse the conscience of the opponent, King explained, you go to jail and stay there. "You have broken a law which is out of line with the moral law and you are willing to suffer the consequences by serving the time."

He did not reckon, however, on the tyranny of racist officials, who clamped him in a malevolent state penitentiary, in a cell for hardened criminals. But state authorities released him when Democratic presidential nominee John F. Kennedy and his brother Robert interceded on King's behalf. According to many analysts, the episode won critical black votes for Kennedy and gave him the election in November. For King, the election demonstrated what he had long said: that one of the most significant steps a black could take was the short walk to the voting booth.

The trouble was that most blacks in Dixie, especially in the Deep South, could not vote even if they so desired. For decades, state and local authorities had kept the mass of black folk off the voting rolls by a welter of devious obstacles and outright intimidation. Through 1961 and 1962, King exhorted President Kennedy to sponsor tough new civil rights legislation that would enfranchise southern blacks and end segregated public accommodations as well. When Kennedy shied way from a strong civil rights commitment, King and his lieutenants took matters into their own hands, orchestrating a series of southern demonstrations to show the world the brutality of segregation. At the same time, King stumped the country, drawing on all his powers of oratory to enlist the black masses and win white opinion to his cause.

Everywhere he went his message was the same.

> The civil rights issue is an eternal moral issue that will determine the destiny of our nation and our world. As we seek our full rights, we hope to redeem the soul of our country. For it is our country, too, and we will win our freedom because the sacred heritage of America and the eternal will of God are embodied in our echoing demands. We do not intend to humiliate the white man, but to win him over through the strength of our love. Ultimately, we are trying to free all of us in America—Negroes from the bonds of segregation and shame, whites from the bonds of bigotry and fear.
>
> We stand today between two worlds—the dying old order and the emerging new. With men of ill-will greeting this change with cries of violence, of interposition and nullification, some of us may get beaten. Some of us may even get killed. But if you are cut down in a movement designed to save

the soul of a nation, no other death could be more redemptive. We must realize that change does not roll in "on the wheels of inevitability," but comes through struggle. So "let us be those creative dissenters who will call our beloved nation to a higher destiny, to a new plateau of compassion, to a more noble expression of humaneness."

That message worked like magic among America's long-suffering blacks. Across the South, across America, they rose in unprecedented numbers to march and demonstrate with Martin Luther King. His singular achievement was that he brought the black masses into the freedom struggle for the first time. He rallied the strength of broken men and women, helping them overcome a lifetime of fear and feelings of inferiority. After segregation had taught them all their lives that they were *nobody*, King taught them that they were *somebody*. Because he made them believe in themselves and in the beauty of chosen suffering, he taught them how to straighten their backs ("a man can't ride you unless your back is bent") and confront those who oppressed them. Through the technique of nonviolent resistance, he furnished them something no previous black leader had been able to provide. He showed them a way of controlling their pent-up anger, as he had controlled his own, and using it to bring about constructive change.

The mass demonstrations King and SCLC choreographed in the South produced the strongest civil rights legislation in American history. This was the goal of King's major southern campaigns from 1963 to 1965. He would single out some notoriously segregated city with white officials prone to violence, mobilize the local blacks with songs, scripture readings, and rousing oratory in black churches, and then lead them on protest marches conspicuous for their grace and moral purpose. Then he and his aides would escalate the marches, increase their demands, even fill up the jails, until they brought about a moment of "creative tension," when whites would either agree to negotiate or resort to violence. If they did the latter, King would thus expose the brutality inherent in segregation and stab the national conscience so that the federal government would be forced to intervene with corrective measures.

The technique succeeded brilliantly in Birmingham, Alabama, in 1963. Here Police Commissioner Eugene "Bull" Connor, in full view of reporters and television cameras, turned firehoses and police dogs on the marching protestors. Revolted by such ghastly scenes, stricken by King's own searching eloquence and the bravery of his unarmed followers, Washington eventually produced the 1964 Civil Rights Act, which desegregated public facilities—the thing King had demanded all along from Birmingham. Across the South, the "WHITES ONLY" signs that had hurt and enraged him since boyhood now came down.

Although SNCC and others complained that King had a Messiah complex and was trying to monopolize the Civil Rights movement, his technique worked with equal success in Selma, Alabama, in 1965. Building on a local movement there, King and his staff launched a drive to gain southern blacks the unobstructed right to vote. The violence he exposed in Selma—the beating of black marchers by state troopers and deputized posse men, the killing of a young black deacon and a white Unitarian minister—horrified the country.

When King called for support, thousands of ministers, rabbis, priests, nuns, students, lay leaders, and ordinary people—black and white alike—rushed to Selma from all over the country and stood with King in the name of human liberty. Never in the history of the movement had so many people of all faiths and classes come to the southern battleground. The Selma campaign culminated in a dramatic march over the Jefferson Davis Highway to the state capital of Montgomery. Along the way, impoverished local blacks stared incredulously at the marching, singing, flag-waving spectacle moving by. When the column reached one dusty crossroads, an elderly black woman ran out from a group of old folk, kissed King breathlessly, and ran back crying, "I done kissed him! The Martin Luther King! I done kissed the Martin Luther King!"

In Montgomery, first capital and much-heralded "cradle" of the Confederacy, King led an interracial throng of 25,000—the largest civil rights demonstration the South had ever witnessed—up Dexter Avenue with banners waving overhead. The pageant was as ironic as it was extraordinary, for it was up Dexter Avenue that Jefferson Davis's first inaugural parade had marched, and in the portico of the capitol Davis had taken his oath of office as president of the slave-based Confederacy. Now, in the spring of 1965, Alabama blacks—most of them descendants of slaves—stood massed at the same statehouse, singing a new rendition of "We Shall Overcome," the anthem of the Civil Rights movement. They sang, "Deep in my heart, I do believe, We have overcome—*today*."

Then, within view of the statue of Jefferson Davis, and watched by cordons of state troopers and television cameras, King mounted a trailer. His vast audience listened, transfixed, as his words rolled and thundered over the loudspeaker:

> My people, my people listen. The battle is in our hands. . . . We must come to see that the end we seek is a society at peace with itself, a society that can live with its conscience. That day will be a day not of the white man, not of the black man. That will be the day of man as man.

And that day was not long in coming, King said, whereupon he launched into the immortal refrains of "The Battle Hymn of the Republic," crying out, "Our God is marching on! Glory, glory hallelujah!"

Aroused by the events in Alabama, Washington produced the 1965 Voting Rights Act, which outlawed impediments to black voting and empowered the attorney general to supervise federal elections in seven southern states where blacks were kept off the rolls. At the time, political analysts almost unanimously attributed the act to King's Selma campaign. Once federal examiners were supervising voter registration in all troublesome southern areas, blacks were able to get on the rolls and vote by the hundreds of thousands, permanently altering the pattern of southern and national politics.

In the end, the powerful civil rights legislation generated by King and his tramping legions wiped out statutory racism in America and realized at least the social and political promise of emancipation a century before. But King was under no illusion that legislation alone could bring on the brave new America he so ardently championed. Yes, he said, laws and their vigorous enforcement were necessary to regulate destructive habits and actions and to protect blacks and their rights. But laws could not eliminate the "fears, prejudice, pride, and irrationality" that were barriers to a truly integrated society, to peaceful intergroup and interpersonal living. Such a society could be achieved only when people accepted that inner, invisible law that etched on their hearts the conviction "that all men are brothers and that love is mankind's most potent weapon for personal and social transformation. True integration will be achieved by true neighbors who are willingly obedient to unenforceable obligations."

Even so, the Selma campaign was the movement's finest hour, and the Voting Rights Act the high point of a broad civil rights coalition that included the federal government, various white groups, and all the other civil rights organizations in addition to SCLC. King himself had best expressed the spirit and aspirations of that coalition when, on August 28, 1963, standing before the Lincoln Memorial, he electrified an interracial crowd of 250,000 with perhaps his greatest speech, "I Have a Dream," in which he described in rhythmic, hypnotic cadences his vision of an integrated America. Because of his achievements and moral vision, he won the 1964 Nobel Peace Prize, at 34 the youngest recipient in Nobel history.

Still, King paid a high price for his fame and his cause. He suffered from stomachaches and insomnia, and even felt guilty about all the tributes he received, all the popularity he enjoyed. Born in relative material comfort and given a superior education, he did not think he had earned the right to lead the impoverished black masses. He complained, too, that he no longer had a personal self and that sometimes he did not recognize the Martin Luther King people talked about. Lonely, away from home for protracted periods, beset with temptation, he slept with other women, for some of whom he had real feeling. His sexual transgressions only added to his guilt, for he knew he was imperiling his cause and hurting himself and those he loved.

Alas for King, FBI Director J. Edgar Hoover found out about the black leader's infidelities. The director already abhorred King, certain that Communist spies influenced him and masterminded his demonstrations. Hoover did not think blacks capable of organizing such things, so Communists had to be behind them and King as well. As it turned out, a lawyer in King's inner circle and a man in SCLC's New York office did have Communist backgrounds, a fact that only reinforced Hoover's suspicions about King. Under Hoover's orders, FBI agents conducted a ruthless crusade to destroy King's reputation and drive him broken and humiliated from public life. Hoover's men tapped King's phones and bugged his hotel rooms; they compiled a **prurient** monograph about his private life and showed it to various editors, public officials, and religious and civic leaders; they spread the word, Hoover's word, that King was not only a reprobate but a dangerous subversive with Communist associations.

prurient An inordinate interest in matters of sex or appealing to that interest.

King was scandalized and frightened by the FBI's revelations of his extramarital affairs. Luckily for him, no editor, not even a racist one in the South, would touch the FBI's salacious materials. Public officials such as Robert Kennedy were shocked, but argued that King's personal life did not affect his probity as a civil rights leader. Many blacks, too, declared that what he did in private was his own business. Even so, King vowed to refrain from further affairs—only to succumb again to his own human frailties.

As for the Communist charge, King retorted that he did not need any Russians to tell him when someone was standing on his neck; he could figure that out by himself. To mollify his political friends, however, King did banish from SCLC the two men with Communist backgrounds (later he resumed his ties with the lawyer, a loyal friend, and let Hoover be damned). He also denounced communism in no uncertain terms. It was, he believed, profoundly and fundamentally evil, an atheistic doctrine no true Christian could ever embrace. He hated the dictatorial Soviet state, too, whose "crippling totalitarianism" subordinated everything—religion, art, music, science, and the individual—to its terrible yoke. True, communism started with men like Karl Marx who were "aflame with a passion for social justice." Yet King faulted Marx for rejecting God and the spiritual in human life. "The great weakness in Karl Marx is right here," King once told his staff, and he went on to describe his ideal Christian commonwealth in **Hegelian** terms: "Capitalism fails to realize that life is social. Marxism fails to realize that life is individual. Truth is found neither in the rugged individualism of capitalism nor in the impersonal collectivism of communism. The kingdom of God is found in a synthesis that combines the truths of these two opposites. Now there is where I leave brother Marx and move on toward the kingdom."

But how to move on after Selma was a perplexing question King never successfully answered. After the devastating Watts riot in August 1965, he took his movement into the racially troubled urban North, seeking to help the suffering black poor in the ghettos. In 1966, over the fierce opposition of some of his own staff, he launched a campaign to end the black slums in Chicago and forestall rioting there. But the campaign foundered because King seemed unable to devise a coherent antislum strategy, because Mayor Richard Daley and his black acolytes opposed him bitterly, and because white America did not seem to care. King did lead open-housing marches into segregated neighborhoods in Chicago, only to encounter furious mobs who waved Nazi banners, threw bottles and bricks, and screamed, "We hate niggers!" "Kill the niggers!" "We want Martin Luther Coon!" King was shocked. "I've been in many demonstrations all across the South," he told reporters, "but I can say that I have never seen—even in Mississippi and Alabama—mobs as hostile and as hate-filled as I've seen in Chicago." Although King prevented a major riot there and wrung important concessions from City Hall, the slums remained, as wretched and seemingly unsolvable as ever.

That same year, angry young militants in SNCC and the Congress of Racial Equality (CORE) renounced

> **Hegelian** Relating to the philosophy or dialectic method of the German philosopher Hegel, in which the thesis, antithesis, and synthesis are used as an analytic tool to approach a higher unity or new thesis.

King's teachings—they were sick and tired of "De Lawd" telling them to love white people and work for integration. Now they advocated "Black Power," black separatism, even violent resistance to liberate blacks in America. SNCC even banished whites from its ranks and went on to drop "nonviolent" from its name and to lobby against civil rights legislation.

Black Power repelled the older, more conservative black organizations such as the NAACP and the Urban League and fragmented the Civil Rights Movement beyond repair. King, too, argued that black separatism was chimerical, even suicidal, and that nonviolence remained the only workable way for black people. "Darkness cannot drive out darkness," he reasoned: "only light can do that. Hate cannot drive out hate: only love can do that." If every other black in America turned to violence, King warned, then he would still remain the lone voice preaching that it was wrong. Nor was SCLC going to reject whites as SNCC had done. "There have been too many hymns of hope," King said, "too many anthems of expectation, too many deaths, too many dark days of standing over graves of those who fought for integration for us to turn back now. We must still sing 'Black and White Together, We Shall Overcome.'"

In 1967, King himself broke with the older black organizations over the ever-widening war in Vietnam. He had first objected to American escalation in the summer of 1965, arguing that the Nobel Peace Prize and his role as a Christian minister compelled him to speak out for peace. Two years later, with almost a half-million Americans—a disproportionate number of them poor blacks—fighting in Vietnam, King devoted whole speeches to America's "immoral" war against a tiny country on the other side of the globe. His stance provoked a fusillade of criticism from all directions—from the NAACP, the Urban League, white and black political leaders, *Newsweek, Life, Time,* and the *New York Times,* all telling him to stick to civil rights. Such criticism hurt him deeply. When he read the *Times*'s editorial against him, he broke down and cried. But he did not back down. "I've fought too long and too hard now against segregated accommodations to end up segregating my moral concerns," he told his critics. "Injustice *any*where is a threat to justice everywhere."

That summer, with the ghettos ablaze with riots, King warned that American cities would explode if funds used for war purposes were not diverted to emergency antipoverty programs. By then, the Johnson administration, determined to gain a military victory in Vietnam, had written King off as an antiwar agitator, and was now cooperating with the FBI in its efforts to defame him.

The fall of 1967 was a terrible time for King, the lowest ebb in his civil rights career. Everybody seemed to be attacking him—young black militants for his stubborn adherence to nonviolence, moderate and conservative blacks, labor leaders, liberal white politicians, the White House, and the FBI for his stand on Vietnam. Two years had passed since King had produced a nonviolent victory, and contributions to SCLC had fallen off sharply. Black spokesman Adam Clayton Powell, who had once called King the greatest Negro in America, now derided him as Martin Loser King. The incessant attacks began to irritate him, creating such anxiety and depression that his friends worried about his emotional health.

Worse still, the country seemed dangerously polarized. On one side, back-lashing whites argued that the ghetto explosions had "cremated" nonviolence and that white people had better arm themselves against black rioters. On the other side, angry blacks urged their people to "kill the Honkies" and burn the cities down. All around King, the country was coming apart in a cacophony of hate and reaction. Had America lost the will and moral power to save itself? he wondered. There was such rage in the ghetto and such bigotry among whites that he feared a race war was about to break out. He felt he had to do something to pull America back from the brink. He and his staff had to mount a new campaign that would halt the drift to violence in the black world and combat stiffening white resistance, a nonviolent action that would "transmute the deep rage of the ghetto into a constructive and creative force."

Out of his deliberations sprang a bold and daring project called the poor people's campaign. The master plan, worked out by February 1968, called for SCLC to bring an interracial army of poor people to Washington, D.C., to dramatize poverty before the federal government. For King, just turned 39, the time had come to employ civil disobedience against the national government itself. Ultimately, he was projecting a genuine class movement that he hoped would bring about meaningful changes in American society—changes that would redistribute economic and political power and end poverty, racism, "the madness of militarism," and war.

In the midst of his preparations, King went to Memphis, Tennessee, to help black sanitation workers there who were striking for the right to unionize. On the night of April 3, with a storm thundering outside, he told a black audience that he had been to the mountaintop and had seen what lay ahead. "I may not get there with you. But I want you to know tonight that we as a people *will* get to the promised land."

The next afternoon, when King stepped out on the balcony of the Lorraine Motel, an escaped white convict named James Earl Ray, stationed in a nearby building, took aim with a high-powered rifle and blasted King into eternity. Subsequent evidence linked Ray to white men in the St. Louis area who had offered "hit" money for King's life.

For weeks after the shooting, King's stricken country convulsed in grief, contrition, and rage. While there were those who cheered his death, the *New York Times* called it a disaster to the nation, the *London Times,* an enormous loss to the world. In Tanzania, Reverend Trevor Huddleston, expelled from South Africa for standing against apartheid, declared King's death the greatest single tragedy since the assassination of Gandhi in 1948, and said it challenged the complacency of the Christian Church all over the globe.

On April 9, with 120 million Americans watching on television, thousands of mourners—black and white alike—gathered in Atlanta for the funeral of a man who had never given up his dream of creating a symphony of brother-hood on these shores. As a black man born and raised in segregation, he had had every reason to hate America and to grow up preaching cynicism and retaliation. Instead, he had loved the country passionately and had sung of her promise and glory more eloquently than anyone of his generation.

They buried him in Atlanta's South View Cemetery, then blooming with dogwood and fresh green boughs of spring. On his crypt, hewn into the marble, were the words of an old Negro spiritual he had often quoted: "Free at Last, Free at Last, Thank God Almighty I'm Free at Last."

A Primary Perspective

JO ANN ROBINSON AND THE WOMEN'S POLITICAL COUNCIL OF MONTGOMERY

Though best remembered as the event that catapulted Martin Luther King, Jr., onto the national stage, the Montgomery bus boycott was a collective effort that involved the city's entire black community. Long before King assumed his Montgomery pastorate, local activists had been planning for just such an occasion. Without their organizational work, the boycott could not have been sustained for a week, much less 13 months. In the selection below, Jo Ann Robinson describes the actions taken by the Women's Political Council to launch the boycott. Her recollections provide a salutary reminder of the vital role women played in the Civil Rights movement.

The Women's Political Council was an organization begun in 1946 after dozens of black people had been arrested on the buses. We witnessed the arrests and humiliations and the court trials and the fines paid by people who just sat down on empty seats. We knew something had to be done.

We organized the Women's Council and within a month's time we had over a hundred members. We organized a second chapter and a third, and soon we had more than 300 members. We had members in every elementary, junior high, and senior high school. We had them organized from federal and state and local jobs; wherever there were more than 10 blacks employed, we had a member there. We were organized to the point that we knew that in a matter of hours we could corral the whole city.

The evening that Rosa Parks was arrested, Fred Gray called me and told me that her case would be [heard] on Monday. As president of the main body of the Women's Political Council, I got on the phone and called all the officers of the three chapters. I told them that Rosa Parks had been arrested and she would be tried. They said, "You have the plans, put them into operation."

I didn't go to bed that night. I cut those stencils and took them to [the] college. . . .

Source: "Organizing Before the Boycott," from *Eyes on the Prize: America's Civil Rights Years* by Juan Williams, introduction by Julian Bond, copyright © 1987 by Blackside, Inc. Used by permission of Viking Penguin, a division of Penguin Group (USA) Inc.

I talked with every member [of the Women's Council] in the elementary, junior high, and senior high schools and told them to have somebody on the campus. I told them that I would be there to deliver them [the handbills]. I taught my classes from 8:00 to 10:00. When my 10:00 class was over, I took two senior students with me. I would drive to the place of dissemination and a kid would be there to grab [the handbills].

After we had circulated those 35,000 circulars, we went by the church. That was about 3:30 in the afternoon. We took them to the minister. . . . The [ministers] agreed to meet that night to decide what should be done about the boycott after the first day. You see, the Women's Council planned it only for Monday, and it was left up to the men to take over after we had forced them really to decide whether or not it had been successful enough to continue, and how long it was to be continued.

They had agreed at the Friday night meeting that they would call this meeting at Holt Street Church and they would let the audience determine whether or not they would continue the bus boycott or end it in one day.

Monday night, the ministers held their meeting. The church itself holds four or five thousand people. But there were thousands of people outside of the church that night. They had to put up loudspeakers so they would know what was happening. When they got through reporting that very few people had ridden the bus, that the boycott was really a success—I don't know if there was one vote that said "No, don't continue that boycott"—they voted unanimously to continue the boycott. And instead of it lasting one day as the Women's Council had planned it, it lasted for 13 months.

The spirit, the desire, the injustices that had been endured by thousands of people through the years . . . I think people were fed up, they had reached the point that they knew there was no return. That they had to do it or die. And that's what kept it going. It was the sheer spirit for freedom, for the feeling of being a man or a woman.

Now when you ask why the courts had to come in, they had to come in. You get 52,000 people in the streets and nobody's showing any fear, something had to give. So the Supreme Court had to rule that segregation was not the way of life. . . . We [met] after the news came through. All of these people who had fought got together to communicate and to rejoice and to share that built-up emotion and all the other feelings they had lived with during the past 13 months. And we just rejoiced together.

QUESTIONS

1. In what ways was King's boyhood different from that of most other black children growing up in the South during the 1930s and 1940s? What childhood experiences made the greatest impression on King?
2. How did the writings of Thoreau and Gandhi influence the development of King's social thought? What did Oates mean when he described King as a "man of contradictions"?

3. Why, according to Jo Ann Robinson, did the Montgomery bus boycott prove so successful? What do her recollections tell us about gender relations within the Civil Rights movement?

4. What were King's greatest strengths as a civil rights leader? Why did King conduct his major campaigns in southern cities that were particularly notorious for their harsh treatment of African Americans? How would you characterize King's relationship with the various groups involved in the Civil Rights movement?

5. Why did King come to believe that legislation alone would provide inadequate protection of black rights? In what ways did King's view of the movement's objectives change during the final years of his life?

6. Could the Civil Rights movement of the 1960s have made the advances that it did without King's leadership? Would W. E. B. Du Bois or Henry McNeal Turner have been able to play a similar role had they been given the opportunity during their most active years? What was King's most enduring achievement as a civil rights leader?

ADDITIONAL RESOURCES

Stephen B. Oates, the author of this essay, also has written a full-length biography of the civil rights leader: *Let the Trumpet Sound: The Life of Martin Luther King, Jr.* (1983). Other biographies include Marshall Frady, *Martin Luther King, Jr.* (2002); Lerone Bennett, Jr., *What Manner of Man: A Biography of Martin Luther King, Jr.*, 6th ed. (1986); and David L. Lewis, *King: A Biography*, 2nd ed. (1978). Four major studies of King's role in the movement for African-American rights are Stewart Burns, *To the Mountaintop: Martin Luther King, Jr.'s Sacred Mission to Save America, 1955–1968* (2004); David J. Garrow, *Bearing the Cross: Martin Luther King, Jr., and the Southern Christian Leadership Conference* (1986); and two works by Taylor Branch, *Parting the Waters: America in the King Years. 1954–1963* (1988) and *Pillar of Fire: America in the King Years, 1963–1965* (1998). A fine retrospective account of the civil rights struggle is Howell Raines, *My Soul Is Rested: Movement Days in the Deep South Remembered* (1977). For a well-crafted survey that moves beyond the King years, see Harvard Sitkoff, *The Struggle for Black Equality, 1954–1992*, rev. ed. (1993). J. Edgar Hoover's harassment of King is examined in David J. Garrow, *The FBI and Martin Luther King, Jr.: From "Solo" to Memphis* (1981), and Kenneth O'Reilly, *Racial Matters: The FBI's Secret File on Black America, 1960–1972* (1989).

Eyes on the Prize is the definitive documentary series on the modern Civil Rights movement. Produced in 1987, the series covers the movement from 1954 through the mid-1980s. *Martin Luther King, Jr.: I Have a Dream* (1986) focuses on the 1963 March on Washington and provides the speech in its entirety. *The Speeches of Martin Luther King, Jr.* (1991) provides edited versions of Dr. King's most famous speeches.

Chapter *15*

Betty Friedan

With the passage of the Nineteenth Amendment in 1920, women appeared ready to assume an increasingly prominent role in American public life. But this was not to be. The movement that gave women the right to vote did not survive the twenties, and by the 1950s many people had forgotten that it ever existed. Meanwhile, as the postwar domestic revival gave the doctrine of separate spheres a new lease on life, women seemed more firmly tied to family and household duties than they had ever been. Yet, beneath the seemingly placid surface of 1950s home life, a number of important changes were taking place—changes that would result in the formation of the modern women's movement.

One important change was the fact that increasing numbers of women were entering the labor force. By 1960, 40 percent of all women over the age of 16 held jobs outside the home. And with each passing year, a growing proportion of these women were married: Whereas 15 percent of wives worked in 1930, 30 percent did so in 1960. This development contributed to the resurgence of feminism by exposing more women to the inequities that made them second-class citizens in the workplace. Everywhere they looked, women ran up against long-standing assumptions that their natural place was in the home; that they were working only to pick up a little "pin money" or to supplement male incomes; that they were in effect casual workers who lacked real commitment to their jobs; and that, as a consequence, they did not have the same rights as their male counterparts.

At the same time, as Betty Friedan soon would show, there was growing discontent among suburban housewives. It is not often that a book has the impact that its author would like. One of those rare exceptions was Friedan's *The Feminine Mystique* (1963). Unlike most books, this one really struck a nerve. In it, Friedan used a number of case studies to examine the alienation felt by many American housewives—to look at what she called "the problem that has no name." These were women who had been told that marriage, family, and the homemaker's role would provide them all that one could reasonably expect from life: a sense of self-worth, dignity, and personal fulfillment. They tried it, and years later they found that they did not feel any of these things. Friedan attempted to explain the discrepancy by looking at the ways in which women's magazines, advertisers, and educators manipulated the feminine mystique to convince women that they could best attain happiness by accepting a "voluntary servitude" within the home.

Those women who responded to Friedan's message did not immediately take their case into the streets. But they did begin to reexamine their lives. Many also began searching, often outside the household, for a means of achieving that sense of fulfillment their domestic lives denied them. And regardless of what they did on their own behalf, they vowed that their daughters would never be put in a similar position. In the essay that follows, David Halberstam examines the process by which Friedan came to write her pathbreaking work, while surveying the developments that made her observations in *The Feminine Mystique* so compelling to suburban housewives of the early 1960s.

Betty Friedan

David Halberstam

It was all part of a vast national phenomenon. The number of families moving into the middle class—that is, families with more than $5,000 in annual earnings after taxes—was increasing at the rate of 1.1 million a year, *Fortune* noted. By the end of 1956 there were 16.6 million such families in the country, and by 1959, in the rather cautious projections of *Fortune's* editors, there would be 20 million such families—virtually half the families in America. *Fortune* hailed "an economy of abundance" never seen before in any country in the world. It reflected a world of "optimistic philoprogenitive [the word means that

Americans were having a lot of children], high-spending, debt-happy, bargain-conscious, upgrading, American consumers."

In all of this no one was paying very close attention to what the new home-oriented, seemingly drudgery-free life was doing to the psyche and outlook of American women. The pictures of them in magazines showed them as relentlessly happy, liberated from endless household tasks by wondrous new machines they had just bought. Since the photos showed them happy, and since there was no doubt that there were more and better household appliances every year, it was presumed that they were in fact happy. That was one of the more interesting questions of the era, for the great migration to the suburbs reflected a number of profound trends taking place in the society, not the least important of which was the changing role of women, particularly middle-class women. Up until then during this century women had made fairly constant progress in the spheres of politics, education, and employment opportunities. Much of their early struggle focused on the right of married women to work (and therefore to take jobs away from men who might be the heads of families). In the thirties a majority of states, 26 of 48, still had laws prohibiting the employment of married women. In addition, a majority of the nation's public schools, 43 percent of its public utilities, and 13 percent of its department stores enforced rules on not hiring of wives. A poll of both men and women in the thirties that asked "Do you approve of a married woman earning money in business or industry if she has a husband capable of supporting her?" showed that 82 percent of the men and women polled disapproved.

During the Depression, large numbers of women went to work because their homes needed every bit of cash they could bring home. In addition women were always welcome in those parts of industry that offered poorer-paying jobs. At the beginning of the New Deal in the garment district of New York, where traditionally workers were the wives of immigrants, women worked 48 hours a week for 15 cents an hour, which meant that after a long, exhausting work week they brought home $7.20.

But in general there was an assumption that as society began to change and more and more women were better educated, there would be more women working in the professions for better wages. World War II dramatically (if only temporarily) changed how the nation regarded the employment of women. Overnight, that which had been perceived as distinctly unfeminine—holding heavy-duty industrial jobs—became a patriotic necessity. Four million additional workers were needed in industry and in the armed forces and a great many of them had to be women. The *Ladies' Home Journal* even put a woman combat pilot on its cover. Suddenly, where women had not gone before, they were very welcome indeed; some 8 million women entered the workforce during the war.

That trend came to a stunning halt in the years after the war. Part of it was the traditional tilt of the society toward men—if there were good, well-paying jobs, then the jobs obviously belonged to men as they came home from the war to head families. Within two months after the end of the war, some

800,000 women had been fired from jobs in the aircraft industry; the same thing was happening in the auto industry and elsewhere. In the two years after the war, some 2 million women had lost their jobs.

In the postwar years the sheer affluence of the country meant that many families could now live a middle-class existence on only one income. In addition, the migration to the suburbs physically separated women from the workplace. The new culture of consumerism told women they should be homemakers and saw them merely as potential buyers for all the new washers and dryers, freezers, floor waxers, pressure cookers, and blenders.

There was in all this a retreat from the earlier part of the century. Now, there was little encouragement for women seeking professional careers, and in fact there was a good deal of quite deliberate discouraging of it. Not only were women now reared in homes where their mothers had no careers, but male siblings were from the start put on a very different track: The boys in the family were to learn the skills critical to supporting a family, while daughters were to be educated to get married. If they went to college at all they might spend a junior year abroad studying art or literature. Upon graduation, if they still had ideas of a professional career, the real world did not give them much to be optimistic about.

The laws about married women working might have changed, but the cultural attitudes had not. The range of what women were allowed to do professionally in those days was limited, and even in those professions where they were welcome, they were put on a lower, slower track. Gender, not talent, was the most important qualification. Men and women who graduated at the same time from the same colleges and who had received the same grades (in many cases the women received better grades), then arrived at the same publishing or journalistic companies only to be treated very differently.

Men were taken seriously. Women, by contrast, were doomed to serve as support troops. Often they worked harder and longer for less pay with lesser titles, usually with the unspoken assumption that if they were at all attractive, they would soon get married, become pregnant, and leave the company. Only someone a bit off-center emotionally would stay the course. It was a vicious circle: Because young women were well aware of this situation, there was little incentive to commit an entire life to fighting it and becoming what was then perceived of as a hard and brittle career woman. ("Nearly Half the Women in Who's Who Are Single," went one magazine title in that period trying to warn young women of the pitfalls of careerism.) If there were short stories in women's magazines about career women, then it turned out they, by and large, portrayed women who were unhappy and felt themselves emotionally empty. Instead, the magazines and the new television sitcoms glorified dutiful mothers and wives.

Even allegedly serious books of the era (for instance, an influential book of pop sociology by a man named Ferdinand Lundberg and his psychoanalyst collaborator Marynia Farnham, entitled *Modern Woman: The Lost Sex*) attacked the idea of women with careers. "The independent woman is a contradiction in terms," Lundberg and Farnham had written. Feminism itself, in their words, "was a deep illness." "The psychosocial rule that takes form, then, is this: The more educated a woman is, the greater chance there is of sexual disorder, more or less severe. The greater the disordered sexuality in a given group of women, the fewer children they have," they wrote. They also suggested that the federal government give rewards to women for each child they bore after the first.

A postwar definition of femininity evolved. To be feminine, the American woman first and foremost did not work. If she did, that made her competitive with men, which made her hard and aggressive and almost surely doomed to loneliness. Instead, she devotedly raised her family, supported her husband, kept her house spotless and efficient, got dinner ready on time, and remained attractive and optimistic; each hair was in place. According to studies, she was prettier than her mother, she was slimmer, and she even smelled better than her mother.

At this particular moment, it was impossible to underestimate the importance and influence of the women's magazines—the *Ladies' Home Journal, Redbook, McCall's,* and *Mademoiselle*—on middle-class young women. Isolated in the suburbs they felt uneasy and lonely and largely without guidance. More often than not, they were newly separated from their original families and the people they had grown up with. They were living new lives, different from those of their parents, with new and quite different expectations on the part of their husbands. Everything had to be learned.

In an age before the coming of midday television talk shows largely designed for housewives, women's magazines comprised the core reading material for the new young suburban wives. If the magazines' staffs at the lower rungs were comprised mostly of women, the magazines were almost always edited by men; in addition, editorial content, much more than in most general-circulation magazines, echoed the thrust of the advertising. Research showed, or seemed to show, that husbands made the critical decisions in terms of which political candidate a family might support, but the wives made the decisions on which refrigerator and which clothes washer to buy. If the advertising was designed to let women know what the newest appliances were and how to use them, then the accompanying articles were designed to show they could not live up to their destinies without them.

This was not done deliberately. There were no editorial meetings where male editors sat around and killed ideas that showed the brave new suburban world as populated with a significant percentage of tense, anxious female college graduates who wondered if they were squandering the best years of their lives. But there was an instinctive bias about what women needed to hear and that it should all be upbeat, and that any larger doubts were unworthy.

The magazines explained their new lives to them: how to live, how to dress, what to eat, why they should feel good about themselves and their husbands and their children. Their sacrifices, the women's magazines emphasized, were not really sacrifices, they were about fulfillment. All doubts were to be conquered.

The ideal fifties women were to strive for was articulated by *McCall's* in 1954: togetherness. A family was as one, its ambitions were twined. The husband was designated leader and hero, out there every day braving the treacherous corporate world to win a better life for his family; the wife was his mainstay on the domestic side, duly appreciative of the immense sacrifices being made for her and her children. There was no divergence within. A family was a single perfect universe—instead of a complicated, fragile mechanism of conflicting political and emotional pulls. Families portrayed in women's magazines exhibited no conflicts or contradictions or unfulfilled ambitions. Thanks, probably, to the drive for togetherness, the new homes all seemed to have what was called a family room. Here the family came together, ate, watched television, and possibly even talked. "When Jim comes home," said a wife in a 1954 advertisement for prefabricated homes, "our family room seems to draw us closer together." And who was responsible ultimately for togetherness if not the wife?

"The two big steps that women must take are to help their husbands decide where they are going and use their pretty heads to help them get there," wrote Mrs. Dale Carnegie, wife of one of the nation's leading experts on how to be likable, in the April 1955 *Better Homes and Gardens.* "Let's face it, girls. That wonderful guy in your house—and in mine—is building your house, your happiness, and the opportunities that will come to your children." Split-level houses, Mrs. Carnegie added, were fine for the family, "but there is simply no room for split-level thinking—or doing—when Mr. and Mrs. set their sights on a happy home, a host of friends, and a bright future through success in HIS job."

Those women who were not happy and did not feel fulfilled were encouraged to think that the fault was theirs and that they were the exception to blissful normality. That being the case, women of the period rarely shared their doubts, even with each other. If anything, they tended to feel guilty about any qualms they had: Here they were living better than ever— their husbands were making more money than ever, and there were ever bigger, more beautiful cars in the garage and appliances in the kitchen. Who were they to be unhappy?

One of the first women to challenge the fallacy of universal contentment among young suburban wives was a young woman from the heartland of the country. Born and reared in Peoria, Illinois, she did well enough in school to be admitted to an elite Eastern women's college, one of the **Seven Sisters schools.** She entered Smith College in 1939, finding everything that she had longed for as a small-town girl in Peoria: a world where women were rewarded for being smart and different instead of being punished for it. She graduated in 1942, summa cum laude, full of optimism about the future even though the war was still going on. Several scholarships were offered her. Ambitious, admired by her classmates, Betty Goldstein was certain

> **Seven Sisters schools** Elite colleges made up of Smith, Mt. Holyoke, Barnard, Vassar, Radcliffe, Wellesley, and Bryn Mawr.

that she would lead a life dramatically different from her mother's. Miriam Goldstein had been a society-page writer for the Peoria, Illinois, paper, before marrying a local storeowner and becoming a housewife. In her daughter's eyes, she took out her own frustrated ambitions by pushing her children to achieve. But at graduation time, Betty Goldstein turned down the fellowships because she was interested in a young man; since he had not been offered a comparable scholarship, she was afraid it would tear their relationship apart if she accepted hers. That decision, she later wrote, turned her instantly into a cliché. Looking back on her life, Betty Goldstein Friedan, one of the first voices of the feminist movement, noted the young man's face was more quickly forgotten than the terms of the scholarship itself.

Instead of getting married, she moved to the exciting intellectual world of Greenwich Village and became part of a group of liberal young people involved in labor issues and civil rights before it was fashionable. The women all seemed to be graduates of Smith, Vassar, and Radcliffe; they were bright and optimistic, eager to take on a static society. Betty Goldstein worked as a reporter for a left-wing labor paper. As a journalist, she had got a reputation of knowing her way around and having lots of contacts. She became the person designated to arrange illegal abortions for involuntarily pregnant friends. This, she found, she was able to do with a few discreet phone calls. The going price was $1,000. Once it was also her job to find a minister for two Protestant friends who wanted to marry. Because the groom was a divorced man, she noted with some irony, it was harder to find a willing minister than an abortionist.

When the war was over, the men returned from Europe and the South Pacific, and the women were gradually squeezed out of their jobs. Betty Goldstein, unsure of her role and her future, not liking the idea of a life alone (she had, she noted, "a pathological fear of being alone"), met a young veteran named Carl Friedan, who seemed funny and charming, and in 1947, two years after the war had ended, they were married. In 1949 they had their first child. When she was pregnant with her second child she was fired from the labor paper, whose radicalism, it appeared, did not yet extend to women's rights. When she took her grievance to the newspaper guild, she was told that the second pregnancy, which had cost her job, was her fault. There was, she later realized, no union term for sex discrimination.

Ms. Friedan soon found herself part of the great suburban migration as she moved further and further away from the Village, which had been the center of her professional and intellectual world. There, ideas had always seemed important. As she and her husband moved to larger and larger living quarters, first to Queens, where the Friedans lived in a pleasant apartment, and then to houses in the suburbs, her time was gradually more and more taken by children and family. As that happened, she was cut off, first physically, from what she had been, and then increasingly intellectually and socially as well. Betty Friedan now poured her energy into being a housewife and mother, into furnishing the apartment and houses and shopping, cooking, and cleaning for her family.

The Friedan family, she later realized, had been almost unconsciously caught up in the postwar migration to the suburbs. It was an ascent to an ever better style of living; but she also began to see it as a retreat as well from her earlier ambitions and standards. She liked doing the domestic things that Americans now did in their new, ever more informal social lives— grilling hamburgers on the outdoor barbecue, attending spur-of-the-moment cocktail parties, sharing summer rentals on Fire Island with friends. Finally, the Friedans bought an old house, worthy of **Charles Addams,** in Rockland County for $25,000 (with $2,500 down), where Betty Friedan, Smith summa cum laude and future feminist leader, spent her time, scraping eight layers of paint off a fireplace ("I quite liked it"), chauffeuring children to and from school, helping to run the PTA, and coming as close as someone as fiercely independent as she was could to being a good housewife, as portrayed in the women's magazines of that day. In some ways her life was full, she would later decide, and in some ways it was quite empty. She liked being a mother, and she liked her friends, but she missed the world of social and political involvement back in New York. She also worried that she had not lived up to her potential. By the time they were living in Rockland County, she had begun to write free-lance for various women's magazines. It was a clear sign, she realized later, that while the domestic side of her life was rich, it was not rich enough.

The deal she made with herself then was a revealing one. It was her job as a writer to make more money than she and Carl spent on a maid— otherwise her writing would be considered counterproductive and would be viewed as subtracting from rather than adding to the greater good of the family. Her early articles, "Millionaire's Wife" (*Cosmopolitan,* September 1956); "Now They're Proud of Peoria" (*Reader's Digest,* August 1955); "Two Are an Island" (*Mademoiselle,* July 1955); and "Day Camp in the Driveways" (*Parents' Magazine,* May 1957) were not exactly the achievements she had had in mind when she left Smith.

She was also very quickly finding out the limits of what could be done in writing for women's magazines at that time. In 1956, when she was pregnant with her third child, she read in a newspaper about Julie Harris, the actress, then starring in a play called *The Lark.* Ms. Harris had had natural childbirth, something that Betty Friedan, who had undergone two cesareans, admired and even envied. She decided, with the ready agreement of the magazines, to do a piece on Ms. Harris and her childbirth. She had a glorious time interviewing the actress and was completely captivated by her. She wrote what she thought was one of her best articles on the joys of natural childbirth. To her surprise, the article was turned down at first because it was too graphic.

Charles Addams Famed cartoonist whose drawings appeared frequently in the *New Yorker.*

That was hardly her only defeat with the magazines. When she suggested an article about Beverly Pepper, just beginning to experience considerable success as a painter and sculptor, and who was also raising a family, the editors of one magazine were scornful. American women, they told her, were not interested in someone like this and would not identify with her. Their market research, of which they were extremely confident, showed that women would only read articles that explained their own roles as wives and mothers. Not many American women out there had families and were successful as artists—therefore it would have no appeal. Perhaps, one editor said, they might do the article with a photograph of Mrs. Pepper painting the family crib.

At the time one of her children was in a play group with the child of a neighboring woman scientist. Ms. Friedan and the woman talked on occasion and her friend said she believed that a new ice age was approaching. The subject had interested Friedan, not normally a science writer, and she had suggested an article for *Harper's*. The resulting article, "The Coming Ice Age" was a considerable success and won a number of prizes. In New York George Brockway, a book editor at Norton, saw the piece and liked it. He called to ask if she was interested in writing a book. She was excited by his interest but had no desire to expand the piece into a book; the scientific work was not really hers, in the sense that it did not reflect her true interests and feelings. It was, she later said, as if she had served as a ghostwriter for another person on it.

Then something happened that changed her life. She and two friends were asked to do a report on what had happened to the members of the Smith class of '42 as they returned for their 15th reunion in 1957. She made up a questionnaire and got an assignment from *McCall's* to pay for her time. The piece was supposed to be called "The Togetherness Woman." The questions were: "What difficulties have you found in working out your role as a woman?" "What are the chief satisfactions and frustrations of your life today?" "How do you feel about getting older?" "How have you changed inside?" "What do you wish you had done differently?" The answers stunned her: She had tapped into a great reservoir of doubt, frustration, anxiety, and resentment. The women felt unfulfilled and isolated with their children; they often viewed their husbands as visitors from a far more exciting world.

The project also emphasized Friedan's own frustrations. All those years trying to be a good wife and mother suddenly seemed wasted; it had been wrong to suppress her feelings rather than to deal with them. The surprise was that there were thousands of women like her out there. As she wrote later in *The Feminine Mystique*:

> It was a strange stirring, a sense of dissatisfaction, a yearning that women suffered in the middle of the twentieth century in the United States. Each suburban wife struggled with it alone. As she made the beds, shopped for groceries, matched slip cover materials, ate peanut butter sandwiches with her children, chauffeured Cub Scouts and Brownies, lay beside her husband at night, she was afraid to ask of herself the silent question—"Is this all?"

As she had walked around the Smith campus during her reunion, she was struck by the passivity of the young women of the class of 1957. Upon graduation, her generation had been filled with excitement about the issues of the day: When Ms. Friedan asked these young women about their futures, they regarded her with blank looks. They were going to get engaged and married and have children, of course. She thought: This is happening at Smith, a place where I found nothing but intellectual excitement when I was their age. Something had gotten deep into the bloodstream of this generation, she decided.

She left and started to write the piece for *McCall's*, but it turned out very different from the one that she had intended to write. It reflected the despair and depression she had found among her contemporaries, and it was critical of women who lived through their husbands and children. *McCall's*, the inventor of "togetherness"—not surprisingly—turned it down. She heard that all the women editors there wanted to run it but that they had been overruled by their male superiors. That did not entirely surprise her, but she was sure someone else would want it. So she sent it to the *Ladies' Home Journal*, where it was accepted. There, to her amazement, it was rewritten so completely that it seemed to make the opposite points, so she pulled it. That left *Redbook*, where Bob Stein, an old friend, worked. He suggested that she do more interviews, particularly with younger women. She did, and sent the piece back to him. He was stunned by it. How could Betty Friedan write a piece so out of sync with what his magazine wanted? Why was she so angry? What in God's name had come over her? he wondered. He turned it down and called her agent. "Look," he said over the phone. "Only the most neurotic housewife would identify with this."

She was, she realized later, challenging the magazines themselves. She was saying that it was wrong to mislead women to think they should feel one way when in fact they often felt quite differently. She had discovered a crisis of considerable proportions, and these magazines would only deny it.

She was angry. It was censorship, she believed. Women's magazines had a single purpose, she decided—to sell a vast array of new products to American housewives—and anything that worked against that, that cast doubt about the happiness of the housewives using such products, was not going to be printed. No one from the advertising department sat in on editorial meetings saying which articles could run and which could not, she knew, but the very purpose of the magazine was to see women first and foremost as consumers, not as people.

At about that time she went to New York to attend a speech by Vance Packard, the writer. He had just finished his book, *The Hidden Persuaders*, about subliminal tactics in advertising. His efforts to write about this phenomenon in magazines had been completely unsuccessful, he said, so he turned it into a book, which had become a major best-seller. The parallels between his problems and hers were obvious. Suddenly, she envisioned "The Togetherness Woman" as a book. She called George Brockway at Norton, and he seemed delighted with the idea.

The economics of publishing were significantly different from those of magazines. Books were not dependent upon ads, they were dependent upon ideas, and the more provocative the idea, the more attention and, often, the better the sales. Brockway knew there had already been a number of attacks on conformity in American society, particularly as it affected men. Here was an attack that would talk about its effect on women, who were, of course, the principal buyers of books. He was impressed by Ms. Friedan. She was focused and, to his mind, wildly ambitious.

She told Brockway she would finish it in a year; instead, it took five years. Later she wrote that no one, not her husband, her editor, or anyone who knew her, thought she would ever finish it. She did so while taking care of three children. She later described herself as being like all the other mothers in suburbia, where she "hid, like secret drinking in the morning, the book I was writing when my suburban neighbors came for coffee . . ."

Her research was prodigious. Three days a week she went to the New York City Public Library for research. The chief villains, she decided, were the women's magazines. What stunned her was the fact that this had not always been true. In the same magazines in the late thirties and forties, there had been a sense of women moving steadily into the male professional world; then women's magazines had created a very different kind of role model, of a career woman who knew how to take care of herself and who could make it on her own.

But starting around 1949, these magazines changed dramatically. It was as if someone had thrown a giant switch. The new woman did not exist on her own. She was seen only in the light of supporting her husband and his career and taking care of the children.

The more Ms. Friedan investigated, the more she found that the world created in the magazines and the television sitcoms was, for many women at least, a fantasy world. Despite all the confidence and happiness among women portrayed in the magazines, there was underneath it all a crisis in the suburbs. It was the crisis of a generation of women who had left college with high idealism and who had come to feel increasingly frustrated and who had less and less a sense of self-esteem.

Nor, she found, did all the marvelous new appliances truly lighten the load of the housewife. If anything they seemed to extend it—there was some kind of Gresham's law at work here: The more time-saving machines there were, the more things there were to do with them. She had stumbled across something that a number of others, primarily psychiatrists, had noticed: a certain emotional malaise, bordering on depression, among many women of the era. One psychiatrist called it "the housewife's syndrome," another referred to it as "the housewife's blight." No one wrote about it in popular magazines, certainly not in the monthly women's magazines.

So, gathering material over several years, she began to write a book that would come out in 1963, not as *The Togetherness Woman*, but as *The Feminine Mystique*. She was approaching 40 as she began, but she was regenerated by the importance of the project; it seemed to give her her own life back. The result was a seminal book on what had happened to women in America. It started selling slowly but word of it grew and grew, and eventually, with 3 million copies in print, it became a handbook for the new feminist movement that was gradually beginning to come together.

A Primary Perspective

THE FEMININE MYSTIQUE

The best way to understand why Friedan's analysis evoked such a strong response is to read what she had to say. In the selection below from her influential work, she discusses that mysterious ailment, "the problem that has no name."

If a woman had a problem in the 1950s and 1960s, she knew that something must be wrong with her marriage or with herself. Other women were satisfied with their lives, she thought. What kind of a woman was she if she did not feel this mysterious fulfillment waxing the kitchen floor? She was so ashamed to admit her dissatisfaction that she never knew how many other women shared it. If she tried to tell her husband, he didn't understand what she was talking about. She did not really understand it herself. For over 15 years women in America found it harder to talk about this problem than about sex. Even the psychoanalysts had no name for it. When a woman went to a psychiatrist for help, as many women did, she would say, "I'm so ashamed," or "I must be hopelessly neurotic." "I don't know what's wrong with women today," a suburban psychiatrist said uneasily. "I only know something is wrong because most of my patients happen to be women. And their problem isn't sexual." Most women with this problem did not go to see a psychoanalyst, however. "There's nothing wrong really," they kept telling themselves. "There isn't any problem."

But on an April morning in 1959, I heard a mother of four, having coffee with four other mothers in a suburban development 15 miles from New York, say in a tone of quiet desperation, "the problem." And the others knew, without words, that she was not talking about a problem with her husband, or her children, or her home. Suddenly they realized they all shared the same problem, the problem that has no name. They began, hesitantly, to talk about it. Later, after they had picked up their children at nursery school and taken them home to nap, two of the women cried, in sheer relief, just to know they were not alone. . . .

Even so, most men, and some women, still did not know that this problem was real. But those who had faced it honestly knew that all the superficial remedies, the sympathetic advice, the scolding words and the cheering words were somehow drowning the problem in unreality. A bitter laugh was beginning to

Source: From *The Feminine Mystique* by Betty Friedan. Copyright © 1983, 1974, 1973, 1963 by Betty Friedan. Reprinted by permission of W. W. Norton & Company, Inc.

be heard from American women. They were admired, envied, pitied, theo-
rized over until they were sick of it, offered drastic solutions or silly choices
that no one could take seriously. They got all kinds of advice from the growing armies of marriage and child-guidance counselors, psychotherapists, and
armchair psychologists, on how to adjust to their role as housewives. No other
road to fulfillment was offered to American women in the middle of the twentieth century. Most adjusted to their role and suffered or ignored the problem
that has no name. It can be less painful, for a woman, not to hear the strange,
dissatisfied voice stirring within her.

It is no longer possible to ignore that voice, to dismiss the desperation of
so many American women. This is not what being a woman means, no matter
what the experts say. For human suffering there is a reason; perhaps the reason has not been found because the right questions have not been asked, or
pressed far enough. I do not accept the answer that there is no problem
because American women have luxuries that women in other times and lands
never dreamed of; part of the strange newness of the problem is that it cannot be understood in terms of the age-old material problems of man: poverty,
sickness, hunger, cold. The women who suffer this problem have a hunger
that food cannot fill. It persists in women whose husbands are struggling
interns and law clerks, or prosperous doctors and lawyers; in wives of workers and executives who make $5,000 a year or $50,000. It is not caused by lack
of material advantages; it may not even be felt by women preoccupied with
desperate problems of hunger, poverty, or illness. And women who think it
will be solved by more money, a bigger house, a second car, moving to a better
suburb, often discover it gets worse.

QUESTIONS

1. According to women's magazines, what qualities were required for the
   ideal woman of the 1950s to achieve happiness and fulfillment? What
   were Friedan's feelings about life in the suburbs? Were they entirely
   negative?
2. Why did the media discourage women from pursuing careers outside the
   home during the 1950s? What obstacles did wage-earning women typically
   confront during the period?
3. Why was the popular image of women's domestic role so positive during
   the 1950s? Why did Friedan decide to challenge that image? What influence did her association with Smith College have on her development as
   a social critic?
4. Why were Friedan's ideas for *The Feminine Mystique* so much more acceptable to a book publisher than to a women's magazine? What did her research
   reveal about the changing portayal of women in these magazines?
5. Why do you think Friedan believed "the problem that has no name" was
   the most apt description of the frustration that many suburban housewives
   felt during the 1950s? Based on the above excerpts from *The Feminine*

Mystique, how would you define "the problem that has no name"? Would Friedan's work have been more or less influential if it had been written 20 years earlier?

6. Do you see any similarities between Friedan, Eleanor Roosevelt, and Margaret Sanger? In what ways did the three women differ? Which of them faced the greatest obstacles? Which of them did more to advance the cause of women's rights?

 ## ADDITIONAL RESOURCES

There are two full-length treatments of Friedan's life and work: Judith A. Hennessee, *Betty Friedan: A Life* (1999), and Daniel Horowitz, *Betty Friedan and the Making of the Feminine Mystique* (1998). In addition, autobiographical observations appear in four of the books Friedan has written: *The Feminine Mystique* (1963); *It Changed My Life: Writings of the Woman's Movement* (1976); *The Second Stage* (1981); and *Life So Far: A Memoir* (2000). Those seeking to learn more about the postwar expansion of suburbia should consult Kenneth Jackson, *Crabgrass Frontier: The Suburbanization of the United States* (1985). For a provocative examination of postwar domesticity, see Elaine Tyler May, *Homeward Bound: American Families in the Cold War Era* (1988). Major studies of the rebirth of feminism during the 1980s include Susan M. Hartmann, *From Margin to Mainstream: American Women and Politics since 1960* (1989), and Sara Evans, *Personal Politics: The Roots of Women's Liberation in the Civil Rights Movement and the New Left* (1980). Two surveys that place these developments in a broader historical context are William Chafe, *The Paradox of Change: American Women in the Twentieth Century* (1991), and Rosalind Rosenberg, *Divided Lives: American Women in the Twentieth Century* (1992).

For the modern women's movement, "Not One of the Boys" (1984) is from the PBS *Frontline* series and examines women in politics. *The Wilmar 8* explores a strike for equal pay in Minnesota during the 1970s, and a *Simple Matter of Justice* looks at the fight for the Equal Rights Amendment.

Chapter 16

Cesar Chavez

*I*n the immediate postwar decades, unions in mass-production industries such as autos and steel achieved impressive advances at the bargaining table. In addition to providing substantial wage increases, union-negotiated contracts contained provisions for paid vacations, health insurance programs, pension plans, cost-of-living allowances, and other security measures. When the United Auto Workers (UAW) established an employer-funded system of supplemental unemployment benefits in 1955, organized labor appeared to be on the verge of obtaining its long-sought goal of a guaranteed annual wage. And when UAW President Walter Reuther later observed that the union movement was "developing a whole new middle class," countless workers doubtless agreed.

But Reuther did not speak for all wage earners. Far away from the nation's mass-production industries, America's agricultural workers continued to live and labor in a world of grinding poverty that had changed little during the previous century. Federal laws mandating collective bargaining did not apply to these workers; and a series of organizational efforts, extending back to the turn of the century, had all been defeated by the politically powerful growers who employed them and who dominated the areas in which they worked. Without protection and often without hope, farmworkers had become

the forgotten people of the American labor force. It was little wonder that when Cesar Chavez decided to organize California farmworkers during the early 1960s, he spoke of the mission as "an all but impossible task."

Yet the sixties were a unique time in American life, when anything seemed possible. Civil rights demonstrators had shown that courage and determination could undermine the most intractable forms of oppression. And Chavez possessed just the qualities needed to channel that movement's energy and hope toward his own ends. An intense man of single-minded purpose, he convinced farmworkers that they too could create a better world for themselves and their children. At the same time, he took steps to mobilize national support for his efforts, thus shattering the isolation that had long abetted growers' exploitation of agricultural laborers. As much a social activist as a labor organizer, Chavez established a union that exhibited the same dual personality.

It was an extraordinary achievement. In the essay that follows, Cletus E. Daniel describes the numerous obstacles that Chavez had to overcome. In the process, Daniel not only provides an insightful examination of the character traits that enabled Chavez to persevere in his seemingly hopeless task; he also offers a judicious assessment of Chavez's strengths and shortcomings as a labor leader.

Cesar Chavez

Cletus E. Daniel

It was, Cesar Chavez later wrote, "the strangest meeting in the history of California agriculture." Speaking by telephone from his cluttered headquarters in La Paz to Jerry Brown, the new governor of California, Chavez had been asked to repeat for the benefit of farm employers crowded into Brown's Sacramento office the farmworker leader's acceptance of a farm labor bill to which they had already assented. And as the employers heard Chavez's voice repeating the statement of acceptance he had just made to the governor, they broke into wide smiles and spontaneous applause.

That representatives of the most powerful special interest group in California history should have thus expressed their delight at the prospect of realizing still another of their legislative goals does not account for Chavez's assertion of the meeting's strange character. These were, after all, men long accustomed to having their way in matters of farm labor legislation. What was strange about that meeting on May 5, 1975, was that the state's leading farm

Source: From *Labor Leaders in America.* Copyright © 1987 by the Board of Trustees of the University of Illinois. Used with permission of the University of Illinois Press.

employers should have derived such apparent relief and satisfaction from hearing the president of the United Farm Workers of America, AFL-CIO, agree to a legislative proposal designed to afford farmworkers an opportunity to escape their historic powerlessness through unionism and collective bargaining.

Beyond investing the state's farmworkers with rights that those who labored for wages on the land had always been denied, the passage of California's Agricultural Labor Relations Act (ALRA) was a seismic event, one that shattered the foundation upon which rural class relations had rested for a century and more. For the state's agribusinessmen, whose tradition it had been to rule the bounteous fields and orchards of California with a degree of authority and control more appropriate to potentates than mere employers, supporting the ALRA was less an act of culpable treason against their collective heritage than one of grudging resignation in the face of a suddenly irrelevant past and an apparently inescapable future. For the state's farmworkers, whose involuntary custom it had always been to surrender themselves to a system of industrialized farming that made a captive peasantry of them, the new law made possible what only the boldest among them had dared to imagine: a role equal to the employer's in determining terms and conditions of employment. Yet if the ALRA's enactment was a victory of unprecedented dimensions for California farmworkers as a class, it was a still greater personal triumph for Cesar Chavez.

More than any other labor leader of his time, and perhaps in the whole history of American labor, Cesar Chavez leads a union that is an extension of his own values, experience, and personality. This singular unity of man and movement has found its most forceful and enduring expression in the unprecedented economic and political power that has accrued to the membership of the United Farm Workers (UFW) under Chavez's intense and unrelenting tutelage. Indeed, since 1965, when Chavez led his then small following into a bitter struggle against grape growers around the lower San Joaquin valley town of Delano, the UFW has, despite the many crises that have punctuated its brief but turbulent career, compiled a record of achievement that rivals the accomplishments of the most formidable industrial unions of the 1930s.

While this personal domination may well be the essential source of the UFW's extraordinary success, it has also posed risks for the union. For just as Chavez's strengths manifest themselves in the character of his leadership, so, too, must his weaknesses. Certainly the UFW's somewhat confused sense of its transcending mission—whether to be a trade union or a social movement; whether to focus on narrow economic gains or to pursue broader political goals—reflects in some degree Chavez's personal ambivalence toward both the ultimate purpose of worker organization and the fundamental objective of his own prolonged activism.

Had his adult life followed the pattern of his early youth, Cesar Chavez need not have concerned himself with the task of liberating California farmworkers from an exploitive labor system that had entombed a succession of Chinese, Japanese, Filipino, Mexican, and other non-Anglo immigrants for more than a hundred years. Born on March 31, 1927, the second child of

Librado and Juana Chavez, Cesar Estrada Chavez started his life sharing little beyond language and a diffuse ethnic heritage with the Chicano—Mexican
and Mexican-American—workers who constitute nearly the entire membership of the United Farm Workers of America. Named after his paternal grand-
father Cesario, who had homesteaded the family's small farm in the north
Gila River valley near Yuma three years before Arizona claimed statehood,
Chavez enjoyed during his youth the kind of close and stable family life that
farmworkers caught in the relentless currents of the western migrant stream
longed for but rarely attained. And although farming on a small scale afforded
few material rewards even as it demanded hard and unending physical labor,
it fostered in Chavez an appreciation of independence and personal sovereignty that helps to account for the special force and steadfastness of his later
rebellion against the oppressive dependence into which workers descended
when they joined the ranks of California's agricultural labor force.

It is more than a little ironic that until 1939, when unpaid taxes put the
family's farm on the auction block, Chavez could have more reasonably
aspired to a future as a landowner than as a farmworker. "If we had stayed
there," he later said of the family's farm, "possibly I would have been a
grower. God writes in exceedingly crooked lines."

The full significance of the family's eviction from the rambling adobe
ranch house that had provided not only shelter but also a sense of place and
social perspective was not at once apparent to an 11 year old. The deeper
meaning of the family's loss was something that accumulated in Chavez's
mind only as his subsequent personal experience in the migrant stream disclosed the full spectrum of emotional and material hardship attending a life
set adrift from the roots that had nurtured it. At age 11 the sight of a bulldozer effortlessly destroying in a few minutes what the family had struggled
over nearly three generations to build was meaning enough. The land's new
owner, an Anglo grower impatient to claim his prize, dispatched the bulldozer
that became for Chavez a graphic and enduring symbol of the power that the
"haves" employ against the "have-nots" in industrialized agriculture. . . .

"When we were pushed off our land," Chavez said, "all we could take
with us was what we could jam into the old Studebaker or pile on its roof
and fenders, mostly clothes and bedding . . . I realized something was happening because my mother was crying, but I didn't realize the import of it at
the time. When we left the farm, our whole life was upset, turned upside
down. We have been part of a very stable community, and we were about to
become migratory workers."

Yet if Chavez's experience was in some ways similar to that of the dispossessed dust-bowl migrant whose pilgrimage to California was also less an
act of hope than of despair, it was fundamentally unlike that of even the most
destitute Anglo—John Steinbeck's generic "**Okie**"—because of virulent racial attitudes among the state's white majority that tended to define all persons "of color" as unequal. For

> "Okie" Poor people of Oklahoma
> who left the "dust bowl" and
> sought a better life in California.

the Chavez family, whose standing as landowners in a region populated by people mainly like themselves had insulated them from many of the meanest forms of racism, following the crops in California as undifferentiated members of a brown-skinned peasantry afforded an unwelcome education. To the familiar varieties of racial humiliation and mistreatment—being physically punished by an Anglo teacher for lapsing into your native tongue; being in the presence of Anglos who talked about you as if you were an inanimate object—were added some new and more abrasive forms: being rousted by border patrolmen who automatically regarded you as a "wetback" until you proved otherwise; being denied service at a restaurant or made to sit in the "Mexican only" seats at the local movie house; being stopped and searched by the police for no reason other than your skin color announced your powerlessness to resist; being cheated by an employer who smugly assumed that you probably wouldn't object because Mexicans were naturally docile.

But, if because of such treatment Chavez came to fear and dislike Anglos—*gringos* or *gabachos* in the pejorative lexicon of the barrio—he also came to understand that while considerations of race and ethnicity compounded the plight of farmworkers, their mistreatment was rooted ultimately in the economics of industrialized agriculture. As the family traveled the state from one crop to the next, one hovel to the next, trying desperately to survive on the meager earnings of parents and children alike, Chavez quickly learned that Chicano labor contractors and Japanese growers exploited migrants as readily as did Anglo employers. And, although the complex dynamics of California's rural political economy might still have eluded him, Chavez instinctively understood that farmworkers would cease to be victims only when they discovered the means to take control of their own lives.

The realization that unionism must be that means came later. Unlike the typical Chicano family in the migrant stream, however, the Chavez family included among its otherwise meager possessions a powerful legacy of the independent life it had earlier known, one that revealed itself in a stubborn disinclination to tolerate conspicuous injustices. "I don't want to suggest we were that radical," Chavez later said, "but I know we were probably one of the strikingest families in California, the first ones to leave the fields if anyone shouted Huelga!—which is Spanish for Strike! . . . If any family felt something was wrong and stopped working, we immediately joined them even if we didn't know them. And if the grower didn't correct what was wrong, then they would leave, and we'd leave." . . .

Although the United Cannery, Agricultural, Packing and Allied Workers of America, a CIO-affiliated union, was conducting sporadic organizing drives among California farmworkers when Chavez and his family joined the state's farm labor force at the end of the 1930s, he was too young and untutored to appreciate "anything of the real guts of unions." Yet because his father harbored a strong, if unstudied, conviction that unionism was a manly act of resistance to the employers' authority, Chavez's attitude toward unions quickly progressed from vague approval to ardent endorsement. His earliest participation in a union-led struggle did not occur until the late 1940s, when the AFL's National Farm Labor Union conducted a series of ultimately futile strikes in the San Joaquin valley. This experience, which left Chavez with an acute sense of frustration and disappointment as the strike inevitably withered in the face of overwhelming employer power, also produced a brief but equally keen feeling of exhilaration because it afforded an opportunity to vent the rebelliousness that an expanding consciousness of his own social and occupational captivity awakened within him. Yet to the extent that unionism demands the subordination of individual aspirations to a depersonalized common denomination of the group's desires, Chavez was not in his youth the stuff of which confirmed trade unionists are made. More than most young migrant workers, whose ineluctable discontent was not heightened further by the memory of an idealized past, Chavez hoped to escape his socioeconomic predicament rather than simply moderate the harsh forces that governed it.

To be a migrant worker, however, was to learn the hard way that avenues of escape were more readily imagined than traveled. As ardently as the Chavez family sought a way out of the migrant orbit, they spent the early 1940s moving from valley to valley, from harvest to harvest, powerless to fend off the corrosive effects of their involuntary transiency. Beyond denying them the elementary amenities of a humane existence—a decent home, sufficient food, adequate clothing—the demands of migrant life also conspired to deny the Chavez children the educations that their parents valiantly struggled to ensure. For Cesar school became a "nightmare," a dispiriting succession of inhospitable places ruled by Anglo teachers and administrators whose often undisguised contempt for migrant children prompted him to drop out after the eighth grade.

Chavez's inevitable confrontation with the fact of his personal powerlessness fostered a sense of anger and frustration that revealed itself in a tendency to reject many of the most visible symbols of his cultural heritage. This brief episode of open rebellion against the culture of his parents, which dates from the family's decision to settle down in Delano in late 1943 until he reluctantly joined the navy a year later, was generally benign: *Mariachis* were rejected in favor of Duke Ellington; his mother's *dichos* and *consejos*—the bits of Mexican folk wisdom passed from one generation to the next—lost out to less culture-bound values; religious customs rooted in the rigid doctrines of the Catholic church gave way to a fuzzy existentialism . . . In the end, Chavez reacted most decisively against the debilitating circumstances of his life by joining the navy, a reluctant decision whose redeeming value was that it offered a means of escape, a way "to get away from farm labor."

The two years he spent in the navy ("the worst of my life") proved to be no more than a respite from farm labor. If Chavez had hoped to acquire a trade while in the service, he soon discovered that the same considerations of race and ethnicity that placed strict limits on what non-Anglos could reasonably aspire to achieve at home operated with equal efficiency in the navy to keep them in the least desirable jobs. Without the training that might have allowed him to break out of the cycle of poverty and oppression that the labor system of industrialized agriculture fueled, Chavez returned to Delano in 1946 to the only work he knew.

Finding work had always been a problem for farmworkers due to a chronic oversupply of agricultural labor in California. The problem became even more acute for migrant families after the war because agribusiness interests succeeded in their political campaign to extend the so-called *Bracero* program, a treaty arrangement dating from 1942 that permitted farm employers in California and the Southwest to import Mexican nationals under contract to alleviate real and imagined wartime labor shortages.

For Chavez, the struggle to earn a living took on special urgency following his marriage in 1948 to Helen Fabela, a Delano girl whom he had first met when his family made one of its periodic migrations through the area in search of work. Being the daughter of farmworkers, and thus knowing all too well the hardships that attended a family life predicated upon the irregular earnings of agricultural work, did nothing to cushion the hard times that lay ahead for Helen Chavez and her new husband, a 21-year-old disaffected farm laborer without discernable prospects.

Chavez met the challenge of making a living, which multiplied with the arrival of a new baby during each of the first three years of marriage, in the only way he knew: He took any job available, wherever it was available. Not until 1952, when he finally landed a job in a San Jose lumberyard, was Chavez able to have the settled life that he and Helen craved. The Mexican barrio in San Jose, known to its impoverished inhabitants as Sal Si Puedes—literally "get out if you can"—was a few square blocks of ramshackle houses occupied by discouraged parents and angry children who, in their desperation to do just what the neighborhood's morbid nickname advised, too often sought ways out that led to prison rather than to opportunity. Long before it became home to Chavez and his family, Sal Si Puedes had earned a reputation among the sociologists who regularly scouted its mean streets as a virtual laboratory of urban social pathology. In the early 1950s, however, the area also attracted two men determined in their separate ways to alleviate the powerlessness of its residents rather than to document or measure it. More than any others, these two activists, one a young Catholic priest, the other a veteran community organizer, assumed unwitting responsibility for the education of Cesar Chavez.

When Father Donald McDonnell established his small mission church in Sal Si Puedes, he resolved to attend to both the spiritual need of his destitute parishioners and their education in those doctrines of the Catholic church relating to the inherent rights of labor. To Cesar Chavez, the teachings of the church, the rituals and catechism that he absorbed as an obligation of culture rather than a voluntary and knowing act of religious faith, had never seemed to have more than tangential relevance to the hard-edged world that poor people confronted in their daily lives. But in the militant example and activist pedagogy of Father McDonnell, Chavez discovered a new dimension of Catholicism that excited him precisely because it was relevant to his immediate circumstances. . . .

More than anyone else, Father McDonnell awoke Chavez to a world of pertinent ideas that would become the essential source of his personal philosophy; introduced him to a pantheon of crusaders for social justice (Gandhi among them) whose heroic exertions would supply the inspiration for his own crusade to empower farmworkers. Yet the crucial task of instructing Chavez in the practical means by which his nascent idealism might achieve concrete expression was brilliantly discharged by Fred Ross, an indefatigable organizer who had spent the better part of his adult life roaming California trying to show the victims of economic, racial, and ethnic discrimination how they might resist further abuse and degradation through organization.

Drawn to Sal Si Puedes by the palpable misery of its Chicano inhabitants, Ross began to conduct the series of informal house meetings through which he hoped to establish a local chapter of the Community Service Organization (CSO), a self-help group that operated under the sponsorship of radical activist Saul Alinsky's Chicago-based Industrial Areas Foundation. Always on the lookout for the natural leaders in the communities he sought to organize, Ross at once saw in Chavez, despite his outwardly shy and self-conscious demeanor, the telltale signs of a born organizer. "At the very first meeting," Ross recalled: "I was very much impressed with Cesar. I could tell he was intensely interested, a kind of burning interest rather than one of those inflammatory things that lasts one night and is then forgotten. He asked many questions, part of it to see if I really knew, putting me to the test. But it was much more than that." Ross also discovered that Chavez was an exceedingly quick study. . . .

The confidence that Ross expressed in Chavez's leadership potential was immediately confirmed. Assigned to the CSO voter registration project in San Jose, Chavez displayed a natural aptitude for the work; so much in fact that Ross turned over control of the entire drive to him. And if his style of leadership proved somewhat unconventional, his tactical sense was unerring. While Ross had relied upon local college students to serve as registrars for the campaign, Chavez felt more could be gained by using people from the barrio. "Instead of recruiting college guys," he said, "I got all my friends, my beer-drinking friends. With them it wasn't a question of civic duty, they helped me because of friendship, and because it was fun." With nearly 6,000 new voters registered by the time the campaign ended, Chavez's reputation as an organizer was established. . . .

After watching his protégé in action for only a few months, Fred Ross persuaded Saul Alinsky that the CSO should employ the talents of so able an organizer on a full-time basis. Becoming a professional organizer, however, was a prospect that frightened Chavez nearly as much as it excited him. Helping Fred Ross was one thing, organizing on his own among strangers was quite another. Yet in the end, his desire to oppose what seemed unjust outweighed his fears.

From the end of 1952 until he quit the organization 10 years later to build a union among farmworkers, the CSO was Chavez's life. He approached the work of helping the poor to help themselves in the only way his nature allowed, with a single-mindedness that made everything else in his life—home, family, personal gain—secondary. For Chavez, nothing short of total immersion in the work of forcing change was enough. If his wife inherited virtually the entire responsibility for raising their children (who were to number eight in all), if his children became resentful at being left to grow up without a father who was readily accessible to them, if he was himself forced to abandon any semblance of personal life, Chavez remained unshaken in his belief that the promotion of the greater good made every such sacrifice necessary and worthwhile. . . .

In the beginning, helping people to deal with problems they felt otherwise powerless to resolve was an end in itself. In time, however, Chavez saw that if his service work was going to produce a legacy of activist sentiment in Chicano neighborhoods, it was necessary to recast what had typically been an act of unconditional assistance into a mutually beneficial transaction. And, when he discovered that those whom he was serving were not just willing, but eager, to return the favor, Chavez made that volition the basis upon which he helped to build the CSO into the most formidable Mexican-American political organization in the state. "Once I realized helping people was an organizing technique," he said, "I increased that work. I was willing to work day and night and to go to hell and back for people—provided they also did something for the CSO in return. I never felt bad asking for that . . . because I wasn't asking for something for myself. For a long time we didn't know how to put that work together into an organization. But we learned after a while— we learned how to help people by making them responsible."

Because agricultural labor constituted a main source of economic opportunity in most Chicano communities, many of those whom Chavez recruited into the CSO were farmworkers. Not until 1958, however, did Chavez take his first halting steps toward making work and its discontents the essential focus of his organizing activities. This gradual shift from community to labor organization occurred over a period of several months as Chavez struggled to establish a CSO chapter in Oxnard, a leading citrus-growing region north of Los Angeles. Asked by Saul Alinsky to organize the local Chicano community in order that it might support the flagging efforts of the United Packinghouse Workers to win labor contracts covering the region's citrus-packing sheds, Chavez embarked upon his task intending to exploit the same assortment of grievances that festered in barrios throughout the state.

His new clients, however, had other ideas. From the beginning, whenever he sought to impress his agenda upon local citizens, they interrupted with their own: a concern that they were being denied jobs because growers in the region relied almost entirely on **braceros** to meet their needs for farm labor. It proved to be an issue that simply would not go away. "At every house meeting," Chavez recalled, "they hit me with the bracero problem, but I would dodge it. I just didn't fathom how big that problem was. I would say, 'Well, you know, we really can't do anything about that, but it's a bad problem. Something

should be done.'" An apparently artless dodger, he was, in the end, forced to make the bracero problem the focus of his campaign. "Finally," he admitted, "I decided this was the issue I had to tackle. The fact that braceros

> **bracero**   A Mexican laborer admitted to the United States especially for seasonal contract labor in agriculture.

were also farmworkers didn't bother me . . . The jobs belonged to local workers. The braceros were brought only for exploitation. They were just instruments for the growers. Braceros didn't make any money, and they were
exploited viciously, forced to work under conditions the local people wouldn't
tolerate. If the braceros spoke up, if they made the minimal complaints, they'd
be shipped back to Mexico."

In attacking Oxnard's bracero problem, Chavez and his followers confronted the integrated power of the agribusiness establishment in its most
forceful and resilient aspect. While farm employers around Oxnard and
throughout the state were permitted under federal regulations to employ
braceros only when they had exhausted the available pool of local farmworkers, they had long operated on the basis of a collusive arrangement with
the California Farm Placement Service that allowed them to import Mexican
nationals without regard to labor market conditions in the region.

Although Chavez and the large CSO membership he rallied behind him
sought nothing more than compliance with existing rules regarding the
employment of braceros, the 13-month struggle that followed brought them
into bitter conflicts with politically influential employers, state farm placement
bureaucrats, and federal labor department officials. Yet through the use of
picket lines, marches, rallies, and a variety of innovative agitational techniques
that reduced the Farm Placement Service to almost total paralysis, Chavez and
his militant following had by the end of 1959 won a victory so complete that
farm employers in the region were recruiting their labor through a local CSO
headquarters that operated as a hiring hall.

Chavez emerged from the Oxnard campaign convinced that work-related
issues had greater potential as a basis for organizing Chicanos than any that
he had earlier stressed. The response to his organizing drive in Oxnard was
overwhelming, and he saw at once "the difference between that CSO chapter
and any other CSO up to that point was that jobs were the main issue." And
at the same juncture, he said: "I began to see the potential of organizing the
Union." . . .

In Chavez's view, nothing less than fanaticism would suffice if farmworkers were to be emancipated from a system of wage slavery that had
endured for a century. When a reporter observed during one of the UFW's
later struggles that he "sounded like a fanatic," Chavez readily admitted the
charge. "I am," he confessed. "There's nothing wrong with being a fanatic.
Those are the only ones that get things done."

In many ways, Chavez's supreme accomplishment as an organizer came
long before he signed up his first farmworker. Attracting disciples willing to
embrace the idea of a farmworkers' movement with a passion, single-
mindedness, and spirit of sacrifice equal to his own was at once Chavez's greatest challenge and his finest achievement. By the fall of 1962, when he formally
established the National Farm Workers Association (NFWA) in a derelict Fresno
theater, Chavez had rallied to "La Causa"—the iconographic designation soon
adopted by the faithful—an impressive roster of "co-fanatics": Dolores Huerta,
a small, youthful-looking mother of six (she would have 10 in all) whose

willingness to do battle with Chavez over union tactics was exceeded only by her fierce loyalty to him; Gilbert Padilla, like Huerta another CSO veteran, whose activism was rooted in a hatred for the migrant system that derived from personal experience; Wayne Hartimire and Jim Drake, two young Anglo ministers who were to make the California Migrant Ministry a virtual subsidiary of the union; Manuel Chavez, an especially resourceful organizer who reluctantly gave up a well-paying job to join the union when the guilt his cousin Cesar heaped upon him for not joining became unbearable. Most important, there was Helen Chavez, whose willingness to sacrifice so much of what mattered most to her, including first claim on her husband's devotion, revealed the depth of her own commitment to farmworker organization.

Working out of Delano, which became the union's first headquarters, Chavez began the slow and often discouraging process of organizing farm laborers whose strong belief in the rightness of his union-building mission was tempered by an even deeper conviction that "it couldn't be done, that the growers were too powerful." With financial resources consisting of a small savings account, gifts and loans from relatives, and the modest wages Helen earned by returning to the fields, the cost of Chavez's stubborn idealism to himself and his family was measured in material deprivation and emotional tumult. Had he been willing to accept financial assistance from such sources as the United Packinghouse Workers or the Agricultural Workers Organizing Committee (AWOC), a would-be farmworkers' union established in 1959 by the AFL-CIO, the worst hardships that awaited Chavez and his loyalists might have been eased or eliminated. Yet, following a line of reasoning that was in some ways reminiscent of the voluntarist logic of earlier trade unionists, Chavez insisted that a farmworkers' union capable of forging the will and stamina required to breach the awesome power of agribusiness could only be built on the sacrifice and suffering of its own membership.

During the NFWA's formative years there was more than enough sacrifice and suffering to go around. But due to the services it provided to farmworkers and the promise of a better life it embodied, the union slowly won the allegiance of a small but dedicated membership scattered through the San Joaquin valley. By the spring of 1965, when the union called its first strike, a brief walkout by rose grafters in Kern County that won higher wages but no contract, Chavez's obsession was on its way to becoming a functioning reality.

Despite the studied deliberateness of its leaders, however, the struggle that catapulted the union to national attention, and invested its mission with the same moral authority that liberal and left-wing activists of the 1960s attributed to the decade's stormy civil rights, antipoverty, and antiwar movements, began in the fall of 1965 as a reluctant gesture of solidarity with an AWOC local whose mainly Filipino membership was on strike against grape growers around Delano. Given the demonstrated ineptitude of the old-time trade unionists who directed the AFL-CIO's organizing efforts among California farmworkers, Chavez had reason to hesitate before committing his still small and untested membership to the support of an AWOC strike. But the strike was being led by Larry Itliong, a Filipino veteran of earlier agricultural strikes and the ablest of the AWOC organizers, and Chavez did not have it in him to ignore a just cause. . . .

The Delano strike, which soon widened beyond the table grape growers who were its initial targets to include the state's major wineries, was a painful five-year struggle destined to test not only the durability of agricultural unionism in California but also the wisdom and resourcefulness of Chavez's leadership. Because growers had little difficulty in recruiting scabs to take the place of strikers, Chavez recognized immediately that a strike could not deny employers the labor they required to cultivate and harvest their crops. Even so, picket lines went up on the first day of the strike and were maintained with unfailing devotion week after week, month after month. Chavez emphasized the need for picketing because he believed that no experience promoted a keener sense of solidarity or afforded strikers a more graphic and compelling illustration of the struggle's essential character. "Unless you have been on a picket line," he said, "you just can't understand the feeling you get there, seeing the conflict at its two most acid ends. It's a confrontation that's vivid. It's a real education." It was an education, however, for which pickets often paid a high price: threats, physical intimidation, and outright violence at the hands of growers and their agents and arbitrary arrests and harassment by local lawmen who made no effort to mask their pro-employer sympathies. Yet, no matter how great the provocation, no matter how extreme the violence directed against them, strikers were sworn by Chavez not to use violence. Chavez's unwavering commitment to nonviolence was compounded from equal measures of his mother's teachings, the affecting example of **St. Francis of Assisi,** and the moral philosophy of **Gandhi.** In the end, though, it was the power of nonviolence as a tactical method that appealed to him. Convinced that the farmworkers' greatest asset was the inherent justice of their cause, Chavez believed that the task of communicating the essential virtue of the union's struggle to potential supporters, and to the general public, would be subverted if strikers resorted to violence. . . .

Winning and sustaining public sympathy, as well as the active support of labor, church, student, civic, and political organizations, was indispensable to the success of the Delano struggles because the inefficacy of conventional strike tactics led Chavez to adopt the economic boycott as the union's primary weapon in fighting employers. Newly sensitized to issues of social justice by the civil rights struggles that reverberated across the country, liberals and leftists enthusiastically embraced the union's cause, endorsing its successive boycotts and not infrequently showing up in Delano to bear personal witness to the unfolding drama of the grape strike. Many unions— from dockworkers who refused to handle scab grapes to autoworkers,

> **St. Francis of Assisi** Founder of the Franciscans and one of the greatest Christian saints.
> **Gandhi** Leader of the Indian Nationalist movement against British rule who advocated nonviolent protest.

whose president, Walter Reuther, not only pledged generous financial assistance to the strikers but also traveled to Delano to join their picket lines—also supported the NFWA. Even the AFL-CIO, which had been sponsoring the rival Agricultural Workers Organizing Committee, ended up embracing the NFWA when Bill Kircher, the federation's national organizing director, concluded that the future of farmworker unionism lay with Chavez and his ragtag following rather than with the more fastidious, but less effective, AWOC. Kircher's assessment of the situation also led him to urge a merger of the NFWA and AWOC. And although their long-standing suspicion of "Big Labor" impelled many of the Anglo volunteers who had joined his movement to oppose the idea, Chavez and the union's farmworker membership recognized that the respectability and financial strength to be gained from such a merger outweighed any loss of independence that AFL-CIO affiliation might entail. With Chavez at its helm and Larry Itliong as its second-in-command, the United Farm Workers Organizing Committee (UFWOC) was formally chartered by the AFL-CIO in August 1966. . . .

"Alone, the farm workers have no economic power," Chavez once observed, "but with the help of the public they can develop the economic power to counter that of the growers." The truth of that maxim was first revealed in April 1966, when a national boycott campaign against its product line of wines and spirits caused Schenley Industries, which had 5,000 acres of vineyards in the San Joaquin valley, to recognize the farmworkers' union and enter into contract negotiations. For Chavez, who received the news as he and a small band of union loyalists were nearing the end of an arduous, but exceedingly well-publicized, 300-mile march from Delano to Sacramento, Schenley's capitulation was "the first major proof of the power of the boycott." . . .

The victories won during the first two years of the Delano struggle, while they propelled the cause of farmworker organization far beyond the boundaries of any previous advance, left Chavez and his followers still needing to overcome table grape growers in the San Joaquin and Coachella valleys before the union could claim real institutional durability. The state's table grape industry, comprised for the most part of family farms whose hardworking owners typically viewed unionism as an assault on their personal independence as well as a threat to their prerogatives as employers, remained unalterably opposed to UFWOC's demands long after California's largest wineries had acceded to them. Thus when Chavez made them the main targets of the union's campaign toward the end of 1967, table grape growers fought back with a ferocity and tactical ingenuity that announced their determination to resist unionism at whatever cost.

While the boycott continued to serve as the union's most effective weapon, especially after employers persuaded compliant local judges to issue injunctions severely restricting picketing and other direct action in the strike region, the slowness with which it operated to prod recalcitrant growers toward the bargaining table produced in farmworkers and volunteers alike an impatience that reduced both morale and discipline. It also undermined La

Causa's commitment to nonviolence. "There came a point in 1968," Chavez recalled, "when we were in danger of losing . . . Because of a sudden increase in violence against us, and an apparent lack of progress after more than two years of striking, there were those who felt that the time had come to overcome violence by violence . . . There was demoralization in the ranks, people becoming desperate, more and more talk about violence. People meant it, even when they talked to me. They would say, 'Hey, we've got to burn these sons of bitches down. We've got to kill a few of them.'"

In responding to the crisis, Chavez chose a method of restoring discipline and morale that was as risky and unusual as it was revealing of the singular character of his leadership. He decided to fast. The fast, which continued for 25 painful days before it was finally broken at a moving outdoor mass in Delano that included Robert Kennedy among its celebrants, was more than an act of personal penance. "I thought I had to bring the Movement to a halt," Chavez explained, "do something that would force them and me to deal with the whole question of violence and ourselves. We had to stop long enough to take account of what we were doing." Although the fast's religious overtones offended the secular sensibilities of many of his followers, it was more a political than a devotional act; an intrepid and dramatic, if manipulative, device by which Chavez established a compelling standard of personal sacrifice against which his supporters might measure their own commitment and dedication to La Causa, and thus their allegiance to its leader. . . .

Those in the union who were closest to Chavez, whatever their initial reservations, found the fast's effect undeniably therapeutic. Jerry Cohen, the union's able young attorney, while convinced that it had been "a fantastic gamble," was deeply impressed by "what a great organizing tool the fast was." "Before the fast," Cohen noted, "there were nine ranch committees [the rough equivalent of locals within the UFW's structure], one for each winery. The fast, for the first time, made a union out of those ranch committees . . . Everybody worked together." Dolores Huerta also recognized the curative power of Chavez's ordeal. "Prior to that fast," she insisted, "there had been a lot of bickering and backbiting and fighting and little attempts at violence. But Cesar brought everybody together and really established himself as a leader of the farmworkers."

While a chronic back ailment, apparently exacerbated by his fast and a schedule that often required him to work 20 hours a day, slowed Chavez's pace during much of 1968 and 1969, the steadily more punishing economic effects of the grape boycott finally began to erode the confidence and weaken the resistance of growers. With the assistance of a committee of strongly pro-union Catholic bishops who had volunteered to mediate the conflict, negotiations between the union and the first defectors from the growers' ranks finally began in the spring of 1970. And by the end of July, when the most obdurate growers in the Delano area collapsed under the combined weight of a continuing boycott and their own mounting weariness, Chavez and his tenacious followers had finally accomplished what five years before seemed impossible to all but the most sanguine forecasters.

The union's victory, which extended to 85 percent of the state's table grape industry, resulted in contracts that provided for substantial wage increases and employer contributions to UFWOC's health and welfare and economic development funds. Even more important, however, were the noneconomic provisions: union-run hiring halls that gave UFWOC control over the distribution of available work; grievance machinery that rescued the individual farmworker from the arbitrary authority of the boss; restrictions on the use of pesticides that endangered the health of workers; in short, provisions for the emancipation of workers from the century-old dictatorship of California agribusiness.

After five years of struggle and sacrifice, of anguish and uncertainty, Chavez and his followers wanted nothing so much as an opportunity to recuperate from their ordeal and to savor their victory. It was not to be. On the day before the union concluded its negotiations with Delano grape growers, Chavez received the distressing news that lettuce growers in the Salinas and Santa Maria valleys, knowing that they would be the next targets of UFWOC's organizing campaign, had signed contracts providing for the Teamsters' union to represent their field workers. In keeping with the pattern of the Teamsters' involvement with agricultural field labor, no one bothered to consult the Chicano workers whose incessant stooping and bending, whose painful contortions in the service of the hated short-handle hoe, made possible the growers' proud boast that the Salinas valley was the "salad bowl of the nation." . . .

The challenge presented by the Teamsters-grower alliance in the lettuce industry forced UFWOC to divert precious resources into the reconstruction of its far-flung boycott network. It also distracted Chavez and his most competent aides at a time when the union was in the process of transforming itself from an organization expert in agitation into one equipped to administer contracts covering thousands of workers in the grape industry. Meeting the demands of the hiring hall and the grievance process, which were the union's greatest potential sources of institutional strength, also became its most worrisome and debilitating problem as ranch committees composed of rank-and-file members struggled against their own inexperience, and sometimes powerful tendencies toward vindictiveness, favoritism, and a residual servility, to satisfy the labor requirements of employers and to protect the contractual rights of their fellow workers.

Although Chavez instituted an administrative training program designed by his old mentor Fred Ross, he rejected an AFL-CIO offer of assistance because of his stubborn conviction that a genuinely democratic union must entrust its operation to its own members even at the risk of organizational inefficiency and incompetence. And when he shifted the union's headquarters 50 miles southeast of Delano to an abandoned tuberculosis sanitorium in the Tehachapi mountains that he called La Paz—short for Nuestra Senora de la Paz (Our Lady of Peace)—Chavez claimed the move was prompted by a concern that his easy accessibility to members of the union's ranch committees discouraged self-reliance. "It was my idea to leave for La Paz," he explained, "because I wanted to remove my presence from Delano, so they could develop their own leadership, because if I am there, they wouldn't make the decisions themselves. They'd come to me." But the move intensified suspicions of internal critics like Larry Itliong, who left the union partly because Chavez's physical isolation from the membership seemed to enhance the influence of the Anglo "intellectuals" while diminishing that of the rank and file. The greatest barrier to broadening the union's leadership and administrative operation, however, was posed neither by geography nor the influence of Anglo volunteers, but by Chavez himself, whose devotion to the ideal of decentralization was seldom matched by an equal disposition to delegate authority to others. Journalist Ron Taylor, who observed Chavez's style of leadership at close range, wrote: "He conceptually saw a union run in the most democratic terms, but in practice he had a difficult time trying to maintain his own distance; his tendencies were to step in and make decisions . . . Even though he had removed himself from Delano, he maintained a close supervision over it, and all of the other field offices. Through frequent staff meetings and meetings of the executive board, he developed his own personal involvement with the tiniest of union details."

If Chavez's deficiencies as an administrator troubled sympathetic AFL-CIO officials like Bill Kircher, they tended to reinforce the suspicion privately harbored by such trade-union traditionalists as federation president George Meany that viable organization was probably beyond the compass of farmworkers, no matter how driven and charismatic their leader. Indeed, what appeared to be at the root of Meany's personal skepticism was Chavez's eccentric style of leadership and somewhat alien trade-union philosophy: his well-advertised idealism, which uncharitably rendered was a species of mere self-righteousness; his overweening presence, which seemingly engendered an unhealthy cult of personality; his extravagant sense of mission, which left outsiders wondering whether his was a labor or a social movement; his apparently congenital aversion to compromise, which, in Meany's view, negated the AFL-CIO's repeated efforts to negotiate a settlement of UFWOC's jurisdictional dispute with the Teamsters. None of these reservations were enough to keep the AFL-CIO in early 1972 from changing the union's status from that of organizing committee to full-fledged affiliate—the United Farm Workers of America—but in combination they were apparently enough to persuade Meany that Chavez was no longer deserving of the same levels of financial and organizational support previously contributed by the federation.

Yet if trade union administration of an appropriately conventional style was not his forte, Chavez demonstrated during the course of several legislative battles in 1971 and 1972 that his talents as a political organizer and tactician were exceptional. When the Oregon legislature passed an anti-union bill sponsored by the American Farm Bureau Federation, Chavez and his followers, in only a week's time, persuaded the governor to veto it. Shortly thereafter, Chavez initiated a far more ambitious campaign to recall the governor of Arizona for signing a similar grower-backed bill into law. And while the recall drive ultimately bogged down in a tangle of legal disputes, Chavez's success in registering nearly 100,000 mostly poor, mostly

Chicano voters fostered fundamental changes in the political balance of power in Arizona.

It was in California, however, that the UFW afforded its opponents the most impressive demonstration of La Causa's political sophistication and clout, and Chavez revealed to friends and foes alike that his ability to influence public debate extended well beyond the normal boundaries of trade-union leadership. With the backing of the state's agribusiness establishment, the California Farm Bureau launched during 1972 a well-financed initiative drive—popularly known as Proposition 22—designed to eliminate the threat of unionism by banning nearly every effective weapon available to the UFW, including the boycott. Having failed the year before to win legislative approval for an equally tough anti-union measure, farm employers were confident that they could persuade the citizens of California, as they had so often before, that protecting the state's highly profitable agricultural industry was in the public interest. Aware that the UFW could not survive under the restrictive conditions that Proposition 22 contemplated, but without the financial resources needed to counter the growers' expensive media campaign, Chavez and his aides masterfully deployed what they did have: an aroused and resourceful membership. In the end, the growers' financial power proved to be no match for the UFW's people power. In defeating Proposition 22 by a decisive margin—58 percent to 42 percent—the UFW not only eliminated the immediate threat facing the union, but also announced to growers in terms too emphatic to ignore that the time was past when farm employers could rely upon their political power to keep farmworkers in their place.

The political battles that occupied Chavez and the UFW during much of 1972 involved issues so central to the union's existence that they could not be avoided. But even in the course of winning its political fights with agribusiness, the union lost ground on other equally crucial fronts. Organizing activities all but ceased as the UFW turned its attention to political action, and further efforts aimed at alleviating the administrative problems that plagued the union's operation in the grape industry and increasing the pressures on Salinas valley lettuce growers were neglected. At the beginning of 1973 the UFW was in the paradoxical situation of being at the height of its political strength while its vulnerability as a union was increasing.

Just how vulnerable the union was became apparent as the contracts it had negotiated in 1970 with Coachella valley grape growers came up for renewal. Chavez had heard rumors that the Teamsters were planning to challenge the UFW in the region, but not until growers made plain their intention to reclaim complete control over the hiring, dispatching, and disciplining of workers did he suspect that a deal was already in the making. The UFW retained the allegiance of a vast majority of the industry's workers, but neither the growers nor the Teamsters seemed to care. As soon as the UFW contracts expired, all but two growers announced that they had signed new four-year agreements with the Teamsters. Hiring halls, grievance procedures, and protections against dangerous pesticides disappeared along with the workers' right to a union of their own choice. . . .

In the face of the Teamsters onslaught, the UFW, reinforced by a familiar coalition of religious, student, liberal, and labor volunteers, resorted to its customary arsenal: picket lines, rallies, marches, boycotts, and appeals to the public's sense of justice. Yet with hundreds of beefy Teamster goons conducting a reign of terror through the region, and UFW activists being jailed by the hundreds for violating court orders prohibiting virtually every form of resistance and protest the union employed, the Chavez forces never had a chance of winning back what they had lost in the Coachella valley, or of stopping the Teamsters when they later moved in on the UFW's remaining contracts with Delano-area table grape growers and the state's major wineries. George Meany, who described the Teamsters' raids as "the most vicious strikebreaking, union-busting effort I've seen in my lifetime," persuaded the AFL-CIO executive council to contribute $1.6 million to the UFW's support. But the money could only ease the union's predicament, not solve it. After five months of bitter struggle, more than 3,500 arrests, innumerable assaults, and the violent deaths of two members—one at the hands of a deputy sheriff who claimed that his victim was "resisting arrest," the other at the hands of a gun-toting young strikebreaker who said he felt menaced by pickets—Chavez, his union in ruins, called off any further direct action in favor of the UFW's most effective weapon: the boycott. The UFW, which only a year before had more than 150 contracts and nearly 40,000 members, was reduced by September 1973 to a mere handful of contracts and perhaps one-quarter of its earlier membership.

In the wake of the UFW's stunning defeat in the grape industry, writing the union's obituary became a favorite pastime not only of its long-time adversaries but of some of its traditional sympathizers as well. Most acknowledged the irresistible pressures that a Teamsters–grower alliance unleashed against the union, but many also found fault with the leadership of Cesar Chavez, especially his real or imagined failure to progress from unruly visionary to orderly trade unionist. Chavez's "charisma," said one sympathizer, was no longer "as marketable a commodity as it once was" . . .

Yet if Chavez left something to be desired as a union administrator, his alleged deficiencies scarcely explained the UFW's precipitous descent. The union's battered condition was not a product of its failure to behave conventionally, or of Chavez's disinclination to abandon his assertedly quixotic proclivities in favor of the pure and simple ethic that informed the thinking and demeanor of the more typical trade-union leader. Rather, the UFW's sudden decline was, for the most part, not of its own making: Grape growers had never resigned themselves to sharing power with their workers, and when the Teamsters proffered an alternative brand of unionism that did not impinge upon their essential prerogatives they happily embraced it.

It was precisely because Chavez was "a bit of a dreamer" that the idea of farmworker organization gathered the initial force necessary to overcome the previously insurmountable opposition of employers, and it was because he remained stubbornly devoted to his dream even in the face of the UFW's disheartening setbacks that those who had rushed to speak eulogies over the momentarily prostrated union were ultimately proven wrong. The resources available to him after the debacle of 1973 were only a fraction of what they had been, but Chavez retained both the loyalty of his most able assistants and his own exceptional talents as an organizer and agitator. As the nationwide boycotts he revived against grape and lettuce growers and the country's largest wine producers, the E. and J. Gallo Wineries, slowly gained momentum during 1974, Chavez reminded his Teamsters-employer adversaries in the only language they seemed to understand that the UFW was not going away no matter how diligently they conspired to that end. . . .

Since 1975 the union's record testifies to a mixed performance on Chavez's part. After reaching a membership of approximately 50,000 by the late 1970s, the union has slowly dwindled in size, comprising roughly 40,000 members by the early 1980s, nearly all of whom, except for isolated outposts in Florida, Arizona, and a couple of other states, are confined to California . . .

It is also the case, however, that the UFW's drift from vitality toward apparent stagnation is partially rooted in a web of complex factors related to the sometimes contradictory leadership of Cesar Chavez: a sincere devotion to democratic unionism that is undermined by a tendency to regard all internal dissidents as traitors at best and anti-union conspirators at worst; a professed desire to make the UFW a rank-and-file union governed from the bottom up that is contradicted by a strong inclination to concentrate authority in his own hands and those of close family members; a commitment to professionalize the administration of the UFW that is impeded by a reliance on volunteerism so unyielding as to have caused many of the union's most loyal and efficient staff members to quit.

In fairness, however, Chavez's performance must be assessed on a basis that encompasses far more than the normal categories of trade-union leadership. For unlike most American labor leaders, who had stood apart from the traditions of their European counterparts by insisting that unionism is an end in itself, Chavez has, in his own somewhat idiosyncratic way, remained determined to use the UFW and the heightened political consciousness of his Chicano loyalists as a means for promoting changes more fundamental than those attainable through collective bargaining and other conventional avenues of trade-union activism. In defining the UFW's singular mission, Chavez once declared: "As a continuation of our struggle, I think that we can develop economic power and put it in the hands of the people so they can have more control of their own lives, and then begin to change the system. We want radical change. Nothing short of radical change is going to have any impact on our lives or our problems. We want sufficient power to control our own destinies. This is our struggle. It's a lifetime job. The work for social change and against social injustice is never ended."

When measured against the magnitude of his proposed enterprise, and against his extraordinary achievements on behalf of workers who were among the most powerless and degraded in America prior to his emergence, Chavez's real and alleged deficiencies in guiding the UFW across the hostile terrain of California's industrialized agriculture in no way detract from his standing as the most accomplished and far-sighted labor leader of his generation.

A Primary Perspective

DOLORES HUERTA

Though their contributions are often overlooked, women have long played a major part in the American labor movement. They continue to do so. With the dramatic rise in dual-income and single-parent families in recent decades, unprecedented numbers of women 'have entered the labor force; and with the displacement of male-dominated manufacturing work by service employment, unions today must pay particular attention to the needs of their female members if they are to regain their position as major actors in American social and economic life. In the excerpt that follows, Dolores Huerta of the United Farm Workers speaks about some of the problems she has encountered in attempting to combine her roles as single parent and labor organizer.

When I first started working with Cesar I had this problem worrying about whether my kids were going to eat or not, because at the time I started work- ing for the union I was making pretty good money, and I knew I was going to start working without *any* money, and I wondered how I could do it. But the kids have never gone hungry. We've had some rough times, particularly in Delano during the strike, because my kids went without fresh milk for two years. They just had powdered milk we got through donations. It's made them understand what hardship is, and this is good because you can't really relate to suffering unless you've had a little bit of it yourself. But the main thing is that they have their dignity and identity.

My family used to criticize me a lot. They thought that I was a traitor to my Raza, to my family, and to everybody else. But I think they finally real- ized that what I'm doing is important and they're starting to appreciate it now. They thought that I was just neglecting my children and that what I was doing was just for selfish reasons.

The criticism came mostly from my dad and other relatives, but my brothers are very understanding. My mother was a very active woman, and I just followed her. She's dead now, but she always got the prizes for regis- tering the most voters, and she raised us without any hang-ups about things like that.

You could expect that I would get a lot of criticisms from the farmworkers themselves, but it mostly comes from middle-class people. They're more hung-up about these things than the poor people are, because the poor people have to haul their kids around from school to school, and the women have to

Source: Dolores Huerta, "Dolores Huerta Talks about Republicans, Cesar, and Her Home Town," in *Awakened Minority: The Mexican-Americans,* ed. Manuel P. Seruin (Beverly Hills, CA: Glencoe Press, 1974), pp. 287–88.

go out and work and they've got to either leave their kids or take them out to the fields with them. So they sympathize a lot more with my problem in terms of my children. Sometimes I think it's bad for people to shelter their kids too much. Giving kids clothes and food is one thing, you know, but it's much more important to teach them that other people besides themselves are important, and that the best thing they can do with their lives is to use it in the service of other people. So my kids know that the way that we live is poor, materially speaking, but it's rich in a lot of other ways. They get to meet a lot of people and their experiences are varied.

I know people who work like fools just to give their kids more material goods. They're depriving their family of themselves, for what? At least my kids know why I'm not home. They know that I'm doing this for something in which we're all working—it makes a whole different thing. My children don't have a lot of material things but they work hard for what they do get, just like everybody else, and that makes them really self-sufficient. They make their own arrangements when they go places. They all have a lot of friends and they don't get all hung-up about having a lot of goodies. I think my kids are very healthy both mentally and physically. All the women in the union have similar problems. They don't have to leave their families for as long as I do. But everybody shares everything, we share the work.

QUESTIONS

1. What influence did Father Donald McDonnell and Fred Ross have on the development of Chavez's social thought? Why did Chavez shift from community to labor organization during the early 1960s?
2. What role did women play in the development of the United Farm Workers? What do Dolores Huerta's general beliefs and reflections on her personal life suggest about her effectiveness as a labor organizer?
3. Why did Chavez urge union members to avoid the use of violence? Why did he make the boycott the union's main weapon against growers? Chavez once observed that walking a "picket line is a beautiful thing, because it does something to a human being." What do you think he meant?
4. How would you characterize Chavez's relationship with mainstream labor leaders such as George Meany? Why did the latter sometimes view Chavez with suspicion?
5. What were Chavez's greatest strengths as a labor leader? What were his most notable shortcomings? In what ways was Chavez similar to Martin Luther King, Jr.? In what ways were the two men different?
6. Given the current emphasis on organizing low-wage workers from diverse cultural backgrounds, what can contemporary labor leaders learn from Chavez's career?
7. Which of the historical figures profiled in Part Three would you most like to write about? What questions would you ask in a study of that person? What types of sources would you consult to answer those questions?

ADDITIONAL RESOURCES

Those seeking additional information on Chavez should consult Griswold del Castillo and Richard Garcia, *Cesar Chavez: A Triumph of the Spirit* (1995); Susan Ferriss and Ricardo Sandoval, *The Fight in the Fields: Cesar Chavez and the Farmworkers Movement* (1997); Joan London and Henry Anderson, *So Shall Ye Reap: The Story of Cesar Chavez and the Farm Labor Movement* (1970); Dick Meister and Ann Loftis, *A Long Time Coming: The Struggle to Unionize America's Farm Workers* (1977); Ronald B. Taylor, *Chavez and the Farm Workers* (1975); and Richard W. Etulain, ed., *Cesar Chavez: A Brief Biography with Documents* (2002). Historical background on efforts to organize California farmworkers can be found in Cletus E. Daniel, *Bitter Harvest: A History of California Farmworkers, 1879–1941* (1981), and Ernesto Galarza, *Merchants of Labor: The Mexican Bracero Story* (1964). Two good general surveys of the Mexican-American experience are Rudolfo Acuna, *Occupied America: A History of Chicanos*, 4th ed. (2000), and Matt S. Meier and Feliciano Ribera, *Mexican Americans/American Mexicans: From Conquistadors to Chicanos*, rev. ed. (1994).

The Fight in the Fields: César Chávez and the Farmworkers' Stuggle was a PBS offering by Rick Tejada-Flores and Ray Telles that examines the life of Chavez and his struggle to organize workers as well as create Chicano activism.

Chapter 17

Ronald Reagan

he immediate post–World War II decades were hard years for American conservatives. Voters may have been skeptical about proposals to extend Franklin Roosevelt's New Deal reforms, but they had fond memories of Roosevelt himself and strongly supported those programs already in place. Many people could still recall the poverty and destitution of the Great Depression and how government had stepped in to relieve the widespread human distress of that terrible period. Politicians who spoke about returning the country to the laissez-faire days of the Harding-Coolidge era had a very tough row to hoe.

Nor was this the only problem then facing the American Right. If they were to become a serious political force again, conservatives also had to overcome a major ideological division within their own ranks. On one side, a group that might be called the libertarian Right championed personal liberty, free enterprise, limited government, and private property. Individualists who resented nearly all forms of external authority, the libertarians had small regard for any laws or institutions that limited personal freedom. On the other side, a group that might best be described as the traditionalist Right emphasized the preservation of order and sought to construct a world based on religion, virtue, and old-fashioned morality. Although not opposed to individualism per se, they did expect individuals to conform to their definition of appropriate moral and ethical standards—an expectation that, needless to say, set them at odds with many libertarians. Despite a shared commitment to the crusade against world communism and the ability of some conservatives to move easily between the two camps, the potential for conflict was enormous.

Conservative political operatives who recognized the breadth of these divisions made little effort to bridge them. Instead, they attempted to transcend them by focusing attention on the activities of common enemies. Two developments during the 1960s made their task easier than it otherwise would have been. One was the expansion of federal authority during the Kennedy and Johnson administrations, which both libertarians and traditionalists viewed with alarm. The second was the emergence of the Civil Rights struggle and related social movements. The effective use of nonviolent direct action by Civil Rights activists and antiwar protesters shocked many libertarians. They had never imagined that their principles might be used to justify civil disobedience by minority groups or the burning of draft cards by college students. When this happened, libertarians began to reconsider their views of external authority and concluded that, under certain circumstances, it might not be such a bad thing after all. As they did, the philosophical gap between libertarians and traditionalists narrowed.

Another event that helped bring the two groups together was the presidential candidacy of Barry Goldwater. There was no place in the world of practical politics for doctrinal quarrels, and once engaged in the Goldwater campaign, conservatives of all ideological persuasions put their differences aside and focused on the common enemy: initially the liberal Republicanism of Nelson Rockefeller, and later the aggrandizing statism of Lyndon Johnson. Although Goldwater went down in flames in the 1964 election, the campaign gave conservatives an opportunity to establish themselves as a real force within the Republican party. As their power grew, no one would benefit more than a one-time actor from California named Ronald Reagan, whose cheerful disposition, superb communication skills, and flexible brand of conservatism made him acceptable to all factions of the American Right. In the essay that follows, James T. Patterson undertakes the difficult task of assessing Reagan's controversial presidency at a time when historians have only begun their examination of it.

Ronald Reagan

James T. Patterson

Evaluating the not-so-distant presidency of Ronald Reagan necessarily leads to a number of tentative conclusions. On the one hand, a fairly clear scholarly consensus persists concerning three aspects of his presidency: the substance

Source: The Reagan Presidency: Pragmatic Conservatism and Its Legacies, eds. W. Elliot Brownlee and Hugh Davis Graham (University Press of Kansas, 2003), pp. 355–71. Reprinted with permission.

of his ideas, the nature of his personality, and the style of his leadership. On the other hand, scholars and others still argue heatedly over his legacy. Thanks to some key developments since his presidency—notably the end of the cold war and the return by the mid-1990s of widespread prosperity and of federal budget surpluses—his reputation among scholars may be marginally higher today than it was in 1989. But we are still too close to the Reagan years to reach assured judgments about his legacy.

Virtually all students of Reagan's ideas agree that long before his successful run for the presidency in 1980, he had been one of the nation's more ideologically committed political figures. Indeed, friends from the 1940s remember him carrying about copies of the *Congressional Record*. At that time, and later, he professed great admiration for FDR, for whom he voted four times. In 1948 he supported Truman, writing a friend after the election, "I'm sure Truman, with a Democratic congress, will do lots to make things better in every way, and what a landslide it was, the votes boy!" In 1950 he backed Helen Gahagan Douglas in her race against Richard Nixon for a Senate seat from California. Thereafter, however, a series of developments—Reagan's anger at high income taxes, his marriage in 1952 to Nancy Davis, his work as traveling spokesman for the General Electric Company from 1952 to 1962— moved him politically to the right. Formally turning Republican in 1962, he served two terms as California governor between 1967 and 1975, and nearly overcame incumbent Gerald Ford in a race for the Republican presidential nomination in 1976.

By then, Reagan was well known as a highly conservative politician. Moreover, we now understand, thanks to the publication in 2001 of some 670 handwritten radio addresses delivered in the late 1970s, how profoundly and ideologically engaged he continued to be in those years, mainly about a fairly small range of concerns. As Godfrey Hodgson put it, "Reagan had a few big ideas, deeply held, and he was brilliantly successful at communicating them."

These ideas were focused on economics and foreign policy. Though he had relished ridiculing hippies while governor of California, he was only sporadically a culture warrior, and his radio addresses after 1974—like his speeches as president—had relatively little to say about social matters such as race, immigration, or religion. These radio addresses are best described as earnest and fact-filled, revealing that he prepared carefully and that he could marshal arguments clearly—he was emphatically not the moron that opponents thought (or said) he was. These speeches were also ideologically predictable, for Reagan was consistent in his beliefs. Like many of his statements as president, they celebrated ideas taken from the well-traveled baggage of antistatist, anticommunist conservatism as set forward in his own time by leading Republicans such as Robert Taft and Barry Goldwater. Passionately, they asserted that the United States must carry out its historic, God-given mission of promoting freedom and liberty, both at home and abroad.

Reagan, indeed, was then and later a regular reader of the conservative publication *Human Events*. Domestically, he aimed to cut back the size of government, abolish excessive regulation, and—above all—reduce taxes. As he expressed this approach (most famously) in his inaugural, "government is not the solution to our problem; government *is* the problem." His foreign policy rested on building up the military so as to enable the United States to negotiate from a position of strength with the Soviet Union. But negotiations would have to follow the buildup. Meanwhile, Reagan repeatedly denounced the Soviet Union, most memorably in 1983 by branding it an "evil empire."

In one way his ideas about foreign and military policy featured a highly personal stamp: his attraction to biblical prophecies about apocalypse, which he foresaw as an outcome of the nuclear arms race. Frightened by the prospect of a nuclear war, he resolved to make America safe from Armageddon. The result was his call in 1983 for a Strategic Defense Initiative (SDI), or "Star Wars," which almost all knowledgeable officials concerned with defense policies found bizarre, except perhaps as a bargaining chip to use in future negotiations with the Soviet Union. As Frances FitzGerald has emphasized, SDI was "way out there in the blue." This belief, and the passionate certitude that animated Reagan's worldview, placed his ideas solidly on the political right.

There is also consensus among scholars concerning Reagan's qualities as a person and as a presidential leader and administrator. It begins with agreement that he was a genial, kindly, and unpretentious man. Perhaps because he was the son of an alcoholic father, he grew up trying hard to please people. As speechwriter Peggy Noonan put it, for the rest of his life, "he thought it was his job to cheer people up." He was unusually optimistic and upbeat—so much so, indeed, that he often came across as a Pollyanna. Garry Wills likened him to **Mr. Magoo.** Maureen Reagan, irritated by her father's unfailing cheeriness, commented, "It's enough to drive you nuts."

Virtually all students of Reagan have also identified a related personal trait: his remarkable self-assurance. Katharine Graham of the *Washington Post* observed that Reagan was perhaps the only modern president who did not worry much about what his critics—or hostile journalists—said about him. Reagan, she wrote, "was so successful [with the press] because he had supreme self-confidence." Wills, too, has highlighted Reagan's self-assurance, noting that he was an oddity—a "cheerful conservative." "What must strike the candid observer," Wills wrote, "is the President's almost preternatural security, the lack of inner division that he maintains despite so much contained diversity."

There is agreement also that Reagan consciously and eagerly sought to stamp this upbeat attitude into the minds of the American people. As a fan of science fiction, he was certain that the future would be better than the past. Again and again he insisted that nothing was impossible for the United States, which in his mind had always been a wonderful, exceptional civilization. Americans needed only to have

Mr. Magoo A cartoon character.

confidence—in themselves and in the nation. "What I'd really like to do," he said in 1981, "is to go down in history as the president who made Americans believe in themselves again."

Most observers also concur that Reagan's cheerful, buoyant demeanor, which contrasted sharply with the grimness of President Jimmy Carter, was a key to the popularity that he enjoyed for most of his years as president. In 1984 the political scientist Austin Ranney exclaimed, "Win, lose or draw, Reagan has made it at least possible for us to look at our leader with a feeling of uplift." Lou Cannon, Reagan's discerning biographer, later added, "Because of his ability to reflect and give voice to the aspirations of his fellow citizens, Reagan succeeded in reviving national confidence at a time when there was a great need for inspiration. This was his great contribution as president."

Scholarly observers tend to agree as well on other, less flattering personal traits of the president. One is his intellectual rigidity concerning most issues. Seventy years of age in February 1981, he was set in most of his ideas. After responding with extraordinary courage and good humor following John Hinckley's attempt to assassinate him in March 1981, he basked in an especially warm glow of popular affection. Thereafter, he seemed even more incurious than earlier, relying on his well-honed talents as a speaker and media presence to sustain his happy political relationship with the public. Friends as well as foes deplored this trait. Clark Clifford, a Democratic insider, memorably labeled him an "amiable dunce." Peggy Noonan added, "Beyond those warm eyes is a lack of curiosity that is, somehow, disorienting." Edmund Morris, Reagan's official biographer, tells how he was warned that the president did not have "hidden depths": "what you see," Reagan's associates said, "is what you get." "Nevertheless," Morris added, "I could not believe how little one indeed 'got,' and how shallow those depths appeared to be."

Both Thomas "Tip" O'Neill, Reagan's adversary as Democratic Speaker of the House, and James Baker, Reagan's top aide during the first presidential term, offered similar opinions. O'Neill commented that the president was "most of the time an actor reading lines, who didn't understand his own programs." Reagan, he cracked, "would have made a hell of a king." Baker recalled the time in 1983 when he left Reagan a thick briefing book on the eve of an economic summit of the world's democratic leaders. The next morning Baker could see that the book lay unopened. He asked Reagan why he had not looked at it. "Well, Jim," the president replied calmly, *"The Sound of Music* was on last night."

Other Reagan officials were quick to complain of the president's inattentiveness and passivity. At meetings he was normally affable, but often—especially in his second term—he scarcely seemed to listen, and he frequently said nothing of substance when conferences came to a close. What had the president decided? aides wondered. As Martin Anderson later wrote, Reagan "made decisions like an ancient king or a Turkish pasha, passively letting his subjects serve him, selecting only those morsels of public policy that were especially tasty. Rarely did he ask searching questions and demand to know why someone had or had not done something. He just sat back in a supremely calm, relaxed manner and waited until important things were brought to him."

Anderson, an adviser and admirer, contended that Reagan normally decided decisively and wisely. Other observers have added that Reagan's style of management, which depended heavily on the ability of loyal aides, usually worked adequately, at least in his first presidential term. Many advisers, however, were even then dismayed. Some resigned or (like Baker) sought government jobs outside the White House. Even before Reagan's presidency ended, ten ex-staffers had published memoirs testifying to their frustrations. Secretary of State Alexander Haig later complained to Cannon, "To me, the White House was as mysterious as a ghost ship; you heard the creak of the rigging and the groan of the timbers and sometimes even glimpsed the crew on the deck. But which of the crew had the helm? Was it [attorney general Edwin] Meese, was it Baker, was it someone else? It is impossible to know for sure."

Members of Reagan's own family also confessed frustration with this curious passivity. To them as to others, it was if he were still on the silver screen, beguiling admirers with his performances but keeping a star's careful distance from his audience. As Nancy Reagan observed, "Although he loves people, he often seems remote, and he doesn't let anybody get too close. There's a wall around him." His son Michael tells perhaps the most distressing—and perhaps best-known—story of this remoteness. After speaking at Michael's high school graduation, Reagan shook hands with some of the students. Facing Michael, who was dressed in cap and gown, he said, "My name is Ronald Reagan. What's yours?"

Examples such as these bolster what is perhaps the most widely held view of Reagan the man and the leader: that he was so much the actor and performer as to be unfathomable as a person. Cannon subtitles his study of Reagan's presidency *The Role of a Lifetime*. The historian Gil Troy cites William Allen White's depiction of President William McKinley as applicable to Reagan: "Living thirty years in politics, McKinley became galvanized with a certain coating of publicity. He lost his private life and his private view. He walked among men a bronze statue, for thirty years determinedly looking for his pedestal."

Seeking to discover the sources of Reagan's remoteness can plunge us into armchair psychology, some of which suggests that Reagan was fundamentally shy and therefore hard to reach. Other speculation has it that harsh life experiences—notably his father's alcoholism and the hurtful breakup of his first marriage—made him profoundly wary of closeness to others. Whatever the roots of Reagan's remoteness, many people have agreed that he was especially "mysterious." No one, of course, has advanced this view more memorably than Edmund Morris, who spent years trying to crack Reagan's shell. When he finally published his "memoir" of Reagan, he complained of the president's "slabby, alabaster-like quality." At the close of the book, Morris confessed that "Dutch [Reagan's boyhood name] remained a mystery to me, and worse still . . . an apparent airhead." Favorably reviewing Morris's book, Reagan's daughter Patti added, "I still don't fully understand my father. After all those years of exhaustive research, even Edmund says the man is a mystery."

Except for a few loyal aides, most careful students of Reagan agree, finally, that as president he was laid-back. Rejecting the workaholic style of Jimmy Carter, he refused to hold early morning staff meetings, and he normally left the Oval Office before five. Easily tired, he was known to doze at meetings in the afternoon. He spent almost a full year of days at his beloved ranch in California, as well as 183 weekends at Camp David. Using humor to disarm critics of these work habits, Reagan told reporters, "I am concerned about what is happening in government—and it's caused me many a sleepless afternoon." On another occasion he quipped, "It's true hard work never killed anyone but I figure, why take the chance?"

Humor was indeed a major source—Cannon called it a "saving grace"—of Reagan's political success. There was no doubt that he had a wonderful gift for telling jokes and stories. Some of these, ridiculing the excesses of Big Government, helped him score political points. He was also quick with one-liners, such as his disarming quip at the 1984 Gridiron dinner about the federal deficit. "I'm not worried about the deficit," he cracked. "It's big enough to take care of itself." Perhaps no quips were more memorable than those he tossed off following the attempt on his life in 1981. As he was being wheeled in for surgery, he joked with the surgeons, "Please assure me that you are all Republicans." Told that he would be happy to hear that the government was running smoothly while he was in the hospital (twelve days), he responded, "What makes you think I'd be happy about that?"

About these matters—the nature of Reagan's ideas, personality, and style of leadership—I reiterate that scholars today do not much disagree. In many other ways, however, scholarly consensus has always remained elusive. Students of Reagan's presidency differ considerably now, as they did in the 1980s, about the legacy of many of his key initiatives—notably his economic and foreign policies. . . .

No issue was closer to Reagan's heart than lowering income taxes. Donald Regan, Treasury secretary in his first term, helps explain why this was so by relating a story that Reagan told about his own experience. "When he was in Hollywood," Donald Regan said,

> he would make about three or four hundred thousand dollars per picture. It took about three months to complete a picture. Reagan would work for three months, and loaf for three months, so he was making between six and seven hundred thousand dollars per year. Between Uncle Sam and the state of California, over 91 percent of that was going in taxes. His question, asked rhetorically, was: "Why should I have done a third picture, even if it was *Gone with the Wind?* What good would it have done me?"
>
> So he loafed for a part of the year. And he said the same thing was happening throughout America. People would reach a certain peak, and they weren't willing to do the extra effort that was needed to keep us a first-class nation.

As this story indicates, Reagan had strongly held personal reasons for his loathing of high taxes, and in the 1970s he became an ardent backer of some of the more extreme and populistic versions of **supply-side economics.** Various ideas within this movement, indeed, were then attracting considerable bipartisan support, for the American economy seemed to be in free fall at the time. By 1980, inflation was running at 13 percent and unemployment at 7 percent. The prime interest rate, averaging more than 15 percent for the year, peaked at over 21 percent in December. Many regulatory policies had come to seem counterproductive in the emergent global and high-tech economy. Popular unrest against high taxes broke out in California and many other places. Once promising "demand side" theories, such as Keynesianism, seemed to be in tatters.

While advocates of supply-side economics differed among themselves, they agreed that tax cuts would stimulate entrepreneurial activity, investment, production, and—the key—economic growth. Most of them, notably Congressman Jack Kemp of New York, were conservative Republicans. Senator Daniel Moynihan, observing this ideological ferment in Republican circles, warned in 1980, "Of a sudden, the GOP has become a party of ideas." But prominent Democrats, too, became true believers. Lloyd Bentsen, chairman of the Joint Economic Committee of Congress, declared in 1980 that America had entered "the start of a new era of economic thinking. For too long we have focused on short-run policies to stimulate spending, or demand, while neglecting supply—labor, savings, investment, and production. Consequently, demand has been over-stimulated and supply has been strangled."

At the time, of course, many critics ridiculed the supply-side approach. George Bush, challenging Reagan for the GOP nomination, famously dismissed it as "Voodoo Economics." Reagan, however, insisted that tax cuts would actually *reduce* government deficits in time, and he demanded sharp reductions in rates for all taxpayers, not just for the wealthy. Thus he wasted no time in 1981 in urging an across-the-board 30 percent tax cut, to be accomplished over three years. In subsequent efforts for these cuts, he impressed Washington insiders with political maneuvering of a high order. Democratic leaders, seriously underestimating his persistence in lobbying congressmen and his ability to articulate his case on television, were stunned. "I'm getting the shit whaled out of me," O'Neill complained. Jim Wright, the House majority leader, commented in a diary entry in June 1981, "I stand in awe . . . of [Reagan's] political skill. I am not sure that I have seen its equal."

Thanks in no small part to Reagan's able leadership, which helped draw forty-eight Democratic congressmen to his side on the final vote, a significant tax bill passed in July 1981. It promised to cut taxes by 23 percent over three years, dropping the top marginal rate for individuals from 70 percent to 50 percent, as well as reducing marginal rates in lower brackets. It was estimated at the time that tax cuts over the next five years would amount to $750 billion. On August 13 Reagan signed both the tax bill and a major budget measure that he said would reduce funding for social programs,

---

supply-side economics Theory that lowering taxes will stimulate investment and promote economic growth.

especially Aid to Families with Dependent Children and Food Stamps, by some $130 billion over the next three years. Scaling back such programs had also been a major goal of Reagan's first year.

Veteran reporters lauded Reagan's leadership on these issues. Hedley Donovan wrote that these two acts represented the "most formidable domestic initiative any president has driven through since the Hundred Days of Franklin Roosevelt." Donovan's praise was echoed again and again in the next few years, as scholars, journalists, and others welcomed Reagan's forceful, assured leadership, which they regularly contrasted with the ineptness that Carter had shown in dealing with Capitol Hill. At last, it seemed, America had a president who could oil the wheels of government.

What many contemporary observers seemed happiest about was the ability of the president to take control of things. Their comments reflected a deep yearning, which had escalated during the troubled 1970s, for a show of presidential forcefulness. Then, and in later years, Reagan's reputation benefited from popular perceptions that he rescued the nation from political gridlock.

Reagan, to be sure, had dazzled Washington insiders, but it remained to be seen whether his economic policies were good for the country. Were they? Now as then, there is no sure answer to that question. Defenders of Reaganomics maintain correctly that the economy grew uninterruptedly between 1983 and 1990. During his presidency, some seventeen million new jobs developed. Thanks mainly to tight monetary policies in the early 1980s, sternly imposed (with Reagan's strong backing) by Federal Reserve Board chairman Paul Volcker, inflation dropped from 13 percent in 1980 to 4.4 percent in 1989. Unemployment fell from 7 percent to 5.5 percent. Statistics like these, jubilantly advertised by supporters of Reagan's policies, contributed greatly to Reagan's personal popularity.

Even then, however, many students of Reagan's economic policies had their doubts. And these doubts have persisted over the years. For a start, the tax and budget acts of 1981 failed to prevent the nation from plunging into a sharp recession in 1981 and 1982, during which unemployment surged to 10 percent. Moreover, it became clear even in 1981 that the budgetary projections used by Reagan and his advisers bore almost no relation to reality. Congressional pork barreling sent these projections even farther off line. David Stockman, Reagan's budget director, famously confessed in late 1981, "None of us really understands what's going on with all these numbers."

The most staggering "numbers," as it turned out, surfaced in the buckets of red ink of federal deficits during the Reagan years. Contrary to Reagan's beliefs, tax cuts did not lead to escalating government revenues. Whopping increases in spending on defense, on entitlements such as Social Security and Medicare, and on interest payments to cover federal borrowing accounted for perhaps two-thirds (tax cuts the other third) of deficits that became huge in every year of Reagan's presidency. Between the fiscal years 1980 and 1989, the national debt tripled from $914 billion to $2.7 trillion. While congressional actions contributed to these deficits, the administration, which never submitted a balanced budget, was far and away the main source of them. By 1989, alarm about deficits was mounting greatly. Lou Cannon concluded at the time, "The deficit is Reagan's great failure."

By then, some people were beginning to suspect that the Reagan administration had deliberately fostered large deficits in order to make it more difficult for liberals to increase spending for social programs. This, they said, was "Reagan's Revenge." Systematic, conspiratorial plotting of this sort cannot be documented. Still, the huge deficits amassed under his watch incited such widespread alarm by the early 1990s that ambitious social plans (such as Clinton's health care proposal in 1993) became politically difficult to sell.

It is also clear that Reagan's economic policies helped to magnify inequality. This was not the result of his tax cuts—income tax progressivity did not change in the 1980s. Moreover, Reagan reluctantly took belated steps to moderate the deficits that the tax cuts of 1981 helped to enlarge, signing income tax increases in 1982 and 1984. In 1983 he approved a bipartisan agreement to hike payroll taxes for Social Security and Medicare. These taxes, regressive in nature, especially affected working-class people and exacerbated income inequality.

Thanks in part to the hike in payroll taxes, Reagan also did not reach his goal of lessening the overall federal tax burden. By 1988 it was estimated that the share of national income that went to the federal government in taxes was 19.3 percent, compared with 19.4 percent in 1980.

Reaganomics also failed to achieve one of the most important goals of the supply-side vision: promoting more rapid economic growth. Real growth in GNP averaged 3.2 percent per year between 1971 and 1978, 3 percent during the worst years of stagflation under Carter, and 3 percent again under Reagan's watch. What the tax cuts seemed to do, instead, was to bolster consumer demand in the short run. They did not appear to motivate many people to work harder, though by the 1990s they may have helped to stimulate the growth in productive investment that some of the supply-siders had anticipated.

To say these things is not to conclude on an altogether negative note about Reagan's tax policies. For one thing, deficits had been growing earlier, promoted in part by decisions in the 1970s that led to large increases in spending on entitlements. Reagan, like his successors, dared not seriously tamper with the largest of these, Social Security and Medicare. Military spending had begun rising considerably in the last year of the Carter administration, though not so rapidly as it was to do under Reagan. Income inequality also started to accelerate before the 1980s, perhaps because of the long-term, disadvantageous effects of economic globalization on those American workers who were relatively unskilled and uneducated. Most of this inequality has shown in pretax incomes, which indicates that forces other than tax reduction have contributed importantly to it. Reagan's policies heightened inequality and delegitimated efforts to reverse it, but they were not the only sources of it.

It is also hard to know whether the huge deficits were an altogether bad thing. To be sure, they led to greatly increased interest payments, thereby diverting money that might have been used for other, more productive purposes. But the Keynesian-style deficits, mounting by the mid-1980s, may have been antirecessionary after 1982. They may therefore have helped significantly to promote the extended and fairly stable economic expansion of the mid- and late 1980s. And, of course, the federal government again managed to show surpluses (thanks in part to tax increases in the early 1990s) in the late 1990s and 2000. However frightening the Reagan era deficits seemed to be at the time, it is arguable that they did not cause great harm in the long run.

Some limitations of Reagan's economic ideas nonetheless stand out. Various of his supply-side aides came up with wildly inaccurate projections. Their most ambitious predictions—a much strengthened work ethic, a lower overall federal tax burden, considerably more rapid growth—were not met, at least not in the 1980s. Moving more cautiously after 1981, Reagan and his advisers shifted a few gears between 1982 and 1984, notably by accepting higher income and payroll taxes. In the second term, he worked with Congress to secure still lower income tax rates, as well as tax reforms. For the most part these lower rates have survived into the early 2000s, perhaps promoting voluntary compliance with the tax code. These are important legacies. But these efforts, too, did not represent serious changes in Reagan's supply-side ideas. By 1989 Reaganomics still commanded the loyalties of true believers. The president's supply-side ideas, however, remained controversial.

Aside from cutting taxes, Reagan cared most deeply about foreign policy and defense issues. And these issues, of course, dominated his second term, during which he revealed considerable strengths, offset by striking weaknesses.

Many of the weaknesses had been apparent in his first term. From the beginning, high-ranking aides were upset by what they considered to be his ignorance concerning important matters relating to foreign and military policy. In early 1983, Brent Scowcroft was astonished to realize that Reagan did not recognize that land-based Soviet **ICBMs** represented the major threat to United States security. A few months later the president staggered a group of congressmen by telling them that bombers and submarines did not carry nuclear missiles. Backing the Strategic Defense Initiative in 1983, he refused to listen to arguments that the policy of nuclear deterrence had helped to keep the peace, or to appreciate that America's submarine-based missiles offered a strong defense that could well make "Star Wars" unnecessary.

His management of foreign policy also caused despair among top aides. Anxious not to offend people, Reagan was ordinarily unwilling to resolve conflicting viewpoints, notably those that divided Secretary of State George Shultz and Defense Secretary Caspar Weinberger. Richard Perle, an adviser, grumbled, "It never ceased to amaze me how inconclusive meetings at the highest levels were. They are almost never decisive."

Reagan's handling of the National Security Council (NSC) especially revealed his weak managerial skills. Until Frank Carlucci became head of it in 1987, the NSC often floundered, mired in turf wars between strong-minded men like Shultz, Weinberger, and CIA Director William Casey. In

> **ICBMs** Intercontinental ballistic missiles.

December 1981, for instance, Reagan, Secretary of State Haig, Weinberger, Baker, Meese, Michael Deaver, and Vice President Bush met to discuss a plan of Casey's to aid the contras in Nicaragua. Most of those at the meeting did not think much of Casey's ideas, but they supported his plan as a way of avoiding *larger* support for the contras, in whom they had little confidence. As Cannon puts it, "A more negative consensus is hard to conceive." Reagan nonetheless set in motion the plan, which ultimately had huge political consequences.

The sometimes chaotic nature of Reagan administration decision making concerning foreign policy matters was especially obvious in what became known as the **Iran-Contra scandal.** Here, Reagan was led astray by his deep personal yearning to arrange for the release of American hostages, by his predilection for covert operations, and—again—by poorly coordinated staff work, this time centering around NSC head Robert McFarlane and chief of staff Regan, who scarcely spoke to one another. Ignoring the views of Shultz and Weinberger (who for once agreed with each other), Reagan encouraged McFarlane to establish connections with so-called moderates in Iran and then to work out various arms-for-hostages deals. These deals were in fact harebrained, doing nothing to advance "moderation" in Iran and resulting in more hostages being taken than were released. When news leaked of the deals, Reagan, who had proudly proclaimed that he would never deal with terrorists, suffered a body blow to his personal popularity, which declined from 67 percent to 46 percent in November 1986.

Reagan knew in advance of the arms-for-hostages deals. Whether he also knew of the activities of NSC aide Colonel Oliver North, who was funneling profits from the arms sales to the contras, remains unknown. In fact, Reagan did not want to engage American soldiers in aid of the contras. Privately denouncing advocates of direct American military intervention, he told his chief of staff in 1988, "Those sonsofbitches won't be happy until we have 25,000 troops in Managua, and I'm not going to do it." But he obviously admired the contras, once calling them the "moral equivalent of our Founding Fathers." He had secretly sought to find money to aid them, notably from the Saudis. North and others were fully aware that the president was eager to offer funding to the contras.

It may well be that Admiral John Poindexter, who succeeded McFarlane as NSC director, had told Reagan what he had authorized North and others to do, before the scandal broke in November 1986. It may also be, however, that Poindexter told the truth when he later fell on his sword and denied having informed the president. Or it may be that Poindexter had told him and that Reagan had forgotten about it. Any of these scenarios, of course, makes the president look bad. Either Reagan knowingly authorized secret payments, in violation of congressional direction, or he was no longer in control of his own administration. Perhaps he was suffering from the early ravages of Alzheimer's disease. Only

Iran-Contra scandal Scheme to sell arms to Iran and use the money to aid rebel forces seeking to overthrow the left-wing government of Nicaragua.

his strong personal standing with the American people—and the absence of a smoking gun to prove that he had knowingly approved the diversion of profits—saved him from possible impeachment proceedings.

Among the events most helpful in bolstering Reagan's standing at that time, of course, were the fruitful series of meetings that he held with Soviet leader Mikhail Gorbachev between 1985 and 1988. These led to the signing in December 1987 (and Senate ratification in May 1988) of the historic Intermediate Nuclear Forces (INF) Treaty, whereby the Soviets and Americans agreed to scrap intermediate-range and short-range nuclear missiles. This was the first time that the two nations had accepted destruction of any nuclear weapons and the first pact approved to establish on-site monitoring. By the time Reagan left office in January 1989, the world was a little safer place.

The thaw that warmed Soviet-American relations in these years has come under near-endless scrutiny, leading many writers to acclaim Reagan as the man who ended the cold war. Librarian of Congress James Billington, a historian of Russia, wrote in 1997, "President Ronald Reagan was the single most important political figure in ending the Cold War without either making concessions or incurring major loss of life on either side. It was an astonishing accomplishment." Francis Loewenheim, a diplomatic historian, added, "Without firing a shot, Ronald Reagan brought down the house that Lenin, Stalin, Khrushchev and Brezhnev had built. . . . That certainly looks like a world-historical achievement."

That Reagan, long an ardent cold warrior, could be lauded for helping to end the cold war could scarcely have been imagined during his first term. Misled by sometimes overheated CIA estimates of Soviet strength, he greatly escalated defense spending—this effort, Raymond Garthoff has written, was a "mindless spending spree." In March 1983, he denounced the Soviet Union as the "focus of evil in the modern world." He then overruled virtually all his top advisers by calling for creation of the Strategic Defense Initiative. "Star Wars," they thought, was unnecessary, unworkable, and provocative. Shultz at first called the idea "lunacy."

Still, as Reagan's defenders point out, the president did prove flexible enough to change course, especially after Gorbachev came to power in 1985. Agreeing to a summit at Geneva in November 1985, he prepared with great thoroughness. Once at the summit, he worked effectively to establish good relations with Gorbachev. The strong personal bond created at Geneva enabled the two men to push ahead, notably at Reykjavik in 1986, for the INF Treaty. Moreover, the strong anticommunist credentials that Reagan enjoyed with the American people gave him the secure political base that he needed to sell his efforts at home. In this sense, his defense buildup had a domestic political payoff. Most important, Reagan's admirers insist, the president's defiant support of SDI frightened Soviet leaders, who are said to have realized that they could no longer afford to keep up with the United States and therefore resolved to cut a deal.

Most scholars of Reagan's policy toward the Soviet Union nonetheless stop well short of giving him all, or even most, of the credit for relaxation of the cold war. Instead, they point to the sad economic condition of the Soviet Union as of the early 1980s. Bleeding from a war in Afghanistan, reeling

economically, the Soviet Union was simply in no position—SDI or no SDI—
to engage in further expansion of the arms race against the United States. It
had become an enormous Potemkin village that Gorbachev was determined
to reform. Reagan's provocative insistence on going ahead with SDI—and on
building up the military in general—may in fact have made it more difficult
for Gorbachev, confronted with hard-liners at home, to be accommodating.

   To focus on Gorbachev's role is not to deny that Reagan played an important part in the relaxation of tensions. Indeed, this relaxation is the most
notable legacy of his presidency. Still, it also seems clear that a key source of
the thaw lay in the Soviet Union. Not everything that improves international
relations has its origins in the United States.

Difficult though it is to pinpoint the still controversial legacies of Reagan's
presidency, a few final stabs in that direction may make a start.

   Those who are impressed with the size of Reagan's shadow often emphasize three general points. First, that he succeeded in resisting what had
appeared to be an irreversible tide of Big Government. Second, that he shoved
politics and political thinking toward the right. And third, that he heightened
popular faith in the nation.

   The first claim is inaccurate insofar as means-tested programs for the poor
are concerned. Though stemmed in 1981, they increased again after 1984, and
welfare spending was higher in 1989 than it had been in 1981. In other ways,
too, this claim is overstated. His own rhetoric to the contrary, Reagan was far
too adept a politician to undertake any serious dismantling of large and popular social programs such as Social Security or Medicare. Although he talked
repeatedly about the evils of federal regulation, he did not scrap important
government agencies. Federal bureaucracy, which had swelled since the 1960s,
emerged unscathed. The number of federal employees increased more rapidly
during his presidency than it had under Jimmy Carter. Federal government
spending as a percentage of gross domestic product was slightly higher under
Reagan than it was to become under Bill Clinton.

   Reagan also failed to overturn, or even seriously to challenge, a number of
highly controversial practices, such as abortion or affirmative action, that he said
he would fight hard against. Though a supporter of school-directed prayers, he
did little to bring them into being. In coping with these matters, as with popular programs of the New Deal, a politically careful Reagan took the path of least
resistance. Knowing that ardent social conservatives would never support liberal Democrats, he gave only lip service to these social conservative causes. He
played symbolic politics very well, enraging many conservatives in the process.

   Reagan also recognized, of course, that reversing existing practices concerning abortion and school prayer would require changes in judicial
interpretation.With that goal in mind, he was careful to name conservatives to
the federal courts. Most observers think that these conservatives were well qualified. But though he ended by naming nearly four hundred federal judges—
almost half of the total on the bench—the courts moved more slowly to the right

in later years than ardent conservatives had hoped. Most of the landmark liberal decisions of the 1960s and early 1970s—concerning school prayers, criminal rights, and reproductive rights—had not been overturned as of early 2003.

The second claim, that Reagan helped move politics and political thinking to the right, seemed to be valid in the early and mid-1980s. In 1980, Republicans captured the Senate for the first time since 1954. The GOP also seemed to be making headway in other ways. In 1980, for instance, polls showed that there was a considerable Democratic edge—of more than 20 percent—in the expressed partisan preference of voters. After Reagan's reelection, however, Republicans were approaching parity with Democrats. The victory of George Bush in 1988 seemed to indicate that Reaganism was promoting a political realignment in the nation.

There is also little doubt that the resurgence of conservative thinking in the Reagan years placed liberal ideas on the defensive. In 1988 Bush effectively demonized the "L" word, liberalism. And Democrats, too, saw conservative handwriting on the wall. Under Bill Clinton, they moved to the right, especially in the areas of welfare and fiscal policy. The recentering of the Democratic Party under Clinton, who understood the force of Reagan's impact on political thinking, was probably a key to the revival of its fortunes in the 1990s.

Another pronounced political development of the 1990s was what Benjamin Ginsberg and Martin Shefter have called the "Reagan Diaspora." Many conservative activists, energized greatly by Reagan's victories in the 1980s, entered electoral politics, some of them leading the GOP electoral bonanza of 1994. They also strengthened a network of organizations—the Christian Coalition, the National Taxpayers Union, the National Rifle Association, various think tanks—that bolstered conservative ideas and pressure groups at all levels of government. On some issues both parties seemed to become more conservative after 1980 than they had been in the 1960s and 1970s.

It was obvious by 2003, however, that Reagan failed to accomplish what FDR had done: create a major realignment of partisan preferences. Democrats maintained firm control of the House of Representatives until 1995, recaptured the Senate between 1987 and 1995, and regained the White House in 1993. In 2000, Al Gore and Ralph Nader won 52 percent of the popular vote for president. Nor is it accurate to credit Reagan alone for the resurgence of the Republican Party. Nixon, after all, had earlier paved the way for a GOP strategy that brought millions of disaffected Democrats, especially southerners, into the Republican column. And conservative intellectuals, founding journals and think tanks, had advanced impressively in the late 1960s and 1970s. As Martin Anderson has stressed, this conservative "Revolution," as he calls it, was well on its way before 1980. Reagan gave a substantial boost to many conservative ideas, to be sure, but he was a beneficiary as well as a mover of the rise of the right.

What, then, of the final claim—that Reagan's greatest legacy was to make Americans feel good again about themselves and the future of the nation? If by this claim it is meant that Reagan—the avowed enemy of Big Government—ironically restored popular faith in the competence of Washington, that is true—to some extent—in two ways. First, as Morris has written, Reagan was "centered and purposeful, a man of unstoppable, slow, inexorable drive." Unusually constant for a politician, he stuck with most of his strongly held convictions. In this sense he was more resolute than most men in public life and therefore personally admired. Second, Reagan was lucky to follow four presidents—LBJ, Nixon, Ford, and Carter—who had stumbled off the national stage with low popular ratings. By contrast, Reagan was fortunate to be president in an era of mostly improving prosperity, and he managed to keep the nation out of major wars. A professional actor whose final approval rating of 68 percent was the best since FDR's, he was a star whom many people applauded.

But Reagan's tenure did not mean that the majority of Americans came to love their government. (Nor, of course, would he have wanted them to love it.) They admired the star, not the play. For one thing, Iran-Contra strengthened a host of already anguished popular doubts about the evils of federal officialdom. For another, many followers of Reagan above all cherished his antigovernment message. We need not agree with Garry Wills that Reagan's antistatism prepared the ground for Rush Limbaugh, the Freemen, and extremists like Timothy McVeigh. Still, polls since 1989 indicate that a majority of Americans have remained suspicious and distrustful of government. Reagan's rhetoric not only fed these feelings; it also helped to kindle antistatist fires that blazed fiercely during the heyday of Newt Gingrich and other right-wing leaders of the mid-1990s.

The larger claim, that Reagan made Americans feel good about themselves and about their country, is in any solidly quantifiable sense unverifiable. But the claim is plausible. Like FDR, he was indeed an optimist and a booster who was fortunate politically in that he entered the White House at a somber time in United States history. Rejecting the notion that America had reached an Age of Limits, the Great Communicator told people again and again that they could still accomplish wonderful things and that the future would be better than the past. In so preaching he made effective use of the bully pulpit of the White House. Though this was often "feel good" leadership, it helped him forge a bond with many Americans. Without this leadership, the malaise of the late 1970s might have persisted.

With the limited hindsight that we now enjoy, however, it is hard to claim too much for the legacy of Reagan's presidency. Though strong as a booster, he was a frequently negligent and incurious manager. Concerning many policy areas—race relations, urban affairs, immigration and population issues, health care, action against AIDS, education, environmental concerns—he was essentially uninterested. Excepting his efforts to lower income tax rates, and— more important—his contributions to the ending of the cold war, he did little in the way of developing new or effective approaches to key problems, some of which were allowed to fester.

To speak, therefore, of a "Reagan Revolution," or of an "Age of Reagan," seems excessive. Grand phrases such as these are best reserved for twentieth-century presidents like Theodore Roosevelt, who did much to promote the activist presidency of our own times; like Franklin Roosevelt, whose New Deal inaugurated the welfare state; or like Harry Truman, whose foreign policies established America's response to the Soviet Union for forty years or more. By contrast to these formidable figures, Ronald Reagan does not seem quite so tall. Still, his legacies in the realms that he cared most about—tax rates and Soviet-American relations—have been durable as well as significant. His large shadow remains.

A Primary Perspective

THE REAGAN REVOLUTION

Was there a "Reagan Revolution"? That is the question with which Patterson concludes his essay. It is also the main topic addressed by David A. Stockman in the selection that follows. A former Michigan congressman who served as Reagan's director of the Office of Management and Budget, Stockman was as well placed as anyone in the administration to comment on the subject. His insightful and provocative observations raise important questions about the nature of the American legislative process as well as the legacy of the Reagan presidency.

The Triumph of Politics: How the Reagan Revolution Failed

Revolutions have to do with drastic, wrenching changes in an established regime. Causing such changes to happen was not Ronald Reagan's real agenda in the first place. It was mine, and that of a small cadre of supply-side intellectuals.

The Reagan Revolution, as I had defined it, required a frontal assault on the American welfare state. That was the only way to pay for the massive Kemp-Roth tax cut.

Accordingly, forty years' worth of promises, subventions, entitlements, and safety nets issued by the federal government to every component and stratum of American society would have to be scrapped or drastically modified. A true economic policy revolution meant risky and mortal political combat with all the mass constituencies of Washington's largesse—Social Security recipients, veterans, farmers, educators, state and local officials, the housing industry, and many more.

Behind the hoopla of the Kemp-Roth tax cut and my thick black books of budget cuts was the central idea of the Reagan Revolution. It was minimalist government—a spare and stingy creature, which offered even-handed public justice, but no more. Its vision of the good society rested on the

Source: From the Prologue (pages 8–9 and 13–14) from *The Triumph of Politics: How the Reagan Revolution Failed* by David A. Stockman. Copyright © 1986 by David A. Stockman. Reprinted by permission of HarperCollins Publishers.

strength and productive potential of free men in free markets. It sought to encourage the unfettered production of capitalist wealth and the expansion of private welfare that automatically attends it. It envisioned a land the opposite of the coast-to-coast patchwork of dependencies, shelters, protections, and redistributions that the nation's politicians had brokered over the decades.

The true Reagan Revolution never had a chance. It defied all of the overwhelming forces, interests, and impulses of American democracy. Our Madisonian government of checks and balances, three branches, two legislative houses, and infinitely splintered power is conservative, not radical. It hugs powerfully to the history behind it. It shuffles into the future one step at a time. It cannot leap into revolutions without falling flat on its face. . . .

By 1982, I knew the Reagan Revolution was impossible—it was a metaphor with no anchor in political and economic reality. I never gave up the supply-side ideology, however. I just put it in my safe, along with other intellectual valuables. It was simply not operationally relevant in the world of democratic fact where the politicians have the last and final say.

So I changed jerseys and joined their side. We succeeded in reducing the size of the nation's fiscal disaster modestly, despite the White House. In four different tax bills, we replenished the revenue coffers by about $80 billion per year. We whittled down defense. I got them to make a few more domestic spending cuts, too. In all, we got the deficit down to $200 billion.

I didn't like joining forces with the congressional politicians at all. I couldn't stand the idea of making all those deals to preserve their booty and waste. I disliked the idea of raising new tax revenues in order to pay farmers not to milk their cows or developers to build a luxury hotel in the ghetto.

But the congressional politicians had one redeeming virtue. They were willing to face economic and democratic reality. The dreamers and public relations men in the White House were not.

In the final analysis, there has been no Reagan Revolution in national economic governance. All the umbilical cords of dependency still exist because the public elects politicians who want to preserve them. So they have to be paid for. That is the unyielding bottom line. Economic and financial disaster is the only alternative.

I joined the Reagan Revolution as a radical ideologue. I learned the traumatic lesson that no such revolution was possible. I end up giving two cheers for the politicians. But only that.

The fact is, politicians can be a menace. They never stop inventing illicit enterprises of government that bleed the national economy. Their social uplift and pork barrel is wasteful; it reduces our collective welfare and wealth. The politicians rarely look ahead or around. Two years and one Congressional District is the scope of their horizon.

There is only one thing worse, and that is ideological hubris. It is the assumption that the world can be made better by being remade overnight. It is the false belief that in a capitalist democracy we can peer deep into the veil of the future and chain the ship of state to an exacting blueprint. It can't be done. It shouldn't have been tried.

QUESTIONS

1. How did a one-time New Deal Democrat like Reagan become a leading conservative spokesperson? Was it simply changes in his own life that prompted him to become such an outspoken proponent of conservative political views and policies?
2. What do you think were the major sources of Reagan's political success? In what ways did Reagan's acting background contribute to his later success as a politician? Was Reagan's reputation as "the Great Communicator" simply a reflection of his acting skills?
3. How would you characterize Reagan's governing style? Why did so many of Reagan's top staffers find working for him to be a frustrating experience? In which instances did the weaknesses of his managerial approach become most apparent? Were there any occasions on which Reagan's governing style seemed particularly appropriate or effective?
4. What did Reagan mean when he said that he would like "to go down in history as the president who made Americans believe in themselves again"? What does the statement reveal about Reagan and his view of the role of government in American life?
5. How much credit do you think Reagan should be given for ending the Cold War? In what ways are new findings about Soviet government and society during the regime's final decade likely to affect assessments of Reagan's role in the fall of communism?
6. What was Reagan's greatest contribution to the late 20th-century resurgence of political conservatism in the United States? Of the presidents who followed him, which one do you think was most similar to Reagan? In answering the question, consider personal characteristics as well as political beliefs.
7. According to David Stockman, what was the central theme of the "Reagan Revolution"? Do you agree with Stockman's assertion that the real Reagan Revolution "never had a chance" of succeeding? What do you think was the most notable legacy of Reagan's administration? Give reasons for your answer.

ADDITIONAL RESOURCES

The secondary literature on Ronald Reagan and his presidency is already extensive and becoming more so with each passing month. Major biographical treatments of "the Great Communicator" include Edmund Morris, *Dutch: A Memoir of Ronald Reagan* (1999), and several books by Lou Cannon: *Reagan*

(1982); *President Reagan: The Role of a Lifetime* (1991); and *Governor Reagan: His Rise to Power* (2003). Garry Wills, *Reagan's America: Innocents at Home* (1988), is an insightful and stimulating early work. Readers might also wish to consult Reagan's autobiography, *An American Life* (1990). Among the better insider accounts of the Reagan presidency are David A. Stockman, *The Triumph of Politics: Why the Reagan Revolution Failed* (1988), and George P. Schultz, *Turmoil and Triumph: My Years as Secretary of State* (1993). For a good recent assessment of Reagan's politics and various aspects of his administration, see the essays in W. Elliot Brownlee and Hugh Davis Graham, *The Reagan Presidency: Pragmatic Conservatism and Its Legacies* (2003).

Chapter *18*

Bill Gates

*I*nformation has long played a significant role in American society. Its importance became particularly clear during the course of industrialization. Beginning in the 1840s, a "communications revolution" transformed the nation's informational environment and established the foundation for a process of ongoing innovation that continues to this day. The infrastructure of this revolution had three main elements: the railroad, the telegraph, and the telephone. Their development not only linked together expanding continental markets but improved the flow of communications within and among units of the multidivisional enterprises that came to dominate the country's industrial landscape.

Meanwhile, as businesses generated a growing mountain of correspondence and reports, a host of other innovations added to corporate efficiency—typewriters made information easier to record, vertical filing systems reduced storage and retrieval problems, devices for mass copying facilitated distribution, and adding and calculating machines enabled executives and office workers to conduct increasingly sophisticated forms of data analysis.

The most important of these industrial age innovations was the development of punched-card tabulating technology. In terms of technical

complexity and their ability to manage and manipulate large quantities of information, these machines provided a vital link to the coming computer era. Many of the major breakthroughs required to get there resulted from work conducted at institutions of higher learning such as Harvard, MIT, and the University of Pennsylvania, where during the 1920s and 1930s researchers constructed increasingly sophisticated calculating devices using vacuum tubes and electricity. Outside the academy, engineers at Bell Labs also made noteworthy advances. In 1939, they devised one of the first electrical relay computers; seven years later, they developed the transistor. With the creation of the integrated circuit (computer chip) during the late 1950s by Jack Kirby at Texas Instruments and Robert Noyce at Fairchild Semiconductor, the technological infrastructure of the modern computer industry was in place.

The main task now was to develop products that would be accessible to a broad range of consumers. For many years, government, industry, and various research institutions had dominated the demand side of the computer market, as the cost and complexity of early machines ruled out home use. It was not until 1977 that the first microcomputers appeared on store shelves. Although IBM did not produce one of these early models, it quickly assumed command of efforts to create a mass market for personal computers. Over the years, the firm had amassed considerable experience in the design, production, and distribution of data-processing technology; it also knew how to provide the support services that technologically challenged computer owners would doubtless need. In 1980, the company assembled a task force to develop a microcomputer that could be manufactured in volume and sold through a network of franchisers. The project proved extraordinarily successful. By mid-decade, PC sales were generating more than $5 billion in annual revenue for IBM.

Several other firms also benefited from IBM's success. One was Andrew Grove's Intel Corporation, which produced the silicon chips that supplied the electrical circuitry for the IBM PCs. The other was Bill Gates's Microsoft Corporation, which created the software that furnished instructions to the machines. In the essay that follows, H. W. Brands describes how Gates took advantage of the IBM opportunity to become a major player in the computer industry, while providing a lively portrait of the individual who in the eyes of many best personifies the information revolution of the late 20th century.

Bill Gates

H. W. Brands

Few firms were closer to the cutting edge of technology than Intel; yet in a fundamental sense what Andy Grove did didn't differ materially from what Andy Carnegie had done a hundred years before. Both were in manufacturing; each produced something tangible that could be weighed, that took up space, that had to be warehoused, that required some physical form of transport to be delivered. Carnegie would have had trouble understanding the electronics of what Grove did, but he would have had no difficulty with the economics.

The success of the other of personal computing's gold-dust twins, Bill Gates, would have been harder to explain to a nineteenth-century industrialist. Gates didn't *make* anything, at least not anything you could drop on your foot. Nor did he quite provide a service, the way J. P. Morgan, for example, had in finance. The closest nineteenth-century analogy to what Gates did might have been Samuel Morse's creation of a standard language for telegraphy, the hot new information technology of the early industrial era. For what Gates *really* did was set standards.

Somebody had to do it. If personal computing had come of age before the arrival of Ronald Reagan and his cadres of deregulators, the standard-setter might have been the same **FCC** that David Sarnoff had tilted with over color television. If the Cold War hadn't been already thawing and on the verge of liquidation, it might have been the Pentagon's counterpart to the procurers who told Henry Kaiser what kind of ships to build. But as things happened, it was a kid from Seattle with a head for computer code and an eye for the main chance.

This latter was what distinguished Gates from a hundred other hackers who matured—or at least got older—while Andy Grove and Intel were working their wonders in silicon. The computer culture that inverted night and day, that thrived on cold caffeine and metamorphic mozzarella, that disdained convention as the refuge of the dim-witted—this was not a culture that took readily to commerce. Gates was initially so rare in this world as to be essentially unique. He could code with the best of the geeks, but he also had an instinct for the marketplace. The top-gun mentality that pervaded the realm of mathematics and hard science—Who's the smartest guy around? (and they were almost all *guys*)—carried over into computers; Gates was one of the few who took it the next step into business. The smartest guy of all would be the one who solved not just this problem on this computer, but everyone's problems on all the world's computers.

It helped that he started early. At six he attended the 1962 World's Fair in his hometown; among the exhibits was one by IBM that projected an

FCC Federal Communications Commission.

Source: From H. W. Brands, "Standard Operating Procedure: Bill Gates," chap. 25 in *Masters of Enterprise* (New York: Free Press, 1999), pp. 315–31.

information revolution based on computers—its own, naturally. The boy was impressed, although at the time more by the monorail and the carnival rides than by the computers. He first encountered computers academically in eighth grade, in the form of a teletype terminal connected via telephone to a General Electric time-sharing mainframe. The teacher was a novice; he later recalled giving Gates's class a fifteen-minute orientation. "And I remember that was the last time I knew more than those guys." Shortly thereafter a parent at the private school—to which Bill had been sent to unwrinkle some behavioral problems—with connections to a computer startup enlisted Gates's group to help shake down a new system. As pay for their assistance they would earn free computer time.

"It was manna from heaven," Gates recalled. In deliberately trying to crash the system, Gates and the others learned the weaknesses and strengths of the BASIC language in which it was programmed; the free computing time afforded opportunity for creativity on their own. Paul Allen, a schoolmate and subsequent cofounder of Microsoft, remembered Gates spending hours on a war game that grew and grew. "I'm not sure if it was ever finished or what it did," Allen said, "but he invested a lot of time trying to figure out how it worked."

Eventually the system was tweaked to the company's satisfaction, and the free time was terminated. But this didn't stop Gates and Allen from hacking their way past system security and cadging additional time—and apparently tampering with the accounting files in the process. When they were caught the school was more upset than the computer company, which chiefly wanted to know how they had done it, to prevent others from doing the same. "Our official position was one of concern," said a company representative. "But in the back room, it was 'Holy mackerel, if kids can do this, imagine what somebody who knew something could do.'"

Through most of high school Gates and Allen begged, borrowed and bootlegged computer time wherever they could. They contracted to write a payroll program, which turned out to be more than they had bargained for. "It was a bitch," Allen said. Other programming jobs included scheduling for their school, which carried the perk for the programmers of getting the classes they wanted at the choice times and with the right classmates, including the maximum number of the most attractive girls and the fewest and least attractive (to the girls) boys.

The most ambitious effort by the budding informational entrepreneurs had them trying to develop a computer system that would track traffic flow for municipalities. Traf-O-Data, as the entity that embodied this effort was called, proved more remarkable for its longevity than for its profitability. The essential hang-up was the hardware rather than the software; this experience probably contributed to Gates's eventual decision to leave the former to others.

While Traf-O-Data struggled, Gates and Allen honed their software skills writing code for the Bonneville Power Administration (the electrical offspring sired by the New Deal out of Henry Kaiser's dams). "It was like a dream come true," Gates said. As a high school senior he was working on state-of-the-art equipment with seasoned engineers—some of whom had serious suspicions of this scrawny kid who looked twelve and frequently acted fourteen. "We had contests to see who could stay in the building like three days straight, four days straight," he recounted with a certain pride. "Some of the more prudish people would say, 'Go home and take a bath.'" Gates subsisted on astronaut tea—Instant Tang—scooped from the jar in unwashed handfuls and eaten dry, which left an ethereal orange glow around the lips and fingernails. "We were just hardcore, writing code."

Gates entered Harvard in the autumn of 1972 and gravitated naturally toward applied mathematics and computer science. He impressed his instructors in a variety of ways. "He was a hell of a good programmer," said the director of Harvard's computer lab. Yet the personal side of the Gates equation left something to be desired. "In terms of being a pain in the ass, he was second in my whole career here. He's an obnoxious human being. . . . He'd put people down when it was not necessary, and just generally not be a pleasant fellow to have around the place."

Gates found college per se no more congenial than it found him. He preferred poker to books, and video games—which were just becoming popular—to classes. He got badly sick at the end of his freshman year, requiring hospitalization for ulcerative colitis. He dropped out, started again, dropped out again. Eventually he gave it up altogether.

Computers were far more fun. In late 1974 Paul Allen showed him a magazine article about a small computer called the Altair 8800, made by an Albuquerque company named MITS and powered by Intel's new 8080 processor. In those days small computers didn't come with software; Gates and Allen proposed to supply the deficiency. In particular they would write a version of the BASIC they had mastered in high school (and whose original authors had obligingly released it gratis into the public domain). Gates and Allen would sell their version to MITS or through MITS to that company's customers. They contacted the president of MITS and apparently—in what would become a Microsoft trademark—promised more than they were prepared to deliver at the moment. But that was fine with MITS, which wasn't ready to accept delivery of the software. "God, we gotta get going on this!" said Gates, in Allen's recollection of the MITS sale.

For the next several weeks the two slaved over their project, adapting the standard BASIC (which really wasn't very standard at all) to the idiosyncrasies of the Altair. Because they didn't own one of the machines, they simulated it on others—getting Gates into trouble with Harvard for unauthorized and excessive use of the university's computer system. Nor could they be certain until Allen flew out to Albuquerque with the program, which was coded on the paper tape that provided that generation's mass storage, that it would really run. The crucial test was simple enough. Allen typed

    PRINT 2 + 2

Because most of their code was required to solve even this trivial problem, Allen knew that if the Altair got it right, the language worked. He held his breath.

    4

printed the computer, leaving Allen to try to hide his relief.

The demonstration led to a deal whereby Gates and Allen received $3000 up front and royalties that ranged from $30 to $60 for each copy of their program that went out with an Altair machine. This agreement marked the beginning of Microsoft, although the name wasn't adopted (in the form "Micro-Soft") for some months yet, and the partnership remained unofficial.

By the time those details had been hammered out—with Gates talking Allen into accepting forty percent, against his own sixty, on grounds that Allen by now had taken a full-time job with MITS and presumably was devoting fewer hours to the partnership than Gates—Gates felt obliged to address an issue critical to the future of the company. In an open letter in the monthly *Computer Notes*, Gates griped that notwithstanding the uniformly enthusiastic response to Altair BASIC, its originators—Allen and himself—weren't making any money. "Why is this?" he demanded, before accusing his readers with the answer: "Most of you steal your software." He complained that coders like himself were left in the cold by the common view of the relationship between hardware and software: "Hardware must be paid for, but software is some-thing to share. Who cares if the people who worked on it get paid?" Gates cared, and he warned that illicit copying of software would serve only to deter software writers from developing good programs. He asserted that he and Allen had run through more than $40,000 worth of computer time perfecting their current product, and he asked rhetorically, "Who can afford to do professional work for nothing?" In closing he urged the guilty to pay up and declared, "Nothing would please me more than being able to hire ten programmers and deluge the hobby market with good software."

Gates's letter elicited a variety of responses from the still-small world of per-sonal computerists. A few fellow programmers applauded his hardnosed stance against piracy, but many others assailed the author as insulting and greedy. They reminded him that BASIC was basically in the public domain; he and Allen were trying to sell something they hadn't originated and didn't own. Sources close to Cambridge leaked that Gates hadn't spent anywhere near the $40,000 cited in the letter, especially as most of the development was done—in the words of one printed version of the story—"on a Harvard University computer provided at least in part with government funds." This report added that there was "some question as to the propriety if not the legality of selling the results."

The software flap provided Gates his first notoriety; it also persuaded him to change Microsoft's approach to selling its products. When MITS needed a revision of BASIC for a new computer, Gates and Allen licensed it to the hard-ware maker—nonexclusively—for a flat fee of $31,200, payable in monthly installments over two years.

After leaving Harvard definitively, Gates joined Allen in Albuquerque, where Microsoft established its first real office and hired real employees. Allen had quit MITS to devote his entire energies to the partnership; nonetheless Gates—much the pushier of the two—managed to modify the earlier pact to increase his share: sixty-four percent to Allen's thirty-six.

Although Microsoft would come to be associated with Seattle, the distinctive style that characterized the company emerged during the Albuquerque days.

"We would just work until we dropped," Allen remembered. "I used to joke that Albuquerque is a repeating pattern of a gas station, a 7-Eleven, and a movie theater." Gates put the matter more formally in an early memo: "Microsoft expects a level of dedication from its employees higher than most companies. Therefore, if some deadline or discussion or interesting piece of work causes you to work extra time some week, it just goes with the job."

In practice the "some week" of Gates's memo became nearly every week. His habit was to find a computer company that needed a customization of BASIC for its machines, to make a sales pitch promising impossibly fast delivery, and then to turn the Microsoft troops loose to meet his promise. The fact that he led from the front—that he worked harder than anyone else, programming even while he was managing, and that he took home the lowest salary in the place—averted what might have become crippling complaints.

But there was something else. In the strange world of computer coders Gates exerted an unusual appeal. By most standards and in many circumstances Gates was socially awkward. He had a curious habit of rocking when he sat or stood, almost like an infant trying to soothe himself. Strolling down a hallway he would spontaneously leap up and touch the ceiling like an adolescent boy testing his physical abilities. (Unstereotypically athletic for a computer nerd, he had a particular skill at jumping, which he liked to demonstrate by bounding from a standstill over armchairs or out of garbage cans.) He was as absentminded as the caricatured professor, constantly misplacing money, airplane tickets, credit cards, clothes and nearly anything else not permanently attached to his person. (Often a cause for amusement, his distraction became worrisome when he got behind the wheel of his sports car, which he drove as hard as he drove himself.)

Gates's managerial style was fully as confrontational as Andy Grove's. In a culture that prized being intelligent over everything else—including being rich—Gates was constantly screaming "That's the stupidest thing I've ever heard" to subordinates who usually considered themselves unusually intelligent. If a listener failed to understand a Gates statement, he typically repeated the same words, only louder. An early Microsoftie described the effect of the technique: "You know, like 'You stupid idiot. This is what I said. Just listen to what I say.'" Another old-timer (admittedly a relative term in the craft of computing) remembered being figuratively struck in the middle of a presentation when Gates began literally banging his head on the table and shouting, "You think I am an idiot! Don't use that logic on me!"

Those who got along best with Gates were the ones who stood their ground and shouted back. Paul Allen's nose-to-nose sessions with his partner became the stuff of company lore. One employee remembered hearing a set-to that started in an office on the eighth floor, spilled into the hallway, continued across the lobby and emptied into the elevator, which carried the screamers down the shaft and mercifully out of earshot. Thinking the peace of the place had been restored, the employee went back to work—just in time to hear Gates and Allen emerge from the entrance on the ground floor, still screaming. They deafened each other in the parking lot for another half-hour, to the amazement, although no longer the surprise, of the neighbors.

The battles eventually wore Allen down. "You'd see Paul go home after one of these marathon screaming sessions that was five hours long, and he wouldn't show up at work for three or four days," recounted one witness. "He was just physically wrung out." But it was something else—Hodgkin's disease—that caused Allen to reconsider his priorities and ultimately, in 1983, retire from Microsoft.

Gates, on the other hand, thrived on the combat, and if it wore Allen out it motivated the other employees. A journalist who for several months played fly-on-the-Microsoft-wall described the chairman in action.

> Although I had attended meetings before at which Gates had exploded in anger, I was mystified now at the palpable nervousness in the room. Gates's guests were terrified. Yet his tantrums had always struck me as a kind of act, a contrivance. His is an odd sort of rage that explodes and subsides instantly, as if it were turned on and off by a toggle switch. When not **expostulating**, Gates sits stock-still in his chair, his gaze directed at the edge of the table in front of him, his mind wholly concentrated on what he is being told. His displays of wrath always seem more Socratic than Hitlerian, designed not to intimidate or insult, but to elicit more thorough thought. It is not uncommon, toward the end of a scream-punctuated meeting, for him to say calmly, "Okay . . . go ahead," as if his tantrum had never taken place.

Contrived or genuine, Gates's wrath worked. Those nervous employees held him in awe. "He has this laserlike ability to hone in on the absolute right question to ask," said one person who made vice president.

> You may think you have everything totally prepared, and the one area you weren't quite sure about, somehow he just finds it right away, and asks you the one right question. He'll know intricate low-level detail about a program, and you wonder, "How does he know that? He has no reason ever to get to that level!" Some piece of code, or some other technology Microsoft isn't even involved in. You just shake your head.

Another top Microsoft executive concurred.

> He's a maniac. Bill knows more about the product than any of us. And you go into the meetings and you come out sweating because, if there is any flaw, he will land on it immediately and pick it to bits. He is just unbelievable.

A third individual wondered at Gates's ability to absorb and integrate information. Gates, this person declared, occupied "the center of one of the information centers of the universe." Gates sucked up information about all sorts of things at a breathtaking speed. "If information were some kind of tribute, he'd be Kubla Khan."

expostulating Dissuading or correcting someone.

Gates admitted that his managerial style sometimes accentuated the negative. "We're always trying to figure things out, look at our mistakes, give ourselves a hard time," he said. "I've always been fairly hardcore about looking at what we did wrong. We're not known for reflecting back on the things that went well." On another occasion he was more direct: "We can be pretty brutal about the parts that don't do well."

Some of his subordinates understood the strategy even as they trembled at the prospect of the next eruption of Mt. William. One described a complement to Gates's habit of venting his unhappiness so forcefully.

> For a guy who's allegedly a brainy nerd, Bill is extremely charismatic. He can really make you want to please him. That's one of the reasons the company works. And when he's not happy, it usually seems like disappointment, like he thought that maybe you understood along with him a direction towards a vision, a grand architecture of some kind, then you came back to him with something flawed.

Gates's vision took time to develop; through the early 1980s he had all he could do simply staying one step ahead of the competition. Until 1981 small computers were small potatoes: toys for hobbyists but not the sort of thing for businesses to take seriously. Only when IBM weighed in with its Personal Computer did the industry win real credibility. Microsoft, as much through Gates's aggressive marketing as through superior software, rode to credibility alongside—or rather inside—the IBM PC. Microsoft wasn't IBM's first choice for an operating system for the PC, but CP/M, the leading operating system, wasn't suited to the IBM architecture, and its owner, Digital Research, wasn't sure it wanted to make the necessary revisions at a price IBM wanted to pay. IBM had been interested in Microsoft's BASIC; now it asked Gates if he had an operating system as well.

He didn't but knew where to get one. Microsoft had moved to Seattle—carrying Gates and Allen back home—after outgrowing its Albuquerque sponsor MITS. Gates knew that Seattle Computer Products, a small firm down the road, had an operating system, a CP/M knockoff it called the Quick and Dirty Operating System. Without telling Seattle Computer what they wanted the system for, Gates and Allen bought QDOS (whose name was cleaned up to DOS: "Disk Operating System") for a total of $75,000. Then they turned around and licensed DOS to IBM. The precise terms of the licensing agreement were never disclosed, but they apparently involved an advance of several hundred thousand dollars against royalties. (The package included BASIC and other Microsoft languages, making the exact contribution of DOS to the deal even more difficult to determine.)

The money, however, was the least important part of the pact. IBM got DOS but not all of DOS: Microsoft withheld the right to license the operating system to other computer makers. As Gates explained afterward:

> Our restricting IBM's ability to compete with us in licensing MS-DOS to other computer makers was the key point of the negotiation. We wanted to make sure only we could license it. We did the deal with them at a fairly low price, hoping that would help popularize it. . . . We knew that good IBM products

are usually cloned, so it didn't take a rocket scientist to figure out that eventually we could license DOS to others. We knew that if we were ever going to make a lot of money on DOS it was going to come from the compatible guys, not from IBM.

Events unfolded as Gates anticipated. In hopes of encouraging the development of software applications, IBM opted for an accessible "open architecture" for the PC; this had the side effect of allowing easy reproduction of the PC's hardware. Cloners like Compaq soon began producing IBM equivalents; more nimble than the computer giant, the cloners eventually overtook the cloned. Conceivably the cloners could have developed their own operating systems, but like IBM they decided it was cheaper to purchase Microsoft's DOS off the shelf. Microsoft held other software firms at bay by pricing its product low—an easy matter because the program was already written—and relying on volume to keep the bottom line solid. As a result DOS became the standard operating system for the industry.

The most important holdout against the ubiquitization of DOS was the Macintosh computer built by Apple. The Macintosh was more intuitive in use than the DOS machines, employing a graphical user interface (GUI, pronounced "gooey") instead of the abstruse and error-intolerant command lines of DOS. In other words—rather, in other pictures—a user with a pointing device (a "mouse," for its round body and long, tail-like wire) could simply point and click and let the computer figure out what was wanted. Especially as proselytized by Steve Jobs, Apple's cofounder and resident guru, and as advertised by a spectacular Super Bowl commercial showing a fearless woman warrior assaulting the Orwellian citadel of computer-corporate conformity (read: IBM), the Macintosh presented itself as the wave of the future.

Which, in a sense, it turned out to be—but as rendered by Bill Gates, not Steve Jobs. Even as DOS became the champion operating system, Gates rowed Microsoft downstream into applications software. To some extent this represented a return to the company's original competency: consumer products for computer users. The first computer users had employed BASIC and other languages to accomplish their esoteric tasks; the much larger and less specialized group that now embraced the PC and the Macintosh demanded spreadsheets, word processors and other real-world tools. To at least an equal extent Microsoft's move into applications was simply a matter of following the money. The VisiCalc spreadsheet and the WordStar word processor proved to be cash cows for Software Arts and MicroPro, respectively, and Gates saw no reason not to poach on the pastures where they grazed.

In 1982 Microsoft released Multiplan, its own spreadsheet, and at the beginning of 1984 an improved version of the same. Unfortunately, the state of the spreadsheet art was improving faster than Microsoft was improving Multiplan; the 1-2-3 program by Lotus leaped into first place among spreadsheets and pulled Lotus into first place among software makers overall.

Microsoft's Word initially encountered a similar reaction. Despite some novel features and a marketing blitz that included the distribution of demonstration diskettes in the 100,000 subscription copies of *PC World*, the word processor started off sluggishly. WordStar was overtaken in the backstretch, but by WordPerfect, a dark horse from Utah, rather than Word.

Yet the success of Microsoft's competitors simultaneously underwrote Microsoft's success. The rapid growth of personal computing (a term that was somewhat misleading, as most of the machines sold during the 1980s were for office, rather than strictly personal, use) depended on the development of attractive applications software. Although Microsoft's applications weren't the most attractive, the company benefited from the overall growth by selling more of its system software.

That system software was constantly being improved, but still it suffered by comparison with the Macintosh system, the gold standard for ease of use by non-specialists. Consequently, even while he defended—somewhat defensively—the precision and power of DOS, Gates guided Microsoft into the world of GUIs.

He did so in a manner that infuriated his rivals and popularized a neologism: "vaporware." At least since Gordon Moore pronounced his law regarding the forever-falling price of computer power, would-be buyers have been sorely tempted to postpone purchases. Wait six months, goes the reasoning, and you'll get a better product for less money. Hardware and software makers alike have exploited this mind-set, repeatedly announcing new products before those products were ready, in hopes of preempting purchases of competitors' products. Gates didn't originate this strategy—IBM had been employing it with mainframes for years—but he developed it into an art form.

In November 1983, two months before the debut of the Macintosh but many months after that newest Apple's essential GUIness was evident, Microsoft announced Windows. This revolutionary new operating system, the company said, would employ a graphical interface that would make it unprecedentedly easy to work with. In other words—words Microsoft took pains to avoid—it would be much like the Macintosh system.

The only problem was that Windows didn't exist. And for all the high-performance, hypertensive atmosphere at Microsoft headquarters, there wasn't a chance in the world it would exist by its projected release date of early 1984. That date came and went with no Windows opening. The spring of 1984 slipped by: no Windows. August was announced, and arrived productless. During that autumn the auguries indicated January 1985; in January they pointed to May. A second hopeful summer faded into autumn with no Windows. Only in November 1985 did Gates finally deliver the new system—not quite soon enough to avoid being awarded *InfoWorld*'s "Golden Vaporware Award" for a product that for so long hadn't been substantial enough even to rate the label "software."

After the prolonged delay, the response to Windows was tepid. "Windows is a slug on 8088 PCs," said one influential reviewer, "an impossibility on floppy-disk PCs." Yet this reviewer, more prescient than many, thought Gates's new product had legs, even if they weren't moving very fast at the moment. "I am a Windows fan, not because of what it is today, but what it almost certainly will become."

Apple also saw a future for the new operating system and naturally reacted differently. Now headed by John Sculley, Apple judged Windows a rip-off of the Macintosh system and sued. Gates and his lieutenants defended their actions and their product, claiming that earlier agreements allowing Microsoft to incorporate the look and feel of the Macintosh system into applications programs implicitly covered the current Microsoft operating system as well. In any event, they pointed out, Apple itself had appropriated the Gill style from Xerox's Palo Alto Research Center. If a style was proprietary, Apple was in trouble too. Apple and Microsoft carried their fight beyond the courtroom to the computer trade shows, with Sculley and Gates getting publicly and repeatedly hot and bothered, to the amusement of the conventioneers and the pecuniary interest of the stock analysts watching from the galleries.

The latter group had been monitoring Microsoft closely since the company went public in 1986. The IPO was a roaring success; overnight Gates became one of the wealthiest people in the country. As a result celebrity inevitably surrounded him. He was feted by *Forbes*, trumpeted by *Time*, profiled by *People* and contextualized by *Fortune*, whose 1987 cover story asserted that the thirty-something (thirty-one, to be precise) sultan of software had "apparently made more money than anyone else his age, ever, in any business." Analogies to business superstars of earlier eras abounded; a favorite in the columns of commentary was Henry Ford, the young tinkerer who struck it big with a design that brought a new technology to the masses and revolutionized America in the process.

Gates knew enough about Ford to know that he too had been sued for stealing other people's ideas, and the fact that Ford had beaten that suit encouraged Gates to keep fighting Apple. The suit went on and on, dragging well into the 1990s before the courts finally decided that Apple's claim—like that of Ford's foes eighty years earlier—was without substantial merit. Apple could copyright code but couldn't monopolize a general approach to computing. It won in an esthetic sense but not in a legal sense.

And not in a business sense. After the yawns that greeted the initial release of Windows, reactions improved as the product improved. Second and subsequent generations ran faster and froze less frequently. Meanwhile third-party programmers found their way around Windows' complexities, and Microsoft's own applications caught on. Although the alliance with IBM expired following the hardware giant's decision to develop its own GUI system, by that time Windows had an insurmountable lead in the operating-systems market for computers modeled on the IBM PC.

By that time as well, Gates's vision for the computer industry was coming into focus. The metaphor of a "desktop" was common currency among program designers and industry pundits, with the computer screen mimicking the appearance of the work surface executives were familiar with. Whether or not the metaphor was any more apt than the "horseless carriage" had been in the early days of cars (which didn't really enter their own until Ford and other automakers abandoned the equine analogy), it provided a vocabulary to describe software. In this idiom, Gates wanted to own the desktop. Computer users would power up with the Windows operating system, then slide seamlessly into one of Microsoft's applications, now bundled into an "office suite" of programs. Through aggressive marketing, Microsoft persuaded leading computer manufacturers to install its line of products in the hardware they sold; consumers could now take their machines out of the box, plug them in and start to work, almost unaware that any alternative to Microsoft existed.

So aggressive was Microsoft's marketing—or simply so successful—that the company's competitors cried foul. One practice that particularly galled rivals was an arrangement whereby computer makers paid Microsoft per computer shipped rather than per software package installed. Microsoft defended this practice as an accounting convenience: It was easier to verify the number of machines that went out the door than the contents of disk drives. But to historically aware observers, the effect recalled the "drawbacks" John D. Rockefeller's Standard Oil got from the railroads on its competitors' shipments. A computer maker might install a program by a Microsoft competitor, but Gates's company had to be paid—as of course did the competitor. Not surprisingly this double duty discouraged the installation of those competing programs. Like John D.'s practice, Gates's eventually provoked such controversy as to force its discontinuance.

By the 1990s Microsoft's hold on computer software matched Standard Oil's grip on petroleum products a hundred years before. "By any normal test, Microsoft is a monopoly," declared the *Economist* magazine. "This software colossus's domination of the personal computer's operating-system market is complete. Microsoft's Windows is to be found on just about every desktop and laptop PC in the world." This London-based advocate of free-market capitalism went on to describe Gates as being simultaneously "admired by consumers as a benevolent dictator who gives the people what they want, and deeply feared by competitors, who must watch him define their own standalone products out of existence, one by one."

The resemblance to Rockefeller surfaced otherwise as well. Like Rockefeller's Standard, Gates's Microsoft produced profits at a rate that outstripped the company's ability to reinvest them in its central business; Microsoft's cash reserves mounted into the several billions. And like Rockefeller's Standard, Gate's Microsoft absorbed or intimidated competition so effectively as to preclude any serious challenge to its predominance. Philippe Kahn of Borland International briefly gave Gates a run for his money in computer languages; during this period Kahn called the Microsoft chairman "Citizen Gates" and asserted that his aim was to control "not just the software industry but the whole world." Yet even Kahn was finally forced to quit the contest. "If I've learned anything, it's not to fight battles I can't win," he said. Referring to firms still in the field, he added, "What I don't understand are the companies that, instead of learning from the past, head straight for disaster."

Often Microsoft's massive war chest sufficed to scare off rivals. Gates was candid about this aspect of his strategy, at least behind the walls of the

Microsoft campus. He told a group of key people working on a multimedia project:

> You know, you basically have to convince the other guys not to spend enough money to compete with us, to keep just making it harder and harder, move the terms up, budgeting, promotion, and quality, we just keep raising the bar, and eventually maybe one of them will try to do stuff with us. But a lot of them will just say, "Forget it."

Those who didn't forget it included only the wariest and most combative. After Netscape stole a march on Microsoft in Internet software, Gates evidently suggested an alliance that would involve some sharing of technology. Netscape chief James Barksdale declined, balking particularly at Gates's condition that Microsoft have a seat on the Netscape board of directors. Barksdale reasoned: "Why would you want a spy on your board? It's a classic Microsoft game. They learn more about you so they can hollow you out to the core. . . . They have a winner-takes-all attitude and anybody who thinks you can buddy up to them is just plain naive." (Precisely who said what between Microsoft and Netscape became a key issue in acrimonious litigation.)

Sun Microsystems wasn't exactly naive, just insufficiently suspicious. Sun promoted the Java language as an alternative to Windows; Gates, after initially dismissing Java as inconsequential, decided to license it for Microsoft. But he insisted on the right to "improve" Java in Microsoft's implementation. Whether the changes Microsoft made constituted improvements was a matter of interpretation; beyond doubt they made it different, to the point of at least partial incompatibility. Because of Microsoft's huge user base, Sun found itself facing the distinct possibility of seeing Microsoft seize the standard-setting role for Sun's own product. Outflanked, Sun sued.

Gates's parade from conquest to conquest spawned a psychological condition that sometimes seemed epidemic among his competitors. Industry pundit Esther Dyson called it "Bill Envy," and explained: "Just about all the guys in the business have it. It makes them feel inadequate and it makes them do stupid things. He's the Rorschach blot of the industry. What people think of Bill tells more about them than it does about him." Not surprisingly, almost no one owned up to the ailment. "I don't have Bill Envy," Sun's Scott McNealy said. "I have a great wife, a nice house, and I'm sure my kid is smarter than his kid." Another rival, who was forced to seek shelter with Sun, reflected rhetorically, "Is there Bill Envy in Silicon Valley?" His answer: "There's money envy in Silicon Valley, and Bill's got a lot of money."

That envy presumably grew as Gates's fortune ballooned. One Billophobic technophile created a site on the World Wide Web that constantly reported the downs and mostly ups of Gates's paper wealth. Another obsessive—blessed in this case with a sense of humor—calculated a "Too Small a Bill for Bill" index, which revealed that, in light of the $16-billion increase in his wealth during a runup of the Microsoft share price in the first half of 1997, if Gates were heading to work and saw a $10,000 bill lying on the street, he should resist the temptation to stop and pick it up. Instead he should proceed straight to the office, where he would make more than $10,000 in those four seconds saved.

Gates generally ignored the personal sniping . . . but he couldn't ignore the intense scrutiny the federal Justice Department applied to Microsoft's marketing strategy. During the 1990s the company constantly fought charges of anticompetitive practices. In the autumn of 1998 the federal government and twenty states joined forces against Gates and Microsoft in inaugurating what pundits called the most important antitrust suit since the breakup of Standard Oil in 1911. Gates, although a less appealing witness than Rockefeller had been, followed John D. in denying all wrongdoing. Microsoft, he said, played hard—and well—but by the rules.

Industry observers often remarked the seeming paradox that Gates acted as though Microsoft was still a startup company long after it had attained behemoth status. Not for Gates any such self-limiting strategy as Alfred P. Sloan had adopted in autos; Microsoft was as uncompromisingly competitive at $10 billion in sales as it had been before it sold its first million.

Gates saw nothing paradoxical in the matter at all. Microsoft might dominate software at the moment, but that was no guarantee of future dominance. "There's not a single line of code here today that will have value in, say, four or five years' time," he told his software developers. Windows was the darling du jour, but that could change overnight. "Today's operating systems will be obsolete in five years."

H. Ross Perot, another computer billionaire, understood what Gates was up against and why he did what he did. "His is an industry where the faster you run the faster you have to run," Perot said. "If he could create software and sit on it for twenty years, he'd probably be bored. But the minute it hits the market shrinkwrapped he'd better be on the next one, right? There is no halftime in his business. You don't even get to go to the locker room and rest."

Compared to Sloan's auto industry—or Andy Grove's semiconductors or Andy Carnegie's steel—Gates's software was a business marked by insubstantial products and immaterial barriers to entry. Gates liked to say that the only thing that stood between Microsoft and mediocrity was the bright ideas of his top thinkers. "Take our twenty best people away," he declared, "and I will tell you that Microsoft would become an unimportant company." It was this possibility that kept him pushing so hard.

Yet immaterial barriers weren't no barriers. Having set the standards for software, Microsoft benefited enormously from those standards. "I really shouldn't say this," he had explained way back in 1981, speaking of the existence of standards, "but in some ways it leads, in an individual product category, to a natural monopoly: where somebody properly documents, properly trains, properly promotes a particular package and through momentum, user loyalty, reputation, sales force, and prices builds a very strong position with that product." By the late 1990s Microsoft had been setting standards for nearly two decades; its position was indeed very strong.

A Microsoft-watcher during most of those two decades summarized Gates's accomplishment—and what it meant for Gates, Microsoft and the industry:

> Microsoft really isn't in the software business; it's in the standards business. Microsoft succeeds not because it writes the best code but because it sets the best standards. Microsoft Windows—the personal computer software that made Gates a septibillionaire—was nurtured and developed to be a standard, not just another operating system.

Somebody had to set the standards; without them the modern computer industry could never have matured as it did. Gates might dispute his critics' charges of megalomania and deny the allegations that Microsoft was the Standard Oil of the information age, but to a considerable degree he had to recognize that such carping came with the territory of standard-setting. He didn't appreciate the criticism, but neither did he give any sign of surrendering the territory.

A Primary Perspective

MICROSOFT AT THE CREATION OF THE IBM PC

As noted, the IBM PC project of the early 1980s hastened the development of a mass market for personal computers. In the excerpt below from his book *The Road Ahead*, Gates explains the initiative's significance for both Microsoft and the computer industry.

The Road Ahead

In the summer of 1980, two IBM emissaries came to Microsoft to discuss a personal computer they might or might not build.

At the time, IBM's position was unchallenged in the realm of hardware, with a more than 80 percent market share of large computers. It had had only modest success with small computers. IBM was used to selling big, expensive machines to big customers. IBM's management suspected that IBM, which had 340,000 employees, would require the assistance of outsiders if it was going to sell little, inexpensive machines to individuals as well as companies anytime soon.

IBM wanted to bring its personal computer to market in less than a year. In order to meet this schedule it had to abandon its traditional course of doing all the hardware and software itself. So IBM had elected to build its PC mainly from off-the-shelf components available to anyone. This made a platform that was fundamentally open, which made it easy to copy.

Although it generally built the microprocessors used in its products, IBM decided to buy microprocessors for its PCs from Intel. Most important for Microsoft, IBM decided to license the operating system from us, rather than creating software itself.

Working together with the IBM design team, we promoted a plan for IBM to build one of the first personal computers to use a 16-bit microprocessor chip, the 8088. The move from 8 to 16 bits would take personal computers from hobbyist toys to high-volume business tools. The 16-bit generation of computers could support up to one full megabyte of memory—256 times as much as an 8-bit computer. At first this would be just a theoretical advantage because IBM initially intended to offer only 16K of memory, 1/64 of the total memory possible. The benefit of going 16-bit was further lessened by IBM's decision to save money by using a chip that employed only 8-bit connections to the rest of the computer. Consequently, the chip could think much faster than it could communicate. However, the decision to use a 16-bit processor was very smart because it allowed the IBM PC to evolve and remain the standard for PCs to this day.

IBM, with its reputation and its decision to employ an open design that other companies could copy, had a real chance to create a new, broad standard in personal computing. We wanted to be a part of it. So we took on the operating-system challenge. We bought some early work from another Seattle company and hired its top engineer, Tim Paterson. With lots of modifications the system became the Microsoft Disk Operating System, or MS-DOS. Tim became, in effect, the father of MS-DOS.

IBM, our first licensee, called the system PC-DOS; the PC was for personal computer. The IBM Personal Computer hit the market in August 1981 and was a triumph. The company marketed it well and popularized the term "PC." The project had been conceived by Bill Lowe and shepherded to completion by Don Estridge. It is a tribute to the quality of the IBM people involved that they were able to take their personal computer from idea to market in less than a year.

Few remember this now, but the original IBM PC actually shipped with a choice of three operating systems—our PC-DOS, CP/M-86, and the UCSD Pascal P-system. We knew that only one of the three could succeed and become the standard. We wanted the same kinds of forces that were putting VHS cassettes into every video store to push MS-DOS to become the standard. We saw three ways to get MS-DOS out in front. First was to make MS-DOS the best product. Second was to help other software companies write MS-DOS-based software. Third was to ensure MS-DOS was inexpensive.

We gave IBM a fabulous deal—a low, one-time fee that granted the company the right to use Microsoft's operating system on as many computers as it could sell. This offered IBM an incentive to push MS-DOS, and to sell it inexpensively. Our strategy worked. IBM sold the UCSD Pascal P-System for about $450, CP/M-86 for about $175, and MS-DOS for about $60.

Our goal was not to make money directly from IBM, but to profit from licensing MS-DOS to computer companies that wanted to offer machines more or less compatible with the IBM PC. IBM could use our software for free, but it did not have an exclusive license or control of future enhancements. This put Microsoft in the business of licensing a software platform to the personal-computer industry. Eventually IBM abandoned the UCSD Pascal P-system and CP/M-86 enhancements.

Consumers bought the IBM PC with confidence, and in 1982, software developers began turning out applications to run on it. Each new customer, and each new application, added to the IBM PC's strength as a potential de facto standard for the industry. Soon most of the new and best software, such as Lotus 1-2-3, was being written for it. Mitch Kapor, with Jonathan Sachs, created 1-2-3 and revolutionized spreadsheets. The original inventors of the electronic spreadsheet, Dan Bricklin and Bob Frankston, deserve immense credit for their product, VisiCalc, but 1-2-3 made it obsolete. Mitch is a fascinating person whose eclectic background—in his case as a disc jockey and transcendental meditation instructor—is typical of that of the best software designers.

A positive-feedback cycle began driving the PC market. Once it got going, thousands of software applications appeared, and untold numbers of companies began making add-in or "accessory" cards, which extended the hardware capabilities of the PC. The availability of software and hardware add-ons sold PCs at a far greater rate than IBM had anticipated—by a factor of millions. The positive-feedback cycle spun out billions of dollars for IBM. For a few years, more than half of all personal computers used in business were IBMs and most of the rest were compatible with its machines.

The IBM standard became the platform everybody imitated. A lot of the reason was timing and its use of a 16-bit processor. Both timing and marketing are key to acceptance with technology products. The PC happened to be a good machine, but another company could have set the standard by getting enough desirable applications and selling enough machines.

IBM's early business decisions, caused by its rush to get the PCs out, made it very easy for other companies to build compatible machines. The architecture was for sale. The microprocessor chips from Intel and Microsoft's operating system were available. This openness was a powerful incentive for component builders, software developers, and everyone else in the business to try to copy.

QUESTIONS

1. Why does Brands believe 19th-century industrialists would have had a difficult time understanding what Gates did? According to Brands, what set Gates apart from most other people in the relatively small programmers' world of the 1970s was his "eye for the main chance." What evidence does Brands provide to support this statement?

2. How would you describe Gates's personality? What was it like working for Gates in the early days at Microsoft? What were Gates's greatest strengths as a manager?

3. Why did Gates feel compelled to follow Apple's lead and develop a graphical user interface system? What does Microsoft's defense against charges that it had stolen Apple's ideas suggest about the nature of software development?

4. On one occasion, Brands relates, Gates told his software developers, "There's not a single line of code here today that will have value in, say, four or five years' time." What does Gates's observation suggest about the nature of competition in the software industry?

5. In what ways did Gates resemble John D. Rockefeller? In what ways did the two men differ? Why do so many of Gates's competitors have such a negative view of him? Is it simply "Bill Envy"?

6. According to one Microsoft-watcher whom Brands quotes near the close of the essay, the company "really isn't in the software business; it's in the standards business." Explain the significance of this observation. What does the remark tell us about the influence that Gates and Microsoft had on the development of the computer industry?

7. Which of the historical figures profiled in Part Three would you most like to write about? What questions would you ask in a study of that person? What types of sources would you consult to answer those questions?

 ## ADDITIONAL RESOURCES

The most thorough biography of Gates's early life is James Wallace, *Hard Drive: Bill Gates and the Making of the Microsoft Empire* (1993), which can be supplemented by Gates's own observations in *The Road Ahead* (1995). Also see Janet Lowe, *Bill Gates Speaks: Insight from the World's Greatest Entrepreneur* (1998). Studies of how the corporation he founded conducts business include Robert Slater, *How Bill Gates and Steve Ballmer Reinvented Their Company* (2004), and Randall E. Stross, *The Microsoft Way: The Real Story of How the Company Outsmarts the Competition* (1997). Three books that take a more critical look at Gates and Microsoft are David Bank, *Breaking Windows: How Bill Gates Fumbled the Future of Microsoft* (2001); Gary Rivlin, *The Plot to Get Bill Gates: An Irreverent Investigation of the World's Richest Man* (1999); and Jennifer Edstrom and Marlin Eller, *Barbarians Led by Bill Gates: Microsoft from the Inside: How the World's Richest Corporation Wields Its Power* (1998). Those seeking to put the communications revolution of the late 20th century in historical context should consult the essays in Alfred D. Chandler, Jr., and James W. Cortada, eds., *A Nation Transformed by Information: How Information Has Shaped the United States from Colonial Times to the Present* (2000).

Photo Credits

p. 3: Stock Montage, Inc.; **p. 23**: Courtesy of the Archives and Special Collections on Women in Medicine, MCP, Hahnemann University; **p. 38**: © Corbis; **p. 55**: Stock Montage, Inc.; **p. 75**: © Bettmann/Corbis; **p. 95**: North Wind Picture Archives; **p. 111**: Stock Montage, Inc.; **p. 129**: © Bettmann/Corbis; **p. 148**: AP/Wide World Photos; **p. 170**: Stock Montage, Inc.; **p. 190**: AP/Wide World Photos; **p. 200**: AP/Wide World Photos; **p. 215**: Stock Montage, Inc.; **p. 233**: Stock Montage, Inc.; **p. 249**: AP/Wide World Photos; **p. 263**: AP/Wide World Photos; **p. 285**: © Bettmann/Corbis; **p. 305**: © Reuters/Corbis